Sustainable Investing

A seminal shift has taken place in the world of investing. A clear and overarching reality has emerged which must be solved: financial considerations must factor in sustainability considerations for ongoing societal success, while sustainability issues equally need to be driven by a business case. As a result, investment practices are evolving, especially towards more positive philosophies and frameworks.

Sustainable Investing brings the reader up to speed on trends playing out in each region and asset class, drawing on contributions from leading practitioners across the globe. Implications abound for financial professionals and other interested investors, as well as corporations seeking to understand future investment trends that will affect their shareholders' thinking. Policymakers and other stakeholders also need to be aware of what is happening in order to understand how they can be most effective at helping implement and enable the changes arguably now required for economic and financial success.

Sustainable Investing represents an essential overview of sustainable investment practices that will be a valuable resource for students and scholars of sustainable banking and finance, as well as professionals and policymakers with an interest in this fast-moving field.

Cary Krosinsky is a noted educator and author on the nexus of sustainability strategy, investing and financial value. He teaches at Yale University, USA; Concordia University, Canada; the University of Maryland, USA; and Brown University, USA; and acts as Senior Advisor to organizations such as the Carbon Tracker Initiative, the Principles for Responsible Investment and Wilshire Associates.

Sophie Purdom is a Henry David Thoreau scholar, the co-creator and instructor of the Theory and Practice of Sustainable Investing course at Brown University, USA, and established the Brown Sustainable Investment Fund. She is currently an Associate Consultant at Bain & Company in Boston and will be attending Harvard Business School, USA.

'*Sustainable Investing* provides a much-needed roadmap that describes where we are and the many paths available to us. We find ourselves at a moment with the potential to take advantage of technology and momentum and the ability to steward our financial resources and social intent toward addressing the issues facing us globally. This book supplies us with the tools to help tackle those critical decisions.'

– Jenny Chan, Senior Investment Officer, Doris Duke Charitable Foundation, USA

'As we make the vital sustainability and low carbon transition, we are finally moving from persuading to doing, from testing to investing. This book gives a great guide to the reasons change is needed, the methods, tools and ideas to make that change, plus all the latest thinking that goes along with that.'

– Dave Gorman, Director of Social Responsibility and Sustainability, Responsible Investment Lead, University of Edinburgh, UK

'Reallocating capital flows towards a more sustainable future is vital if we are to safeguard this planet for future generations. This book provides a very helpful overview of this emerging field and demonstrates how this crucial financial innovation is taking place.'

– Jules Kortenhorst, CEO, Rocky Mountain Institute, USA

'Those of us responsible for maximizing the long-term prospects of the funds we manage must have a strong understanding of the theory and practice of sustainable investing. As fiduciaries, we cannot afford to passively accept what the market gives us. We must assert our influence to promote sustainable behavior at the companies we invest in and throughout the economy.'

– Seth Magaziner, General Treasurer for the State of Rhode Island, USA

'Krosinsky and Purdom have assembled a prodigious and original set of pieces on the crucial issue of how businesses, institutions, governments and individuals can and must shift their investments in a much more sustainable direction. One-stop-shopping for useful and provocative ideas on greening finance, brilliantly timed.'

– J. Timmons Roberts, Ittleson Professor of Sociology and Environmental Studies, Co-Founder, Climate and Development Lab, Institute at Brown for Environment and Society, Brown University, USA

'The market need for sustainable solutions is accelerating and big, as is the growing universe of investable solutions. This fresh look at sustainable investing organized by Krosinsky and Purdom is must reading for every investor seeking to align his or her sustainability values with superior investment returns.'

– Jackson Robinson, Vice Chair & Portfolio Manager, Trillium Asset Management, USA

'Sustainable investing has come a long way in the past decade. From the start, Krosinsky has been an astute observer and participant. In this new book, Krosinsky and Purdom provide a detailed 360-degree view of emerging priorities and practices. Impressive in depth and breadth, this sophisticated, practical volume is essential reading.'

– Paul Shrivastava, Executive Director, Future Earth, Canada

'Asset owners, asset managers and investment consultants will all greatly benefit from *Sustainable Investing*. This book focuses on taking the reader from understanding into an investor perspective. Turning that perspective into an investment approach, as the book notes, is where the rubber will meet the road for investors.'

– George Wong, Special Investment Officer, New York State Common Retirement Fund, USA

Sustainable Investing

Revolutions in Theory and Practice

Edited by Cary Krosinsky
and Sophie Purdom

First published 2017
by Routledge
2 Park Square, Milton Park, Abingdon, Oxon OX14 4RN

and by Routledge
711 Third Avenue, New York, NY 10017

Routledge is an imprint of the Taylor & Francis Group, an informa business

British Library Cataloguing in Publication Data
A catalogue record for this book is available from the British Library

Library of Congress Cataloging in Publication Data
Names: Krosinsky, Cary, editor. | Purdom, Sophie, editor.
Title: Sustainable investing : revolutions in theory and practice / edited by Cary Krosinsky and Sophie Purdom.
Description: Abingdon, Oxon ; New York, NY : Routledge, 2017. | Earlier edition: 2008. | Includes index.
Identifiers: LCCN 2016027624| ISBN 9781138678606 (hb) | ISBN 9781138678613 (pb) | ISBN 9781315558837 (ebk)
Subjects: LCSH: Investments--Environmental aspects. | Investments--Social aspects. | Social responsibility of business. | Investment analysis.
Classification: LCC HG4521 .S847 2017 | DDC 332.6--dc23
LC record available at https://lccn.loc.gov/2016027624

ISBN: 978-1-138-67860-6 (hbk)
ISBN: 978-1-138-67861-3 (pbk)
ISBN: 978-1-315-55883-7 (ebk)

Typeset in Goudy Old Style and Gill Sans
by Saxon Graphics Ltd, Derby

Contents

Illustrations

Figures

Tables

Boxes

Contributors

Harold Bracy is a sophomore at Brown University, USA, pursuing a degree in applied mathematics–economics and Energy Sector Chair for Brown's Socially Responsible Investment Fund. After Brown, he hopes to attain a Ph.D. in economics so that he can eventually bring his knowledge back to the rocky coasts of Maine, where he was raised by his deaf parents, and improve the economic opportunities for that state's youth.

Kathryne Chamberlain is a senior at Brown University, USA, studying biomedical engineering and conducting independent research on microfluidic diagnostic devices. She spent the previous two summers as an investment banking intern in New York City. Beyond the classroom, Kathryne is a coordinator of Brown Elementary Afterschool Mentoring (BEAM), an organization dedicated to teaching a variety of subjects to elementary school students in Providence, Rhode Island. Kathryne is from San Diego, California, and enjoys travelling, having recently returned from a semester abroad in Dublin, Ireland.

Sagarika Chatterjee is Associate Director of Policy and Research for the Principles for Responsible Investment (PRI), based in London, UK, where she leads PRI's work on investor action on climate change. This includes convening global PRI signatory support for the Paris Agreement and the Montreal Carbon Pledge, supported by 120 investors (US$10 trillion). Sagarika collaborates closely with PRI's UN partners, UN Global Compact and UNEP FI, as well as with CDP, IIGCC, INCR and IGCC. She serves in a personal capacity on the investment committee of the Joseph Rowntree Foundation, an independent organization working to inspire social change. Prior to PRI, Sagarika worked for over ten years at BMO Global Asset Management, focusing on engagement with companies and ESG incorporation into investment practices. She has served as Vice-Chair of UKSIF and trustee of environmental research charity Earthwatch. She started her career at Kingfisher plc in a commercial role, sourcing timber for B&Q. She has an M.Sc. in development studies from the University of London, UK, a management studies diploma from the University of Oxford, UK, and a B.A. in social and political sciences from the University of Cambridge, UK.

Jeff Cherry is Executive Director of Conscious Venture Lab and a thought leader in the emerging discipline of Conscious Capitalism®. Jeff expanded on the ideas of Conscious Capitalism® to form Concinnity Advisors, a hedge fund focused on identifying and investing in companies operating from a more holistic, long-term value mindset. More recently, he helped create Conscious Venture Fund to do seed stage investments in places such as West Baltimore, MD; Cleveland, OH and Detroit, MI, connecting these cities and their citizens to opportunities where they are most needed.

Lillian Childress is a student at Yale College, USA, graduating in 2017 as an environmental engineering major. She works as a research assistant at the Yale Center for Industrial Ecology and helps manage the *Journal of Environmental Investing*.

Todd Cort is a faculty member at the Yale School of Management and Yale School of Forestry and Environmental Studies, USA. He also serves as the faculty co-director of the Yale Center for Business and the Environment (CBEY) and adjunct faculty member of the Columbia University Earth Institute, USA. He holds a Ph.D. in civil and environmental engineering, masters and bachelors degrees in biochemistry and a professional engineer's license in California. Todd previously served as Director of Sustainability Advisory Services for TUV (Terra Alpha Investments) Rheinland and Det Norske Veritas, where he consulted on sustainability matters including metrics, risk management and auditing practices.

The **Dwight Hall SRI Fund** is an initiative of Yale's Dwight Hall which serves as a model for the Social Innovation Laboratory. A committee of twenty Yale College, USA, students manages the $85,000 fund with guidance from the Dwight Hall at Yale Board of Directors and Trustees. The committee aims to educate students at Yale and beyond about the potential of ethical investing to shift corporate behaviour. It seeks to fulfil its goals though a market-driven portfolio that makes investments in community development, socially responsible mutual funds, REITs and ETFs, while also organizing conferences on emerging practices and trends in the industry.

Ali Edelstein is Senior Sustainability Analyst for YUM! Brands and recently graduated from the Tufts University Fletcher School of Law and Diplomacy, USA, with a masters in international business. She was a credit analyst for Breckenridge Capital Advisors from September 2015 through April 2016.

Dan Esty is the Hillhouse Professor at Yale University, USA, with primary appointments in Yale's Environment and Law Schools and a secondary appointment at the Yale School of Management. He serves as Director of the Yale Center for Environmental Law and Policy and on the Advisory Board of the Yale Center for Business and Environment, which he founded in 2006. He is also the author and/or editor of ten books and dozens of articles on environmental protection, energy, and sustainability – and their connections to policy, corporate strategy, competitiveness, trade, performance measurement and economic success. His prizewinning volume, *Green to Gold: How Smart Companies Use Environmental Strategy to Innovate, Create Value, and Build Competitive Advantage*, has recently been named the top-selling 'green business' book of the past decade. From 2011 to 2014, he has served as Commissioner of Connecticut's Department of Energy and Environmental Protection, where he earned a reputation for bringing fresh thinking to both energy and environmental policymaking, including such innovations as the launch of Connecticut's first-in-the-nation Green Bank and a 'LEAN' restructuring of all of Connecticut's environmental permitting programmes to make the state's regulatory framework lighter, faster, more efficient and effective. Prior to taking up his Yale professorship in 1994, he served in a variety of senior positions at the US Environmental Protection Agency (where he helped negotiate the 1992 Framework Convention on Climate Change) and was a senior fellow at the Peterson Institute for International Economics in Washington, DC.

Elodie Feller joined the UNEP Finance Initiative in January 2013 as the Investment Commission Coordinator responsible for the UNEP FI investment work programme. She was a lead author of the UNEP FI and Principles for Responsible Investment (PRI) report, *Fiduciary Duty in the 21st Century*, and is currently leading the Fiduciary Duty in Asia project, a joint initiative between UNEP FI, PRI and the Generation Foundation. Prior to joining UNEP FI, Elodie worked for Lombard Odier Investment Managers as a product specialist and ESG analyst in its Fixed Income department. Elodie graduated in international relations from the Graduate Institute in Geneva, Switzerland.

Stéfanie D. Kibsey is Program Coordinator for the David O'Brien Centre for Sustainable Enterprise in the John Molson School of Business at Concordia University, Canada. She holds a Master of Environmental Studies (M.E.S.) degree in environment and resource studies from the University of Waterloo, Canada. Her research interests are interdisciplinary in nature and include science–practice–policy interfaces, natural resource management, environmental change and governance, sustainable financial systems and emerging risks. Previously, Stéfanie has worked in responsible investing and environmental risk management at La Caisse de Dépôt et Placement du Québec, Canada's second largest pension fund manager.

Jules Kortenhorst works as an investment analyst at Vision Ridge Partners, an investment firm committed to pairing transformative environmental impacts with outstanding financial performance. Previously, he interned at the Society for Nature and the Environment in the Netherlands, which provides public- and private-sector environmental consulting services. His interests include sustainable food systems, wilderness-based therapy and Nietzsche. He holds a B.A. with honors in philosophy and economics from Brown University, USA.

Winston Kortenhorst studies economics at Brown University, USA. He was a summer analyst at Greentech Capital Advisors, an investment bank focused on transactions in the sustainable infrastructure space. Additionally, his previous experience includes time at asset management firms. In addition to environmental finance, Winston's interests include basketball and hiking. Winston is originally from the Netherlands.

Cary Krosinsky teaches, writes and advises with a special focus on business and investment strategies that achieve both superior shareholder value and societal benefit. At Brown University, USA, he co-taught with Sophie Purdom and the Investment Office on the Theory and Practice of Sustainable Investing for the purpose of creating a new fund within the endowment, and he continues to teach at Yale, USA, the University of Maryland, USA, and Concordia University in Montreal, Canada. His previous books include *Sustainable Investing: The Art of Long Term Performance* (Routledge, 2008) and *Evolutions of Sustainable Investing* (Wiley, 2011). He provides senior advisory services to organizations such as the Carbon Tracker Initiative, dMass, the Network for Sustainable Financial Markets, RLP Wealth Advisors and Wilshire Associates. Teaching, writing and advising on sustainability and investing is his third career after a first career in technology, followed by his creation of the world's first sustainability and investor relations business and the first fully global institutional ownership database for which he remains a recognized expert.

Winnie Lau, Ph.D., is officer of International Ocean Policy for the Pew Charitable Trusts. Previously she was Climate Change Science and Technology Advisor at USAID, working in Sri Lanka. In this role, she designed and managed multi-million dollar USAID climate change adaptation projects in the Maldives focused on water security and marine resource protection, and advised USAID/Sri Lanka and Maldives Mission on climate change and science and technology issues. She has also been Program Manager of Marine Ecosystem Services at Forest Trends. She is an expert on marine payment for ecosystem services (PES) and other innovative financing mechanisms, and has developed conceptual frameworks and tools, facilitated a global community of practice, collaborated with local partners in on-the-ground PES demonstration projects in Colombia and Mexico, published articles and primers on marine PES, and facilitated and hosted conferences and training workshops. She has a Ph.D. in oceanography from University of Washington, USA.

Stephanie Lee is an undergraduate student at the John Molson School of Business, Canada, majoring in finance. She is a research assistant at the David O'Brien Centre for Sustainable Enterprise. Her research interests include sustainable finance and social enterprise, mergers and acquisitions, as well as technical analysis.

David Lubin has more than twenty-five years of experience successfully founding and managing both public and private technology and business analytics companies. He currently serves as Managing Director of S3 LLC, a climate data and sustainability research firm. He also serves as Founding Director of the Palladium Group, a global leader in business analytics. Previously, he served as Chairman of the Sustainability Innovators Working Group (SIWG), a research consortium of global corporations who are world leaders in sustainability. He has also served as Vice Chairman of Zefer, a leader in internet business strategy and technology development, acquired by NEC in 2001. Beginning in 1991, he served as Co-Founder, Co-Chairman and Managing Director of Renaissance Worldwide, a pioneer in enterprise performance management and IT services which grew to become a publicly traded company with over 6,000 employees around the world. David was a member of the faculties at both Tufts and Harvard University, USA. He is a frequent speaker and writer, whose work includes 'Bridging the Sustainability Gap' (with Daniel Esty, *MIT Sloan Review*, 2014) and 'The Sustainability Imperative' (with Daniel Esty, *Harvard Business Review*, 2010).

Will Martindale is Head of Policy at Principles for Responsible Investment. Since joining PRI, Will has led major programmes on fiduciary duty, investment beliefs and mandates, and investor engagement in public policy. He is the author/co-author of *Fiduciary Duty in the 21st Century* (with UNEP FI, UN Global Compact and the UNEP Inquiry into the Design of a Sustainable Financial System), *How Asset Owners Can Drive Responsible Investment: Beliefs, Strategies and Mandates* and *Policy Frameworks for Long-Term Responsible Investment: The Case for Investor Engagement in Public Policy* (with the UNEP Inquiry into the Design of a Sustainable Financial System, London). Prior to joining PRI, Will was a business manager for BNP Paribas' credit trading desk and an associate at J. P. Morgan. Will read Maths at King's College London, UK, and has a Masters degree in Comparative Politics from the London School of Economics.

Brian McFarland is the Director of Carbonfund.org Foundation's Project Portfolio where he identifies, conducts due diligence, and structures the financial support for global climate change mitigation projects. Brian is also the Director of Project Origination for CarbonCo, where he identifies, designs and advises on the implementation of several REDD+ projects throughout Brazil and Indonesia. Brian earned a dual graduate degree in business administration and global environmental policy from American University, USA. Brian has published twenty-two articles and a book entitled, *REDD+ and Business Sustainability: A Guide to Reversing Deforestation for Forward Thinking Companies*. Brian also has a forthcoming book tentatively entitled *Conservation Finance: An Historical Review of International Finance for Tropical Forest Conservation*.

Mirova is the Responsible Investment division of Natixis Asset Management, and has developed an engaged approach which aims to combine value creation with sustainable development. Their philosophy is based on the conviction that integrating sustainable development themes in investment approaches can generate solutions that create value for investors over the long term.

Jason Mitchell is a sustainability strategist and thought-leader whose articles and comments have appeared in the *Huffington Post, Wall Street Journal, Institutional Investor, 7x7, Bloomberg, Global Times, Aftenposten, Euromoney, Nikkei, Responsible Investor, Hedge Fund Journal*, AIMA *Journal* and *Investment Europe*. He oversees Man GLG's sustainability investment strategies, including the Global Sustainability strategy and the Virgin Climate Change strategy. Prior to that, he spent two years as advisor to the UK government on infrastructure development across sub-Saharan Africa and as COO of Hydrotech International. He has been Chair of the United Nations Principles for Responsible Investing (UNPRI) Hedge Fund Steering Committee since 2014, and participates on the boards of the Plastic Disclosure Project and Hub Culture. Jason co-manages the GLG Global Equity and EAFE strategies. Prior to that he worked at Andor Capital and Pequot Capital, where he covered telecoms and technology. He began his career with Credit Suisse First Boston's technology equity research team. He graduated from the London School of Economics and Political Science, UK, with a M.Sc. in international political economy and the University of California–Berkeley, USA, with a B.A. in english literature and classics, and is a fellow of the British American Project and part of the Milken Institute's Young Leaders Circle. He was chosen as one of *Institutional Investors*' rising stars of 2011.

Sophie Purdom is a Henry David Thoreau Scholar, the co-creator and instructor of the Theory and Practice of Sustainable Investing course at Brown University, USA, and established the Brown Sustainable Investment Fund. She is currently an Associate Consultant at Bain & Company in Boston and will be attending Harvard Business School, USA.

Mimi Reichenbach graduated from Yale College, USA, in 2016 with a B.A. in environmental studies with specialization in renewable energy and human health. She is Associate Editor of the *Journal of Environmental Investing*, where she writes about innovations in clean technology and financial vehicles. Mimi has worked for Braemar Energy Ventures, Trillium Asset Management, Sunvestment Energy Group and the Yale Office of Sustainability. She is a member of the Nexus Global Youth Summit Working Group on Climate Change, as well as the Yale Net-Zero Think Project. Mimi is an alumna of Phillips Exeter Academy, USA.

Nick Robins is Co-Director of the UNEP Inquiry into the Design of a Sustainable Financial System. The inquiry aims to advance policy options that align the financial system with long-term sustainable development. Nick has over twenty years' experience in the policy, research and financial dimensions of sustainable development. Before joining UNEP, he was head of the Climate Change Centre of Excellence at HSBC in London, UK, from 2007 to 2014, where he produced investment research on issues such as clean tech growth, climate vulnerability, green stimulus and stranded assets. Prior to HSBC, Nick was first head of SRI research and then head of SRI funds at Henderson Global Investors. At Henderson he published the first ever carbon audit of an investment fund and co-designed the Industries of the Future fund. Nick has also worked for the International Institute of Environment and Development, the European Commission's Environment Directorate and was part of the original Business Council for Sustainable Development. Nick has authored two books – *The Corporation that Changed the World: How the East India Company Shaped the Modern Multinational* (2006) and *Sustainable Investing: The Art of Long-Term Performance* (with Cary Krosinsky, 2008). He is also an adviser to a number of groups including the Climate Bonds Initiative, the Carbon Tracker Initiative and WHEB Asset Management, and is a trustee of the Resurgence Trust.

Emily Rutland received her B.A. in English from Yale University, USA, in 2015 where she focused on sustainability from a business and environmental perspective. She currently lives in New York City where she works as a business analyst for a financial technology startup and remains a freelance writer, contributing articles centred on sustainable cities and communities.

Morgan Smiley is a senior at Yale University, USA, from Long Island, New York. She is majoring in ethics, politics and economics and is concentrating on the energy industry within the major. Morgan is one of the co-chairs of the Dwight Hall Socially Responsible Investment (DHSRI) Fund and is a former co-president of the New Haven Urban Debate League. She has also worked as a research assistant in Yale's Department of Political Science, USA. Morgan was a 2016 Summer Analyst at an investment bank and will be returning as a full-time analyst upon graduation.

Bud Sturmak is the founder of BlueSky Investment Management, established in 2015. As an investment consultant and partner at RLP Wealth Advisors, Bud spent nearly a decade immersed in the field of sustainable investing, performing detailed due diligence on existing investment managers and recommending solutions to institutions and high net worth investors. Over the course of eighteen months, Bud and his team undertook a massive research project to scientifically explore the relationship between environmental, social and governance (ESG) and investment performance, which led to the undeniable conclusion that companies performing well on ESG measures also produce superior financial returns. Recognizing the lack of existing ESG-integrated investment products designed to enhance investment performance, Bud and his team established BlueSky Investment Management. He is a Certified Financial Planner practitioner and an Accredited Investment Fiduciary. Bud graduated from Dickinson College, USA, in 1995 with a B.A. in history. He was a contributing author to the 2012 book *Evolutions in Sustainable Investing*. Bud is a member of the Network for Sustainable Financial Markets.

Rory Sullivan is an internationally recognized expert on responsible investment, climate change, human rights and development issues. He has over twenty years' experience in these and related areas. His recent projects include working with the Principles for Responsible Investment initiative on its *Fiduciary Duty in the 21st Century* report, with the UN Global Compact to develop advice for companies on the strategies they can adopt to manage the impacts of investor short-termism on corporate sustainability (the *Coping, Shifting, Changing* report), and with a number of UK and US investment managers on the development and implementation of their responsible investment strategies. He has written seven books and many papers, reports and articles on responsible investment, climate change, human rights and development issues. His books include *Valuing Corporate Responsibility: How Do Investors Really Use Corporate Responsibility Information?* (2011), *Corporate Responses to Climate Change* (editor, 2008) and *Business and Human Rights: Dilemmas and Solutions* (editor, 2003).

Terra Alpha Investments LLC is an advocacy investment firm established in 2014 that operates on the premise that environmental productivity (the efficiency by which companies use and impact natural resources) will enhance business and investor risk-adjusted returns. Specifically, Terra Alpha uses environmental data to focus on energy, water and natural materials efficiencies as a key factor in finding profitable companies that will bring competitive returns in their investment fund.

Gabriel Thoumi, CFA, FRM, is a senior fellow at Climate Advisers, where he provides global financial analysis for mitigating systemic climate risk while advising on 'greening' capital markets for clients and coalitions. He has fifteen years of experience managing and deploying frameworks to improve global capital markets sustainability through risk mitigation and return enhancement. Previously, for Calvert Investment Management, he valued global equity, index and fixed income portfolios and their component positions in the utilities, energy, materials, chemicals and financial sectors. He has an M.B.A. and M.Sc.

from the University of Michigan, USA, where he was a Consortium and Erb Institute fellow. He is a frequent speaker, author and lecturer for various universities.

Thomas Walker is a professor in the Department of Finance and Interim Director of the David O'Brien Centre for Sustainable Enterprise at Concordia University in Montreal, Canada. His current research focuses on sustainable investing, environmental litigation and green venture capital. In addition, he frequently publishes in the area of corporate governance, risk management and securities litigation. He has over thirty peer-reviewed publications and received several outstanding paper awards. Prior to assuming the directorship of the David O'Brien Centre for Sustainable Enterprise, he was chairman of Concordia's Finance Department, served on the university's Senate Finance Committee, and sat on the steering committee of the Professional Risk Managers' International Association (PRMIA). He currently serves on the academic advisory board of two sustainability centres and on Concordia University's Joint Sustainable Investment Advisory Committee.

Mujtaba Wani is an undergraduate student at Yale College, USA, majoring in political science and the humanities, expecting graduation in May 2017.

Ella Warshauer is a senior at Brown University, USA, where she is pursuing her bachelors degree in economics, with a focus in environmental studies.

John Waugh is the Director for Climate and Environment at Integra LLC, a professional services firm in international development. He has worked at the interface of environment and development since 1980, primarily as an analyst and adviser on conservation strategies and planning for resilient communities. John is an expert in participatory planning, with experience in participatory mapping and participatory social network analysis. As a WWF project manager and Peace Corps volunteer, he developed one of the earliest co-management agreements for a protected area in Africa (1987). He continues this work, advising the Bonobo Conservation Initiative on benefit sharing mechanisms for community managed protected areas in the Democratic Republic of the Congo. His current focus is on the uses of information in decision-making, on sustainable finance, benefit sharing, participatory planning for climate adaptation and post-conflict natural resource management.

Helene Winch has spent the last twenty years in finance, with various responsibilities including commodity trading, investment management, pension management and public policy. She has worked in the private and NGO sector, holding the role of Head of Policy at the £40 billion BT Pension Scheme as well as at the United Nations supported Principles for Responsible Investment (PRI). Her current role with Low Carbon Ltd is focused on facilitating institutional investment in renewable energy at scale and managing the associated UK energy policy risk.

Christopher Wright Ph.D. is head of sustainability at Norges Bank Real Estate Management. He is responsible for ensuring that sustainability risks and opportunities are properly assessed and integrated into the real estate investment process. Previously, he was a senior analyst in Norges Bank Investment Management, providing advice on climate change risk management across asset classes. He has a background as an academic and consultant in the area of sustainable finance and policy.

The views expressed by the contributors and endorsers are their personal views only. They do not reflect the views of the affiliations listed.

Acknowledgments

Thanks first and foremost to Nick Robins, not only for his ongoing sage counsel but for his suggestion in late 2015 of a follow-up third book on what sustainable investing needs to look like over the next five to ten years, which led directly to this effort.

Also to Kate Chamberlain for her excellent and hard work editing and adapting chapters that helped us meet a very aggressive deadline. And to the other amazing students at Brown and Yale we've come to know so well over the recent months and years. To Frederic Lamontagne for your video conferencing efforts, to Dana Le for spearheading our speaker series so very capably, to Marta Pysak and Solveig Xia for corralling our mentors and judges, and to all the mentors, judges, speakers, students and participants in PLCY 1710 at Brown: your collective efforts led to a very special class that we will never forget. We are very fortunate to have some of your writing in this book. To all the amazing speakers we've been fortunate to have sharing their knowledge and experience with all of our classes. To the Junto for Sustainable Investing for inspiring some fresh thinking, and to Keith Brown for helping make our Brown class happen at the last minute.

To Brown University President Christina Paxson for your support in creating the Brown University Sustainable Investment Fund. To Jane Dietze and Molly Landis for your excitement at trying something new and for putting all of the pieces of this big puzzle together.

And to the wonderful students we have come to know and love at Yale. There are too many students to mention and we feel bad leaving anyone not mentioned who should be. But to Alexander Vernoit whose sage, tempered wisdom is already badly missed, and to Gabe Rissman, well, we basically owe you everything.

And to Sophie Purdom, thanks for welcoming me into your special world, what a pleasure and honor it was to teach with you.

Introduction

The future of investing is sustainable

Cary Krosinsky and Sophie Purdom

It is a rare moment that one realizes that they are at a turning point in history. The technological onslaught of modern life coupled with the intensifying pressure to make a living and be most productive consume most working people on a global and day-to-day basis, as well as many eager students, while systemic shifts creep by completely unnoticed. Between this all-consuming short term and the omnipresent long term, who has the bandwidth and perspective to determine turning points in history until they've already happened? Yet we find ourselves today at such a seminal shift in the history of business. Are investment practices ready for these seminal shifts already taking place? If not, what needs to change, and can investing enable the necessary transitions already underway at scale, and how?

There is much discussion about short-term investment perspectives and strategies versus the long term. The reality is that there is no such thing as a long-term investor. The long term is merely a series of short terms. What has changed is that these short terms will need to shift, both gradually and with intentionality, to get us where we need to be in a generation's time at the very most. Move too fast and you can get sucked right into a cleantech bubble – move too slow and you are left behind by the next Tesla. How to get this balance just right? That's what we hope to provide in the chapters that follow.

There is one clear and overarching reality that needs solving, and now:

Financial considerations now must factor in sustainability considerations for ongoing societal success, while sustainability issues equally need to be driven by a business case.

These two historically opposing parties are coming to realize the necessity of a deeply entwined partnership for mutual – and global – success and survival. One without the other destines both for failure. The good news is that this necessary combination of financial and sustainability success is starting to happen across the board, and the world needs this to be accelerated, given ongoing environmental and societal trends, in haste. Sustainability without a business case is just philanthropy, which while a fine and noble thing unto itself, is insufficient for the problems at hand. Finance without sustainability is a recipe for environmental and social disaster (i.e., climate change, fresh water shortages, increased levels of inequity and inequality).

We are actually quite confident of success – because if outperformance can only come through both sustainability and finance together, then this *will* happen, and sooner than you might think, forcing investor hands, creating a necessary positive dynamic of sustainability for financial and societal success, with those not participating being left behind in a Darwinian race for both financial and societal benefit. Skeptics beware. If positive approaches are what resonates and what actually works, this is what will win out at the end of the day. How to make this happen with urgency will be the laser focus of this book.

We will also assume that you have some knowledge of climate science and ESG (environmental, social and governance) considerations, but if you want a concise guide, check out the Appendices.

Much has been tried in so far as integrating ESG into investment, but the field also remains quite nascent at solving societal challenges. Given the rapidly increasing challenges we face, and the parallel rise in interest in solving societal problems through finance, we will move as quickly as possible in this book to a sharp focus on where investing needs to get to over the next five to ten years looking at what actually works, can work and needs to work right now, cutting across regions, systems and implementation strategies across a variety of fresh, global solutions-oriented perspectives.

Fortunately, there are rapid changes underway in our favor, such as the dramatically lower costs of renewable energy and challenges to the traditional high-carbon ways of doing business; but there are also many distractions to avoid.

Interest in factoring ESG considerations into investment itself is at record levels as we speak, given increasing concerns about the environmental and social challenges that we face as a global society. But as we discuss in the first chapter that follows, different 'tribes' have formed.

What is most exciting is that we appear to be on the threshold of a sustainable investing tipping point where capital itself can move environmental and social issues from areas of concern into positive solutions that also provide every chance of financial outperformance.

Arguably, the first waves of socially responsible investing were implemented too soon, were at times too politically focused, and attempted to use poor to non-existent data, which often resulted in somewhat poorly constructed, ineffective negative screens. Is it any wonder more sophisticated investors looked the other way? Not really, not when financial returns were poor to meeting benchmark performance at best.

Crucially, we are seeing the sustainable investing ship turn from values-focused to value-driven, from delivering negative messages to finding solutions, from poor financial performance to exceptional, and starting to move capital in more positive directions, on the scale that is required, helping enable the necessary increased pace towards social improvement and the low-carbon future that we require.

The rest of this book lays out arguments for what's needed across asset class, across region, across investment strategy and how to develop your plans accordingly.

One could argue that the COP 21 climate negotiations in Paris and subsequent Paris Agreement represented the necessary 'observation of the system' moment which was required. Such a coming together was needed to start to globally unify previous disconnects that existed between sustainability and finance. The very good news is that the revolution is already underway, bringing these two modes of thinking together and resulting in just good investing.

We wrote this book to mark the turning of what has largely been a negative into what needs to become a positive; to bring light to the financially outperforming practices of positive sustainable investing and the meeting of the worlds of mainstream finance and sustainable investing, and to help both sides realize that these goals are now one and the same.

Part I

How

Chapter 1

The seven tribes of sustainable investing

Cary Krosinsky

As we start to consider sustainable investing and what it needs to become, a first essential step is to establish and clarify the state of the field and all of its varying practices. Very specific strategies are often quite different and distinct within the field, and are all too often lumped into a single 'I'm likely to give up returns' umbrella by those less familiar with it. Sustainable investing is very much not returns-jeopardizing, fortunately. Think about the difference between funds with a religious mandate and funds seeking to invest in water infrastructure for just one of many examples of how different strategies can be.

Also, as you will see in the next chapter, when you really dig in and compare and contrast strategies, investors can seek maximum financial performance without needing to sacrifice financial returns, and positioning portfolios towards the future may well also become a source of alpha.

Here for us is where the rubber hits the road, and the confusion which remains on terminology and performance needs to be better understood by anyone in an investment decision-making position of authority.

And so for the sake of this clarification, we introduce here the concept of:

The seven tribes of sustainable investing

Sustainable investing and *impact investing* are the two most frequently heralded terms referencing seven separate investment strategies which are in actuality very different in both practice and performance.

These 'seven tribes' include:

1 *Values first* – the roots of the field, practiced first as implementations of religious mandates, manifested as negative screens typically on sectors such as alcohol, tobacco, weapons, more recently South African apartheid, Sudan, and fossil fuel. This area remains two thirds of the $21 trillion of assets under management factoring in environment, social and governance (ESG) factors in some way as of 2014 (GSIA, 2015). It is often also called *ethical investing* (also the main manifestation of *responsible investing* as well as the now more

antiquated term *socially responsible investing*). *Islamic or sharia finance* is often practiced as a form of negative screening, but in its pure form is a version of the shared economy, with shared ownership constructs at its heart. Values first investing is less interested in financial performance, and many studies show it often at best meets benchmark performance, leading to a broader perception of the entire field being philanthropic in nature, and as a result not fit from a fiduciary duty standpoint.

2 *Value first* – championed by the likes of Generation Investment Management and Parnassus Investments, both of whom have gained over $US10 billion in assets in recent years, value first investing using ESG as among primary considerations has gained in strength given its ability to encourage societal improvement while allowing for the potential for financial outperformance. Some call for value first investing to be called *sustainable investing*, which if scaled, could create the missing dynamic allowing for profit and societal benefit to be truly scalable simultaneously. Generation has beaten its benchmarks over its first 10 years while most active fund managers underperformed, yet has capped its fund, so scalability can be a challenge. Parnassus grew over the past eight years from under $1 billion to $15 billion in assets under management.

3 *Community/impact* – *community investing* has a long-established history of investing with intention to improve the wellbeing of a specific region and group of targeted individuals. So-called 'bottom of the pyramid' focuses and implementations of microfinance are also in this sphere, as is much of the history of *social business*. More recently, *impact investing* has risen as a lens for investors seeking to have positive societal and environmental effect with their investments through intentionality. For example, a First Nation in Canada financing a wind farm would create a local, environmental and community benefit. Most impact investments have been implemented within the realms of access to medicine, housing, education and healthcare for the world's poorest, though some use an overarching definition of impact investing to include all of the possible strategies listed here. Chapter 3 provides further detail.

4 *Thematic investing* – typically private equity or venture capital in nature, but also available through some mutual funds (including the largest ESG fund in Europe, Pictet Water Fund), thematic investments are often focused on areas such as *cleantech*/renewable energy or water among other related innovations and categories of environmental finance (such as conservation). This would be the extreme case of sustainable investing on the one hand seeking positive intentionality, with the other extreme being a negatively screened public company fund based on a large cap global liquid index. Climate/green bonds are a growing area of interest within the space of thematic investing, as is the nascent area of green infrastructure, and arguably green real estate can also fit here. Chapter 11 and Chapters 11a–11g go into further detail on how investors focus thematically.

5 *ESG integration* – generally carried out by analysts, asset managers and investors, bringing in ESG data from one or more external providers and using that as one more set of criteria to analyze the strength of a business among a variety of more traditional factors, is also on the rise. Some, for example, have been known to use bottom performance on ESG as scope for further research when potentially committing to lending as part of due diligence. Asset owners also use bottom performers to decide on engagement activities (active ownership is the process of exercising your rights as a shareholder to influence management and performance). ESG integration needs to combine data access with specific strategies to be effective.[1] We provide examples of a few investors in the chapters that follow, and our previous book *Evolutions in Sustainable Investing* also detailed methodologies used in practice.

6 Engagement/advocacy – the field of *shareholder engagement* is practiced both openly through shareholder resolution and public discourse on issues such as stranded asset risk, as well as on compensation, tax and many other issues. It is also often practiced quietly, with agreements not to go public after extensive dialogue. Record levels of participation are being seen in climate change shareholder resolutions alongside all-time-high quantities of resolutions being filed. Arguably the most successful strategy deployed to date by investors attempting to facilitate positive change (see Chapter 7 on the PRI Climate Change Asset Owner Framework and related case studies and Chapter 15 on the various strands of activity surrounding positively focused shareholder activism). This also includes engaging with policymakers, and asset owners with their outsourced fund managers where such are used.

7 *Norms-based screening* – mainly a Northern European strategy, typically involves using United Nations (UN) principles, including the UN Global Compact and the UN Guiding Principles on Business and Human Rights, as a minimum standard for investment.

Combinations of the above seven strands of activity are often deployed by investors when seeking to address specific issues; for example, the Principles for Responsible Investment (PRI) in 2015 created a Framework for Asset Owner Climate Change Strategy combining additional specific allocations of capital with engagement in three ways – with corporates, on policy and with outsourced fund managers, as well as selling companies for which there is no perceived business case.

Social issues can be resolved best through intentional investing and multi-stakeholder dialogue. Governance is often addressed through attempting to improve bottom performers as identified through ESG data and analysis.

Financial performance also widely differs, based on which of these strands are deployed. We understand those who assume they will leave returns on the table when deploying negative screening, and the academic literature is filled with cases where such strategies were suboptimal.

Separately, positive sustainable investing has been a major source of financial performance as well, as we will see in the next chapter detailing the work of our class at Brown University, and as we discussed at length in our first two books on this subject.

Note

1 For example, see Chapter 34 of *Evolutions in Sustainable Investing* (ed. Cary Krosinsky, Nick Robins and Stephen Viederman, New York: Wiley, 2011) on Insight Investment Management and their designed ESG strategy process.

Reference

GSIA (Global Sustainable Investment Alliance) 2015. 'Global Sustainable Investment Review 2014'. www.gsi-alliance.org/members-resources/global-sustainable-investment-review-2014/ (accessed 8 September 2016).

Chapter 2

From far-fetched theory to best practice

Sustainable investing at Brown University

Sophie Purdom

It started metaphorically: caught in tangled electrical appliance cords in the dark under my high school teacher's desk.

I emerged with data in hand and an epiphany brewing in my mind. By unplugging unused appliances, my school could save electricity being drawn as phantom load for very little effort and a high impact. We got to work on a sustainability program that through carefully communicated behavioral change succeeded in reducing our high school's electricity consumption enough to hire two new teachers.

At the core of the program is the theory of the sustainability/financial value nexus – that same epiphany that I had unplugging cords in the dark, that saving energy is great for the world and all of us in the long run but saving money is great for the individual right now. If we are to achieve the necessary and immediate transition to a low-carbon economy that will save our planet from catastrophic anthropogenic warming, sustainability must learn the logic and language of finance because, for good or for bad, economics is the universal language of the present and we need universal action now.

Brown University complicated that. I arrived on campus to a sea of passionate and critical students rising up to challenge the Brown Administration to be a leader around fossil fuel divestment. Through clever public actions, rallies, high-profile lectures, and mass petitions with over 2,000 signatories Brown Divest Coal demanded that Brown 'divest from the 15 filthiest coal companies'. Their actions brought to campus mountain top removal activists, bioethics professor Peter Singer, the CEO of Duke Energy, and Bill McKibben of 350.org. Students, faculty, staff, alumni, and the Brown community at large coalesced behind the demand to divest from coal for ethical reasons including human rights, intergenerational equity, and environmental justice. On February 6, 2013, the Advisory Committee on Corporate Responsibility in Investment Policies (ACCRIP) recommended that the university assume Brown Divest Coal's demands 'given the well documented human and environmental impacts of the coal industry'.

On October 27, 2013 President Christina Paxson released a letter[1] to the Brown Community announcing the Brown Corporation's decision to not divest from coal. Her letter tipped a hat to Brown Divest Coal for revealing the social and environmental harm caused by coal but continued, 'The existence of social harm is a necessary but not sufficient rationale for Brown to divest' and 'by the fact that coal is currently necessary for the functioning of the global economy' a judgment call that divestment would improve such social ills would be 'a difficult one at that'. She then suggested:

> The second question to consider is whether divestiture would help correct the social harm by speeding the transition away from coal. It is clear that divestiture would not have a direct effect on the companies in question. Brown's holdings are much too small for divestiture to reduce corporate profits. Furthermore, because the profits of these companies are determined primarily by the demand for their products rather than their stock prices, divestiture would not reduce profits even if Brown's holdings were orders of magnitude larger.

In sum, the financial impact of divestment on coal companies had been lost in the emphasis on social harm. The sustainability/financial value nexus had not been proven.

With the precedent of Divest Coal in mind, I set out in search of the sustainability/financial value nexus. As a part of many teams we wrote the Sustainable Providence plan, passed the Resilient Rhode Island climate change Act, and held fossil fuel executives on message at the UN Framework Conventions on Climate Change. I interned in Boston with Ceres, seeking to prove that the Carbon Asset Risk from high-carbon, high-capital expenditures made by certain public fossil fuel companies was worth engaging company management about. The idea stuck and now Ceres, the Carbon Tracker Initiative, and students from Yale University are leading the conversation with investor networks engaging with carbon majors on climate risks.

This idea that analytical incorporation of material information on environmental, social, and governance (ESG) could drive superior financial performance while doing good for the planet and people drew me to the Brown Socially Responsible Investment Fund (SRIF). A student group managing $50,000 of the university's current use funds, SRIF put this ESG theory to practice in managing a concentrated portfolio of public equities. In order to be added to the SRIF portfolio each stock must meet financial and ESG performance standards. Each week the SRIF team met to deliver a presentation on a target with the intention of garnering enough votes from peers in the audience for the stock to pass on both finance and ESG. Over the course of my time with SRIF our standards for what made a successful ESG company developed as we integrated materiality assessments from leaders like SASB, a breadth of scientific, market, and social understanding from our diverse team, and data from MSCI ESG Analytics. Our investment approach began to shift too. Rather than metrics we focused on materiality. Rather than short-term fads, we followed long-horizon trends. We practiced what we preached about corporate governance and invested in our expanding membership through trainings, career networking, and mentoring. We expanded our leadership suite from a small homogeneous group to a 15-person board inclusive of all years, majors, and personal backgrounds.

It paid off. The Brown Administration decided that our performance proved that ESG investing warranted equal support to that of traditional investing and increased our assets under management to over $120,000 to match the seed funding of the Brown Investment Group. With a 13.5 percent return in 2014 and performance beating the S&P 500 each year since, SRIF has consistently outperformed 80–90 percent of money managers through a difficult period.

For all of SRIF's successes, one of its greatest achievements was the opportunity it afforded students to begin a dialogue with the Brown Investment Office. Due to the work of Brown Divest Coal, the Investment Office's attention had pivoted towards socially responsible investing. With the encouragement of President Paxson, the Investment Office began to take action to achieve the goal of significantly incorporating ESG considerations across the endowment. I was brought on as an intern to share SRIF's experience. The divestment discussion had highlighted an immediate and pressing demand for a fossil fuel free endowed option. As an immediate win that would go beyond such a demand and establish Brown as a leader in the space, we began to develop the nation's first institutional endowed sustainable investment donor option. The Brown University Sustainable Investment Fund will seek to drive long-term capital appreciation for the Brown Endowment by making investments well-positioned to mitigate the systemic risks associated with environmental, social, and governance issues and maximize the opportunities generated by a transition to a low-carbon sustainable economy.

Over time, turnover at SRIF improved year over year, as did the continued range of backgrounds of students joining the club as an alternative to traditional investment options offered on campus. With the interest of the Administration piqued by sustainable investing and no course offerings that mixed finance with sustainability issues, I got the go-ahead to write the syllabus for a course on sustainable investing with the ultimate goal of educating the next generation of thought-leaders and practitioners in sustainable investing. Thanks to an introduction from Yale Dwight Hall SRI, Cary Krosinsky and I connected to join forces and make the course a reality. With Cary's experience and my foot into various workings of Brown, we got the green light on official approval of the syllabus and course just one day before the start of the 2016 spring semester. The Theory and Practice of Sustainable Investing got off to a running start when over 100 students showed up to the first day of lectures, eager to join our brand-new 25-person seminar. We had clearly hit a nerve of interest by the sheer number and diversity of interested students. We eventually built a class of 45 with a range of experience from aspiring oil and gas investment bankers to first-years unclear on the S&P 500, and weathered environmental justice activists to renewable energy engineers.

The class and the fund dovetailed throughout the semester in the fashion of true engaged scholarship. Students wrote a tear sheet for the Brown Sustainable

Investment Fund (see Box 2.1 below) and suggested best-fit fund managers based on an analysis mimicking that of the Investment Office itself. Amazingly, the most popular student-selected fund manager matched the choice of the Investment Office after they conducted an independent analysis. At the conclusion of the class, students pitched extensively researched presentations of ESG leading companies for inclusion into a suggested BUSIF concentrated portfolio. Incorporating lessons from throughout the semester and interviews with pitched companies' c-suites, the visiting judges remarked that the students' presentations were more impressive than those of professional investors. In fact, our final class portfolio representing the five most popular stocks as voted on by the class went on to be +25.95 percent vs. the S&P 500 +8.16 percent between March 31 and August 30, 2016.

Box 2.1 Brown University Sustainable Investment Fund tear sheet

Objective

The Brown University Sustainable Investment Fund seeks to drive long-term capital appreciation for the Brown Endowment by making investments well-positioned to mitigate the systemic risks associated with Environmental, Social, and Governance (ESG) issues and maximize the opportunities generated by a transition to a low-carbon sustainable economy.

Overview

The Fund posits that ESG factors are presently undervalued by the market, and thus represent an optimal financial investment for the long term. The Fund positively screens for investments by identifying macroeconomic, technological, and societal trends that drive shareholder value and social benefit. Each investment will be vetted to determine whether its activities align with the Fund's established ESG objectives.

Portfolio transparency, community participation, and accessibility are core operating values of the Fund. Its returns, investments, and policies are made publicly available online. Given the Fund's position within the larger Brown Endowment, student input through engaged scholarship is of significant value to and encouraged by the Brown Investment Office. The Fund accepts donations regardless of amount.

Box 2.2 Hannon Armstrong pitch

By Kathryne Chamberlain

As a student of the Theory and Practice of Sustainable Investing, co-taught by Cary Krosinsky and Sophie Purdom, I was asked to research and pitch a publicly traded company for the Brown University Sustainable Investment Fund (BUSIF). Working as a team of three, we decided to recommend Hannon Armstrong, a company that specializes in the debt and equity financing of renewables and energy efficiency projects. The initial selection of the company reflected our in-class discussions regarding investment not only in companies that are positioned for success during the transition to a low-carbon economy, but in companies responsible for driving the inevitable energy revolution.

With the encouragement of our mentor Jules Kortenhorst, CEO of the Rocky Mountain Institute, my team contacted Hannon Armstrong directly to assess the intangible assets of the company, including the maintenance of respectable cultural values. In alignment with the engaged scholarship principle of the course, we spoke directly with Brendan Herron, CFO, and briefly with Jeff Eckel, CEO, to complete our due diligence and enhance the quality of our pitch. The conversation revealed an unexpected commitment to ESG standards, from Hannon Armstrong's business model to the personal values of its executives.

We attribute the success of our presentation and first-place ranking to this phone call – not only was my team able to understand the company beyond their financial reports, but our peers and the Brown University Investment Office were also able to sense the trustworthiness and passion that was so evident through our phone call. Following our pitch, we circulated our presentation to Mr. Herron and received immediate congratulations along with interest in discussing career opportunities for students on this course. Engaged scholarship drove our learning beyond the confines of a classroom, serving as the bridge to build professional relationships that we will take with us even as this course becomes just another academic credit on our transcripts.

The class was heralded as a success by students who cited it as their favorite course at Brown, employers who hand-selected nearly one third of our students directly into sustainable investing positions, and outsiders who hoped to replicate our example at their institutions. The Investment Office appreciated the materials and momentum generated by the class and will benefit from well-trained future student interns who can continue to propel ESG integration at the endowment.

With the Brown University Sustainable Investment Fund cleared for an impending public launch, I and many of my peers from SRIF, Fossil Free Brown, and the class are graduating with a complex and deep understanding of how to bring sustainable investing into the future and out into the world.

Brown's revolution in sustainable investing though unique has relevant lessons to share. Debates over the morality of our institution's implicit propagation of climate change indirectly set the stage for a tangible and actionable creation of a thoughtfully fossil fuel free fund: Brown has proven that social and environmental values not only coincide with finance but actually drive smart investment decisions.

From activists to economists, from first years to alumni, from student clubs to the Brown Investment Office, diverse stakeholders held the movement accountable for tangible results: Brown has proven that it takes an army to spark the revolution from negative screening/divestment to active sustainable investing.

But perhaps Brown's most important lesson has been the necessity of creating space to discuss and learn together as a community throughout. Hence why we are writing this book: to arm you, the future revolutionary, with a variety of approaches that will lead sustainable investing into the future.

Note

1 www.brown.edu/about/administration/president/2013-10-27-coal-divestment-update. Accessed September 8, 2016.

Chapter 3

Impact investing

Thomas Walker, Stéfanie D. Kibsey and Stephanie Lee

History and definition

Since the 2008 financial crisis, the viability, effectiveness, and social utility of the financial market system has been repeatedly questioned. In reaction to the crisis, academics, regulators, and practitioners have explored a variety of ways in which the markets can be structurally changed to avoid excessive risk taking, the widespread focus on short-term performance, self-serving behavior, and outright fraud. In fact, with ongoing revelations of fraudulent behavior such as the recent Libor and Forex market manipulations (O'Toole 2012; Vaughan et al. 2013), an increasing number of market participants are questioning the viability and social purpose of the traditional financial markets. Indeed, the old maxim of maximizing shareholder returns has broadened in scope to encompass a larger mission: one that includes achieving social and environmental objectives, alongside financial returns.

It is in this context that impact investing has gained momentum. The term 'impact investing' has been around for nearly a decade. Coined by the Rockefeller Foundation in 2007 (Harji et al. 2014; Rockefeller Foundation 2016), impact investing is most commonly defined as 'investments intended to create positive impact beyond financial returns' (O'Donohue et al. 2010, 7). In other words, impact investors anticipate both a positive social or environmental return in addition to a financial return on their investment (Harji et al. 2014). Investees are typically expected to develop a sustainable business model that is both financially sound and provides a measurable positive impact in order to receive funding (Harji et al. 2014).

Overview

Impact investing occurs throughout many different asset classes, with fixed income instruments such as social impact bonds and private equity being the two most popular asset vehicles for impact investors (Svedova et al. 2014; Saltuk et al. 2015). Impact investing also occurs in many different sectors, with microfinance having attracted the most attention and capital from investors. Other popular sectors include sustainable agriculture, renewable energies, and healthcare (Saltuk et al. 2015).

The United Kingdom is the clear global leader in impact investing, likely because of its financial innovations such as the introduction of impact bonds (Svedova et al. 2014). At the time of writing in spring 2015, the UK government supports the sector, providing tax relief of up to 30 percent for social investments (UK Cabinet Office and HM Treasury 2015). The United States is not far behind and President Obama has voiced his support for the sector (Svedova et al. 2014). The United States has also traditionally been very open to market-based strategies to tackle social problems.

While the total amount of impact capital invested is fairly evenly split between developed and developing markets, over three-quarters of organizations that make impact investments are located in North America, Europe, and Oceana (Mudaliar et al. 2016). This suggests that much of the money flows from developed to developing markets where there is more opportunity for each dollar invested to create meaningful impact (Mudaliar et al. 2016).

Impact investors

Impact investors are a diverse group: they range from high net-worth individuals like George Soros to foundations (with the Rockefeller Foundation arguably the most high-profile advocate) to public institutional investors (Svedova et al. 2014). Socially conscious investors are classified into two categories: investors willing to accept lower returns in order to achieve the social impact they aim for, and investors unwilling to make concessionary returns, i.e. so-called 'mission investors' (Brest and Born 2013). Most socially motivated investors fall into the latter category.

How do impact investors invest their money? From a strategic investment perspective, impact investors can take many different routes. A 2016 survey by the Global Impact Investing Network (GIIN) (Mudaliar et al. 2016), reveals that most impact investors aim to benefit a specific population. They do so by investing either in businesses that sell products or provide services that have a positive impact on the targeted population, or by investing in businesses that provide direct employment for the targeted population. These investment strategies have cropped up to provide new solutions to pressing societal problems which traditional methods such as governmental or philanthropic aid cannot address.

Growth

Impact investing, while still in its early stages of development, is experiencing enormous growth. A recent survey by the GIIN and J. P. Morgan revealed that the 157 investors surveyed had invested over 15.2 billion dollars through impact investments (Saltuk et al. 2015). Of course, because the field is so new and the definition of impact investment is very broad, the actual amount that is actively invested via impact investment strategies is difficult to estimate with accuracy.

Of course, any strong growth pattern should be questioned with respect to its sustainability. According to a study by the Canadian Responsible Investment Association (Lanz et al. 2015), assets under management in impact investing experienced a 9.5 percent growth in Canada from 2012 to 2013. Globally, the GIIN study shows that investors who invested in impact investments in 2014 planned to invest 16 percent more in that sector in 2015 (Mudaliar et al. 2016).

Despite this growth and the increasing interest from individual investors, impact investing still plays only a very small role in the global institutional investment arena. For example, pension funds, the largest investors in responsible investments in Canada, have 15.49 billion dollars invested in responsible investments, but only 0.26 percent of it is invested in impact investing (Lanz et al. 2015). Indeed, of all the global pension funds surveyed by Canadian Responsible Investment Association, none reported having a distinct impact investing strategy. There is still much room for impact investing to grow, and pension funds do recognize this. In that vein, an earlier report by the World Economic Forum (Drexler and Noble 2013) suggests that 64 percent of U.S. based pension funds expected to make an impact investment in the future, which was in huge contrast to only 6 percent that had already made an impact investment by 2013 (Drexler and Noble 2013). Anecdotal evidence suggests that the number of pension funds that are considering impact investment strategies or have already implemented them has grown significantly since then.

Motivation

There are many reasons why impact investing should be encouraged. Perhaps one of the main motivations is that private investment in societal problems can create immense positive change. When impact investors were asked about their motivations, they widely reported a desire to contribute to their local community, an interest in sustainable development, and a desire to align their investment strategy with their personal values (Saltuk et al. 2015). Many also responded that financial opportunity was an important aspect to consider when impact investing. Moreover, it isn't just impact investors who are motivated to create change – in a 2015 investor survey, Morgan Stanley's investors believed that around 46 percent of their portfolio should be invested sustainably (Morgan Stanley 2015).

Interestingly, this growth is in large part due to increasing client demand for impact investing. A 2012 report on sustainable and responsible investing trends by the U.S. Forum for Sustainable and Responsible Investment (U.S. SIF) revealed that demand from clients is the main reason that asset managers are increasingly implementing ESG criteria in their investments (Voorhes et al. 2012). Similarly, in the 2016 GIIN survey, money managers reported that the most prominent reason for including impact investments in their portfolio was client demand (Mudaliar et al. 2016). This trend is not likely to stop anytime soon. In fact, according to a 2015 wealth management study that explored the investment needs of millennials, Deloitte's Luxembourg office (Kobler et al. 2015) showed that millennials' aggregated global wealth will reach between 19 and 24 trillion dollars by 2020, roughly doubling from 2015. The report also points out that millennials increasingly demand socially responsible investments, including impact investments, creating a market for new innovative financial products.

A similar change in investor demands is observed by a 2015 Morgan Stanley study which argues that 'millennials are twice as likely to invest in companies or funds that target specific social or environmental outcomes' compared to the overall investor population (Morgan Stanley 2015, 4). Through these generational changes, the market for impact investing is set to explode in the near future.

Overcoming challenges

While impact investing shows a lot of promise, there are many obstacles to its widespread use. These challenges include a shortage of quality deals, a lack of appropriate capital available, and a lack of incentives for investment advisors to recommend impact investments (Saltuk et al. 2015). At the root of the problem is the serious lack of regulatory framework in which impact investing can thrive. Without this, there is a huge hurdle to changing the persistent misconception that impact investing necessitates below-market returns or 'concessionary returns' (Brest and Born 2013; Saltuk et al. 2015).

According to a recent J. P Morgan study (2015), 55 percent of impact investors seek a competitive, market-equivalent rate of return when impact investing, suggesting that financial returns are as important to these investors as social and environmental returns. Similarly, Drexler et al. (2013) find that 79 percent of impact funds aim to achieve market returns. Although these findings show that a large majority of funds are actually striving for market-equivalent returns, this fact is not well known to most investors. There is a widespread misconception that impact investing correlates with lower financial returns. A recent Wharton study finds that 'market-rate-seeking impact investments in [the study's] sample [...] may be financially competitive on a gross basis with other equity investing opportunities' (Gray et al. 2013, 6). Gray et al.'s study thus dispels the misconception, and suggests that financial returns are not conceded in exchange for social and environmental gain. Rather, both can be achieved concurrently.

It is only when the expected financial returns of these investments become more certain that investors will take more of an interest in impact investments. So, how can these challenges be overcome? Knowing the benefits of impact investing, several mechanisms can be put in place to drive growth in the areas of social enterprise. Awareness is the key to growth: with greater awareness about the benefits of impact investing, there can also be a push for public policy changes that will incentivize investors towards the social enterprise model, and make it more profitable for all those involved.

While impact investing is gaining traction, there is one factor that is prohibiting it from really taking off: the difficulty for investors to exit investments (Mendell and Barbosa 2013). In their article, Mendell and Barbosa find that without a secondary market and with insufficient liquidity, institutional investors do not want to commit large sums of money to impact investing. Thus, there is a pressing need to find a common platform to connect investors and investees. Financial intermediaries that create a channel between investors and investees are in scarce supply, but with growing demand their number is slowly increasing.

Impact investing desperately needs innovation in order to ensure its continuity and to solve pressing social problems. There is a huge amount of capital in the world that could potentially be deployed in a more meaningful manner. Investors, philanthropists, and institutions are only beginning to understand the powerful ability of market-based tools to solve the most important social and environmental challenges, and impact investing is one of the best ways to confront many of these issues. With increasing research, capital, and more effective intermediaries, impact investing is poised to upheave the traditional investing world, improve existing philanthropic models, and create new resources for many in need. Impact investing improves society as a whole, and will do so for years to come.

Box 3.1 Social business

The world is facing new and ongoing challenges such as poverty, climate change, and political instability, yet traditional approaches continually fail to resolve these social and environmental problems. With limited funds available through government aid and philanthropy, a number of innovative social business constructs have emerged in recent years which both fill the funding gap and directly address these problems.

Social business, as defined by Mohamad Yunus, 2006 Nobel Peace Prize laureate, is a business designed to meet a social goal without paying any dividends, yet is financially sustainable (Yunus and Weber 2007). Though not all businesses may wish to give up their profits, there are a number of different models that allow a company to be more socially responsible.

Benefit corporations are a new type of legal entity that allow firms to pursue a long-term mission in addition to maximizing their shareholders' wealth. As such, they are ideal for entrepreneurs who seek to run a profitable business without compromising their social and environmental values (Wilburn and Wilburn 2014; B Lab 2016a). Such values must be embedded in the company's legally defined goals, and are therefore equally important as turning a profit. Several American states and countries such as Italy now recognize benefit corporations, with several more states and countries considering similar legislation (Schwartz 2013; B Lab 2016b; 2016c).

B Corps are another example. According to Patagonia's CEO Rose Marcario, 'The B Corp movement is one of the most important of our lifetime, built on the simple fact that business impacts and serves more than just shareholders – it has an equal responsibility to the community and to the planet' (B Lab 2016d). Unlike benefit corporations, which self-report their performance, B corps are for-profit companies that must meet set standards on social and environmental performance, accountability, and transparency in order to become certified by the non-profit organization B Lab (NBIS 2012; B Lab 2016e). Furthermore, any private company worldwide is eligible for B Corp certification.

While B Corps and benefit corporations have the potential to make positive social and environmental impacts where other approaches have failed, there are also significant drawbacks. For example, B Corps and benefit corporations often have difficulty raising capital. One possible solution is the London-based Social Stock Exchange, a financial intermediary created for investors and social businesses to provide access to capital (cf. Social Stock Exchange 2016). As the first regulated exchange of its kind, the Social Stock Exchange is an innovative mechanism for companies seeking to both raise capital and make a positive social or environmental impact.

The social business system is frequently referred to as 'enlightened capitalism' (Yunus and Weber 2007). While the traditional capitalist system is not likely to radically change anytime soon, there is a definitive push for a gradual transition, and incorporating social and environmental values in the old system has already begun.

References

B Lab (2016a) 'What Is a Benefit Corporation?' B Lab (http://benefitcorp.net/FAQ). Accessed June 1, 2016.

B Lab (2016b) 'International Legislation', B Lab (http://benefitcorp.net/international-legislation). Accessed June 1, 2016.

B Lab (2016c) 'State by State Status of Legislation', B Lab (http://benefitcorp.net/policymakers/state-by-state-status). Accessed June 1, 2016.

B Lab (2016d) 'Why B Corps Matter', B Lab (www.bcorporation.net/what-are-b-corps/why-b-corps-matter). Accessed June 1, 2016.

B Lab (2016e) 'What Are B Corps?' B Lab (www.bcorporation.net/what-are-b-corps). Accessed June 1, 2016.

Network for Business Innovation and Sustainability (2012) 'B Corporations, Benefit Corporations and Social Purpose Corporations: Launching a New Era of Impact-Driven Companies', NBIS, October 2012.

Schwartz, A. (2013) 'Delaware Just Made It a Whole Lot Easier for Socially Responsible Companies to Exist', Fast Company & Inc., July 23, 2013. www.fastcoexist.com/1682654/delaware-just-made-it-a-whole-lot-easier-for-socially-responsible-companies-to-exist. Accessed September 8, 2016.

Social Stock Exchange (2016) 'Profit with Progress', Social Stock Exchange, (http://socialstockexchange.com/). Accessed June 1, 2016.

Wilburn, K. and Wilburn, R. (2014) 'The Double Bottom Line: Profit and Social Benefit', *Business Horizons*, vol. 57, no. 1, 11–20.
Yunus, M. and Weber, K. (2007) 'Creating a World Without Poverty: Social Business and the Future of Capitalism', New York: Perseus Books.

References

Brest, P. and Born, K. (2013) 'When Can Impact Investing Create Real Impact?' *Stanford Social Innovation Review* (http://ssir.org/up_for_debate/article/impact_investing). Accessed May 16, 2016.

Drexler, M. and Noble, A. (2013) *From the Margins to the Mainstream: Assessment of the Impact Investment Sector and Opportunities to Engage Mainstream Investors*, World Economic Forum Industries and Deloitte, September 2013. www3.weforum.org/docs/WEF_II_FromMarginsMainstream_Report_2013.pdf. Accessed September 8, 2010.

Gray, J., Ashburn, N., Douglas, H., Jeffers, J., Musto, D., and Geczy, C. (2013) 'Great Expectations: Mission Preservation and Financial Performance in Impact Investing', Wharton Social Impact Initiative, University of Pennsylvania. https://socialimpact.wharton.upenn.edu/wp-content/uploads/2013/11/Great-Expectations_Mission-Preservation-and-Financial-Performance-in-Impact-Investing_10.7.pdf. Accessed January 14, 2014.

Harji, K., Best, H., Jeyaloganathan, M., Gauthier, K., Reynolds, J., Martin, E., Ulhaq M., Odendahl, S., Hera, J., Rose, L., Burns, A., and Milne, J. (2014) 'Financing Social Good: A Primer on Impact Investing in Canada', Royal Bank of Canada, June 2014.

Kobler, D., Hauber, F., and Ernst, B. (2015) 'Millennials and Wealth Management: Trends and Challenges of the New Clientele', Deloitte Luxembourg. www2.deloitte.com/content/dam/Deloitte/lu/Documents/financial-services/lu-millennials-wealth-management-trends-challenges-new-clientele-0106205.pdf. Accessed September 13, 2016.

Lanz, D., Abbey, D., Smeh, D., Wentzell, D., and Mneina, E. (2015) *The 2015 Canadian Responsible Investment Trends Report*. Canadian Responsible Investment Association.

Mendell, M., and Barbosa, E. (2013) 'Impact Investing: A Preliminary Analysis of Emergent Primary and Secondary Exchange Platforms', *Journal of Sustainable Finance and Investment*, vol. 3, no. 2, 111–123.

Morgan Stanley (2015) 'Sustainable Signals: The Individual Investor Perspective', Morgan Stanley Institute for Sustainable Investing, February 2015.

Mudaliar, A., Schiff, H., and Bass, R. (2016) *Annual Impact Investor Survey*, Global Impact Investing Network, May 2016.

O'Donohoe, N., Leijonhufvud, C., Saltuk, Y., Bugg-Levine, A., and Brandenburg, M. (2010) 'Impact Investments: An Emerging Asset Class', J. P. Morgan, November 2010.

O'Toole, J. (2012) 'Explaining the Libor Interest Rate Mess', CNN, July 10, 2012.

The Rockefeller Foundation (2016) 'Innovative Finance' (www.rockefellerfoundation.org/our-work/initiatives/innovative-finance/). Accessed May 21, 2016.

Saltuk, Y., Idrissi, A., Bouri, A., Mudaliar, A., and Schiff, H. (2015) 'Eyes on the Horizon: The Impact Investor Survey', J. P. Morgan, May 2015.

Svedova, J., Cuyegkeng, A., and Tansey, J. (2014) 'Demystifying Impact Investing', Centre for Social Innovation and Impact Investing, Sauder School of Business, University of British Columbia, April 2014.

United Kingdom Cabinet Office and HM Treasury (2015) '2010–2015 Government Policy: Social Investment' (www.gov.uk/government/publications/2010-to-2015-government-policy-social-investment/). Accessed May 25, 2016.

Vaughan, L., Finch, G., and Choudhury, A. (2013) 'Traders Said to Rig Currency Rates to Profit off Clients'. Bloomberg News, June 12, 2013.

Voorhes, M., Humphreys, J., and Soloman, A. (2012) *Report on Sustainable and Responsible Investing Trends in the United States 2012* (www.ussif.org/files/publications/12_trends_exec_summary.pdf). Accessed May 21, 2016.

Chapter 4

How Paris became the capital of climate finance

Nick Robins

From la Bourse to Le Bourget

Ten kilometers northeast from the Place de la Bourse, the historic epicenter of France's financial system, lies the airport of Le Bourget. It was here on December 12, 2015 that the Paris Agreement on Climate Change was gaveled to conclusion with a striking green hammer by France's foreign minister Laurent Fabius. From the beginning, money has loomed large in global climate negotiations, focusing on two tightly interlinked questions: first, how to raise the capital needed to decarbonize the global economy, one that is also protected from the impacts of a disrupted climate; and second, who should pay for this transition both within and between nations.

This time around, the matter of finance also dominated proceedings at Paris, but with new dynamics in play. The outcome was a package of commitments and pledges that straddled both the traditional government negotiations and the wider financial system. As a result, the future of world finance will now need to be looked at afresh in the context of cutting net emissions from fossil fuels to zero this century – a huge goal, but one that could help renew the underlying purpose of the financial system: to serve society's greatest ambitions.

This chapter traces the evolution of the 'networked solution' to finance that came together at Paris, linking the formal negotiations with a broader set of actions by financial regulators, by financial institutions and also by civil society. It explores the creative dynamic between France's efforts to stimulate action within its own domestic financial system, and the international steps harnessing the financial system for climate security. It closes with reflections on how this new approach can be deepened in the year ahead.

Old arguments, new dynamics

For much of the past quarter century, the finance agenda in the UN climate negotiations had boiled down to the transfer of public funds from richer industrialized countries to poorer developing nations. The rationale was twofold. First, industrialized countries had contributed the bulk of the stock of carbon pollution in the atmosphere and, according to the 'polluter pays principle', should therefore support those developing countries most impacted by climate shocks. The second reason was that underlying poverty in developing countries can be a major constraint to the adoption of higher capital cost, low-carbon technologies, a viability gap that international transfers could help overcome. In 2009, this highly politicized agenda achieved new clarity with the adoption of a commitment to transfer US$100 billion each year from industrialized to developing countries by 2020 from a variety of sources.

This commitment covered a multitude of uncertainties and disagreements, however: how much money should be public and how much private? Should it be new money, in addition to existing flows of development aid? And what should count as climate finance anyway? Bringing in private capital from banks, insurers and investors was also considered in these discussions – but generally in indirect ways, as a byproduct of putting a price on carbon pollution or introducing policies to promote low-carbon alternatives such as renewables and energy efficiency.

The Paris negotiations were designed to reach the first global agreement on climate change since the Kyoto Protocol of 1997. After the failed talks in Copenhagen in 2009, a more expansive view of climate finance began to be taken, one that encompassed the global financial system, with its more than US$300 trillion in assets. This reflected the realization that holding global warming below the accepted 2°C target would require an unprecedented reallocation of capital. Estimates suggested that over US$1.1 trillion per year would need to be invested in clean energy alone, and most notably in energy efficiency (UNEP, 2015). Funds would also have to flow away from carbon-intensive assets, most notably coal, oil and gas. If existing investment patterns did not change, then the financial system could be left with as much as US$100 trillion in stranded fossil fuel assets by 2050, according to US investment bank Citigroup (2015). Extra investment was also required to protect communities from increasing natural hazards exacerbated by climate change. Ultimately, if these reallocations were not made, then the financial system would be on the road to ruin. According to an assessment made by the Economist Intelligence Unit, a worst-case scenario of 6°C warming could lead to a present value loss of US$13.8 trillion of manageable financial assets, roughly 10 percent of the global total (EIU, 2015).

This refocusing of the climate finance agenda from the billions to the trillions meant a broadening of the ambition for Paris. It meant not just getting agreement from governments on the traditional public finance priorities, but also winning real commitments from new actors such as central banks and financial regulators as well as commercial banks, investors and insurers. All of this came as the financial system itself was undergoing major repair and reorganization following the credit crisis of 2007–8. After an initial phase of fiscal stimulus – including 'green stimulus' efforts notably in China and the US – governments were clamping down on public spending through a new wave of austerity measures. Clearly one target for these cutbacks could be – and was – the US$452 billion in subsidies that G20 countries provide each year for fossil fuels, many multiples of what is given to the clean energy sector (ODI, 2015).

If finance was going to be found for the climate transition, it would mostly have to be private capital and channeled through a new set of market rules. Early in 2015, Fabius made his intentions clear for the year ahead: 'it is essential that the financial system as a whole takes climate risk into account, anticipates ambitious targets and integrates this into investment decisions'. So, around the traditional hub of the financial negotiations within the UN Framework Convention on Climate Change (UNFCCC), a novel model of reform was carefully constructed. For France, finance was a key part of the 'action agenda' that it wanted to develop alongside the formal government-to-government talks. This chimed well with the active cultivation of the financial community by the UNFCCC, notably by its executive secretary Christiana Figueres, who appreciated that the owners, bankers and insurers of capital were one of the key swing factors in the process of change. Back in 2014, she had warned institutional investors that ignoring climate risk could increasingly be seen as breaching their fiduciary duty to ultimate savers and beneficiaries (UNFCCC, 2015).

France's financial ecosystem

A powerful dynamic was now set in motion between France's actions to green its own financial system at the domestic level and its wider efforts to place climate factors as part of the overall architecture of global finance en route to Paris.

From the turn of the century onwards, France had taken steps to make its financial institutions take account of environmental and social factors. As in other industrialized countries, these steps were tentative at first, focused mostly on improving corporate disclosure of sustainability issues – so that financial institutions could make better decisions. In 2010, asset managers in France were required to report on the ways they tackled the trinity of Environmental, Social and Governance (ESG) issues.

Beyond these regulatory steps, a distinctive financial ecosystem was also evolving in France, gathering together the buying power of public pension funds and the creativity of commercial players, as well as the stimulus of social enterprises and think tanks (See 2 Degrees Investing Initiative (2015) and I4CE (2015) for examples). To take one example, Paris was not the first financial center in Europe to promote sustainable and responsible investment (SRI). But over the last decade, Paris had overtaken London in terms of the volume of SRI funds under management, which had reached €22 billion by May 2015 (Extel/UKSIF, 2015). Paris was now also home to the top three banks rated by European investors in terms of their investment research on sustainability issues.

The approach of the Paris negotiations galvanized this process in two main ways: first, the sheer scale of the climate challenge meant that private finance could no longer be regarded as a sideshow to the traditional policy focus on setting carbon prices and subsidizing clean energy; and second, France itself felt it needed to demonstrate that it was a leader across the climate finance agenda in order to accumulate the political capital required to close the deal.

Certainly, France scaled up its commitments of public climate finance to developing countries, pledging that it would increase its spending to €5 billion per year by 2020. More broadly, in February 2015, France's president François Hollande commissioned a rapid review of how to find new ways to mobilize climate finance, co-chaired by former development minister Pascal Canfin and the economist Alain Grandjean. The commission looked far beyond the traditional confines of the UNFCCC to explore how the key institutions that govern the financial system – such as the International Monetary Fund (IMF) and the World Bank – needed to raise their game. The report laid down ten ways in which this could happen – from making all development banks develop a '2°C investment roadmap' to requesting the Basel-based Bank for International Settlements to include climate risks in its rules for banks and insurance companies (Canfin-Grandjean Commission, 2015). And by the time their report was published in the middle of June, major steps forward had already been made both at home and abroad.

With growing numbers of investors recognizing the strategic nature of climate change, in April France's finance minister Michel Sapin requested that the Financial Stability Board (FSB) should examine how global warming could affect the fate of finance. Set up in the wake of the 2008 credit crunch to restore integrity and credibility to global capital markets, the FSB had never before looked at the environmental agenda. Yet by the start of 2015, climate was increasingly viewed as a potentially transformational issue for financial management. What made Sapin's intervention significant was that the chair of the FSB was the Bank of England's governor, Mark Carney. Back in the autumn of 2014, Carney had admitted that the 'vast majority of fossil fuel reserves are unburnable' if the world was to meet the 2°C target. Recognizing that both financial institutions and regulators suffer from a 'tragedy of the horizon' that constrained their ability to deal with long-term threats such as climate change, Carney initiated the world's first assessment of the implications of climate change for financial safety and soundness, focusing on the UK's insurance sector. Sapin's diplomatic démarche bore fruit and in Washington, DC, G20 finance ministers gave their approval for an FSB stocktaking exercise.

Back in France, the final revisions were made to a far-reaching package of legislation to drive the transition to a low-carbon energy system. The law contained many innovative measures – not least setting a trajectory for the country's carbon tax for the next fifteen years, rising to €100 per ton in 2030. Importantly, measures to harness the financial sector were viewed as a core part of the reforms. Again, improving disclosure was the focus both on the corporate and the investor sides. Climate reporting requirements by companies were tightened to ensure that investors had the information to make informed choices on firms' exposure to and management of climate-related issues. Disclosure was also extended to investors themselves, with new requirements to report their own exposure to climate-related risks and the alignment of their portfolios with the 2°C target.

Disclosure is the first step in a process of change in financial behavior, however. This data then needs to be analyzed and assets reallocated. The new French law also included a commitment to develop 'stress tests' which would incorporate climate factors, which would assess how the lending books of banks could be impacted by changing physical, political and technological scenarios, and eventually lay out the exposure of France's banking sector to climate developments. Alongside these institutional actions, other steps were taken to enable individual citizens to play their part through the development of consumer-facing labels for investment funds, one focused on the 'energy transition' and another more broadly on social responsibility (Trésor Direction Générale, 2016).

What helped to bring these measures onto the statute book was a leading group of French financial institutions that demonstrated it was practicable to reflect climate factors in investment decisions. For example, Europe's largest fund manager, Amundi, had pioneered new ways for cautious pension funds to cut the exposure to carbon risk in their portfolios, while maintaining the risk and reward profile of mainstream indices. Importantly, these steps within France were part of much wider changes in the international financial community, where leading institutions were starting to reduce their holdings in fossil fuels, boost allocations to sustainable investments (such as green bonds) and push for greater climate accountability from corporations. Behind these moves lay a surge in smart analytics and public advocacy from global groups ranging from Carbon Tracker to Greenpeace and 350.org, all highlighting the seismic shifts in capital required for climate security to be achieved.

In France, these efforts came together on May 22, less than six months before COP21. At a global climate finance conference hosted in Paris, Sapin was able to declare that the National Assembly had just passed – in an all-night sitting – the new disclosure requirements. Minutes later, Henri de Castries, CEO of insurance giant Axa, announced a wide-ranging package of measures, including exiting €500 million of coal-related investments, a tripling of green investments to €3 billion by 2020 and the publication of a carbon footprint of all its investments. Castries also released new measures to extend insurance protection in developing countries, making it clear that a '2°C world might be insurable, a 4°C world certainly would not be'.

A networked solution

So by the time the formal climate negotiations took place at Le Bourget in the first two weeks of December, the three key aspects of this new model of climate finance were coming together: the inner circle of the formal negotiations, the next ring of actions from financial system regulators and the outer circle of actions from the financial sector itself.

The multilayered Paris Agreement (Article 2c, 2015) gaveled to conclusion by Fabius on December 12 included right up front the goal of 'making financial flows consistent with a pathway towards low greenhouse gas emissions and climate-resilient development'. This explicit focus on finance was then reinforced by a set of strategic signals to bring finance behind this twin task of decarbonization and resilience.

The first signal was the agreement of the long-term goal to hold the increase in global average temperatures to 'well below 2°C above pre-industrial levels', with the aspiration to pursue 'efforts to limit temperature increase to 1.5°C'. The practical implication of this is the need to bring net emissions from fossil fuels down to zero well before the end of the century (Oxford Martin School, 2015). In a net-zero world, for every ton of carbon dioxide released, a ton must be permanently removed from the atmosphere. Decarbonization was thus confirmed as a mega-trend that would reshape the world's capital markets, throwing into doubt conventional financial projections that extrapolate today's energy system into the future.

What made this long-term goal credible for global markets was the presentation of national climate plans by nearly every country, known as the Intended Nationally Determined Contributions (INDCs). The Agreement was clear that these plans would not deliver the 2°C goal, let alone the 1.5°C ambition. Analysis produced by UNEP suggested that full implementation of current commitments would result in 3°C of warming. Yet, even if the pledges contained within the INDCs were not enough to deliver climate security, they were a substantial improvement on the 4°C feared when the Paris process began (UNFCCC, 2015). And for the financial world, the divergence from a 'business as usual' pathway was clear. One estimate suggested that by 2030, even the insufficient pledges contained within the INDCs could deliver a 5 percent contraction in global coal demand by 2030 from 2012 levels (Spencer, 2015).

The Agreement also set out steps to refocus the financial system so that it responds to the increasing impacts of climate change, particularly in developing countries. One growing concern was that the growing physical impacts of climate change could result in increased risk aversion by global investors, cutting developing countries off from capital markets. A new alliance of finance ministers from developing countries had formed the Vulnerable 20 group (V20) in October 2015 just before COP21. Chaired by the Philippines, the V20 brought together countries from all continents – from Afghanistan through Kenya to St. Lucia and Tuvalu. Their collective experience was stark: climate shocks were already exceeding their national capacity to respond, bringing annual losses from climate change of at least 2.5 percent of their GDP. Financial losses were estimated at US$45 billion a year since 2010 – a number expected to increase nearly tenfold to close to US$400 billion by 2030 (V20 Communiqué, 2015). Based on existing regional initiatives in Africa and the Caribbean, the V20 committed to create a new climate risk pooling mechanism. This focus on blending private expertise from the insurance sector with public purpose was ultimately reflected in the Agreement (Article 8, 2015) itself. In addition, all major national and international financial institutions were asked to report on how their programs incorporated climate-proofing measures (COP21, Article 43).

Reducing the consequences of climate impacts was one thing; identifying who might be liable is quite another. In unusually clear text, the Agreement stated that there was no basis for 'any liability or compensation' between states for loss and damage caused by the adverse impacts of climate change (COP21, Article 52). Litigation has been a major tool within nations to drive governments and business to take action on climate change (Global Justice Program, 2016). It is also rising up the financial agenda as a risk for banks, pension funds and insurance companies that fail to take climate risk seriously – with the potential to become a new asbestos-scale threat.

In terms of hard cash, the road to Paris generated a growing chorus of public finance pledges from industrialized countries and the world's development banks: in October, for example, the World Bank committed to boost climate finance to US$16 billion per annum by 2020, some 28 percent of all lending. By the time of Paris, the new Green Climate Fund had received US$10 billion in pledges from 40 countries. A review by the OECD suggested that climate finance flows mobilized by developed countries in 2014 had reached US$62 billion per annum (OECD, 2015). However, many developing countries, notably India, challenged this estimate on both analytical and process grounds (India Ministry of Finance, 2015). In the end, the Paris Agreement shifted the way in which the iconic US$100 billion target was seen – no longer as the ceiling, but now as a floor for international flows. Industrialized countries committed to continue mobilizing the iconic US$100 billion and a new goal would be set in 2025.

Financial innovation got a bad name following the credit crisis, but the Paris Agreement also held out the prospect of new thinking to realize the 'social, economic and environmental value of voluntary mitigation actions and their co-benefits for adaptation, health and sustainable development' (COP21 Article 108; see also Sirkis et al., 2015). In France, debate was already under way on the innovative potential for monetary policy to support the energy transition. For example, in February 2015, France Stratégie – the former Commissariat au Plan and think tank of the prime minister – published a proposal for financing low-carbon investment in Europe using the quantitative easing program of the European Central Bank (ECB).

Looking just at the text of the Agreement, however, misses much of the significance of the overall Paris package on climate finance. The second ring of action involved financial system rule-makers – and Paris became the symbolic location for the launch of a new FSB task force on climate disclosure. On the back of the G20's mandate to explore climate risks back in April, the FSB held a consultation with governments and private sector experts in London in September. Drawing heavily on the Bank of England's identification of three key climate risks facing the financial system – physical, transition and litigation risks – in November, the FSB's chair Mark Carney proposed the creation of a new industry-led disclosure task force to enable a better understanding of these risks (Bank of England, 2015). The task force was modeled on the FSB's Enhanced Disclosure Task Force (EDTF) that had been set up to bring clarity to often opaque financial reporting after the crisis. The new climate disclosure task force would also be industry-led and focus on drawing up voluntary guidelines to bring consistency to the world of reporting so that it was useful to lenders, insurers, investors and also financial regulators (FSB, 2015). For Carney, 'companies would disclose not only what they are emitting today, but how they plan their transition to the net-zero world of the future' (Carney, 2015).

After overcoming initial doubts from some members, the G20 gave the go-ahead at its summit in Antalya. The task force was then announced by Carney within the Le Bourget negotiating halls, under the chairmanship of former New York mayor and financial information guru Michael Bloomberg. Nowhere in the Paris Agreement is there any mention of the new FSB task force or the role of financial regulation. But financial regulation was now accepted as a critical dimension of the overall solution set, something unthinkable a year earlier. The governor of the Banque de France, François Villeroy de Galhau, also chose the Paris negotiations as the moment to give for the first time his own perspective of the implications of climate change for central banking. For him, the challenge boiled down to two key questions: 'how to ensure that investors and financial intermediaries are aware of their actual exposure to risks? And how to prevent a misallocation of capital to carbon-intensive sectors or stranded assets?' (Villeroy de Galhau, 2015). Importantly, Villeroy de Galhau went beyond the normal discussions of climate finance to explore the implications for monetary policy, arguing that 'climate change is likely to affect the price of goods and services ... and monetary policy will have to play its role of contributing to a smoother rebalancing of price structures, in line with its price stability mandate'. He also highlighted that responding to environmental factors is already part of the mandate for the eurozone (ESCB, Statute Article 2). Until now, however, this explicit requirement that the ECB align its policies to sustainable growth, 'respecting the environment', had not led to any formal policy moves.

And beyond these first steps from the regulatory community lay the third circle of commitments from financial institutions themselves. Collective action by investors to support global climate policy had started in the late 2000s in the run-up to the 2009 Copenhagen negotiations (IIGCC, 2008). Now, institutional investors with assets of more than US$24 trillion gave their backing to an ambitious deal in Paris, including the introduction of far-reaching carbon pricing. On top of this statement of strategic intent, financiers launched a host of more specific initiatives to change the actual allocation of capital.

Twenty-eight leading billionaire investors – such as Bill Gates, Vinod Khosla, Jack Ma and George Soros – came together in the Breakthrough Energy Coalition to place private capital behind innovative clean technologies coming out of the public research pipeline. A further US$11 trillion of investment capital also pledged to support policies to grow the green bond market, which had emerged as one of the most promising ways of allocating capital for specific climate finance solutions (Climate Bonds Initiative, 2016b). French bond issuers, including municipalities such as the Île de France and corporations like EDF, had been in the vanguard of the green bond growth, supported by French banks such as Crédit Agricole.

Investors were also opening up to greater scrutiny of their own climate performance. Just 10 years earlier in 2005, the first carbon footprint of an investment fund had been published. Now in Paris, institutions with more than US$10 trillion in assets committed themselves to this basic step in transparency, with the first signatory to this pledge being a French pension fund (ERAFP) (PRI, 2014). Going beyond this, the Portfolio Decarbonization Coalition (PDC) had mobilized an alliance of 25 investors committing to reduce the carbon footprint of US$600 billion of assets under management. Initiated by a Swedish and a French pension fund (AP4 and FRR) along with a French asset manager (Amundi) and managed by UNEP's Finance Initiative, the PDC had gathered more than six times the amount expected when the Coalition was launched in September 2014. All of this was part of the NAZCA platform of pledges made by non-state actors – with 425 of the more than 10,000 pledges made by financial institutions.

Financing the transition

As 2016 started, trading screens across the world initially turned red, not green, as markets took fright over the prospects for the global economy. Little connection was made between these short-term fears and the long-term climate agreement reached just weeks before.

Yet what came out of Paris can be seen not just as an environmental deal, but as the outline of a strategy for harnessing the financial system behind a new phase of global development. Looking back, the networked solution on financing climate action is a powerful expression of Nobel Prize-winning economist Elinor Ostrom's insight that the future lay in a 'polycentric' model of governance (Ostrom, 2015). In Paris, the package of solutions came not just from different levels of government, but also from different parts of the policy arena, stretching far beyond classic climate policies to the public and private rules that govern global capital.

Clearly, the value of this networked model of financing climate action will be shown in how capital is actually deployed in the real world far from the conference hall. As President Hollande highlighted, 'the agreement is not an end, but just a beginning'. Its elements remain new and fragile – and subject to the usual problems of any negotiated agreement: backtracking, inertia and relegation by other newer issues on the political agenda. Yet at its heart, the package is based on the recognition that the structure of the financial response to climate change must reflect both the hard logic of climate science as well as the complexity of the financial system itself.

The likely resilience of the Paris financial package to the normal battering that comes to any climate agreement lies in its networked model, drawing on the dynamic, distributed nature of global finance. Much still needs to be done to make climate a routine factor in the work of central banks, financial regulators, commercial banks and insurance companies. Most central banks and regulators have yet to work though their role in enabling the orderly transition to a zero carbon, zero damage world. But the sense of a new agenda is apparent both among policy makers and capital markets. China has placed green finance at the heart of its 13th Five-Year Plan – and across the Channel, the City of London has launched its own Green Finance Initiative to rapidly expand issuance of green bonds and other instruments.

The year 2015 showed that a new strategic approach to financing climate action was possible. For 2016 and beyond, a number of actions can be taken to accelerate the momentum to make financial flows 'climate consistent'. In Paris itself, a key focus will be on implementing the new Energy Transition law, both the new investor disclosure requirements as well as setting out how climate factors could be included in banking sector stress tests. France although passing the presidency of climate negotiations over to Morocco during November 2016, remains fully engaged on these issues.

At the system level, this embryonic networked approach needs to be fleshed out and deepened. Internationally, three priorities stand out: strategy, tools and rules. An ungainly phrase, but the INDCs were one of the real successes of COP21. The next step is to take the high-level policy directions and translate them into more detailed 'green finance strategies', working through the specific mix of incentives, standards, regulations and alliances needed to mobilize both domestic and international capital, particularly for developing countries (Callaghan, 2015). Here, the new Green Infrastructure Investment Coalition is one expression of a new desire from both governments and investors to develop long-term pipelines of green assets that simultaneously support national ambitions and also meet investors' risk/return requirements (Climate Bonds Initiative, 2016a).

To deliver these strategies, financial institutions and policymakers will need new tools to make climate and wider sustainability factors a routine part of financial decisions. Markets work best when the right information is available – and the new FSB task force has moved quickly to set out its initial thoughts on the fundamental principles of effective disclosures. In its first report, the task force made clear that transparency can reduce the potential for large, abrupt corrections in asset values that can destabilize financial markets (FSB, 2016). The FSB task force will publish its final report in February 2017. Better disclosure will also be essential to build confidence in the new wave of commitments that financial institutions have made on carbon footprinting and carbon reduction. And tools need capacity – pointing to the importance of building the right skills and behaviors among the hundreds of thousands of financial professionals across the world.

Beyond disclosure, new rules of the road are also needed to place climate change at the heart of financial governance. The road to Paris helped to fundamentally shift the burden of proof on how environmental, social and governance factors, exemplified by climate change, relate to core investor responsibilities such as fiduciary duty. Based on real-world experience, the new consensus is that 'a failure to consider long-term drivers of investment value including environmental, social and governance issues in investment practice is a failure of fiduciary duty' (PRI,

2015). This conclusion has ramifications beyond common law jurisdictions where fiduciary duty drives investment practice – and speaks to the structural task of making sure that the consideration of climate factors becomes part of the governance of all financial institutions. For example, traditional definitions of prudence in banking will need to be rethought so that climate factors become part of routine definitions of risk appetite, prefigured by France's extension of conventional stress tests to the environmental sphere. This question of governance also has a profound social dimension. Inclusion has become an accepted goal of global financial policy – for climate action, the challenge is to now think through the changes in financial incentives and duties so that the capital required becomes accessible to all.

The networked solution that came together in Paris needs all these elements to work together – markets that anticipate future shocks, public finance that pulls forward private capital and regulation that extends the notion of financial stability to incorporate the new imperative of decarbonization and resilience. In the end, the Paris package does not guarantee that the finance will flow. But it makes it possible – in a new framework that has a real potential to shift the trillions.

References

14CE (2015) Landscape of a Climate Finance (www.i4ce.org/download/landscape-of-climate-finance-2015-edition/). Accessed September 8, 2016.

2 Degrees Investing Initiative (2015) Assessing the Alignment of Portfolios with Climate Goals (http://2degrees-investing.org/IMG/pdf/2dportfolio_v0_small.pdf). Accessed September 8, 2016.

Bank of England (2015) Prudential Regulatory Authority: The Impact of Climate Change on the UK Insurance Sector (www.bankofengland.co.uk/pra/documents/supervision/activities/pradefra0915.pdf). Accessed September 8, 2016.

Breakthrough Energy Coalition (www.breakthroughenergycoalition.com/en/index.html). Accessed September 8, 2016.

Callaghan, I. (2015) Climate Finance After COP21. InvestorWatch. (http://calltoactiononclimatefinance.net/site/data/000/000/Climate_Finance_After_COP21_Final_011215_MG2.pdf). Accessed September 8, 2016.

Canfin-Grandjean Commission (2015) Mobilising Climate Finance (www.elysee.fr/assets/Report-Commission-Canfin-Grandjean-ENG.pdf). Accessed September 8, 2016.

Carney, M. (2015) Breaking the Tragedy of the Horizon – Climate Change and Financial Stability. Bank of England (www.bankofengland.co.uk/pra/documents/supervision/activities/pradefra0915.pdf). Accessed September 8, 2016.

Citigroup (2015) Energy Darwinism II (climateobserver.org/wp-content/uploads/2015/09/Energy-Darwinism-Citi-GPS.pdf). Accessed September 8, 2016.

Climate Bonds Initiative (2016a) Green Infrastructure Investment Coalition (www.climatebonds.net/files/files/Launch_COP21_Green%20Infrastructure%20Investment%20Coalition-Dec%202015.pdf). Accessed 14 September, 2016.

Climate Bonds Initiative (2016b) The Paris Green Bond Statement (www.climatebonds.net/resources/press-releases/Paris-Green-Bonds-Statement). Accessed September 8, 2016.

COP21 Agreement (2015) Article 43, 52, 108. (https://unfccc.int/resource/docs/2015/cop21/eng/l09.pdf). Accessed October 18, 2016.

EIU (2015) Recognizing the Cost of Inaction (www.economistinsights.com/financial-services/analysis/cost-inaction). Accessed August 12, 2015.

European System of Central Banks (ESCB), Statute Article 2.

Extel/UKSIF (2015) Mobilising Climate Finance (www.extelsurveys.com/Panel_Pages/PanelPagesBriefings.aspx?FileName=Extel-UKSIF_SRI_Report_2015). Accessed September 8, 2016.

France Stratégie (2015) (http://blog.en.strategie.gouv.fr/2015/02/policy-brief-proposal-finance-low-carbon-investment-europe/). Accessed September 24, 2015.

FSB (2015) Proposal for a Disclosure Task Force on Climate-related Risks (www.fsb.org/wp-content/uploads/Disclosure-task-force-on-climate-related-risks.pdf). Accessed September 8, 2016.

FSB (2016) *Phase I Report of the Task Force on Climate-Related Financial Disclosures* (https://www.fsb-tcfd.org/wp-content/uploads/2016/03/Phase_I_Report_v15.pdf). Accessed September 8, 2016.

Global Justice Program (2016) Yale University (http://globaljustice.macmillan.yale.edu). Accessed September 8, 2016.

IIGCC (2008) Investor Statement on a Global Agreement on Climate Change (www.iigcc.org/files/publication-files/Investor_statement_on_a_global_agreement_2008.pdf). Accessed September 8, 2016.

Ministry of Finance, Government of India (2015) Climate and Finance – An Analysis of a Recent OECD Report (http://finmin.nic.in/the_ministry/dept_eco_affairs/economic_div/ClimateChangeOEFDReport.pdf). Accessed September 8, 2016.

ODI and Oil Change International (2015) Empty Promises (www.odi.org/sites/odi.org.uk/files/odi-assets/publications-opinion-files/9957.pdf). Accessed September 8, 2016.

OECD (2015) Climate Finance in 2013–14 and the USD 100 Billion Goal (www.oecd.org/environment/cc/OECD-CPI-Climate-Finance-Report.pdf). Accessed September 8, 2016.

Ostrom, E. (2009) *A Polycentric Approach for Coping with Climate Change*. Policy Research Working Paper 5095.

Oxford Martin School (2015) Working Principles for Investment in Fossil Fuels (www.oxfordmartin.ox.ac.uk/publications/view/2073). Accessed September 8, 2016.

Paris Agreement (2015) Article 2c, 8. (http://unfccc.int/files/essential_background/convention/application/pdf/english_paris_agreement.pdf). Accessed October 18, 2016.

Portfolio Decarbonization Coalition (PDC) (2016) (http://unepfi.org/pdc/category/news/). Accessed September 8, 2016.

PRI (2014) Montreal Climate Pledge (http://montrealpledge.org/). Accessed September 8, 2016.

PRI, Global Compact, UNEP Finance Initiative and UNEP Inquiry (2015) Fiduciary Duty in the 21st Century (www.unepfi.org/fileadmin/documents/fiduciary_duty_21st_century.pdf). Accessed 14 September, 2016.

Sirkis, A., Hourcade, J.-C., Dasgupta, D., Studart, R., Gallagher, K., Perrissin-Fabert, B., Eli da Veiga, J., Espagne, E., Stua, M. and Aglietta, M. (2015) *Moving the Trillions: A Debate on Positive Pricing of Mitigation Actions*. Rio de Janeiro: BrasilClima (www.centrobrasilnoclima.org/precificacao-de-carbono/). Accessed September 8, 2016.

Spencer, T. (2015) The Future of Coal: The Long Comedown. EnergyPost (www.energypost.eu/future-coal- long-comedown/). Accessed September 8, 2016.

Trésor Direction Générale (2016) (www.tresor.economie.gouv.fr/12541_cahier-des-charges-du-label-isr-soutenu-par-les-pouvoirs-publics-). Accessed September 8, 2016.

UNEP (2015) The Emission Gap Report (http://uneplive.unep.org/media/docs/theme/13/EGR_2015_301115_lores.pdf). Accessed September 8, 2016.

UNEP Inquiry (2015) The Coming Financial Climate (http://unepinquiry.org/wp-content/uploads/2015/05/Aligning_the_Financial_System_with_Sustainable_Development_4_The_Coming_Financial_Climate.pdf). Accessed September 8, 2016.

UNEP Inquiry and 14CE (2015) France's Financial (Eco)system (http://unepinquiry.org/publication/france-country-report/). Accessed September 8, 2016.

UNFCCC (2015) Synthesis Report on the Aggregate Effect of the INFCs (http://unfccc.int/resource/docs/2015/cop21/eng/07.pdf). Accessed September 8, 2016.

United Nations (UNFCCC) (2015) Safeguarding Future Retirement Funds – Time for Investors to Move Out of High-Carbon Assets Says UN's Top Climate Official (https://unfccc.int/files/press/press_releases_advisories/application/pdf/pr20140115_ceres_final1.pdf). Accessed September 8, 2016.

V20 Communique (2015) (www.v-20.org/v20-communique/). Accessed September 8, 2016.

Villeroy de Galhau, F. (2015) Climate Change – The Financial Sector and Pathways to 2°C (www.bis.org/review/r151229f.htm). Accessed September 8, 2016.

Chapter 5

The value of everything[1]

Cary Krosinsky

Introduction

Discussions regarding the global financial system often happen without a complete and robust understanding of the total value, impact and relevance of all stocks and flows. Indeed, even the 'value of everything' is not known, insofar as that being measured as the total present-day market value of all global capital assets, let alone the relevance of ongoing flows of commerce as they impact the system.

The purpose of this chapter is to begin the process of clarifying global asset value, especially as may be affected by the sustainability (or lack thereof) of financial systems, and not just that which is represented by institutional assets under management.

Often such attempts to assess the value of financial markets only look at total managed assets in certain asset classes as are reported by financial institutions, or for example through attempts to assess somewhat isolated international money flows.

This chapter, therefore, will answer the question of what is the actual total value of all global asset classes individually, and in aggregate, towards helping inform money flows that relate to the overall global stock, and how do they or can they influence total value, as well as how should these stocks and flows shift to enable the financial system to become truly sustainable and how to measure for that.

Attempts have been made to assess the value of global assets but they are always insufficient for purpose, either missing categories such as the value of state-owned enterprises, the value of people's homes, the true nature of cash in the market and more. Such partial analysis has revealed useful aspects of this single total value figure, which we will make good use of, but our picture will be holistic and complete, or will certainly attempt to be so.

The first place to start, then, is in establishing categories of assets needed to be understood in order to fully assess a static, present-day value of everything.

The three largest categories of assets by value are publicly traded companies, fixed income, and property owned by individuals or in managed portfolios. State-owned enterprises and the total value of infrastructure portfolios, both through direct investment and project finance, are critical to this analysis. Private equity and venture capital are rising in relevance and will be assessed alongside the value of so-called real assets encompassing forests and commodities and the value of issued dollars in the market both in cash and in the nominal value of instruments not directly tied to assets.

This analysis represents a first single static value of everything, in effect the total value of global assets.

Public equity

Companies which trade on public markets have shares outstanding, either traded or sitting in their treasuries, and multiplying this by the current share price gives a total value figure of public equity as an asset class. Care needs to be applied to ensure double counting is avoided, such as where companies trade on multiple stock exchanges or are represented by American depositary receipts (ADRs) which are not separate entities from the underlying corporation in question.

Analysis determined this figure to be US$65 trillion as of early 2008 (Krosinsky, 2008), before stock valuations sank in the wake of the subsequent Global Financial Crisis (GFC). This analysis followed the aforementioned process, that is, looked at one company at a time, calculated the market capitalization of each individual company listed on a global stock exchange, and aggregated the values into one figure.

To the present day, there have not been significant new issuances of securities through IPOs or secondary offerings to dramatically change this picture. Markets have largely recovered their valuations up to date of the finalization of this book. The MSCI World representing 85 percent of global market capitalization is in effect directly even since this time (MSCI, 2016). McKinsey's Global Institute (MGI) also approximated US$64 trillion at the end of 2007, directly correlating with this analysis. The MSCI Emerging Markets Index also remains largely flat since the GFC (MSCI, 2016).

Global IPO issuance has largely slowed down in recent years, Alibaba having been an outlier of sorts, and just over US$200 billion of new issuance occurring as a result, up almost 50 percent from the year prior (Renaissance Capital, 2014). This represented the highest level of issuance since 2010, with little occurring in 2008–9 due to the GFC. It can be estimated that at most an additional US$1 trillion of new public company stock has been issued since the GFC, making the total value of global public equity now between US$65 and 70 trillion (EY, 2014). Thus, US$67 trillion will be used as an acceptable present-day estimate, and with market valuations not having moved much since, this figure still stands as valid. Such figures change not only daily due to price variability, but millisecond to millisecond, based on the presently accepted share price of each company due to its own midpoint of buyer and seller sentiment at any moment.

Fixed income

Fixed income is more difficult to assess, because it represents an overall pool of cash lent out to other parties. Therefore, placing a dollar value on fixed income has some caveats, namely that the owner of a fixed income instrument or portfolio does not own the underlying company unless it were to go bankrupt. Consequently, fixed income as an overall asset class represents both a stock and a flow in the global financial system. That said, the total value of all fixed income instruments in issue can be readily calculated, with US values at US$35 trillion, developed excluding the US at US$50 trillion, and emerging market debt valued at US$14 trillion for a total of US$99 trillion (J. P. Morgan, 2015). This figure includes corporate, sovereign, treasuries, high yield and municipal debt in all countries.

The nature of global lending

Beyond estimates of the value of fixed income as a global assets class, the true size of global lending is not well understood. For example, as seen above, the value of fixed income is approximately US$100 trillion, the largest global asset class of all, while direct lending and other forms of loans are increasingly not visible. This lack of transparency could be a result of black market means as typically observed in the developing world or through aggregations of loans to public and private companies from banking operations that otherwise are not accessible in the public domain.

Categorization of global lending is needed, along with an estimation of areas that are not readily transparent, in order to get a first, full grasp of the size of global lending. Ultimately, there is lending to individuals and families, loans to organizations including public companies, and debt issued by governments on a national and regional basis. Some of this debt will be listed on exchanges and fully transparent, while much lending is direct between a source of funds and the recipient in question, sometimes but not always involving regulated institutions.

SIFMA recently listed US debt at just under US$39 trillion across municipal, Treasury, mortgage-related, corporate debt, other federal agency and asset-backed securities, with an additional US$5.8 trillion issued in 2014 and with outstanding issuance rising roughly US$1 trillion per year, implying almost US$5 trillion per year of debt having settled or otherwise reaching maturity.

Much of the value of everything is in the so-called 'real economy'. Property and infrastructure are in the real economy and non-real economy or purely financial aspects of public companies can be estimated at 20 percent of the total value, or $13.4 trillion, for example. Fixed income, cash, and derivatives by definition are not part of the real economy of physical things. (Thereby, the 'real economy' portion of the value of global capital assets can be estimated at US$225 trillion or exactly half of the value of everything.)

To further understand the effect of lending on the real economy, then lending needs to be broken down further into its components. A significant portion of lending is performed for the purpose of building infrastructure, providing mortgages for homes and otherwise providing capital to businesses for the purpose of creating goods. Therefore, annual new levels of lending should be understood in the context of how it supports and fosters health and growth in the real economy.

If 80 percent of existing fixed income goes into supporting the real economy, then it is apparent that US$80 trillion is supporting US$225 trillion in value as a first observation, and that an ongoing flow of new lending is needed to support both existing and future flows and valuations of the real economy.

In the US, per the SIFMA analysis above there was over US$5 trillion of new debt, mostly offset by retiring debt, for a net increase of just over US$1 trillion. The Bank for International Settlements (BIS) is an especially good resource for financial flow data, with their March 2015 Highlights of Global Financial Flows showing at the end of September 2014 that credit in US dollars to non-bank borrowers outside the United States is approximately US$9.2 trillion, an increase of 9 percent over the previous year, representing an increase of over 50 percent since the end of 2009. The breakdown of this US$9.2 trillion is reflected by US$4.2 trillion of debt securities and US$4.9 trillion of bank loans.

Furthermore, net of repayments, cumulative international debt securities issuance in 2014 was US$178 billion for advanced economies and US$359 billion for emerging markets, suggesting a net additional US$1 trillion was seen in 2014 in both the US and separately, outside the US, for a total of US$2 trillion in net new global lending in 2014.

Property

Often ignored in conversations about the value of global assets is the value in people's homes. In the US, for example, after the various Enron, WorldCom, Adelphia and other accounting scandals of the early 2000s, many individuals sought to maximize the value of their homes having lost trust in public stock markets. In fact, many pension funds at best broke even in such markets during the 2000s. By a combination of the domino effect of decreased trust in markets with a race to seek value in real estate, which was also encouraged by looser forms of credit to encourage home ownership, the value of home-owned property proceeded to collapse. Many homeowners walked away from 'underwater' mortgages. Property markets as a result can be quite volatile and difficult to estimate, but best efforts show that approximately US$75 trillion of value is owned by global individuals in their homes. When combined with the additional US$20 trillion of property (including commercial real estate) owned by pension funds, endowments, and similar, the total value in owned properties becomes US$95 trillion. Thus, while fixed income is the largest global asset class, the total value of global property is comparable.

State-owned enterprises

Harder still to value are state-owned enterprises as well as government assets overall, as these are by definition not publicly traded. However, assessing these assets as if they were to go public enables the calculation of an estimate for the value of state-owned enterprises. This category forms an important proportion of global value, whether considering fossil fuel reserves owned by governments or the companies which represent such interests. It is important to prevent double counting, as some organizations have publicly listed shares representing a very small fraction of the overall value. A best estimate of this category is US$35 trillion, understanding that without such companies being privatized and traded, this figure will remain nebulous by definition, but must without question be considered in this analysis.

Privately owned companies

Privately held companies, as well as earlier stage venture capital supporting such potential value creation, represents a rapidly growing segment of markets. They were valued at US$3.8 trillion in June 2014 (Preqin, 2015), and so given continued growth in this space we will use US$4 trillion as our present estimate. While efforts are under way to build social enterprises, such as B Corporations, impact investments and other forms of 'social capital', these remain in the margin of error of this larger figure. However, moves from public companies such as Natura and possibly Unilever are encouraging.

Infrastructure

Infrastructure is one of the more important, yet at times overlooked asset classes. Representing myriad business activities, estimates for increased infrastructure investment show upwards of an additional US$50–75 trillion of new capital going into this segment by 2030 (MGI, 2013). A gap exists in funding for such investment, despite the clear emerging need for infrastructure to help enable any necessary 'green transition'.

Infrastructure is generally thought to include highways, railways, ports, energy, water, airports and sometimes also telecommunications infrastructure. In some ways, the sunk costs of global infrastructure are not nearly as important as the future directionality of new spend on this asset class. One estimate shows that over US$2 trillion of investment went into new global infrastructure from 2008 to 2011.

Infrastructure which remains in use has only existed in these categories for the most part for the past 50 years, and given depreciation of longer-term assets built some time ago, the value of many projects can be said to be less significant and there is an understandable focus to maximize existing assets both from an efficiency savings and extending of use perspective. From 1992 to 2011, China became the largest contributor to the total US$30 trillion of investment that went into infrastructure, before depreciation (MGI, 2013). While McKinsey estimated existing infrastructure to be valued at US$50 trillion as of 2012, this does not appear to represent depreciated value. Instead, US$35 trillion will be used as a global proxy for the total present value of global existing infrastructure owned in portfolios and by governments.

Real assets

Additional categories of owned assets include land, forests, gold and other tradable commodities, including fossil fuel projects outside of public companies or state-owned enterprises in private hands. The value of each subcategory of these commodities can be estimated, as can the total value of these in managed portfolios. Currently, an estimate of this value is approximately US$10 trillion.

Cash

Three pools of capital must be considered in regards to cash: cash deposits in banks, cash in issuance including foreign exchange, and the value of money market funds. Cash deposits in banks were US$54 trillion in 2010 (MGI, 2011), foreign exchange reserves roughly US$12 trillion in 2013 (IMF, 2014), and the value of money market funds in the US roughly US$2.6 trillion (ICI, 2016), adding to global cash in circulation. An estimate of US$75 trillion will be maintained as an overall figure representing global cash.

Aggregating with the aforementioned categories, the total value in the stock of global assets becomes US$420 trillion.

Other nominal value of instruments

However, the current Age of Securitization has led to derivatives and other forms of creative finance forming an additional layer of 'value'. The BIS put the total value of derivatives outstanding at over US$1,000 trillion in 2013 (BIS, 2015), or a factor of approximately three times the value of every other asset class combined (which upon first recognition, should be cause for concern). Given levels of leverage involved in establishing these derivatives (another area of concern), US$50 trillion of value can be deduced given an approximate average of 20 times leverage being deployed (Nguyen, 2014). Another estimate reveals US$12 trillion of cash tied up in derivatives markets (AmericaBlog, 2013). Additional research must be conducted to accurately determine the underlying value of these instruments, currently an analysis beyond public scrutiny. Consequently, by including another US$30 trillion in the value of everything, the total becomes US$450 trillion.

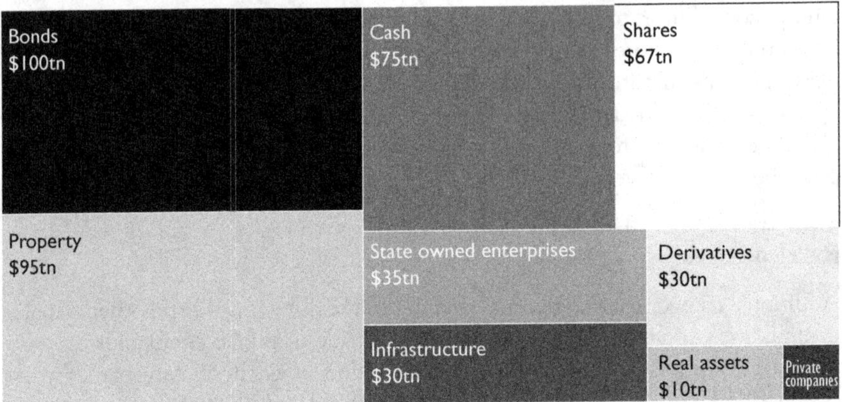

Figure 5.1 The value of everything.
Source: UNEP Inquiry/Krosinsky.

Black market banking

Similarly, black market banking, lending and trading is a rising phenomenon beyond public scrutiny. Dark pool trading in public equities is not a factor in the value of global assets from a stock perspective, but levels of underground banking and commerce do factor in and can be difficult to quantify. The World Bank has made attempts to do just this (Korea Institute of Public Finance, 2005). Given that this represents in effect 'illegitimate' activities, it will not be considered in the value of global legitimate assets.

Understanding institutional investment – half of the value of everything

Half of the value of everything, or US$225 trillion, falls under the ownership of institutional investors, managed either actively or passively, representing a higher figure than is often cited publicly.

This US$225 trillion includes a majority proportion of public companies (the largest 1,000 public companies make up a significant proportion of global market capitalization) and are 70 percent institutionally owned, as high as 73 percent in 2010 (TCB, 2010) up from a minority position a generation ago (Conference Board, 2000).

Most fixed income is also commonly owned by institutional investors. Furthermore, managed portfolios of properties, infrastructure, and real assets can be considered largely managed, as would be the entirety of the notional value of derivatives. Cash is excluded alongside 'valuing nature' and other types of consideration.

Further discussion: infrastructure to drive a low-carbon economy

A further examination of the value of everything is in order, especially as pertains to the need for more infrastructure investment. There is over $1 trillion of net new fixed income issued annually, while estimates vary on the predicted increase in infrastructure spending. However, much future financial action will focus on fixed income and infrastructure, further enhancing the importance of how green these allocations become. Such investments are by definition long term, commonly varying from 20 to 100 years in intended life. It is much harder to change the environmental footprint of existing organizations, projects, and previously issued debt, shifting the area of interest towards the nature of new investment allocations.

Therefore, how to guide future infrastructure investment becomes a major source of both opportunity and concern.

It is first important to determine the expected value of future investment in infrastructure. KPMG estimated the value of infrastructure investment to rise to $78 trillion by 2025 in a report entitled the *Infrastructure 100 World Markets Report* (2014), but the same report predicted that, for example in the US, investment is lagging behind optimal levels. A more recent KPMG report on *Assessing the Value of Infrastructure Investment* (2016) identified investment shortfalls emerging in China as well, with up to a 40 percent gap in private investment. This estimate implies an additional $48 trillion over 10 years, significantly greater than the probable amount of investment given the state of national economies and budget shortfalls that exist today. Even if the additional spend was in the range of $25 trillion, $2.5 trillion of new investment would be necessary each year.

The UNEP Inquiry report, *The Financial System We Need* (UNEP 2015) claims that: '$5–7 trillion will be needed every year to achieve the SDGs on infrastructure, clean energy, water, sanitation and agriculture. In the developing world alone, the financing gap is estimated at $2.5 trillion a year.' Thus, the figures presented above are consistent with independent sources.

And so, key concerns emerge both over where the necessary spending will originate, as well as how it will be spent.

A variety of groups are attempting to tackle the question of green infrastructure, such as the PRI, the IFC and IMF, and new efforts such as those by the Aligned Intermediary, the Asian Infrastructure Investment Bank (AIIB), and the World Bank. However, these efforts often constitute insignificant amounts as compared to the trillions needed, failing to reach the pace of the transition to a low-carbon economy.

This reality drives the concern surrounding whether the money is actually available for this transition. The $100 trillion value of fixed income is money that has already been lent out and, similarly, the $70 trillion value of public companies is baked into their share prices. While they do have $2–3 trillion of cash on the books and hiding in offshore domiciles, this amount is not significant enough to help pay for this sort of effort.

Therefore, if we need to ensure that the transition to a low-carbon economy happens at the pace required, a form of 'green stimulus' may well be needed to make this happen. If approximately $50 trillion is needed to fully finance the necessary low-carbon transition, one approach could be to print that money and deflate value accordingly. If the value of everything were $500 trillion instead of $450 trillion that would be just over a 10 percent deflation and profit over time from the new infrastructure could pay this money back to governments.

Arguably a more applicable approach would be a global public–private partnership to generate this $50 trillion of new spend, including $25 trillion from a green stimulus over time and another $25 trillion from private investors, who again would be paid back over time as part of a long-term investment program. This would deflate the value of everything even less, by just over 5 percent. Again the payback would be significant, as would mitigating the loss of existing value due to the avoidance of climate change and its negative financial effects.

If completed over 20–25 years, then approximately $1 trillion per year on average from both sides of this equation would pay for this transition in full. Inevitably, this transition and funding requires careful planning, and the development of a process of checks and balances involving every category of stakeholders from local communities to global leaders.

The first thing to do is make sure we all agree on its necessity.

Note

1 Adapted by Kathryne Chamberlain.

References

AmericaBlog (2013) Worldwide Derivatives Market Could Be Over $1.2 Quadrillion in Notional Value (http://americablog.com/2013/03/the-worldwide-derivatives-market-could-be-over-1-2-quadrillion-in-notional-value.html). Accessed September 8, 2016.

Bank for International Settlements (BIS) (2015) IS Quarterly Review, September 2015 (www.bis.org/statistics/dt1920a.pdf). Accessed September 8, 2016.

EY (2014) *Global IPO Trends Report* G4 (2013) (http://www.ey.com/Publication/vwLUAssets/EY_-_Global_IPO_Trends_Q4_2013/$FILE/EY-Global-IPO-Trends-Q4-2013.pdf). Accessed October 18, 2016.

International Monetary Fund (2014) *Annual Report* (www.imf.org/external/pubs/ft/ar/2014/eng/pdf/a1.pdf). Accessed September 8, 2016.

Investment Company Institute (ICI) (2016) Frequently Asked Questions About Money Market Funds (www.ici.org/mmfs/basics/faqs_money_funds). Accessed September 8, 2016.

J. P. Morgan (2015) (www.jpmorganfunds.com/blobcontent/750/453/1323371472246_MI-GTM- 1Q2015_Mar_highres-37.png). Accessed September 8, 2016.

Korea Institute of Public Finance (2005) Underground Economy: Causes and Sizes (siteresources.worldbank.org/PSGLP/Resources/UndergroundEconomyPark.pdf). Accessed September 8, 2016.

KPMG (2014) *Infrastructure 100 World Markets Report* (www.kpmg.com/Global/en/IssuesAndInsights/ArticlesPublications/infra100-world-markets/Documents/infrastructure-100-world-markets-report-v3.pdf). Accessed September 8, 2016.

KPMG (2016) Assessing the Value of Infrastructure Investment (home.kpmg.com/content/dam/kpmg/pdf/2016/02/value-of-infrastructure-investment.pdf). Accessed September 8, 2016.

Krosinsky, C. (2008) *Capital Bridge*. MSCI 2016 MSCI World Index (USD) (www.msci.com/resources/factsheets/index_fact_sheet/msci-world-index.pdf). Accessed September 8, 2016.

McKinsey Global Institute (MGI) (2013) *Infrastructure Report* (http://www.mckinsey.com/~/media/McKinsey/Industries/Capital%20Projects%20and%20Infrastructure/Our%20Insights/Infrastructure%20productivity/MGI%20Infrastructure_Executive%20summary_Jan%202013.ashx). Accessed September 8, 2016.

MGI (2011) Mapping Global Capital Markets (www.mckinsey.com/industries/private-equity-and-principal-investors/our-insights/mapping-global-capital-markets-2011). Accessed September 8, 2016.

MSCI (2016) MSCI Emerging Markets Index (USD) (www.msci.com/resources/factsheets/index_fact_sheet/msci-emerging-markets-index-usd-net.pdf). Accessed September 8, 2016.

Nguyen, A. (2014) Unpublished paper, Yale.

PR Newswire (2016) (www.prnewswire.com). Accessed September 8, 2016.

Preqin (2015) *Global Private Equity and Venture Capital Report* Sample Pages (https://www.preqin.com/docs/reports/2015-Preqin-Global-Private-Equity-and-Venture-Capital-Report-Sample-Pages.pdf). Accessed September 8, 2016.

Renaissance Capital (2014) Global IPO Market: 2014 Annual Review (www.renaissancecapital.com/profile/showpdf.aspx?filename=2014GlobalReview). Accessed September 8, 2016.

The Conference Board (TCB) (2010) *Report: Institutional Investors Owning More of Larger Companies* (http://tcbblogs.org/governance/2010/11/23/report-institutional-investors-owning-more-of-larger-companies/). Accessed October 18, 2016.

UNEP (2015) *The Financial System We Need*. The UNEP Inquiry report. (www.unep.org/inquiry). Accessed September 8, 2016.

Part II

Systems and systemic solutions

Chapter 6

Thinking in systems

Cary Krosinsky

It is increasingly clear that environmental, social and corporate governance concerns are largely systemic issues and as a result, these challenges require systemic solutions. These issues won't be solved by investment alone, or by companies alone, or by just policymakers for that matter. All parties will need to move in tandem if any significant shift – say in low-carbon energy – at the scale required is to occur, supported by a consensus of scientists coupled with robust grassroots awareness and the average person insisting on required change through asking the right kind of questions.

Right now we don't have any of these things. We have attempts to invest in a sustainable manner that are insufficient, we have some companies making significant moves, again a minority, and policymakers are just getting started.

Nor are enough people asking the right kind of questions.

Through examining the entirety of the global system of commerce, combined with an understanding of system dynamics and systems thinking, we can start to envision the right kind of solutions that can be enabled through insistence in the right strategies for change.

When you consider the value of everything, and the ownership patterns of all of the asset classes which relate, one realizes how entrenched the current system is, and even more so when you consider the entrenched nature of the status quo.

Climate change is embedded in all of commerce, indeed in all of everyday life. Fossil fuels are in our plastic bottles and many other petrochemical-derived products. Fossil fuels are the strong majority of the transportation that occurs within the supply chains of the products we buy, in the heating of buildings where we live and work and much more.

Consider also that there is often a cost incurred for switching from what you have to instead own something new, whether a car, a building or a power plant. The expected carbon emissions from the status quo of cars that will continue to be driven, buildings that will continue to be operated inefficiently by, say, wealthy families who choose not to act on climate change, and power plants that burn fossil fuel and were designed for 50 years of use are enough alone to bust the carbon budget, let alone the additional new coal plants being planned in many parts of developing Asia.

Transitioning away from current levels of use of coal, oil and gas will take time and a gigantic, global, simultaneous wedge of hundreds of concurrent solutions all coming together in time and in the right way, including the leapfrogging of developing countries on energy.

What will be needed in China alone to scale renewable energy at the levels that seem required will take implementation, enforcement, connectivity, integration, resolve, cooperation, money and much more all happening in parallel. India will be even harder, and Indonesia and Malaysia will be no walk in the park. But we can leave no stone unturned.

If we need to build the system that can provide the transitions required, can we learn from systems thinking to understand what actually works from a system perspective?

In some ways this is everything.

Fundamentally important is the work of the late Donella Meadows. If you read one book on this subject, it should be the posthumously published *Thinking in Systems*.

Questions arise from this classic book, starting with what is a system.

- Can you identify the parts of any system?
- Do the parts affect each other?
- Do the parts together produce an effect that ends up being different from the effect of each part on its own?
- Does the effect, the behavior over time, persist in creating various outcomes?

Systems also quickly and clearly become a series of stocks and flows. Much as in a forest, one needs a balance of new trees being born and maturing at a rate which counteracts any logging business which might also be active, for the ongoing health of the system. This same dynamic plays out in other longer-term contexts, such as how to maintain rainforests in perpetuity, how to revitalize the oceans, how to maintain a balanced atmosphere and climate, all much more complicated issues as you bring in all aspects of any system, but this understanding is crucial to avoid unwanted delayed outcomes.

One key tenet of thinking in systems is that physical systems cannot grow forever in a finite environment, which is in effect our finite planet. Healthy systems require one reinforcing loop driving growth and at least one constraining loop for needed balance. We don't have that constraining loop, and this is a major concern for the longer term, and is also what efforts such as global climate negotiations are attempting to establish.

Stocks include resources in the ground such as zinc, copper, phosphorus, fossil fuel reserves and resources. Flows include financial measures such as those which go into calculations of GDP, which by definition exclude consideration of stocks. Does GDP measure the longer-term effects of carbon emissions that result in eventual financial risk, even catastrophic risk? GDP does not do that, and is therefore by definition insufficient for modern purpose. GDP has its place but it is misused, misunderstood, misinterpreted and arguably therefore dangerous as a concept, yet we lack anything better and more encompassing.

We also must consider the concept of the 'tragedy of the commons'.

For those not aware, picture a pasture open to all farmers. Each farmer, if acting solely for their own financial benefit, is more likely than not to try and keep as many cattle as possible on this common pasture. If the utility of adding one head of cattle is fully enjoyed by the farmer in question, who receives the entire proceeds of adding that head of cattle, and there is no other disincentive, each farmer is likely to reach the same conclusion, wanting to receive these proceeds. The effect of overgrazing ends up being paid for by all, and the pasture in question ends up being a system that is doomed to fail unless other steps are taken.

When thinking about climate change, it becomes clear from the science and the insufficient pace of the climate negotiations and the necessary low-carbon transition that we are locked into a similar system dynamic involving shareholders and the companies they own.

The key question then becomes:

How can we avoid a tragedy of the shareholder commons?

Separately, Meadows was a master at identifying categories of strategy which can both least and most make a difference in creating needed system change. Her archives provide her view on 'Places to Intervene in a System'[1] in order of effectiveness:

12 Constants, parameters, numbers (such as subsidies, taxes, standards).
11 The sizes of buffers and other stabilizing stocks, relative to their flows.
10 The structure of material stocks and flows (such as transport networks, population age structures).
9 The lengths of delays, relative to the rate of system change.
8 The strength of negative feedback loops, relative to the impacts they are trying to correct against.
7 The gain around driving positive feedback loops.
6 The structure of information flows (who does and does not have access to information).
5 The rules of the system (such as incentives, punishments, constraints).
4 The power to add, change, evolve or self-organize system structure.
3 The goals of the system.
2 The mindset or paradigm out of which the system – its goals, structure, rules, delays, parameters – arises.
1 The power to transcend paradigms.

One can quickly see for starters that static data is the least effective means of creating change.

Transparency can be helpful but static data, especially in a world of data challenges as per Chapter 9, doesn't inform on whether change has been successfully achieved. As you work down this list, more effective than static data is the understanding and managing of flows, especially when driving positive feedback loops as opposed to harnessing negativity, one of our own key tenets of investing as well. Continue down the list and you see that the people making the rules can be more important than the rules themselves. People have the power to transcend paradigms, but it will take mass awareness, willpower, and asking the right questions while developing the right positive culture and incentives.

Meadows' book reaches its crescendo in a fascinating way, in consideration of how to accomplish paradigm change.

In effect, the best way to achieve a paradigm shift is to:

- Keep pointing at the anomalies and failures in the present system.
- Design a new system and point out benefits.
- Make them clear and digestible.
- Insert people with the new paradigm in places of influence, people who are active change agents.
- Keep oneself unattached to all paradigms.
- Stay flexible – no paradigm is 'true'.
- Every paradigm is by definition, including yours and mine, a tremendously limited understanding of the world (infinity, purpose).
- Beyond human comprehension.
- There are paradigms, and to 'get' at a gut level the understanding that this in itself is a paradigm – and getting that this is extremely funny – let go into 'not knowing' – know what you don't know.

What does this mean for investors?

Surely, at minimum, that a tipping point could cause dramatic shifts in value, and are you ready for that or overweight in the wrong areas? Can sustainable investing become its own positive paradigm for change? This is what we seek. Impact investing attempts to be this, but is not close to the scale required to shift the balance of environmental and social outcomes. Sustainable investing at scale, we believe, is our main hope for achieving a system pointed at outcomes using capital to facilitate the changes we need.

Systemic risk also continues as a focus of other efforts, including The Investment Integration Project[2] (TIIP), which

> aims to help asset owners and managers better understand how systemic frameworks can be enhanced in order to fortify investments; communicate with corporations and other entities providing investment opportunities to further align their policies and practices with the maintenance of healthy

systems; and work with peers to enhance the integrity of the financial community and encourage disclosure of social and environmental data relevant to investment issues.

TIIP aims to make clearer both what the systemic impacts of portfolios are, as well as what systems effects will affect portfolios; it is the latest interesting brainchild of Steve Lydenberg, who previously helped give birth to SASB and who was the first ESG researcher back at the firm KLD (Kinder, Lydenberg and Domini), now part of MSCI ESG Research.

The Principles for Responsible Investment have been considering whether to add a seventh principle on systemic risk. Systems thinking appears to be deeply embedded as a concern and an opportunity to help find what arguably need to be systemic solutions to otherwise intractable sustainability challenges.

Calls for implementation of the Paris Agreement are themselves systemic, but will not be easily achieved, unless all parts of the system come together and act in unison, including through investing.

This is the Manhattan Project of our time – it needs envisioning and mechanisms for implementation, strategic planning, prioritization, shared incentives, assurance and seasonal recalibration.

The value of everything needs to look a certain way by 2030, by 2025, by 2020, aligned with tweaked strategies along the way to get us from here to there every five years.

This book is about the transitions that need to start to occur in earnest and in parallel, and this will need to be recalibrated every five years to get us where we need to go with intentionality and to see how we are doing versus what the science is telling us.

We don't have five years to wait. Let's go.

Notes

1 http://donellameadows.org/archives/leverage-points-places-to-intervene-in-a-system/. Accessed September 8, 2016.

2 www.investmentintegrationproject.com/. Accessed September 8, 2016.

Chapter 7

On reducing emissions and developing a climate change strategy[1]

Cary Krosinsky/Principles for Responsible Investment

PRI Climate Change Strategy Project

The asset management strategy introduced in this chapter is adapted from two publications from the PRI Climate Change Strategy Project: 'Discussion Paper: Reducing Emissions Across the Portfolio' (2015) and 'Developing an Asset Owner Climate Change Strategy: Pilot Framework' (2015).

The PRI Initiative is a UN-supported international network of investors working together to put the six Principles for Responsible Investment into practice. Its goal is to understand the implications of sustainability for investors and support signatories to incorporate these issues into their investment decision-making and ownership practices. In implementing the Principles, signatories contribute to the development of a more sustainable global financial system.

The Principles are voluntary and aspirational. They offer a menu of possible actions for incorporating ESG issues into investment practices across asset classes. Responsible investment is a process that must be tailored to each organization's investment strategy, approach and resources. The Principles are designed to be compatible with the investment styles of large, diversified, institutional investors that operate within a traditional fiduciary framework.

Drivers for action range from protecting financial value and managing risk to social values. There is growing consensus that considering environmental, social and governance (ESG) topics, including climate change, is supportive of fiduciary duty. Asset owners with diversified, long-term portfolios will be exposed to costs associated with climate change risks. With governments and companies increasingly taking action and fiduciary duty beginning to reflect the necessity for sustainable investment, asset owners have a positive and unique role to play in tackling climate change.

Responses must be tailored to an asset owner's investment approach and asset class mix.

A strong case for asset owner action on climate change

With scientific concerns about the effects of carbon emissions settled, asset owners are increasingly interested in understanding their carbon exposure and learning what role they can play to achieve a safe environment for future generations.

Globally, pressure is mounting.

The IPCC's 5th *Synthesis Report* from November 2014 cited 1,000 Gt of remaining carbon budget before we reach likely tipping points (IPCC, 2014). The IEA's executive director, Dr. Fatih Birol, most recently spoke to this global carbon budget expiring in 2040 (IEA, 2014).

The Carbon Tracker Initiative's carbon budget analysis (2013) findings are similar, and PwC recently estimated that we have approximately 20 years left of annual carbon emissions at present rates before this budget is completely spent. It will be harder to stay within the global carbon budget the longer we do not take action. Additional information on climate science can also be found in Appendix A of the PRI Climate Change Strategy Project Discussion Paper: 'Reducing Emissions across the Portfolio'.

For carbon reductions to occur at the level required, corporate strategy, public policy, and investment strategy need to work in concert, each informing the other's needs. Companies such as BP and Unilever are speaking publicly about a need for action on climate change and a growing number are calling for stronger carbon pricing, including most recently six major European energy companies (United Nations, 2015). Over 90 companies have committed to one or more business leadership initiatives on climate change ahead of COP21 and an increasing number of companies, including Unilever, Nestlé, AXA Group, Allianz and Honda, have committed to adopting a GHG emissions reduction target (CDP, 2016).

Policy is needed to support investor strategy, for example by leveling the playing field on energy through subsidies as per the IEA's four steps to keep us within 2 degrees (IEA, 2013). Policy is also needed to help support corporate strategy, such as long-term fixed incentives to inspire renewable energy investment. Companies have been frustrated where incentives such as feed-in tariffs are established and then removed too soon.

Governments worked towards COP21 in Paris and the subsequent Paris Agreement in December 2015 through bilateral agreements, high-level discussions and other lead-up gatherings. The Climate Change Convention – effectively a planetary risk management treaty – aims to manage climate change within acceptable limits. Parties to the Convention agreed in Cancun in 2010 to 2°C as the upper limit of acceptable warming. Governments will make a significant contribution by calling for a minimum 60 percent reduction in global emissions by 2050 from 2010 levels (consistent with the IPCC range of a 40–70 percent reduction).

However, even if governments fail to fully ratify the Paris Agreement, the potential impacts of climate change on the economy and the global carbon budget mean that asset owners still need to consider their carbon risk exposure and the full range of possible actions to reduce emissions. Their portfolios are inevitably exposed in some way to costs from climate change.

Large, institutional owners typically have diversified and long-term portfolios are broadly representative of the overall capital markets. They can play a positive role in influencing companies and policy makers to minimize their exposure to these costs (Thamotheram and Wildsmith, 2007). Asset owners are already taking concrete actions. Examples include the Aiming for A (Investors on Climate Change, 2016) coalition and other shareholder resolutions on climate change, as well as the growth in green bonds (Climate Bonds Initiative, 2015), whereby proceeds are earmarked for projects with environmental and/or climate benefits.

New platforms such as the Non-Actor Zone for Climate Action (NAZCA) are tracking a range of new commitments to measure, engage and reallocate to low-carbon investments.

Whilst climate change poses risk to the environment, investment in new energy sources and new technologies represents opportunities for investors.

Fiduciary duty

Fiduciary duty has long been a fluid concept, and there is little reason to expect the interpretations and definitions of prudence and loyalty to not continue to evolve. The UK Law Commission (2014) has been looking at the relationship between ESG and fiduciary duty, and other jurisdictions are paying close heed to such developments in fiduciary duty laws and interpretations.

Asset owners such as CalPERS have developed investment beliefs that include recognition that fiduciary duty is multi-generational (CalPERS, 2016). The University of California has undertaken similar work (UCnet, 2015) and other asset owners including the Pensions Trust and the BT Pension Scheme have established belief sets or equivalent investment policies. Increasingly across the globe there is an understanding that part of an investor's fiduciary duty is to manage risks, that include long-term risks such as environmental, social and governance risks.

There may come a time when trustees and others in charge of pools of investable assets will need to be seen as positively addressing climate change or risk being found in breach of their own fiduciary duty. Sarah Barker, of Australian law firm Minton Ellison, identifies three trends: a proactive stance on governance on climate change is consistent with financial wealth interests; boards must actively engage with the issue of climate change impacts on their operations, risk and strategy; and a passive approach to climate change governance may be inadequate to satisfy directors' duties of due care and diligence (Barker, 2015).

The key factors to consider when setting an emissions reduction goal

Asset owners are diverse and drivers for action will vary, ranging from financial value to social values, with actions and outcomes flowing from these. Each asset owner will need to develop a goal appropriate to their organization profile, including headquarters and operational countries, portfolio size, breakdown of AUM by asset class and market, investment strategy and relevant regulation. Additionally, an asset manager's strategy will be reflective of the responsible investment beliefs, policy, goals, and objectives of the organization.

Understanding carbon exposure on a per member basis is critical to developing an applicable plan for reducing carbon intensity. This risk should be assessed through quantitative measurement (i.e., a portfolio carbon footprint) and qualitative review by portfolio managers. Finally, seeking opportunities to reduce emissions is dependent on investor and public policy engagement, investment strategy, and ongoing discussion with portfolio managers and investment consultants.

The development and implementation of a unique emissions goal must be considered in conjunction with the asset owner's priority areas for carbon reduction, fund asset classes, and investment approach.

For some asset owners, divestment will be part of a risk management strategy or a way to align investment beliefs and values, while many organizations are finding that alternatives to divestment, such as engagement and reinvestment into low-carbon initiatives, are effective.

Priority areas for emissions reduction

We will run out of a carbon budget around 2040 (or sooner) if no substantial changes are implemented against current levels of ongoing emissions. However, switching to a lower carbon economy could result in lower average carbon emissions over periods of time, allowing for a gradual transition to occur successfully, keeping us within this budget by 2050.

For example, one potential decadal carbon emissions reduction scenario presents an initial reduction from the 185 Gt released between 2011 and 2015 to 150 Gt (30 Gt/year) from 2016 to 2020.

Over the next three decades, this goal for the reduction of yearly carbon emissions predicts an emission of 25 Gt/year between 2021 and 2030, 20 Gt/year between 2031 and 2040, and finally 10 Gt/year until 2050. This outline thus presents the ability to achieve total carbon emissions of only 885 Gt through 2050.

Production and use will both need to be addressed to achieve this annual emissions reduction. Potential actions include changing the source of electricity generation, maximizing energy efficiency of buildings, building infrastructure for electric vehicles and alternative forms of transportation, facilitating a shared industrial economy, and encouraging better deforestation standards in agriculture and land use.

Additionally, in '4 Steps to Keep Us Within 2 Degrees', the IEA suggested transitioning from coal use, removing energy subsidies, maximizing energy efficiency, and capturing methane in natural gas extraction (and perhaps other processes). Embedded in here are new policies that would be required and which investors need to be advocating for, as well as financial opportunities in energy efficiency and methane capture. Examples can be seen in the UN Global Compact's Value Driver Model (2013).

Finally, thought must be given to an appropriate timeframe for setting goals, taking into account the IPCC/IEA/Carbon Tracker Initiative consensus on a global carbon budget of about 900–1100 Gt expiring around 2040. Asset owners will need to agree targets and timeframes with portfolio managers. Corporate examples could be useful guides. The Unilever Sustainable Living Plan, for example, was launched in 2010 and set out a 'blueprint for sustainable growth' by 2020 focusing on three main goals (health and well-being, reducing environmental impact and enhanced livelihoods) underpinned by nine commitments. Unilever reports on its website whether the target is achieved, on-plan, off-plan and the percentage of the target achieved, providing strong transparency to customers.

Asset classes

Adoption of a strategy for the reduction of carbon emissions and embodiment of ESG values should be tailored to the asset classes covered by a manager. Specifically, the major asset classes for consideration are listed equity, fixed income, private equity, infrastructure, property, and commodities.

Listed equity

Responsible investment practices including active ownership and ESG incorporation are typically most advanced in listed equity. For actively managed mandates, investment analysis may help identify opportunities in companies well positioned for climate change and those offering low-carbon or adaptation solutions. For actively managed and passive mandates, active ownership on climate change is likely to be an important approach, including voting on climate change-related shareholder resolutions and dialogue with companies and public policy makers on climate change. As highlighted below, portfolio carbon footprint measurement is most advanced in equities.

Fixed income

Integrating climate change into issuer analysis is possible and underway to some degree in government issuers, emerging market debt investors, corporate (non-financial) issuers and in covered bonds. Some large fixed income owners find they have increasing influence by engaging directly with the issuing company to address future potential credit risk. Climate bonds are designed to lower the footprint of sectors such as energy generation and transportation. More climate bonds are being developed and issuers could increase appetite for the asset class. Measuring the carbon footprint of new issues is an important short-term focus. For examples of climate change integration, engagement and green bonds, see PRI's Fixed Income Investor Guide.

Private equity

Little-to-no useful data are available on either privately-owned or state-owned companies, although work is underway by at least one provider and asset owner to measure the carbon footprint of a private equity portfolio. CalPERS has called for equity to be considered as a single asset class, regardless of whether privately or publicly held, which would boost an investor's ability to ask for data so that assessments can be made.

Infrastructure

Bespoke analysis on infrastructure is essential. It is an important area of future focus, with calls for replacing trillions of dollars of energy and transportation infrastructure in the years to come including grid, storage, airports/aviation and much more that will have a direct bearing on the carbon footprint of global society. Solutions must also be found to properly fund energy innovation.

Property

Standards such as LEED and BREEAM are somewhat useful, as is the move to benchmark buildings in cities. In general, cities are expected to lead on reducing their carbon emissions, with many planning to both mitigate and adapt through direct investment, including forms of energy efficiency financing that can create jobs. There is a clear opportunity for carbon reporting of portfolios to be performed over time, with targets that can be measured and reported.

Commodities

There is no method to measure a carbon footprint for the vast majority of commodities, whether ecosystem-related or resource-related. A spectrum of Sustainability Standards is being developed at the sourcing level, varying in strength and credibility. Palm oil standards (e.g. RSPO) are a work in progress to mitigate deforestation. Work has been done on sustainable fisheries and sustainable gold, amongst other resources, but these are typically traded by certificate without the ability to discern which are actually sustainable and which are not. Conservation of critical areas remains an important concern, including wetlands, forests, oceans, fisheries and, from a carbon reduction perspective, preserving, enhancing and restoring carbon sinks. Conservation finance does not provide enough cases to make techniques financially viable for investors at sufficient scale to address the underlying issues.

Investment approaches

Active ownership through investor engagement with companies on climate change has been underway for some time. As one recent example, Norges Bank Investment Management has published 'Climate Change Strategy Expectations to Companies' (Norges Bank, 2014) which aims to serve as a basis for constructive dialogue between investors and companies. Positive developments for company–investor dialogue include the Aiming for A coalition's shareholder resolution, 'Strategic Resilience for 2035 and Beyond', which received support from company management and over 98 percent of shareholders at the 2015 annual general meetings of BP, Royal Dutch Shell and Statoil.

The Carbon Asset Risk Initiative involves engagement with fossil fuel companies to use shareholder capital prudently. Meanwhile, a recent shareholder resolution filed by As You Sow and Arjuna Capital called on Chevron to increase return dividends in light of spending on high-cost, high-carbon projects; the resolution received support from 4 percent of shareholders . There are also calls for forceful stewardship, whereby investors would press companies to present 2-degree-compliant business plans and vote for resolutions to change business models.

Institutional investment makes up over 65 percent of equity ownership in publicly traded companies – up from 35 percent over the past few generations. If institutional investment – whether invested actively or passively, directly or through outsourced relationships – were to act collectively and collaboratively on carbon emissions, this may present the largest available opportunity to address the climate challenge at hand. Through 'Carbon Action', investors have engaged collectively with companies on disclosing an emissions reduction target, and the PRI has launched a collaborative engagement program on corporate climate lobbying. This engagement is aimed at encouraging responsible company practices on climate change-related policy activity, focusing on Australia, Canada, Europe and the USA.

Furthermore, there is a move in the market towards lower fee investing, especially passively managed public equity. Passive investment does not mean passive ownership. As large investors with substantial voting rights, passive investors are well placed to influence companies. As they invest across the whole market, passive investors have an interest in raising standards beyond the individual company level and through engagement with regulators. Passive investment can be done through separate accounts and other low-cost index strategies to ensure that asset owners are able to tilt their portfolios towards lower-carbon assets when clients request this within the mandate. Further work is needed with some asset managers on how to provide this basic service within pooled, passive mandates.

Finally, dialogue and engagement with portfolio managers and external managers is essential as well. This may include asking for portfolio carbon footprints as well as integrated analysis and active ownership on climate change. Portfolio managers must demonstrate the necessary knowledge of and capacity to address climate change factors in order to meet goals for portfolio measurement, asset allocation and engagement strategy.

Many asset owners work with third-party providers such as external fund managers, hedge funds and consultants. The Global Investor Coalition on Climate Change's (IIGCC, 2015) recent 'Climate Change Investment Solutions' guide includes guidance on how asset owners can engage with fund managers, including on measuring emissions and carbon intensity, integrating within investment decision-making, voting and engagement, setting targets to reduce portfolio carbon intensity and exposure to fossil fuel reserves, and incorporating climate change in mandate design.

Fossil fuels and divestment

For some asset owners divestment is a way to align investment beliefs with invested dollars. A classic example would be the outright sale of a sector, such as the selling of tobacco companies due to health concerns and liability considerations. Another practice would be selling a targeted company after years of engagement have failed to achieve a result. Norges Bank Investment Management, for example, has a specific process for, and history of, selling companies they have failed to make engagement progress on.

For other asset owners, divestment will conflict with investment beliefs linked to active ownership and ESG integration. Furthermore, the global use of fossil fuels may be seen as being so embedded in commerce, household consumption and society that it would be unclear where to stop divesting to remove fossil fuels from one's portfolio.

Asset owners considering their approach to fossil fuels are encouraged to consider carbon mitigation measures recommended by the IPCC and in the Low Carbon Investment Registry. The range of approaches for reducing or removing exposure to fossil fuel reserves includes: placing a percentage cap on exposure to fossil fuel extraction, or excluding fossil fuel industry groups; using low-carbon indices to measure and manage portfolios against a benchmark that integrates climate change into its weighting methodology; and for passively managed funds applying a tilt away from higher carbon assets to lower carbon ones.

How measuring a carbon footprint can assist in reducing emissions

A portfolio's carbon footprint is the sum of a proportional amount of each portfolio company's emissions (proportional to the amount of stock held in the portfolio). A carbon footprint is a useful quantitative tool that can inform the creation and implementation of a broader climate change strategy and help asset owners build an understanding of the emissions of companies owned in the portfolio. It is also a useful tool for engaging with portfolio managers and companies, and can help set priorities for addressing emissions.

Measuring the carbon footprint of a portfolio means you can compare it to global benchmarks, identify priority areas and actions for reducing emissions and track progress in making those reductions. There are caveats that carbon footprinting is not yet available for unlisted assets, does not include Scope 3 emissions and that different estimation methodologies exist. Nevertheless, investors who have already measured the carbon footprint of portfolios say that doing so can improve their own understanding of the portfolio risks and opportunities that climate change presents, gives them answers to stakeholder questions on climate change and allows them to demonstrate publicly their commitment to tackling climate change.

For any investor considering portfolio carbon footprinting, it is essential to understand where emissions specifically come from. Carbon dioxide is an ongoing outcome from a variety of primarily human activities, but especially from electricity generation; energy use in the ongoing functioning and maintenance of buildings; modes of transportation; industrial processes; and agricultural processes, land use and deforestation.

As a result of ongoing use patterns, greenhouse gas emissions are embedded throughout the functioning of the entire system of global business and society. Ongoing use of energy patterns can be mapped exactly to ongoing production globally and by region.

Globally, percentages of energy use and production vary by region, with coal use being the largest proportion in the Asia/Pacific region, while oil and gas are the largest by percentage everywhere else. 'Leapfrogging' the developing world on renewable energy then becomes a critical factor for achieving a successful global low-carbon transition.

Energy use is the majority source of global carbon emissions, with agriculture and land use the next most significant cause. Understanding the presently locked-in patterns of global production and is an essential step towards seeing how carbon footprinting can inform investment strategy, as both production and use of energy are arguably of equal relevance to this.

Measuring a portfolio carbon footprint by asset class

The most thorough example of measuring the carbon footprint of a portfolio would be measuring the greenhouse gas emissions onsite at particular facilities, getting them verified by reliable external parties and then combining them into a single corporate number of absolute production emissions. This could extend across all operations, and to a company's suppliers and further down the supply chain, all the way to the raw materials procured for use in production processes. Such ongoing production and process emissions can be monitored by software, allowing for a dynamic picture of carbon emissions to be developed.

Equity

Off-the-shelf and customized services exist for measuring an equity portfolio's carbon footprint. It may consider not only carbon but also natural capital, fossil fuel reserves and exposure to stranded assets. A carbon footprint is typically constructed by the following steps:

1. Obtain carbon emissions data on companies or projects owned in a portfolio, either from verified disclosure or from estimated/interpreted sources.
2. Choose an appropriate benchmark.
3. Calculate the total emissions of the owned percentages of each company and add them together, resulting in a total owned carbon emissions figure per portfolio.
4. Normalize the results, typically using factors such as annual revenue or market capitalization.
5. Perform the same calculation on the chosen benchmark, assuming the same dollar amounts are owned by that alternative set of companies. The percentage difference can be expressed as a result.
6. Further refinements and analysis can be considered within and across sectors and regions.

Fixed income

Providers exist for measuring carbon footprints of fixed income portfolios, though how best to do this is still under development and discussion. The aim is to allocate greenhouse gas emissions according to accounting rules, following the GHG Protocol, and including an ownership principle. If an investor holds both the stock and a bond of a company, emissions can be split to avoid double-counting. For government bonds, it is possible to compare climate protection policies and how they are enforced.

Other asset classes

Measurement techniques are under development in private equity. They are not available easily for unlisted assets, but can be conducted on a best-efforts basis.

Data challenges

Carbon footprint measurements can be cradle-to-gate or cradle-to-cradle. Cradle-to-gate means understanding a company's footprint up to the point it sells a product to a consumer, after which any related emissions become part of their footprint. For example, if Toyota sells a car, the footprint for using the car becomes the purchaser's, not the company's. On the contrary, cradle-to-cradle would consider the whole lifecycle of a product, from sourcing of raw materials, through the use phase, and to the eventual disposal.

Much of the emissions impact of a product is therefore not captured by cradle-to-gate analysis of the company that produces them. ACCA reported in 2011 that ignoring a company's indirect emissions, those that fall under Scope 3 of the GHG Protocol, can result in 75 percent of the carbon emissions being missed by analysis (ACCA, 2011).

Box 7.1 GHG Protocol

GHG emissions and scopes

The GHG Protocol has been accepted as a global standard and divides emissions into three scopes: *Scope 1*, the operations portion of a company's products and services; *Scope 2*, purchased electricity; and *Scope 3*, indirect emissions of a company across 15 categories, including aspects from raw materials procured to external investments made by a company, to the use and disposal of a company's products:

1. purchased goods and services
2. capital goods
3. fuel- and energy-related activities
4. upstream transportation and distribution
5. waste generated in operations
6. business travel
7. employee commuting
8. upstream leased assets
9. downstream transportation and distribution
10. processing of sold products
11. use of sold products
12. end-of-life treatment of sold products
13. downstream leased assets
14. franchises
15. investments.

Source: www.ghgprotocol.org

For example, Ford has completely analyzed its business and found that 90 percent of its footprint comes from the use of its cars and trucks. Therefore the design of its future products, along with the development of new technologies and infrastructure for electric cars and trucks using lower carbon energy, would be a clear relative priority over making improvements to Scope 1 and 2 emissions.

Companies continue to report their greenhouse gas emissions to varying degrees of quality and detail, with some reports being verified by external parties and others not. Companies often do not understand the full nature of their supply chain relationships, even if they do want to report on their Scope 3 emissions. For example, first tier suppliers are understood, but raw material providers may not be, nor all sources of transportation within multiple levels of a supply chain.

Scope 3 analysis tends to be from estimates such as industry averages, in the absence of measured and verified data. For a comprehensive account of the emissions of any company, it is necessary to combine voluntarily reported, partially verified data with estimations across some or all of Scopes 1, 2 and 3, using a variety of modeling techniques. Such approaches include Economic Input-Output Life Cycle Assessment (EIO-LCA) models (Carnegie Mellon University, 2016).

Measuring portfolio carbon footprints is now roughly ten years old, dating back to Henderson's June 2005 'How Green Is My Portfolio?' and their 'The Carbon 100' reports. In the case of this first Henderson footprint, the Henderson Global Care Income Portfolio was found to be 32 percent lower carbon than its chosen FTSE All-Share benchmark at the time. Investors measuring their carbon footprint today include Green Century, Calvert, Pax World and signatories to the Montreal Carbon Pledge. In May 2015, the French government voted to amend article 48 of the Energy Transition Law and to require institutional investors (insurance companies, public institutions and public pension funds) to report on risks arising from climate change and GHG emissions associated with assets owned.

Using a portfolio carbon footprint

A portfolio carbon footprint improves understanding of emissions in the portfolio for equities and fixed income, and can be used as a tool for engaging with fund managers and companies on climate change risks, opportunities and reporting. It can also be used as a tool to inform further action, including emissions reduction. However, it needs to be complemented by discussion with portfolio managers and companies, particularly where data is less reliable.

Many asset owners are using portfolio carbon footprinting to inform actions. The Dutch healthcare pension fund PFZW has committed to increasing sustainable investments fourfold, to at least €16 billion, while reducing the carbon footprint of its entire portfolio by 50 percent by 2020. Sustainable investments will include direct investments in green energy, clean technology, sustainable climate-related solutions, food security, and measures against water scarcity. The footprint will be halved by comparing companies in each sector and picking the best performers, using data from four service providers. Similarly, ASN Bank has worked with Ecofys to develop a Carbon P&L methodology. This Carbon P&L concept attempts to proportion out lower carbon investments (the P of their P&L) versus traditional emissions intensive investments (the L side of the ledger) with a goal of balancing this ledger by 2030. ASN are also driving a coalition to make similar commitments.

The Environment Agency Pension Fund and Local Government Super use carbon footprints to inform priority engagement with companies, including on emissions disclosure and performance, and works with bond managers and Trucost to monitor the total environmental footprint of its corporate bond fund. Analysis identifies bonds linked to high-impact activities, and, where practical, these are replaced in the portfolio where another bond can meet the same portfolio needs but with less impact. Finally, the Portfolio Decarbonization Coalition commits members to two interconnected targets: measuring and disclosing the carbon footprint of US$500 billion of assets under management and committing US$100 billion to decarbonization. There are nearly 20 coalition members. The Montreal Carbon Pledge is the delivery mechanism for the carbon footprinting component of the Portfolio Decarbonization Coalition.

Therefore, a strong case exists for asset owners to play an effective role in reducing emissions, alongside government and business, consistent with fiduciary duty. Asset owners are encouraged to take steps to understand their carbon risk exposure by measuring their portfolio carbon footprint and to mitigate this by setting a goal to reduce emissions, appropriate for their individual organizations. The following section introduces a strategy for asset managers to adopt these practices.

Three steps to developing a climate change strategy

This framework focuses on investment actions to mitigate climate change – how actions by asset owners can reduce their exposure to climate change risk in their investment portfolios and also support the reduction of emissions in the real economy.

To tailor the steps below to their own needs, asset owners should select suitable strategies from the framework below and adapt them to fit their own motivations, objectives and investment approaches. Strategies will likely differ based on at least asset owner type (corporate/public pension funds, university endowments, charitable foundations or others), active/passive management and responsible investment maturity level.

Step 1: Measure

Understand your portfolio exposure.

Step 2: Act

Gather commitment from throughout the investment chain. Choose appropriate strategies and execute them – engage, invest, avoid.

Step 3: Review

Monitor and report on effectiveness.

Step 1: Measure

Evaluating portfolio exposure to climate change risk and opportunity, and reviewing portfolio emissions, are practical starting points for addressing climate change. Climate change risk and opportunity refers to how well-positioned the investment portfolio is for risks such as water scarcity, and for investment opportunities such as energy efficiency. Portfolio emissions refer to the actual or estimated emissions of companies held within the investment portfolio.

In addition to determining portfolio emission and carbon footprint, there are different approaches for assessing exposure including sector analysis, stranded assets analysis, low-carbon exposure, and quantitative investment modeling.

SECTOR ANALYSIS

This method can identify exposure to high-carbon sectors and assess individual company performance on an absolute and relative basis, as well as on their ability to manage climate change-related risk. Sector analysis focused on physical climate risk would evaluate risks associated with the physical impacts from climate change that could impact companies. For example, these could include operational risks and the costs of physical damage from wildfires, significant flooding or drought.

UNEP FI and WRI's publication (2015), 'Carbon Asset Risk Discussion Framework', focuses on three carbon risk factors: policy and legal, technology, and market/economic. Policy and legal risk refers to policies or regulation that could impact the operational and financial viability of companies an asset owner invests in. Technology risk includes development in the commercial availability and cost of alternative and low-carbon technologies that could impact a company's choice of technology and costs. Furthermore, market and economic risk relates to changes in market or economic conditions that could impact companies, such as changes in consumer preferences or in fossil prices.

As a practical example of sectoral analysis, a portfolio manager may consider how well sectors are positioned to withstand or respond to the impacts of a changing climate on business operations and of variation in cost of capital and the prices of resources (i.e., energy, water, raw materials). Additionally, portfolio managers may also assess opportunity for low-carbon product development, regulation risk on business operations in specific markets, and volatility in company reputation due to the ratings of issuers.

STRANDED ASSETS ANALYSIS

Applied to fossil fuel companies, this can assist in analyzing the implications of not adjusting investment in line with what is needed to limit global warming.

The Carbon Tracker Initiative's definition of stranded assets is:

> fossil fuel energy and generation resources which, at some time prior to the end of their economic life (as assumed at the investment decision point), are no longer able to earn an economic return (i.e. meet the company's internal rate of return), as a result of changes in the market and regulatory environment associated with the transition to a low-carbon economy.

Stranded risks include regulatory stranding due to change in policy or legislation, economic stranding due to a change in relative costs and prices, and physical stranding due to flood or drought. Asset owners can work with portfolio managers or providers to analyze exposure to stranded asset risks.

LOW-CARBON EXPOSURE

Low-carbon investments can be considered as 'hedge' against high-carbon investments. Low-carbon investments can involve risk though, including policy and technology change, which needs to be evaluated. Asset owners can work with portfolio managers or providers to identify companies in the portfolio that derive a significant portion of revenues from, for example, clean tech, energy efficiency and green buildings.

QUANTITATIVE INVESTMENT MODELING

Risk assessment can draw on quantitative investment modeling incorporating climate change, including asset class sensitivity over 35 years, as in the modeling provided by Mercer (2015) in its study entitled *Investing in a Time of Climate Change*. This study looks at risk factors associated with technological developments, resource availability, the impact of a changed climate and policy decisions. It includes consideration of scenarios, as well as sensitivity of regions, assets and sectors.

The UK Environment Agency Pension Fund's 'Policy to Address the Impacts of Climate Change' (2015) is an example of an asset owner using risk analysis combining emissions risk and carbon footprinting, low-carbon exposure and investment modeling. The policy commits to ensuring the investment portfolio and processes are compatible with 2°C. It includes a target of 15 percent of the fund invested in low-carbon, energy efficient and other climate change mitigation opportunities. It also includes a decarbonization target for the fund's equity portfolio: reducing the fund's exposure to 'future emissions' by 90 percent for coal and 50 percent for oil and gas by 2020 (compared to the exposure in the underlying benchmark as at March 31, 2015).

Step 2: Act

There is a variety of options available to asset owners seeking to reduce exposure to climate risk and encourage the transition to a low-carbon economy. In deciding on appropriate strategies, asset owners can draw on the framework below covering three main strategies: engage, invest and avoid.

ENGAGE

Public policy affects the sustainability and stability of financial markets; policy engagement is therefore a natural and necessary extension of an investor's fiduciary duties to the interests of beneficiaries. On climate change, supportive public policy is essential to leveling the playing field for new forms of energy and energy efficiency, and for scaling up low-carbon investment. Investor engagement with companies is a critical tool for encouraging an orderly transition to a low-carbon economy.

INVEST

Climate change should be integrated into investment decision-making and identify low-carbon opportunities. Carbon is a risk that needs to be considered within investment analysis, including in analyzing company value in equity investing and assessing credit risk in fixed income. Low-carbon investment opportunities include 'green' infrastructure, climate and green bonds, as well as positive or thematic sustainable investing in public and private equity.

AVOID

Investments could be avoided, through screening or reallocation, for reasons such as financial risk, where dialogue with companies does not succeed, for market signaling, or for alignment with an asset owner's specific mission.

Strategy 1: Engage

Engage with policy makers

Engagement with policy makers can influence policy, thus reducing uncertainty for investors, and build an investor's understanding of the direction of policy, which may impact on investments in future.

Recent investor focus areas include asking policy makers to provide stable, reliable and economically meaningful carbon pricing that helps redirect investment commensurate with the scale of the climate change challenge and strengthen regulatory support for energy efficiency and renewable energy. Policy makers should support innovation in, and deployment of, low-carbon technologies by financing clean energy research and development, developing plans to phase out subsidies for fossil fuels, and encouraging governments to incentivize private finance where it can be useful. Finally, policy makers must consider the effect of unintended constraints from financial regulations on investments in low-carbon technologies and in climate resilience.

Strategy evaluation

PROS

Influence policy outcomes and understand future policy direction, helping to achieve a level playing field.

CONS

Effective policy engagement requires resourcing, board-level support and investor collaboration at a domestic and global level.

TIMEFRAME

Medium- to long-term, although policy responses to COP21 in December 2015 are a key opportunity in the short term.

TRACKING AND MEASURING PERFORMANCE

Performance indicators have tended to focus on the number and execution of engagements, but ultimately only policy outcomes and stability matter.

Asset owners can engage with policy makers by supporting the following public initiatives:

Global Investor Statement on Climate Change Investors can sign this to send a clear message to governments that there is strong investor support for a global agreement on climate change.

CDSB Statement on Fiduciary Duty This seeks to include climate change-related information in mainstream corporate reporting as a matter of fiduciary duty.

We Mean Business Coalition This is focused on smart policy frameworks to enable ambitious climate action.

Engage with companies

Investors have been engaging with companies on climate change for some time, and this has a key role to play in encouraging companies to transition to a low-carbon economy. Clearly defined objectives are essential for effective engagement. Asset owners need to monitor engagement outcomes, focusing on whether companies are providing satisfactory responses to investor concerns. Asset owners need to decide how long engagement dialogue should continue, and what investment decisions will be taken if companies provide an unsatisfactory response.

Investor–company engagement can consist of asset owners engaging individually (or with/through external managers and service providers) or in collaboration with other asset owners. Organizations coordinating collaborative engagements include the PRI, the Institutional Investors Group on Climate Change, the Investor Group on Climate Change and the Investor Network on Climate Risk, among others. The agenda of these conversations should include corporate strategy and the transition to a low-carbon economy, emissions reduction targets, carbon asset risk, energy efficiency, and political lobbying. Effective engagement may require dialogue at both board and operational level through different approaches, such as letters, phone or in-person meetings, co-filing, or voting on shareholder resolutions. Furthermore, investors may see benefits of engagement being public and vocal or discreet and confidential, depending on their objectives.

One recent development includes the Aiming for A coalition's shareholder resolution (2012) 'Strategic Resilience for 2035 and Beyond', which received support from company management and over 98 percent of shareholders at the 2015 annual general meetings of BP, Royal Dutch Shell and Statoil. Similarly, the Carbon Asset Risk Initiative (Ceres, 2016) led engagement with fossil fuel companies to use shareholder capital prudently. The As You Sow and Arjuna Capital shareholder resolution (2015), supported by 4 percent of shareholders, called on Chevron to return dividends in light of spending on high-cost, high-carbon projects. Finally, calls for 'forceful stewardship' are gaining traction, in which investors press companies to present business plans compliant with a maximum 2°C rise in global temperature and vote for resolutions to change business models.

Strategy evaluation

PROS

Influence improvements in high-carbon companies' strategy, policies and emissions performance.

CONS

Effective engagement needs resourcing, but outcomes can take time and be difficult to attribute specifically to investor engagement.

TIMEFRAME

Commitments to carbon reduction actions can have immediate effect, although more typically it takes time to build a consensus and for companies to take action and make changes.

TRACKING AND MEASURING PERFORMANCE

Indicators can focus on the number of companies engaged (directly, collaboratively and via service providers), the number of cases where a company changed its practices or made a commitment to do so following engagement, and votes cast on any shareholder resolutions.

In addition to individual engagement, asset owners can join the PRI investor working group on Climate Corporate Lobbying, the Investor Expectations initiative on Corporate Climate Risk Management, the CDP Carbon Action group, or the Ceres Shareholder Initiative on Climate and Sustainability to augment their engagement practices.

Engage with the broader finance community

This form of engagement could involve dialogue on how challenges can be overcome, such as barriers to green infrastructure investment. It could also include dialogue on company disclosure and reporting requirements with stock exchanges. In addition, it could involve engagement with academic researchers to deepen investor understanding and knowledge of climate change.

Strategy 2: Invest

Invest with climate change integrated into decision-making

Integration of ESG factors is 'the systematic and explicit inclusion by investment managers of environmental, social and governance factors into traditional financial analysis' in order to enhance investment decision-making (New Climate Economy, 2015). Integrated analysis of climate change can assist in understanding sector- and company-specific risks. Although not in itself a way to reduce emissions in the real economy, this is essential to informing investor engagement and investment decisions. Integration is a more suitable strategy for actively managed than passively managed funds, given the latter do not involve stock-picking or under/over-weighting companies compared to a benchmark. Integration practices within equities are presently more advanced than in other asset classes such as fixed income.

Actively managed equities: Integration can involve identifying and analyzing material climate change-related issues, quantifying these to adjust value driver assumptions, and as a result making better-informed investment decisions. Climate change can be considered within different stages of investment decision-making, including idea generation, company analysis, the investment case, and portfolio construction. As integration practices become embedded, asset owners can work with portfolio managers to measure the impact of ESG factors on valuations. For example, one manager, Robeco, has calculated that on average, ESG factors account for 5 percent of the target price, with the impact on valuation ranging from −23 percent to +71 percent (Robeco, 2015).

Fixed income: Integration can involve analyzing issuer exposure to material climate change risk and financial implications, pricing the risk and determining whether the bond represents good investment value, and as a result having a more informed assessment of issuer credit risk and creditworthiness. Climate change can be considered for corporate bonds at a sector and company level. It can also be considered for government, municipal and supranational bonds, focusing on exposure and resilience to climate change impacts, for example. Credit rating agencies such as S&P have work underway on sovereign risk and climate change.

Strategy evaluation

PROS

Systematically include evaluation of climate change risks and opportunities in the investment decision.

CONS

Effective in identifying carbon risk at the company and sector level, but challenging to aggregate this meaningfully across an entire portfolio, and some data challenges too.

TIMEFRAME

Developing a robust process for integrated analysis can be resource-intensive initially, but will likely bring better-informed investment decisions on an ongoing basis.

TRACKING AND MEASURING PERFORMANCE

Performance indicators can focus on how a portfolio manager actively incorporates climate change factors into core decision-making processes, including idea generation for actively managed equities, and creditworthiness for fixed income. Indicators may include evidence of specific investment decisions or analysis adjusted as a result of integration of climate change risks and opportunities, at a sector, company or issuer level.

Portfolio managers could be encouraged, through discussions in performance review meetings, surveys or formal wording in mandates, to integrate climate change risk and opportunities within sector analysis and report on the portfolio manager's evaluation of the fund's exposure to climate change risks and opportunities. For actively managed equities, portfolio managers can integrate climate change factors into idea generation, including through assessment of company strategy, management quality including innovation, financial reports and valuation tools. On the contrary, managers of fixed income integrate climate change risk factors into credit risk assessment.

Invest in low-carbon solutions

Investing in solutions to climate change helps finance the transition to a low-carbon economy, and is essential to addressing ongoing global emissions. Priority areas include transportation, electricity generation, property, industrial processes, sustainable agriculture, and forestry.

Investment opportunities exist across asset classes and investment approaches. These include low-carbon indices, thematic funds, climate-aligned bonds, green infrastructure, real estate, and private market opportunities.

LOW-CARBON INDICES

These aim to reflect a lower carbon exposure than the broad market by overweighting companies with low-carbon emissions. This may involve investing in best-in-class companies in carbon intensive sectors, or companies with positive environmental impact, such as those leading in mitigating the causes of climate change.

THEMATIC FUNDS

They seek to focus investment ideas on environmental themes, typically solutions to environmental problems. Thematic funds focused on climate change may invest in renewable energy, energy efficiency, clean technology, water and waste management.

CLIMATE-ALIGNED BONDS

They aim to finance or re-finance projects to address climate change, ranging from wind, solar, hydropower to rail transport. New issuance is often multiple times subscribed and the total climate-aligned bonds universe stands at US$597.7 billion (as at July 2015), a 20 percent year-on-year increase. The *Climate Bond Standard*, supported by the Climate Bonds Initiative assists in demonstrating such bonds are genuinely 'green.'

GREEN INFRASTRUCTURE

An estimated US$57 trillion new investment in infrastructure is needed between 2013 and 2030, while infrastructure planning needs to be aligned with a 2° objective. GRESB Infrastructure assessment offers asset owners an assessment tool for evaluation and industry benchmarking of infrastructure assets, including specific indicators for climate change risk and resiliency. In the longer term, asset owners may need to work with stakeholders on investment-grade green infrastructure investment opportunities.

REAL ESTATE

Buildings generate 40 percent of global primary energy consumption, with significant opportunities to reduce emissions in new buildings and existing property, particularly through energy efficiency. Tools such as The Global Real Estate Sustainability Benchmark can assist asset owners in understanding performance in energy and greenhouse gas emissions.

PRIVATE MARKET OPPORTUNITIES

These can include funds investing in clean tech, energy efficiency and water, for example. They can invest in infrastructure and private equity.

Strategy evaluation

PROS

Investment in low-carbon solutions significantly assists financing the transition to a low-carbon economy and uses the portfolio to address emissions.

CONS

Concerns exist about how low-carbon investments can demonstrate a genuine contribution to solving climate change, liquidity and diversification, and about the investment pipeline, specialist skills and resourcing needed. Additionally, resourcing and screening is needed to assess previously unseen opportunities, such as new technologies, which can be a barrier for many asset owners.

TIMEFRAME

Direct investment and asset allocation can start having an impact on climate change relatively soon, especially if achieved at a meaningful scale.

TRACKING AND MEASURING PERFORMANCE

A fund could commit to having a particular percentage of its total assets under management in low-carbon, energy-efficient and other climate mitigation investments. The UK Environment Agency Pension Fund published such a target in 2015. Further performance metrics have yet to be developed.

Portfolio managers and consultants should review opportunities in line with asset allocation and other investment objectives, and factor climate change into asset allocation decisions. Resources include the Low Carbon Investment Registry, a new global, public, online database of low-carbon and emissions-reducing investments made by institutional investors, including the type and value of investment, destination region and manager (Investors on Climate Change, 2015).

See the end of this chapter for case studies supporting the assessment of climate risk in a portfolio and investment in low-carbon solutions.

Strategy 3: Avoid

Avoid high-carbon companies

Where an asset owner is exposed to companies dependent on fossil fuel reserves (conventional and unconventional oil, gas and coal), reallocation is a way to reduce this exposure. Typically, an investor will review the possibility by first measuring their exposure to high-carbon or fossil fuel companies and then assessing the impact on investments of removing or reducing this exposure. Such a review will also require assessing implications for tracking error, volatility and returns.

It is important to consider excluding carbon intensive companies such as coal and/or oil sands and no longer using a percentage-threshold for extraction of fossil fuels. Additionally, beneficiary and stakeholder views, the local policy trajectory, and the risk of underperforming in the market during commodities' up-cycles are critical areas of focus.

Strategy evaluation

PROS

Reallocation based on carbon, financial risk exposure or values, lowers emissions in the portfolio and sends a signal to the market on investor concern about carbon risk.

CONS

Reallocation has potential short-term performance implications, and does not reduce carbon usage if ownership is simply transferred to another asset owner.

TIMEFRAME

Reallocation has an immediate impact in lowering emissions in the portfolio, although the impact on the overall global carbon budget is unclear.

TRACKING AND MEASURING PERFORMANCE

A carbon footprint can assess emissions in the portfolio against a baseline (including year-on-year changes) and benchmark.

Asset owners can undertake reallocations reviews internally, or with consultants or providers, drawing on input from beneficiaries and other stakeholders to decide on reallocation options. Furthermore, foundations can consider joining the Divest-Invest Philanthropy Coalition.

Selecting an appropriate strategy

To decide on appropriate strategies to engage, invest, and avoid, senior decision-makers, beneficiaries and stakeholders, and portfolio managers need to be engaged.

Early discussions with the Board, trustees and chief investment officer can cover the case for action on climate change, focusing on climate science implications, fiduciary duty, and alignment with the investment horizon and liabilities. Along with providing an overview of possible strategies these discussions should address consistency with investment objectives and the risk and volatility appetite of the end-beneficiaries, as well as how peers are responding to climate change and how to employ new performance indicators for monitoring and evaluating success.

The fast-moving public debate on climate change makes it important to engage with beneficiaries, staff, supporters (in the case of charities) and external stakeholders. Asset owners need to communicate with members on climate change risks associated with their investments and how these are being managed in line with their long-term interests. Mechanisms could include surveys, focus groups, workshops, members' annual general meetings or events focused on climate change and communication through regular reporting and use of social media regarding proposed strategies.

Early dialogue with portfolio managers is essential to deciding and executing actions on climate change, whatever strategy the investor considers appropriate. This may include understanding a portfolio manager's capacity to: conduct portfolio carbon footprinting and/or other kinds of risk assessment evaluation processes; engage with companies and policy makers; conduct integrated analysis; or consider options for low-carbon-themed investment or reallocation from high-carbon holdings. Portfolio managers will need to confirm their willingness to work with their asset owners on significant new requirements.

Discussions should include how managers can evolve their approach to meet new requirements over an agreed time period. Portfolio managers and consultants will need to formally review any new strategies for risk management or emissions reduction impacting on the mandate. They will need to give a clear view on the implications for asset allocation, the investable universe, tracking error, liquidity, time horizons and financial return expectations, as well as outlining the portfolio manager's capability to meet the new requirements.

Including climate change-related requirements in the processes of selecting, appointing, and monitoring managers is an important way to ensure that expectations are clear and delivered on. Climate change-related requirements can be integrated into requests for proposals, questionnaires, discussions and evaluation criteria used to select managers, as well as into contract terms and side letter agreements that aid in the appointment of managers. Evaluation frameworks to monitor managers can incorporate climate change-related performance indicators, while agreements can specify the nature and frequency of reporting.

Discussions in performance review meetings or in written correspondence should cover which investment activities have already been undertaken to respond to climate change risk and opportunity, and to manage emissions risk. Specific areas to discuss include:

Climate change risk and opportunities What kind of sectoral, stranded assets or other analysis can be used to understand exposure to climate change risks and opportunities?

Emissions risk measurement What methods of emissions monitoring can be undertaken, such as carbon footprinting, and how can the findings be used?

Engagement What kind of voting and engagement with companies and policy makers can be undertaken, including setting objectives and measuring outcomes?

Investment How can the investment process be developed to incorporate climate change risk and opportunity at a sector and company level?

Avoidance Could reallocation or reduced portfolio exposure to emissions-intensive fossil fuel holdings be incorporated, and with what implications for the fund and how it is managed? What is the current fossil fuel exposure of the fund compared to the benchmark?

Step 3: Review

Asset owners can put processes in place to assess how effective they are in implementing their chosen strategies. As well as the specific performance indicators suggested within each strategy (see further below), there are broader tools for monitoring and reporting, including those outlined below. Further work is needed on how an individual asset owner can assess their contribution to emissions reduction in the real economy.

The PRI reporting framework

From 2016, this will provide for mandatory indicators and voluntary annual disclosure on investor practices on climate change, including measurement, engagement, low-carbon investment and thematic investment. The public *Transparency Report* generated for each investor that completes the framework can be used in internal reviews. In future years, confidential assessments may include climate change.

The asset owner disclosure project:

This provides an independent and in-depth assessment of disclosure, covering transparency, risk management, low-carbon investment, active ownership and investment chain alignment (AOD Project, 2016).

Balanced scorecards

These are well accepted among Fortune 500 companies, and included in the Value Driver Model work of the UN Global Compact and the PRI. An asset owner could adopt a similar approach by developing performance indicators with metrics for internal understanding, culture and training in relation to climate change, and to ability and success at working with externally appointed managers on climate change. Asset owners should assess the level of success in investor engagement with companies and policy makers, as well as distance from target on established goals, for example on quantitative carbon emissions.

The Investors on Climate Change platform for climate action

In 2015, the Investors on Climate Change online platform was launched to identify and record publicly the wide range of actions on climate change being undertaken by the global investor community. It lists investors taking action in four primary action areas, including measurement (e.g. carbon footprinting of portfolios), engagement (e.g. with fossil fuel and energy-intensive companies), reinforcement (e.g. with public policy makers) and reallocation (including investment in low-carbon assets and shifting capital away from emissions-intensive activities).

Case study on assessing carbon risks in equity portfolios: Allianz SE

This case study highlights how carbon and energy risks can be leveraged for stock picking in key sectors, such as cement and dairy. This can be used to assess and price-in potential risks, before and after a company responds to these risks, and to inform company engagement.

Allianz SE is an international financial services company with 85 million customers, offering products and solutions in insurance and asset management. Allianz Global Investors, a subsidiary of Allianz SE, is a global asset manager that provides a wide range of actively managed investment strategies and solutions across the risk/return spectrum. Its investment teams manage €446 billion of assets on behalf of clients across equity, fixed income, alternative and multi-asset strategies. Allianz Climate solutions GmbH is the competence center on climate change of Allianz SE.

In 2014, Allianz Global Investors and Alliance Climate Solutions in partnership with the CO-Firm and WWF Germany ran a pilot to model carbon and energy risks for stock-picking. The pilot focused on the cement and dairy industries in the USA (California), China (Guangdong Province) and Germany. The aim was to assess the financial impact associated with carbon and energy regulation – as the most material short-term risk from scaled-up climate policy – on corporate return. The model develops plausible development paths for that regulation, resulting in scenarios that can be used for stress-testing purposes. This is not captured by conventional financial analysis.

The study found that to a large extent the margin impact is a function of a company's ability to adjust operations, carbon exposures and business models to a changing regulatory environment. As might be expected, the pilot study found that margin effects are strongest in the energy-intensive industries and in particular in an environment where the ability to pass costs through to consumers is limited. In a scenario based on politically plausible increases in carbon and energy prices over the next five years, regulatory costs might lower current margins by more than 70 percent (see Table 7.1, column 2: 'margin at risk'; in the case of Germany, €12.4/t of cement).

As indicated in the table below, if a cement company anticipates regulatory changes and takes operational measures, for example by investing in waste heat recovery (a key technical improvement lever among a sample of measures), the negative margin impact is reduced and can even turn into a gain. It allows the company to improve margins in the selected scenario by €4.7/t cement (Germany), €1.6/t cement (USA, California) and €2.1/t cement (China, Guangdong) respectively (see Table 7.1, column 3: 'margin improvement potential'). There is a total margin improvement potential of €+1.1/t cement in China, Guangdong, for example. This is the result of adding the margin at risk (€–1/t) and the improvement potential (€2.1/t) in China, Guandong.

Therefore, this approach takes a bottom-up view on risk, allowing investors to identify the factors that differentiate future corporate performance (such as alternative technological or business strategies) and thus make better investment decisions. This differentiation capability will allow investors to price-in potential risks associated with the use of energy and GHG emissions, engage industries and companies on mitigating strategies (e.g. upgrading technologies), and support stock-picking.

Table 7.1 Enhancing financial analysis with carbon risk measurements

Region	*Margin as of today (€/t)*	*Margin at risk (€/t cement)*	*Margin improvement potential (€/t cement)*
Germany	17.3	−12.4	4.7
USA – California	20.3	−3.2	1.6
China – Guangdong	12.0	−1.0	2.1

Case study supporting low-carbon solutions: AP7

This case study illustrates how long-term investors can support solutions to climate change, and emphasizes that supportive public policy is essential to scaling up such investments.

AP7 is the default fund in the Swedish premium pension system managing US$36 billion in assets. As a government pension fund, its values are based on democratic decisions taken in the parliament and enforced by the government. AP7 follows an index and consequently owns a small part of the entire global stock market, and its portfolio reflects the risks and opportunities embedded in the whole global economy, with a 30–40-year investment horizon. AP7 has multiple climate change strategies: carbon footprinting, active ownership and €1.5 billion invested in environmental technologies.

AP7 believes that it can invest in climate change solutions while making a return. Pure venture is not viable as the losses are too great, while it is difficult to find less risky buyout investments. Private equity clean tech is a good space; although savers reaching retirement age are less keen on such investments, the younger generation of savers and millennials are very positive about them.

AP7's clean tech private equity program started in 2007. It has US$200 million invested in unlisted clean tech companies, with two outsourced managers. Most of the investments are in the USA, and the remainder in Scandinavia. AP7 was one of the first investors in Tesla Motors (a successful investment) and co-invested with a Swedish buyout fund in Nordic recycling company Norskgjenvinning. It currently invests in SolarCity, a company with a technological edge in solar panel manufacturing.

In order to successfully invest in clean tech, it is important to have long timeframes, use realistic returns targets, diversify, and employ specialist knowledge. Private equity programs typically run for five to ten years, but clean tech investments are often even longer, requiring strong support from the board. Initially, AP7 required private equity investments to outperform public equity by 2 percent per year, but modified this requirement for clean tech because returns were 5 percent below public equity returns. Additionally, AP7 could not find enough attractive investments in the Scandinavian region so had to diversify to international investments. Finally, AP7's in-house specialist had over ten years' experience in private equity and eight years' in clean tech.

Clean tech is maturing. Five years from now, AP7 expects that there will be more investment opportunities, and is investigating how it can increase financing solutions. However, AP7 cannot scale up its investment significantly as the current returns would risk capital for savers. A key reason is the time lag between start-up technologies and monetizing their value, although US companies are better at this than companies in other markets.

AP7 believes that in order to scale up clean tech investment the funding gap must be closed through government financing of companies during the middle gap, between start-up and achieving more financially successful scale, when a large asset owner can invest in a company. Additionally, in the long run, investors need companies with new technologies that make it on their own, driven by consumer demand and not over-dependent on government subsidies. AP7 also strongly believes a price on carbon is needed, so that there is a financial driver for alternative power generation and clean tech.

Additional examples of recent investor action aligned with the PRI framework include:

- The New York State Common Retirement Fund, with a goal of shifting assets towards a low-carbon future, established a new $2-billion low-carbon fund in partnership with Goldman Sachs and FTSE Russell with a tracking error of 25 basis points, with a parallel goal of the carbon footprint of the resulting portfolio being 70 percent less than benchmark, with the potential for this allocation within the public equity mandate to change over time. A separate $1.5 billion has been allocated to positive sustainable investing alongside divestment from pure coal and ongoing shareholder advocacy.
- One of Europe's largest pension funds, ABP, seeking to align its investments with the ongoing transition to a future low-carbon economy, developed a plan which will be implemented through 2020, allocating $66 billion up from a $32.5 billion investment commitment into a 'clean world', including $4.5 billion into renewable energy, and reducing its carbon footprint by 25 percent. ABP also introduced a carbon budget of $110 billion in equity from 2016 as part of a complete redo from scratch of their entire public equity portfolio, rejecting the previously held notion of universal ownership. One of the other largest pension funds in Europe, PGGM/PZFW, is taking similar steps towards more solutions-based investing.
- The Yale Endowment is managed by David Swensen, the most heralded figure in the history of endowment investing due to Yale's dramatic rise in asset value. Swensen asked his external managers for an understanding of climate risk, which was provided. Upon further engagement, two positions in unprofitable coal- and tar sands worth $10 million were sold.
- Another active participant in this PRI working group, AXA, committed to divesting internally managed assets from companies most exposed to coal-related activities in order to de-risk their investment portfolios and align with AXA's corporate responsibility strategy, while tripling green investments to €3 billion by 2020.

Note

1 Adapted by Kathryne Chamberlain.

References

ACCA (2011) The Carbon We're Not Counting: Accounting for Scope 3 Carbon Emissions (www.accaglobal.com/content/dam/acca/global/PDF-technical/climate-change/not_counting.pdf). Accessed September 8, 2016.

AOD Project (2016) (www.aodproject.net). Accessed September 8, 2016.

As You Sow (2015) Chevron Shareholders with $7.75 Billion in Stock Vote to Increase Dividends to Protect Investor Capital in the Face of Risky Investments in Costly Carbon Reserves (www.asyousow.org/wp-content/uploads/2015/05/release-chevron-shareholders-with-7-75billion-in-stock-vote-to-increase-dividends.pdf). Accessed September 8, 2016.

Barker, S. (2015) Directors' Personal Liability for Corporate Inaction on Climate Change. *Governance Directions*, 67(1), 21–25.

CalPERS (2016) (www.calpers.ca.gov/index.jsp?bc=/investments/policies/invo-policy-statement/home.xml). Accessed February 2016.

Carbon Tracker (2013) Carbon Tracker's Carbon Budget Q&A (www.carbontracker.org/wp-content/uploads/2014/08/Carbon-budget-checklist-FINAL-1.pdf). Accessed September 8, 2016.

Carnegie Mellon University (2016) EIO-LCA: Free, Fast, Easy Life Cycle Assessment (www.eiolca.net/index.html). Accessed September 8, 2016.

CDP (2012) Why We're 'Aiming for A' (www.cdp.net/en-US/News/Pages/why-aiming-for-a.aspx). Accessed December 12, 2015.

CDP (2016) (www.cdp.net/en-US/Pages/HomePage.aspx). Accessed September 8, 2016.

Ceres (2016) Carbon Asset Risk (www.ceres.org/issues/carbon-asset-risk). Accessed September 8, 2016.

Climate Bonds Initiative (2015) Final 2014 Green Bond Total Is $36.6bn (www.climatebonds.net/2015/01/final-2014-green-bond-total-366bn-%E2%80%93-that%E2%80%99s-more-x3-last-year%E2%80%99s-total-biggest-year-ever-green). Accessed September 14, 2016.

Finance UNEP Initiative, World Resource Institute (2015) Carbon Asset Risk: Discussion Framework (www.unepfi.org/fileadmin/documents/carbon_asset_risk.pdf). Accessed September 8, 2016.

IIGCC (2015) Climate Change Investment Solutions: A Guide for Asset Owners (www.iigcc.org%2Ffiles%2Fpublication-files%2FClimate-Change-Investment-Solutions-Guide_IIGCC_2015.pdf&usg=AFQjCNHB6zSNStAewjqG3pgwhksRsUXtwQ). Accessed October 18, 2016.

International Energy Agency (2013) *World Energy Outlook Special Report 2013: Redrawing the Energy Climate Map* (www.iea.org/publications/freepublications/publication/weo-2013-special-report-redrawing-the-energy-climate-map.html). Accessed September 8, 2016.

International Energy Agency (2014) Signs of Stress Must Not Be Ignored, IEA Warns in Its New World Energy Outlook (www.iea.org/newsroomandevents/pressreleases/2014/november/signs-of-stress-must-not-be-ignored-iea-warns-in-its-new-world-energy-outlook.html). Accessed September 8, 2016.

Investors on Climate Change (2015) Low Carbon Registry (http://investorsonclimatechange.org/portfolio/low-carbon-registry/). Accessed September 8, 2016.

Investors on Climate Change (2016) Aiming for A (http://investorsonclimatechange.org/portfolio/aiming-for-a/). Accessed September 8, 2016.

IPCC (2014) *Climate Change 2014: Synthesis Report. Contribution of Working Groups I, II and III to the Fifth Assessment Report of the Intergovernmental Panel on Climate Change*. Core writing team R.K. Pachauri and L.A. Meyer (eds.). IPCC, Geneva, Switzerland, 151 pp. (www.ipcc.ch/report/ar5/syr/). Accessed September 8, 2016.

Law Commission (2014) Fiduciary Duties of Investment Intermediaries (www.lawcom.gov.uk/project/fiduciary-duties-of-investment-intermediaries/). Accessed September 8, 2016.

Mercer (2015) *Investing in a Time of Climate Change*. Report (www.mercer.com/content/dam/mercer/attachments/global/investments/mercer-climate-change-report-2015.pdf). Accessed September 8, 2016.

Norges Bank Investment Management (2014) Climate Change Strategy: Expectations to Companies (www.nbim.no/globalassets/documents/climate-change-strategy-document.pdf?id=5931). Accessed September 8, 2016.

Robeco (2015) Measuring ESG Impact, Part 1: Valuation (www.robeco.com/images/measuring-esg-impact-part-1-valuation-may-2015.pdf). Accessed October 18, 2016.

Thamotheram, R. and Wildsmith, H. (2007) Increasing Long-Term Market Returns: Realising the Potential of Collective Pension Fund Action. *Corporate Governance: An International Review*, 15(3) 438–454.

The New Climate Economy Report (2015) (http://newclimateeconomy.report). Accessed September 8, 2016.

UK Environment Agency Pension Fund (2015) Policy to Address the Impacts of Climate Change (www.eapf.org.uk/~/media/document-libraries/eapf2/climate-change/policy-to-address-the-impacts-of-climate-change.pdf?la=en). Accessed September 8, 2016.

United Nations Framework Convention on Climate Change (2015) Six Oil Majors Say: We Will Act Faster with Stronger Carbon Pricing. Open letter to UN and governments (http://newsroom.unfccc.int/unfccc-newsroom/major-oil-companies-letter-to-un/). Accessed September 8, 2016.

United Nations Global Compact (2016) Implement the Value Driver Model (www.unglobalcompact.org/take-action/action/value-driver-model). Accessed September 8, 2016.

University of California UCnet (2015) Office of the CIO's 10 Investment Beliefs (http://ucnet.universityofcalifornia.edu/news/2015/02/cio-10-beliefs.html). Accessed September 8, 2016.

Chapter 8

Why divestment is the outcome of a thoughtful investment process

Cary Krosinsky

Having been intimately involved with the founders of the Carbon Tracker Initiative since 2006, I've seen the entire history of the so-called 'stranded assets argument', the turf war that resulted, and the now wide and growing acceptance of the premise that most of the world's remaining fossil fuel needs to remain in the ground for the world to retain a chance of avoiding a likely series of global climate catastrophes triggered by the effects of climate change over the next decades.

Less clear is how to get to safety and success, but that is what this book is largely about.

Much clearer is the fact that divestment is a stance which individuals and organizations can take on moral/ethical/political grounds, but for most investors, divestment is the end result of a thoughtful process.

Going back to 2011, a small group of us at the Carbon Tracker Initiative first published the *Unburnable Carbon* report,[1] for which I am listed as a peer reviewer. Those listed in the report were in effect the entirety of the Carbon Tracker team at the time, which has always 'punched above its weight'.

Our original premise in 2006 was to create something called the Investors Disclosure Project.

Back in 2005, I first met Mark Campanale and Nick Robins in London, and we were working together then on combining institutional ownership data with a view on observing which investors were taking on the most climate risk and potentially making that more transparent. While this didn't happen at the time, we had started the move towards building an organization, and also took close note of the Potsdam Institute/Meinhausen piece which appeared in *Nature* in 2009,[2] noting that greenhouse gas emission targets could start to be associated with probabilities of restricting global warming. On the back of this, the idea for the Carbon Tracker Initiative was given life and our first report was launched to great acclaim some five years ago.

With this in mind, I had been attending some high-level events at the Garrison Institute, and had access to Bill McKibben, who I emailed in June 2011 to see if he would be interested in reading our research, which was to be released in July. McKibben's subsequent July 2012 *Rolling Stone* piece entitled 'Global Warming's

Terrifying New Math'[3] went viral[4] and helped spawn the divestment from fossil fuel movement.

There are a number of problems with the choice McKibben made (apparently a close decision with a few advisers involved including Naomi Klein and Bob Massie and not many others) to go with a full coal, oil and gas divestment strategy.

First of all, fossil fuel use is extremely systemic. Oil itself is in everything from chemicals to transportation of goods and well beyond. Fossil fuels are complex, with each of coal, oil and gas arguably needing separate treatment.

In fact, the Carbon Tracker Initiative is not behind the idea of across-the-board straight divestment.

In its 2015 report on gas, the organization states that

> Carbon Tracker is not an advocate of a pure divestment approach to fossil fuels. Rather we advocate engagement, correctly pricing the risk premium associated with fossil fuels, transparency and the closure of high cost, high carbon projects – project level divestment. We look to identify the most economically rational path for the fossil fuel industry to fit within the carbon budget.[5]

The move away from fossil fuel consumption will be difficult, and a narrower lens of prioritization is needed to stop unneeded production, which requires investor involvement and shareholder engagement, meaning investors need to own these companies so they can retain their voice.

The alternative is that less interested owners will retain speculative positions, encouraging what could be unnecessary capital expenditure. An orderly transition will require a combination of innovation, regulation, investor encouragement and corporate cooperation, combined with a grass roots individual and consumer voices pressuring for the right actions.

Keep in mind that oil is needed to keep the current economy going. After Superstorm Sandy the first thing people begged for was for oil to return to the gas stations so they could go back to work. Aviation for now requires jet fuel. An orderly transition will be hard, but we need to prioritize lower-cost resources that make sense to harvest, versus those that need to stay in the ground.

Most fortunately, there is a correlation between high-cost coal, oil and gas and high carbon, so by focusing on lower-cost production we encourage better economic vitality and growth, in combination with the steps needed to encourage the necessary transition to lower carbon consumption in transportation, buildings, industrial processes and energy production, as well as to lower production of the other greenhouse gases – especially by methane efficiency within agriculture, land use and oil and gas production – as well as stopping deforestation in its tracks.

That's how to divest from the high-carbon economy. It will take an organized transition on both the production and consumption side of the equation.

Fortunately most of the greenhouse gas in the ground is in the form of coal, so focusing on leapfrogging China and India from coal to renewables is a very clear and important goal, so it is great that organizations such as the Rocky Mountain Institute are working on this very question.[6] And much of the capital expenditure that is at financial risk is in the oil space,[7] particularly in the Arctic and in the tar/oil sands of Alberta, Canada. Engagement on the back of these issues has been performed by leading investors through organizations such as Ceres surrounding Carbon Asset Risk, asking for companies to return cash to shareholders rather than waste it on high-cost projects that are not needed in a 2-degree world.

Companies who do not agree to such requests, after being given time to respond, have either been sold by many leading organizations such as AXA, Allianz, Norges Bank, or such activities have been turned away from within lending practices of the largest banks such as Bank of America, and coal has also been a focus due to the lack of any reasonable business case.

In this way, divestment becomes the result of a thoughtful investment process.

At the PRI in 2015 we established a Climate Change Asset Owner Framework, working with some of their largest signatories including the aforementioned AXA and Allianz, as well as Aegon, some of the superannuation funds in Australia, one of the large Swedish AP pension funds, and the University of California system among others.

The resulting project was a success, as detailed in the previous chapter, with a first report on the complexities of addressing climate change as investors forming a foundation for understanding how a transition to low carbon could be achieved, entitled *On Reducing Emissions*.[8] The final *Framework Report*[9] laid out the three very clear actions that investors can take regarding climate change:

1 Increase allocations to positive sustainable investing across asset class, including in public equity, as we discuss throughout this book, as well as in solutions that may be available in private equity, venture capital and beyond.
2 Engage with corporations as well as policymakers, and your outsourced fund manager partners where you have them.
3 Sell companies once there is no business case and engagement has failed.

The *Framework Report* is full of case studies of successful actions.

Hence we believe the orientation of our class at Brown lays out exactly the foundation and path for divestment where and when warranted. The fund managers we have chosen for BUSIF are fossil fuel free, not originally by design, but as an outcome of their investment processes, either when seeking to invest in the best workplaces (Parnassus Endeavor), or when seeking companies which are best positioned for a sustainable future (other funds such as Mirova Global Sustainable Equity).

The divestment debate has raged on university campuses in North America and beyond for years now, and it may have taken a while but the path forward is now clear.

Our sustainable investing process works and has been outperforming. It fits neatly within the PRI framework and positions our portfolio for an ideal future, while helping to create a leading positive sustainable investment option for donors, and stands as a thought leadership example for the entire sustainable investing field for other endowments and asset owners to consider.

Notes

1 www.carbontracker.org/wp-content/uploads/2014/09/Unburnable-Carbon-Full-rev2-1.pdf. Accessed September 9, 2016.
2 www.nature.com/nature/journal/v458/n7242/full/nature08017.html. Accessed September 9, 2016.
3 www.rollingstone.com/politics/news/global-warmings-terrifying-new-math-20120719. Accessed September 9, 2016.
4 http://planetsave.com/2012/07/29/global-warmings-terrifying-new-math-gets-half-a-million-views-my-thoughts/. Accessed September 9, 2016.
5 www.carbontracker.org/wp-content/uploads/2015/06/CTI-gas-report-Final-WEB.pdf. Accessed September 9, 2016.
6 www.rmi.org/reinventing_fire_china. Accessed September 9, 2016.
7 www.carbontracker.org/wp-content/uploads/2015/11/CAR3817_Synthesis_Report_24.11.15_WEB2.pdf. Accessed September 9, 2016.
8 http://2xjmlj8428u1a2k5o34l1m71.wpengine.netdna-cdn.com/wp-content/uploads/PRI_Discussion-Paper-on-Reducing-Emissions.pdf. Accessed December 12, 2015.
9 http://2xjmlj8428u1a2k5o34l1m71.wpengine.netdna-cdn.com/wp-content/uploads/PRI_Climate-Change-Framework1.pdf. Accessed December 12, 2015.

Chapter 9

The data challenges which remain

Dan Esty and Todd Cort

Introduction

This chapter explores the data challenges that constrain those interested in corporate sustainability from an investor perspective, first reviewing the need for refined metrics that respond to the diverse set of use cases for which investors want sustainability guidance. Second, it explores the environmental, social and governance (ESG) indicators available to investors in today's marketplace and identifies the shortcomings of virtually all of these data sets. Finally, it highlights a path forward for those seeking to bring a sustainability lens to their analysis.

The need for more robust ESG data has come into focus as a result of growing interest from investors who want information on a different set of factors to those on which traditional investors rely.

Investors bring very divergent interests and values to their focus on sustainability. The range of issues that fall under the sustainability rubric can be very broad, meaning no two investors would highlight the exact same list of ESG metrics. Investors differ widely in how much they prioritize optimizing financial returns versus having their portfolios aligned with their values concerning the environment, social justice, and other issues.

The existing ESG data meets the needs of these investors with varying degrees of success. As the longest standing category is traditional SRI investors, most of the data providers offer carefully constructed negative screens. However, those who want to invest in companies that are offering their customers sustainability solutions have even fewer metrics to deploy with any degree of comprehensive coverage. And those interested in the *social return* of companies have virtually nothing in the way of metrics upon which to rely.

Data needs of mainstream investors

The existing corporate sustainability metrics are so narrowly focused or methodologically flawed that they do not really permit a thoughtful and strategic approach to climate change exposure or other environmental goals. A number of issues can be identified in this regard.

Operational versus reputational metrics

Is Dow a sustainable company? Dow has a long legacy of pollution and might be excluded from some *sustainability*-screened portfolios. But in recent years, Dow has become a recognized leader in sustainability. The company has a globally recognized safety program, multiple sets of specific, quantifiable sustainability targets ranging from operational efficiency to innovation and supporting the global circular economy. Dow also reports that 10 percent of sales ($5.8 billion) now come from products that 'are highly advantaged by sustainable chemistry'.[1]

So if one looks at Dow from an operational perspective rather than a reputational one, the company emerges as a sustainability leader. Yet little of the available ESG data with its backward-looking focus captures these recent accomplishments or Dow's forward-looking potential to benefit from delivering sustainability solutions to its customers. Despite this apparent increase in value, the market has not shown a concomitant increase in Dow's share price. This could be because investors do not see the value of Dow's green chemistry push. However, as we discuss below, it is more likely that investors *cannot* see the value of Dow's green chemistry push because the data is absent or flawed.

Footprints versus handprints

To the extent that the current ESG framework offers metrics on current performance, almost all of the data would center on the environmental impacts – or *footprint* – of the companies being scored. While all of these elements are useful to know, they paint an incomplete picture of the sustainability of a company. As in the case of Dow discussed above, it is often equally important to know a company's *handprint* – how a company affects the sustainability of its customers.

To be more specific, an investor who is trying to understand how Dow will fare in the face of the emerging sustainability challenges and opportunities (Lubin and Esty, 2010) needs data on the market transformation that Dow is delivering in energy efficiency, safety, waste reduction, and other product categories. As a longstanding industrial company, Dow's legacy of pollution is real but much less relevant to its prospects in the marketplace than its current sustainability leadership, especially its focus on meeting customer needs for energy and environmental breakthroughs.

In some industry categories, moreover, the footprint is so light and the handprint so heavy, that a traditional ESG analysis focused on direct company impacts will severely warp any sustainability comparison. Software companies, for example, would be better judged by the sustainability gains made possible by the apps they develop rather than just the level of electricity consumed by the computers they run. Salesforce.com makes the case that network IT solutions have reduced the carbon emissions of its customers by 95 percent compared to on-premises applications.[2]

Beyond risk to growth and productivity: opportunities as well as downside exposure

Most ESG metrics are *risk*-focused. Data sets that provide a gauge of companies' carbon footprint are now available. These greenhouse gas emissions scorecards allow an investor to identify which corporations or sectors might be exposed if CO_2 emissions were priced or faced more severe regulation. But there is little information available on *upside* climate change exposure that might allow an investor to go long on companies or sectors that will thrive as carbon pricing becomes more widespread.

At least some sustainability-minded investors thus need data that records environmental activities and strategies. In particular, data on sustainability-related growth, including both top-line expansion of sales and bottom-line profitability from environmental efforts, is needed. Ideally, ESG data providers would offer metrics – even indicative or qualitative ones – that provide a sense of the scope of a company's sustainability vision and its capacity for execution.

Materiality

While materiality is a well-established concept and is present in every major sustainability management system standard, disclosure guideline and risk management framework, it has yet to effectively drive strategic decision-making and data disclosure on ESG issues by companies, despite work by the Global Reporting Initiative (GRI),[3] the Global Environmental Management Initiative (GEMI, 2015), and the Sustainable Accounting Standards Board (SASB).[4] Fundamentally, the structure of ESG reporting and data comparison needs to be recast to capture what is important or *material* to each company and its industry.

Despite the growing interest in a broader framework of sustainability data, the current set of metrics largely reflects the historic interests of *values* investors, including, most notably, the (rather narrow) concerns of environmental groups. As a result, much of the information that is collected is superficial and reputation-oriented. To make corporate sustainability metrics more meaningful, much more focus needs to be given to what really matters in terms of environmental impacts – and the structure of metrics needs to re-geared to reflect this *materiality* analysis.

Uniform reporting frameworks versus industry-specific metrics

Because industries differ widely in terms of which sustainability issues will be most salient, what metrics should be reported, tracked and compared will also vary by industry. Industry-specific metrics are now becoming more widespread, but for much of the recent sustainability data history too much emphasis was put on uniform reporting requirements. Prior to the latest iteration in its reporting framework (GRI G4), GRI long rewarded companies for the volume of reporting by designating Application Levels of A, B and C (where level A was reserved for those companies that reported on the most aspects). This led to highly immaterial reporting such as a US real estate company reporting on human rights issues, or a global consultancy reporting on living wage efforts. Even within sectors, the various guidance frameworks can be blunt. For the oil and gas industry, many frameworks ask for metrics from exploration and production to refining, despite the fact that very few oil and gas companies are integrated from upstream to downstream assets.

Some common metrics across all industry categories will be needed to allow for industry-versus-industry comparisons. It will be of interest to some investors that Citibank has a more robust sustainability profile than Bank of America, but others will want to know how the financial services category does as a whole in comparison to utilities or other industries (Srinivas, 2015). So metrics that facilitate intra-industry benchmarking and ones that make cross-industry comparisons possible are important.

Additional methodological issues

Concerns about the existing ESG data arise not simply from *what* is being collected but also from *how* the metrics are constructed. Despite the growth in interest in ESG data over the years, little progress has been made on a series of basic methodological challenges in the sustainability domain.

Required versus self-reported data

In the United States, the Environmental Protection Agency (EPA) requires reporting of data under regulations within the Clean Water Act and the Clean Air Act, and include a wide range of industrial environmental impacts from release of toxic compounds into the air to stormwater and surface run-off into water. Other agencies such as the Energy Information Agency (EIA) collect additional mandatory energy data, including from domestic and imported fuel inputs, as well as energy consumption data from a wide variety of industries. To the extent that these data are publicly available, the ESG analytic companies take advantage of them. Thus, the metrics on chemical spills, discharges of toxic chemicals to air and water, while still prone to error and suffering from severe constraints on boundary which impedes comparability, are nevertheless reasonably accurate when compared to other ESG data because they are built on government data sets. But beyond these narrow categories, companies report when and how and to whom they deem it to be convenient. In addition, because much of the data in the ESG arena comes from voluntary company responses to surveys, additional inconsistencies and gaps plague the data sets (Clarkson et al., 2011).

Coached results and conflicts of interest

Survey data can be further distorted if those collecting the information offer consulting services to help companies understand how to respond to the questions being asked. Several data providers have historically had related consulting companies that would provide such coaching. Zurich-based Sustainable Asset Management, one of the earliest entrants into the corporate sustainability metrics world, saw its credibility suffer as a result of the perceived conflict of interest between its consulting business and its data collection efforts. Most of today's firms collecting, analyzing, and rating ESG data also provide paid benchmarks and consulting services around that data, making the line between *objective data collection* and *data consultation* very blurry.

Monitored versus estimated data

Some of the ESG data that is available comes from measured results (e.g., actual levels of air pollution analyzed using monitoring equipment). Unfortunately, measurement-based data on critical environmental factors is surprisingly scarce. Rather, much of the data is also compiled based on estimates, which range from reasonably accurate to wild speculation depending on who is doing the estimating, what incentives for accuracy exist, and whether the tools even exist to measure errors associated with the estimates.

There are a few environmental data sets that are nominally measurement-based. For instance, air emissions data from large smokestacks in the United States must follow strict measurement requirements using in-line monitors that record the presence of chemicals such as sulfur dioxide, nitrous oxides and volatile organic compounds. However, even these data sets quickly run into serious methodological issues. For example, smaller stacks and combustion sources are allowed to estimate emissions based on fuel type and volume burned, or provide no data whatsoever. Even for highly regulated sources such as large smokestacks, a single company might be reporting emissions from operations in multiple countries where the sampling protocols, error rates and boundaries of reporting vary significantly.

Even in a widely used category such as greenhouse gas emissions, most of the data comes from estimations and not actual monitoring or measurement. Almost all of the CO_2 data used by the major ESG data companies comes from a single source: CDP (formerly the Carbon Disclosure Project), which gets its data from the companies themselves.[5] The reporting companies estimate their emissions – usually from energy consumption, which can be tracked. Some do the estimations with care. Others do not. Some companies cross-check their numbers both internally and externally. Others do not. Some seek accuracy; and others massage the numbers to protect their image.

Accurate estimation of other sustainability data is even harder to do – and more open to data manipulation and reporting abuse. An improved corporate sustainability metrics framework thus needs to prioritize more measured data that can be collected on a methodologically consistent basis.

Verification

A little over half of the largest companies in the world that produce sustainability reports are pursuing some form of third-party audit (KPMG, 2013). Of these audited reports, however, most verification only covers a small portion of the information in the reports (Hubbard, 2009). When this data is collected and reported by ESG analytic firms, it is unclear which metrics and which data points have been verified, if any at all. By and large, the data analytics firms rely only on the data from the companies themselves with no additional checks on accuracy. If sustainability metrics are to win the confidence of the investor community, much more has to be done to clarify what data has been verified either by government agencies or third-party, trusted verification entities.

Coverage

Currently, there are somewhere between 80,000 and 100,000 publicly listed companies in the world. As of 2015, just over 5,000 corporations (predominantly public) around the world report their emissions to CDP, representing less than 5 percent of companies (GRESB, 2015). Even fewer offer metrics on other critical issues. GRI, the largest voluntary reporting guideline, provides a database listing the number of companies that have reported against each of its disclosure recommendations (based on companies that submit their report to GRI). As of late 2015, the database included 1,395 companies (less than 2 percent of publicly traded companies).[6] This spotty coverage limits the accuracy and usefulness of the existing ESG data sets, particularly for intra-industry comparative analysis.

Gap filling

Most of the ESG data providers try to fill the gaps in their data matrices. But how gaps get filled varies widely – often with little transparency on what sort of imputation or extrapolation is being done. Some data providers report where particular numbers have come from (i.e., who has provided data), and what data is missing. Others simply fill in the blanks. ESG data companies use a variety of gap-filling strategies – and sometimes, but not always, provide a methodological appendix that details how the gaps in their data matrix were filled. Some fill gaps based on imputation from other data that is available and careful analysis of what other indicators best predict the missing datapoints. Many others *average around* gaps, giving non-reporters an average score – or sometimes the average score of similarly situated companies. Some penalize non-reporters, but often, whether and how this is done is not transparent. While penalizing the imputed score of non-reporters may seem arbitrary, it may well be that non-reporters have strategically chosen not to report for fear that (or with the knowledge that) their actual numbers are much worse than the average.

Reporting consistency and methodological rigor

With no government-mandated or even industry-established reporting standards, companies put forth data in various categories in ways that are convenient from their own internal point of view. This inconsistency creates many problems. As noted above, some companies take great care in gauging their greenhouse gas emissions – and report the results faithfully. Others approach reporting with the primary goal of making themselves look good. To instill confidence in corporate sustainability data and to give investors data that makes systematic comparisons possible will require much greater methodological rigor in how data is collected, reported, and verified.

Normalization

Even if everyone were equally committed to accuracy, the lack of common reporting standards would be a problem. For instance, with regard to greenhouse gas emissions, some companies report just Scope 1 (emissions resulting from direct burning of fuels), others report Scopes 1 and 2 (adding emissions resulting from imported energy such as electricity or steam) and a small number report Scopes 1, 2, and 3 (including all other indirect emissions, other than Scope 2, that occur in the value chain of the company). The lack of consistency creates a real problem for benchmarking, as those who report just Scope 1 may appear to be better performers than those reporting Scopes 1 and 2. And likewise, a company reporting all three Scopes might have what seems to be a bigger carbon footprint than its competitor who reports just Scopes 1 and 2, even though a *normalized* comparison might reveal otherwise.

Likewise, metrics that track the number of legal violations, enforcement actions, reputation or any other indicator that is likely to follow corporate scale need to be normalized. Otherwise, the indicator simply offers a proxy measure for enterprise size and not a useful gauge of attentiveness to sustainability issues.

More generally, the value of sustainability comparisons across companies or among industries depends on the metric in question being a meaningful gauge of differences, which requires that other factors that might confound the analysis be held equal. If these potentially confounding factors are not normalized, then any resulting benchmark would not be accurate. For instance, as noted above, if a comparison of notices of violation is not *denominated* by company size (using sales, or number of employees, or value-added as a denominator) then the comparison will say more about corporate scale than sustainability.

Outcomes versus inputs

In the absence of good data on actual environmental outcomes, such as emissions levels coming out of a smokestack or a measure of contaminants in effluent, ESG data companies provide the *best available* data. But these attempts to get around data limitations can lead to further distortion and bias. For example, rather than providing a real gauge of a company's environmental performance, data on size of the company's environmental budget or staffing sometimes gets relied upon. While in some instances such proxy indicators are better than nothing, data users should insist, over time, that the framework of corporate sustainability metrics evolve away from inputs – such as money spent or projects undertaken – toward outcomes such as emission levels or ambient quality measures.

Analysis

Additional issues arise in the context of data analysis. Some data providers are quite transparent about how they do comparisons. Others offer numbers with little sense of context (Delmas and Blass, 2010). Trucost for instance, which compiles and sells environmental metrics data sets, has had difficulty getting traction in the ESG data arena, in part because it reveals little about its analytic methods. Data users thus worry about whether the data coming out of Trucost's 'black box' are reliable (Cranston, 2014). This same black box challenge continues to plague major sustainability rankings from the *Newsweek* ranking of 'Most Sustainable Companies' to the Dow Jones Sustainability Index.

Aggregation and weighting

Another series of contentious issues that have emerged is the context of how multiple sustainability metrics get combined into an over-arching index. If the scorecard is based on ten individual factors (such as CO_2 emissions, air pollution, waste, etc.) should they all be given the same weight in the aggregation? Or are some factors deemed to be more important than others and therefore given more weight? Should the distribution of scores in each underlying metric be equalized (using, for instance, a technique called Z-scores) to avoid the result that some metrics implicitly get more weight than others? Should outliers be eliminated? Or should other statistical techniques to *trim the tails* be deployed? There are no easy answers to these questions. Indeed, Ph.D. dissertations have been written on how best to grapple with these issues.[7]

In the end, the issues of aggregation and weighting are as much art as science. Or to be more precise, the right way to aggregate depends on what you are trying to do. What is critical is that the data providers be transparent about what they are doing. More fundamentally, as mainstream investors take more of an interest in sustainability metrics, they will likely want to rethink the underlying methodological choices that have been used in the past to meet the needs of the SRI investor community.

Path forward

Growing interest in corporate sustainability, particularly from mainstream investors, argues for more care in how ESG metrics are designed, how the underlying data are collected, and the methods by which the numbers get combined for purposes of comparison. More statistical rigor is possible and greater transparency in terms of what assumptions are being made is essential. As the *use cases* for sustainability metrics expand, new data will be required and existing data sets will need to be refined. Broader coverage is needed to make both intra-industry and market-wide comparisons more accurate and meaningful.

Most importantly, the expanding needs of investors and the inability of current ESG metrics to meet these needs argues strongly for a fundamentally restructured framework of sustainability metrics and some level of government structure – including some degree of mandatory data reporting, rules to ensure methodological consistency and metrics comparability, and required verification. Fewer standards and more focused guidelines for collecting, reporting, and verifying sustainability data would also help to sharpen the focus and improve the consistency and rigor of ESG metrics. Such consolidation should build on the principle of materiality from an investor perspective.

With a sharper picture of the elements of sustainability that translate into superior financial performance, better data, and scorecards designed with specific investment purposes in mind, more mainstream investors may find that some degree of sustainability assessment makes sense as part of their market analysis.

Notes

1 Dow, 'Our 2015 Sustainability Goals', www.dow.com/en-us/science-and-sustainability/sustainability-reporting/sustainable-chemistry/
2 For more information, see the Salesforce webpage, 'Salesforce.com and the Environment: Reducing Carbon Emissions in the Cloud', www.salesforce.com/assets/pdf/misc/WP_WSP_Salesforce_Environment.pdf
3 For more information, see the Global Reporting Initiative's website, www.globalreporting.org/Pages/default.aspx
4 For more information, see Sustainability Accounting Standards Board, 'Materiality', www.sasb.org/materiality/important/
5 For more information, see the Carbon Disclosure Project's website, www.cdp.net/en-US/Respond/Pages/companies.aspx
6 For more information, see the Global Reporting Initiatives' database on sustainability disclosures for full list, http://database.globalreporting.org/benchmark
7 See, for example, Tanja Srebotnjak, 'The Development of Composite Indicators for Environmental Policy: Statistical Solutions and Policy Aspects', Yale University Publication #3293388 (2007).

References

Clarkson P., Overell, M. and Chapple, L.L. (2011) 'Environmental Reporting and Its Relation to Corporate Environmental Performance', *Abacus*, 47, 1, 27–60.

Cranston, G. (2014) 'Back to Basics: Demystifying Natural Capital Valuation', *Huffington Post* (October 15, 2014), www.huffingtonpost.com/gemma-cranston/back-to-basics-demystifyi_b_5990034.html. Accessed September 9, 2016.

Delmas, M. and Blass, V.D. (2010) 'Measuring Corporate Environmental Performance: The Trade-Offs of Sustainability Ratings', *Business Strategy and the Environment*, 19, 4, 245–260.

GEMI (Global Environmental Management Initiative) (2015) 'Quick Guide: Materiality'. September. http://gemi.org/wp-content/uploads/2015/09/GEMI-MaterialityQuickGuide-2015.pdf. Accessed October 18, 2016.

GRESB (2015) *2015 Report*. https://www.gresb.com/results2015/global_trends. Accessed September 9, 2016.

Hubbard, G. (2009) 'Measuring Organisational Performance: Beyond the Triple Bottom Line', *Business Strategy and Environment*, 19, 3, 177–191.

KPMG (2013) 'Survey of Corporate Responsibility Reporting 2013', www.kpmg.com/sustainability. Accessed September 9, 2016.

Lubin, D. and Esty, D. (2011) 'The Sustainability Imperative', in *Evolutions in Sustainable Investing*, ed. C. Krosinsky, N. Robins and S. Viederman. New York: Wiley, 2012. And in *Harvard Business Review*, 88 (May 2010), 42–50.

Srinivas, S. (2015) 'Citigroup to Invest $100bn in Tackling Climate Change', *The Guardian*, February 18, 2015. www.theguardian.com/sustainable-business/2015/feb/18/citi-100bn-investment-climate-change-banks-environment. Accessed September 9, 2016.

Chapter 10

Scaling the sustainable trillion

'Top-down' investment strategies

Cary Krosinsky

What could be called 'the sustainable trillion' is an approximate new trillion dollars of sustainable investing commitments that have emerged during 2015 into 2016. This new money has the potential to transform the way business is accomplished, making it more sustainable in a race for more environmentally and socially intentional investment capital, and creates the potential to scale sustainability even further into the trillions as appears to be required.

A top-down, bottom-up race for attracting sustainable investing dollars is arguably most attractive as it incentivizes creativity while using the natural forces of capitalism for good.

Many categories of organization thrive when competition is healthy and creativity is maximized, such as you see in the race to the top underway at present at universities and among public companies in many sectors to show sustainability leadership. In many ways, investors have just begun this race themselves.

Universities very much have a spotlight on them these days regarding sustainability; often this is the top question incoming students ask of such institutions in so far as 'What are you doing on this subject?' Millennials increasingly want to make a positive impact on the world, as many studies show. Similarly, when graduating students choose places to work, they increasingly want to work in environments where they can most make a difference while also making money while getting their careers underway. So there is a race for talent and quality which includes establishing who are the most sustainable organizations, and this too is starting to play out in the world of investing, which is fantastic to see.

Bank of America is in my recent experience perhaps the most 'all in' of the large US financial institutions attempting to grow their business on the back of sustainable and impact investing. They claimed recently to manage a new $10 billion of assets with sustainability or impact as a primary goal, and actively seek to align clients with their values, with dozens of internal staff.[1]

Bank of America's CEO Brian Moynihan has recently been quite vocal about the need to solve for climate change at major events[2] and the bank has, per a recent press release, 'upped its pledged to increase the company's current environmental business initiative from $50 billion to $125 billion in low-carbon business by 2025 through lending, investing, capital raising, advisory services and developing financing solutions for clients around the world'.[3] The bank has provided more than $39 billion in financing for low-carbon activities since 2007, including $12 billion in 2014 alone, of which:

- Forty percent went to renewable energies – solar, wind, hydro, geothermal, advanced biofuels or mixed portfolios.
- Thirty-three percent went to financing energy efficiency.

Bank of America has also played a lead role in helping develop the expanding green bond market, issuing a first benchmark-sized corporate green bond in 2013 which was a $500 million offering, followed by a second tranche[4] in the spring of 2015.

According to Bloomberg New Energy Finance, Bank of America was the largest underwriter of green bond issuance in 2014.

Its efforts include dozens of employees having worked directly on these questions, as well as training their internal advisors, and so Bank of America sees sustainable investing as a key driver of their own future success. It is important for the success of sustainable investing writ large that such firms as these which commit resources and demonstrate expertise are rewarded with market share.

Goldman Sachs, with a well-earned reputation for focusing on making money, has committed $150 billion to clean energy financing through 2025,[5] as large a commitment to sustainable finance as any institution in the world, quadrupling its previous goals. The clean energy transition requires capital and creative thinking from financial experts, so it is great to see this level of funding commitment emerge.

Back in July, Goldman previewed this step a bit when they joined a White House effort to 'get US businesses to act on climate change',[6] joining Alcoa, Apple, Bank of America, Berkshire Hathaway Energy, Cargill, Coca-Cola, General Motors, Google, Microsoft, PepsiCo, UPS, and Walmart with stated goals at the time of increasing energy efficiency (a key necessary wedge in the climate transition, needing to be as much as $1 trillion per year in new investment globally according to the IEA), boosting low-carbon investing and making solar energy more accessible to low-income American families. Further, the New York State Common Retirement Fund is working with Goldman now to create a $2-billion low-carbon public equity fund.

These initiatives help move Goldman down a more sustainable path than before, and they also often point to their Environmental Policy Framework which further locks in their activities pertaining to climate mitigation, climate adaptation, climate risk management and their own operations.[7]

All of the large banks are in this game. Citibank recently announced a ten-year, $100 billion commitment to sustainable growth,[8] while Morgan Stanley and J. P. Morgan have created new wealth management platforms to service clients interested in sustainability and impact.

J. P. Morgan produces leading reports on impact investing with the support of the Rockefeller Foundation.[9] Morgan Stanley's Institute for Sustainable Investing has been increasingly busy and outspoken, publishing regular thought leadership on the value of real estate, diversity and many other sustainability topics.[10] These institutions have also been rapidly hiring, whereas ten years ago you couldn't find a single employee on this subject at any of their New York City offices. (I know, because I tried to find them to invite to an event in 2006 on sustainability – there were basically none.)

This top-down race is exactly what is needed; let all such firms compete with better services and experience increased market share so that they do more not less going forward, and sustainable investing increasingly becomes mainstreamed, which is and should be one but not the only goal, for there is a parallel, urgent need for bottom-up solutions, innovations and new thinking which would help push the large players to do even better.

Collaboration opportunities also abound and arguably may end up being most important. Public–private partnerships (sometimes called P3s) have the potential to create the double-digit trillions of dollars that appear necessary for the longer-term task at hand, but we need to start with individual commitments and case studies of what works. A number of collaboration efforts have already begun that can build this roadmap, such as Paul Lussier has underway at Yale.[11]

The rest of this new sustainable trillion is found within new commitments to sustainable investing from large pension funds such as ABP and PGGM in the Netherlands, among many other similar global efforts underway now at pace, along with record levels of renewable energy investment, as is reliably measured by Bloomberg New Energy Finance,[12] which they reported recently to be well over $300 billion in 2015.

Also needed is global competitiveness, so it is great to see firms such as Mirova, part of France's largest fund manager Natixis, set up shop in the USA on the back of their thoughtful processes and thinking about how to invest in a sustainable manner. See their Global Sustainable Equity fund for example – a very thoughtful illustration of value-first investing which we were taken with during our analysis of available funds in our class at Brown. Mirova's carbon footprinting methodology is also the best we have found, as it takes into account all of Scopes 1, 2 and 3,[13] and in the chapter that shortly follows.

It would be great to see more value-first investment product emerge, as there doesn't appear to be enough choice in the market – one example would be a public-facing version of the funds managed by Generation Investment Management or Inflection Point Capital Management as per the case studies from our previous book *Evolutions in Sustainable Investing*. Inflection Point subsequently received $1 billion of new capital to manage from French pension fund La Française, and this is how the bottom-up side of this dynamic can start to succeed, building better products and experiencing success which then inspires further top-down thoughtful initiatives. Hence, to complete the needed top-down/bottom-up dynamic, it is critical to see more and more new attempts to create innovative investment initiatives from a startup perspective, and let the best solutions win.

These solutions are popping up all over the place so it can be hard to keep track, but a few examples would include Terra Alpha and BlueSky Investment Management, whose case studies directly follow as just two of what are many emerging new examples.

Notes

1 www.ustrust.com/publish/ust/capitalacumen/summer2014/insights/investments-values.html. Accessed September 9, 2016.
2 www.ceres.org/investor-network/investor-summit/speakers/brian-moynihan. Accessed September 9, 2016.
3 http://newsroom.bankofamerica.com/press-releases/environment/bank-america-announces-industry-leading-125-billion-environmental-busines. Accessed October 18, 2016.
4 http://about.bankofamerica.com/en-us/green-bond-overview.html. Accessed September 9, 2016.
5 http://fortune.com/2015/11/02/goldman-sachs-clean-energy/. Accessed September 9, 2016.
6 https://www.whitehouse.gov/the-press-office/2015/07/27/fact-sheet-white-house-launches-american-business-act-climate-pledge. Accessed September 9, 2016.
7 www.goldmansachs.com/citizenship/environmental-stewardship/epf-pdf.pdf. Accessed September 9, 2016.
8 www.citigroup.com/citi/news/2015/150218a.htm. Accessed September 9, 2016.
9 https://thegiin.org/assets/documents/pub/2015.04%20Eyes%20on%20the%20Horizon.pdf. Accessed September 9, 2016.
10 www.morganstanley.com/what-we-do/institute-for-sustainable-investing. Accessed September 9, 2016.
11 https://environment.yale.edu/profile/paul-lussier/. Accessed September 9, 2016.
12 http://about.bnef.com/. Accessed September 9, 2016.
13 www.mirova.com/Content/Documents/Presse/va/PR%20Mirova%20Carbone%20 4_%20EN.pdf. Accessed September 9, 2016.

Chapter 10a

'Bottom-up' strategy

Water as an investment consideration

Terra Alpha Investments

Water is a resource everyone needs, but even in the face of scarcity few companies or investors have adequately valued water or planned for limited access. Limited or no access to water was once a distant concept to businesses; it has now become reality for many and a near-term challenge globally. The impacts of water stresses reach across sectors – all companies may face physical, regulatory, or reputational risks if they operate or rely on operations in any water-stressed area. Yet managed risks can become opportunities. Preparing for the reality of water stresses can position companies to reduce vulnerabilities and outperform competitors. When companies measure their water footprints and disclose this information, both companies and investors benefit. Companies can benchmark against their peers while providing material information to investors. Investors can make informed decisions that maximize returns by incorporating water risks and opportunities into their valuation methods.

Terra Alpha makes the case that both businesses and investors need to be cognizant of the reality, risks, and opportunities of water stresses, and sees a variety of fundamental factors related to water in a portfolio. The basic takeaways are:

- Identify material amounts of potentially stranded assets due to water risks.
- Identify operational risks due to availability of water or changing weather patterns that could disrupt production facilities and supply chains.
- Identify operational opportunities of a company versus its peers and/or in terms of improvements in operations to lower costs related to water.
- Incorporate efficiency factors into earnings forecasts.
- Incorporate balance sheet and operational risks into valuation processes.

Once a company has collected data on its water usage, risks, and opportunities, it can take initiative to optimize water efficiency and minimize water risk. Terra Alpha believes any investor can and should use this information to make better investment decisions. Investors who incorporate water and natural resource impacts into their investment analysis and portfolio creation process can reduce risks and improve returns.

Global backdrop: Global water resources are becoming increasingly stressed due to a variety of factors

Countries, communities, and companies already are feeling the effect of this stress, which will become progressively more impactful in the future. The effects of growing global consumption – compounded by a changing climate – are straining all freshwater supplies.The World Economic Forum called global water crises 'the biggest threat facing the planet over the next decade' (World Economic Forum 2015). The effects of water stresses are already being felt around the world, as global demand for water is increasing rapidly, and global supply is becoming more variable and unreliable.

Only 2.5 percent of Earth's water is freshwater (USGS 2016). Between 2007 and 2025, water use is predicted to increase 50 percent in developing countries and 18 percent in developed countries (Zabarenko 2015). By 2030, there is projected to be a 40 percent gap between global supplies of and demand for freshwater (Berntell 2014). By 2025, 67 percent of the world's population is expected to be living in water-scarce regions, versus nearly 20 percent in 2015 (Buerkle 2007). Water infrastructure worldwide is outdated and inefficient. In the U.S. alone, infrastructure losses amount to 2.1 trillion gallons of water each year (Schaper 2014). Rising global temperatures can cause faster glacial melting, more evaporation, and less snowfall, all of which increase the risk of droughts (Miller 2016). The severity and frequency of extreme droughts and floods are increasing (Solomon et al. 2007).

A water-constrained future will undoubtedly affect businesses, and the impacts are already being felt today. In 2015, 405 global companies reported detrimental water challenges that totaled more than $2.5 billion to CDP (formerly the Carbon Disclosure Project) in their annual water survey (CDP 2015).

Understanding water-associated risks is fundamental to mitigating potential losses and creating opportunities.

Water risks to business: Water risks may be physical, reputational, or regulatory and will have significant financial implications

Of the world's water supply, 90 percent is used by agriculture and industry (UNESCO 2003). Water risks can have significant financial implications both in terms of direct costs and opportunity costs: higher operating costs, an inability to continue production, tarnished product and brand image, and regulations affecting corporate water access. Companies that fail to regularly assess water risk along their value chains will be exposed to unfavorable business impacts. In company data collected by CDP, 65 percent of companies reported exposure to substantive water risk, and 27 percent reported seeing negative water risk impacts in the past year (CDP 2015). For investors, this translates to a high level of risk exposure in their portfolios.

Every company, regardless of sector, is dependent on water at some point along its value chain. These risks come with a price tag. It is becoming increasingly clear that disregarding water-related risks can result in losses, while preparing for and disclosing the steps taken to manage these risks can create opportunities for growth.

Water risks are driven by competition for water, weak regulation, aging and inadequate infrastructure, water pollution, and changing weather patterns. These factors combine to create risks that affect businesses throughout their value chains and pose a substantive threat to financial performance. Risks to a company's secure access to water fall into three main categories: *physical*, *reputational*, and *regulatory*.

Physical risks

Operational continuity will be hindered by any change in a company's water supply – water is fundamental to stable business operations. Significant changes in water supply and quality will affect businesses in all sectors in a variety of ways. Disregard for the physical risks from water scarcity exposure can lead to insufficient amounts of water for production, irrigation, processing, cooling, cleaning, or even cause an office building to close its doors (UNGC 2016). A company is vulnerable if it relies – at any point along its value chain – on operations in a water-stressed area.

Physical risks from global water stress expose companies to: too much water (e.g., floods); too little water (e.g., droughts); contaminated water; and/or changes in water price. Physical risks can have large financial implications for corporations and can create downward pressure on the stock price as a result of missed earnings guidance or expectations.

With the increasing frequency of severe weather events, companies are exposed more than ever to water-stress-related events.

- The U.S. agricultural sector alone lost $2.2 billion due to the 2015 Californian drought (Howitt 2014, 9).
- Droughts in the U.S. in 2011 halved the production of cotton, causing cotton prices to spike. Gap Inc.'s share price fell 17 percent after cutting its full-year profit forecast by 22 percent due to the scarcity of cotton (Roy 2011).

The following examples illustrate damaging business impacts from unmonitored exposure to too much water:

- In 2010, flooding of a Sasol Synfuels plant caused Sasol Limited production losses of approximately $15.6 million (CDP 2012, 18).
- Munich Re suffered a 38 percent decline in quarterly profits in 2010 after receiving claims worth more than $350 million due to severe flooding that closed 75 percent of coal mines in Australia (Peace et al. 2013).

- Extreme rainfall in 2011 caused severe disruptions to Anglo American's mining activity in Chile; copper production decreased by 8 percent as a result of shutdowns (Peace 2013).

Box 10a.1 Flooding in Thailand

In 2011, higher than average rainfall aligned with other factors to cause Thailand's worst floods in 50 years. Almost 40 percent of the world's hard disk drive (HDD) production and manufacturing facilities were located in the Chao Phraya River valley, a known floodplain. The severe floods caused massive evacuations, factory shutdowns, and supply chain disruptions for all industrial processes located in the valley (Associated Press 2012). Hard drive shipments fell 30 percent below demand (Mearian 2011).

- Emerson Electric saw net income fall 23 percent after costs rose and sales decreased due to supply chain disruptions (Van de Voorde 2012). The negative impact also affected the stock price: Emerson shares were down close to 3 percent relative to the S&P 500 Index on the report date.
- The world's biggest hard drive maker, Western Digital Corp., was forced to close its Thai factories, where it made 60 percent of its hard disk drives. Its operations and ability to meet customer demand were seriously impacted. Shares dropped 7 percent in one day (Tibken 2011).
- The global shortage of HDDs added $5 to $10 to the cost of each hard drive, as reported by Lenovo Group Ltd., the world's second-biggest maker of PCs (Associated Press 2012). Other industries were also affected.
- Toyota, Honda, Nissan, and Ford all felt the effects of the floods on their earnings; the floods caused these companies to close their Thai plants, and the shortages of parts slowed manufacturing around the world. Honda faced costly repairs to its flood-damaged factory; it was forced to delay model releases, and it reported negative earnings that quarter. In 2011, Honda's stock was down 28 percent. Toyota reported an 18.5 percent net income drop, a 4.8 percent decline in revenue, and a 32.4 percent fall of operating profit. Toyota's stock was down 22 percent following the negative earnings report (Whipp 2011).

These floods were not hydrologically unprecedented (Meehan 2012); companies should have been prepared for flood risk losses from operational and supply chain disruption

The remaining sources of clean and usable water around the globe are rapidly becoming polluted. In many industrial production systems, the quality of process water is critical, but the remedies for contaminated water are limited and costly. Often businesses face unforeseen capital expenditures and higher costs to purify contaminated water. Treatment options can be time consuming or in some cases not feasible at all.

Semiconductor production requires large amounts of highly purified water. Were the quality of available water to deteriorate, companies would face increased treatment costs. A J. P. Morgan report estimated that if water costs doubled, it would reduce the earnings per share of Texas Instruments and Intel by almost 5 percent each (using 2008 data) (Levinson et al. 2008). If costs are too high or treatment is not feasible, production will be interrupted or require relocation (Morrison et al. 2009). Contaminated water supplies can also limit opportunities for growth if businesses are looking to expand in an area with poor water quality.

Reputational risks

Reputational risk stems from public perception of water mismanagement. According to a study conducted by the World Economic Forum, three-fifths of chief executives said they believed corporate brand and reputation represented more than 40 percent of their company's market capitalization (Brigham and Linssen 2010).

Strong brand reputational value means higher profits; conversely, reputational damage translates to actualized financial damage. As communities, investors, and consumers become more aware of the physical risks from water scarcity, they are more likely to form opposition to real or perceived inequalities in water use. Heightened criticism can have severe implications for business performance and competitiveness. Reputational risks include: damaged brand value and consumer perception; increased difficulty expanding into new markets; loss of a company's license to operate; alienation of investors; and damaged share price.

One source of reputational damage can come from water scarcity and quality disputes between local communities and companies over water needs. Local resistance resulting in loss of profits and operational shutdowns have occurred already:

- Community opposition forced Nestlé Waters to cancel its plans to operate the country's largest water bottling plant in California in 2009. Protesters believed that Nestlé was illegally taking water from drought-stricken regions in California (Barton 2010). Nestlé also suffered significant reputational damage after citizens in Michigan believed that Nestlé was improperly withdrawing water and competing with the local water supplies, regardless of the fact that authorities ruled in favor of Nestlé (Morrison et al. 2009).
- In 2014, local officials in northern India ordered Coca-Cola to close a bottling plant over its water use. The plant had been the object of local protests for years, as villagers blamed lowering groundwater levels on the bottling plant.

In addition to interrupting operations, the episode caused losses on a planned $24 million expansion of the bottling plant (AFP 2014; Chaudhary 2014).

- The Canadian miner, Barrick Gold, faced intense public opposition after proposing to shift glaciers in Chile, which were the local communities' only source of fresh water, in order to mine gold and silver located beneath the glaciers. The project would have resulted in at least $11.5 billion in gold extraction, but the community's resistance prevented the project from occurring (Chaudhary 2014; Wadi 2014).

Regulatory risks

Businesses thrive in stable regulatory environments. Clean water is progressively being recognized as a finite resource and is therefore attracting greater regulation of its use and impacts.

Businesses are exposed to regulatory risk if any part of their value chain operates in a water-stressed region, where updated regulation may limit water use, tighten wastewater standards, or increase the price of water. Regulatory risks often occur as a result of events triggered by physical and reputational risks: water scarcity and public scrutiny put pressure on authorities to implement more stringent water policies. Businesses are exposed to regulatory risks if they are operating in an area devoid of water-related laws, where sudden, unexpected changes in regulations can create unanticipated costs or loss of assets. Regulatory risks include: increases in the price of water; stricter efficiency, reuse, or recycling requirements; more pollution restrictions or higher wastewater quality standards; changes to withdrawal rights; new process or product standards; and revocation of license to operate. These risks often have large effects on corporate water use and likely will cause a loss of revenue and/or hinder industrial production:

- In 2013, Exelon was forced to retire one of its nuclear plants ten years earlier than planned due to the costs required to upgrade it to meet more stringent water permit conditions, which would have amounted to $800 million (CDP 2012).
- Merck was forced to pay $20 million in 'fines, environmental improvements, and cleanup costs' as a consequence of polluting local drinking water supplies with chemical discharge (Morrison et al. 2009).
- Chilean courts fined Barrick Gold $16 million in 2014 after the company failed to put in place legally required wastewater discharge treatment systems in its new Pascua-Lama mine. Barrick Gold did not have a viable system for treating contaminated water or preventing rainwater contamination. Construction of the mining project was suspended while the company was stuck in legal proceedings with the Chilean government. The stock fell 15 percent that year (Castaldo 2015; BBC News 2013).
- In 2015, California passed a bill that imposed water restrictions due to the severe drought affecting the state. The goal of the bill was to reduce water usage

by 25 percent statewide; non-compliance would result in punitive measures. In September, Starbucks' water supplier Sugar Pine Spring Water was fined by California for 'making the state's drought worse', allegedly tapping into dry springs in one of California's worst drought regions (Nagourney 2015).

Water opportunity: Higher efficiency can lead to higher returns – operational, strategic, and market – for businesses and investors

While the risks to companies and investors posed by water stress are undeniable, these same stresses also create opportunities for outperformance. Companies that capture these opportunities better position themselves to outperform their peers. In CDP's 2015 Global Water Report, 73 percent of respondent companies stated that water offers 'operational, strategic, or market opportunities'. Nearly 77 percent of that subgroup stated that these opportunities will be realized in the next three years. All of these opportunities can add significant value for both businesses and investors. Those who fail to capitalize on these trends will be left behind.

Operational opportunities

Improving operational efficiency has traditionally been a core strategy for many businesses to realize significant and long-term financial savings; improving the water efficiency of a company's operations is no different. There are substantial opportunities for companies to reduce operational water intensity while saving money. Xylem, Inc. estimates that carbon emissions – from wastewater management energy use – could be cut nearly in half by installing high-efficiency wastewater treatment technologies that exist today, at $0 or negative cost (Xylem 2015). Given that in California today, about 20 percent of the state's electricity is used to transport and treat water and wastewater, and nationally about 2 percent ($24.1 billion) (EIA 2011) of total energy consumption is used for drinking water and wastewater treatment services, (Pabi et al. 2013) reducing water usage or increasing the efficiency of these systems would lead to immediate cost reductions. Operational opportunities may come from cost savings as well as increased sales.

- SAB Miller undertook a water-risk assessment of their facilities in 2010 worldwide and have since implemented actions to reduce water use, helping them to realize cost savings of $300 million over five years (CDP 2015, 28).
- AB InBev reduced overall water use by 5.4 percent in 2013 and saved the company $2.5 million – equivalent to the water needed to make more than 6 billion cans of its products. Water reduction efforts saved the company $5 million the following year and more than $12 million since 2012 (AB InBev 2013, 21).
- More than 70 percent of Anglo American mining group's operations are located in water-stressed basins. To address this issue, they launched the

'Water efficiency target tool' in 2011 and achieved their 2020 corporate water reduction target by 2014. This reduction resulted in annual cost savings of $3.6 million (2030 Water Resources Group 2016a).

- In 2007, Levi Strauss & Co. became the first apparel company to conduct a lifecycle assessment, measuring the overall environmental impact of its jeans. Sustainable water management has been a major priority for Levi Strauss, especially after floods in Pakistan and droughts in China in 2011 hurt crop yields and drastically increased cotton prices. The company plans to source 75 percent of its cotton from Better Cotton Initiative by 2020, which trains cotton farmers to use significantly less water. Its 'Water<Less™' program resulted in over one billion liters of water saved from 2011 to 2014. Recently, the company produced 100,000 pairs of women's jeans at a plant in China using recycled water. It is in the process of implementing this standard around the world.

Among the companies in CDP's 2015 *Water Report*, Pfizer Inc., Johnson Controls, and Lockheed Martin Corporation all reported increased sales from more effective water management, while Assa Abloy, Biogen Inc., and Marriott International Inc. all cited increased cost savings from their efforts to reduce water usage.

There is growing evidence showing the financial benefits of reducing water use. A 2013 UK Environment Agency report on FTSE 100 companies found that the most profitable companies in the oil and gas, basic resources, construction and materials, and insurance sectors had the lowest average water intensities in their sector (Environment Agency 2013). As the consistency of reported water data improves, and as water becomes more accurately priced, the relationship between operational water efficiency and profitability will become increasingly evident.

Strategic opportunities

Water risks can pose serious hazards to companies' long-term plans, but those that reduce their water intensity will place themselves at a competitive advantage relative to their peers.

Evaluating and reducing supply chain operations' vulnerability to water stress will help protect operational continuity, improve supply chain resiliency, and boost investor confidence. Strategic opportunities also include the benefits of increased brand value and community goodwill stemming from reduced environmental impact. Companies across sectors are already moving to capture these opportunities and improve their market position in doing so:

- Ford determined that 24 percent of its operations are in regions considered to be at risk of water scarcity now. In order to strategically reduce water consumption now, before significant price increases, they have implemented new technologies to reduce water use per vehicle by 30 percent from 2009 to 2015. More specifically, from 2000 to 2013, Ford reduced water use per vehicle by 58 percent at its Cuautitlán, Mexico facility, located in a water-scarce region (Ford 2016).

- Holmen Paper has developed advanced technology to use treated municipal wastewater in its mills and became the first mill in Europe to manufacture paper operating entirely on 'recovered water'. This not only bolstered its operational security against future water stress, but also increased goodwill within the community (Holmen 2015).
- In the beverage industry as of 2008, it took 12 liters of water to prepare 1 liter of drinkable beverage. Building on innovations from another bottler, Pepsi was able to reduce this ratio to 2.2 liters of water per liter of beverage. This innovation has cut its operating expenses, reduced its impact on the surrounding community, and increased its resilience to water scarcity (Matthews 2016).
- In 2006, Rio Tinto expanded its facility in Western Australia and took the opportunity to overhaul the site's water management structures. The end result was a 96 percent reduction in water abstraction from a nearby lake, a reduced cost of pumping water, and the ability to recycle 40 percent of the site's water. These improvements drastically decreased Rio Tinto's demand on local water resources and helped to fortify its operations against future droughts and community backlash (2030 Water Resources Group 2016b).

Even companies who have experienced the detrimental effects of water risk first-hand can still turn this risk into an opportunity.

Box 10a.2 PepsiCo India goes full circle

PepsiCo India provides both a cautionary tale on water-related risks, as well as an example of how a company can strategically reposition itself through increased water responsibility. Many areas of India suffer from water scarcity, and more than 130 million Indians live in areas with poor water quality (Shiao 2015). While PepsiCo only accounts for about 0.04 percent of India's industrial water use, it has still received criticism over its water use (Brady 2007).

Protests over the company's water footprint occurred in areas with depleted groundwater, resulting in reputational damage, interruptions to operations, and fewer sales. In response, PepsiCo sought to offset the water footprint of its Indian operations. In 2009, it achieved a 'positive water balance', replenishing and recharging water through a variety of projects around the country. Its efforts have included rainwater harvesting, dam building, and a number of agricultural interventions. PepsiCo has maintained a 'positive water balance' since 2009, and offsetting its water footprint remains a major priority (PepsiCo India 2013).

Companies addressing specific risks are already capturing benefits. However, in order to maximize potential opportunity gain, companies are best positioned when they have assessed their entire supply chain.

Box 10a.3 General Mills assesses all risk

General Mills measures the water footprint of its entire supply chain and, in partnership with the Nature Conservancy, assessed the health of the 60+ watersheds worldwide critical to its operations. This resulted in the identification of eight key, at-risk watersheds (Nature Conservancy 2012).

In the El Bajio watershed in northern Mexico, General Mills determined that due to human use and climate change, the watershed could potentially be unsuitable for large-scale agriculture by 2035. With this knowledge, General Mills facilitated multi-stakeholder collaboration between companies, government agencies, and NGOs to develop a conservation plan for the watershed. General Mills has begun issuing interest-free loans to local broccoli and cauliflower farmers to expedite the adoption of drip irrigation practices. So far, these practices are estimated to be saving 1.1 billion gallons of water a year in the region (Nature Conservancy 2012).

General Mills is also pursuing conservation plans in the other seven at-risk watersheds. With its extensive information on water risk exposure and open dialogues with local stakeholders in at-risk watersheds, General Mills is better positioned to withstand (or avoid) future impacts of water stress.

Market opportunities

With water stresses increasing over the coming decades, companies who can minimize water risk and/or help customers to minimize their risk, will be better positioned to succeed. Due to the localized nature of water scarcity, companies who reduce the water impacts of their direct operations will be the least limited by their physical location. More directly apparent are the market opportunities created by water security and efficiency solutions.

The global water sector is estimated to be a $450–500 billion global market, with growing demand across the globe (Dray 2011). In the U.S. alone, leaks from old or faulty infrastructure cause roughly $10 billion a year in private property damage, highlighting the tremendous need for new investment (Pechet 2015). In China, the market for current membrane technology used to clean wastewater will grow more than 30 percent annually over the next two decades (Boccaletti et al. 2009).

McKinsey & Company estimates that over the next two decades between $50 and $60 billion will need to be invested annually in deploying water productivity improvements across the globe to 'close the gap between water supply and demand'. The private sector is expected to make up as much as half of this spending, with many of these investments yielding positive returns in three to four years (Boccaletti et al. 2009). This tremendous demand for capital provides a large opportunity for companies and investors to get ahead of this curve as well as participate in or offer solutions for others.

Some companies are already beginning to anticipate strategic opportunities and offer these solutions.

- COOPERNIC (a sourcing alliance of major European retailers) funded the adoption of more efficient irrigation systems at farms in India, Guatemala and Madagascar. These systems helped farmers to reduce water abstraction by 69 percent and increase agricultural productivity by 41 percent. This increased productivity translated into greater surpluses, which farmers could not only sell to suppliers but also now could sell at their local market (2030 Water Resources Group 2015).
- Advansa implemented a pilot program at its chemical plant in Adana, Turkey, which reduced cooling water use by over 150,000m^3/year. The project payback period was less than six months and now returns cost savings of over $100,000 a year. Most importantly, these improvements comply with stricter EU water regulations, giving Advansa access to the neighboring EU market (2030 Water Resources Group 2016c).
- Jain Irrigation Systems has developed micro-irrigation and drip irrigation systems that use only 30 percent as much water as traditional systems, and has deployed these technologies to farmers in India. The technology aims to reduce agricultural water use and to improve the efficiency of smallholder farmers, who account for 75 percent of all agricultural producers in India. Over the past five years, Jain's investment in this new market has led to its growth at an annual rate of 72 percent (Jain Irrigation 2016).

Conclusion: businesses and investors must adapt to a water-stressed future

Global water resources are undeniably becoming more stressed. All across the world, companies and investors alike have already felt the impacts of these stresses. Water stresses pose a variety of financial risks, ranging from the more palpable physical risks to more intangible regulatory and reputational risks that have serious financial consequences. Dynamic water challenges also present opportunities. By proactively adapting their operations, supply chains, product mixes and investment strategies, both companies and investors can better position themselves to compete and succeed in a changing and constricted environment. In order to capture these opportunities, companies must first measure their water footprint. Companies that measure will invariably be better able to manage their risk and position their businesses for success. Organizations and processes for measuring, managing and reporting on water are already available and can help companies identify risk areas and develop management strategies.

Investors need to demand this information from companies and incorporate it into their investment processes to gain better insight. Many of the same organizations that offer disclosure, measuring and management tools for businesses can also be tools for investors to ensure the water security of their investments.

References

2030 Water Resources Group (2015) 'Micro-Irrigation for Food Security' (www.waterscarcitysolutions.org/new-micro-irrigation-for-food-security/). Accessed February 2016.

2030 Water Resources Group (2016a) 'Corporate Water Efficiency Targets in the Mining Industry' (www.waterscarcitysolutions.org/corporate-water-efficiency-targets-in-the-mining-industry/). Accessed February 2016.

2030 Water Resources Group (2016b) 'Mine Water Recycling' (www.waterscarcitysolutions.org/mine-water-recycling/). Accessed February 2016.

2030 Water Resources Group (2016c) 'Reducing Water and Energy Consumption in a Chemical Plant' (www.waterscarcitysolutions.org/wp-content/uploads/2016/02/A-Reducing-Water-and-Energy-Consumption.pdf). Accessed February 2016.

AB InBev (2013) *Global Citizenship Report – Environment* (www.ab-inbev.com/content/dam/universaltemplate/abinbev/pdf/sr/download-center/2013_GSR_REPORT_Environment.pdf). Accessed September 2016.

AFP (2014) 'Indian Officials Order Coca-Cola Plant to Close for Using Too Much Water'. *Guardian* (www.theguardian.com/environment/2014/jun/18/indian-officals-coca-cola-plant-water-mehdiganj). Accessed September 2016.

Associated Press (2012) 'Thai Flooding Impact on Tech Companies, Suppliers' (http://news.yahoo.com/thai-flooding-impact-tech-companies-suppliers-004001255.html). Accessed February 2016.

Barton B. (2010) *Murky Waters? Corporate Reporting on Water Risk*. Ceres (www.ceres.org/resources/reports/corporate-reporting-on-water-risk-2010). Accessed September 2016.

BBC News (2013) 'Chile Fines Barrick Gold $16m for Pascua-Lama Mine' (www.bbc.com/news/world-latin-america-22663432). Accessed February 2016.

Berntell A. (2014) 'How Can We Save Water and Avoid a Crisis?' World Economic Forum. (https://www.weforum.org/agenda/2014/03/water-growth-challenge-minding-demand-supply-gap-2/). Accessed September 2016.

Boccaletti G., Grobbel M., and Stuchtey M.R. (2009) 'The Business Opportunity in Water Conservation'. McKinsey & Company (www.mckinsey.com/business-functions/sustainability-and-resource-productivity/our-insights/the-business-opportunity-in-water-conservation). Accessed September 2016.

Brady D. (2007) 'Pepsi: Repairing a Poisoned Reputation in India'. *Bloomberg* (www.bloomberg.com/bw/stories/2007-05-31/pepsi-repairing-a-poisoned-reputation-in-india businessweek-business-news-stock-market-and-financial-advice). Accessed September 2016.

Brigham A. and Linssen S. (2010) 'Your Brand Reputational Value Is Irreplaceable. Protect It!' *Forbes* (www.forbes.com/2010/02/01/brand-reputation-value-leadership-managing-ethisphere.html). Accessed September 2016.

Buerkle T. (2007) 'Making Every Drop Count: FAO Heads UN Water Initiative'. *FAO Newsroom* (www.fao.org/Newsroom/en/news/2007/1000494/index.html). Accessed September 2016.

Castaldo J. (2015) 'Barrick Gold Makes Big Changes to Become a Smaller Company'. *Canadian Business* (www.canadianbusiness.com/lists-and-rankings/best-stocks/investor-500-2015-barrick/). Accessed September 2016.

CDP (2012) *CDP Global Water Report 2012* (https://www.starwoodhotels.com/Media/PDF/Corporate/CDP-Water-Disclosure-Global-Report-2012.pdf). Accessed October 18, 2016.

CDP (2015) *CDP Global Water Report 2015* (www.cdp.net/CDPResults/CDP-Global-Water-Report-2015.pdf). Accessed October 18, 2016.

Chaudhary A. (2014) 'Farmers Fight Coca-Cola as India's Groundwater Dries Up'. *Bloomberg* (www.bloomberg.com/news/articles/2014-10-08/farmers-fight-coca-cola-as-india-s-groundwater-dries-up). Accessed September 2016.

Dray D. (2011) 'Investing in the Global Water Sector'. Citigroup Global Markets (www.waterinnovations.org/PDF/presentations/Dray-0927p.pdf). Accessed September 2016.

EIA (2011) 'Consumer Expenditure Estimates for Energy by Source, 19701–2010; Annual Energy Review'. U.S. Energy Information Administration (www.eia.gov/totalenergy/data/annual/pdf/sec3_11.pdf). Accessed January 2016.

Environment Agency (2013) *Environmental Disclosures: The Fourth Major Review of Environmental Reporting in the Annual Report and Annual Accounts of the FTSE All-Share Companies*. Environment Agency (www.gov.uk/government/uploads/system/uploads/attachment_data/file/290052/Disclosures_full_report_04c911.pdf). Accessed September 2016.

Ford (2016) 'Operating in Water-Scarce Regions' (http://corporate.ford.com/microsites/sustainability-report-2013-14/water-scarce.html). Accessed February 2016.

Holmen (2015) 'Sustainability – Raw Materials – Water'. The Holmen Group (www.holmen.com/en/Sustainability/Raw-materials/Water/). Accessed September 2016.

Howitt R. (2014) 'Economic Analysis of the 2014 Drought for California Agriculture'. Center for Watershed Sciences, University of California–Davis. (https://watershed.ucdavis.edu/files/biblio/Economic_Impact_of_the_2014_California_Water_Drought_1.pdf). Accessed September 2016.

Jain Irrigation (2016) 'Jain Irrigation Saves Water, Increases Efficiency for Smallholder Farmers'. Shared Value Initiative (https://sharedvalue.org/examples/drip-irrigation-practices-smallholder-farmers). Accessed February 2016.

Levinson M., Lee E., Chung J., Huttner M., Danely C., McKnight C., and Langlois A. (2008) 'Watching Water: A Guide to Evaluating Corporate Risks in a Thirsty World'. J. P.Morgan and World Resources Institute (http://pdf.wri.org/jpmorgan_watching_water.pdf). Accessed September 2016.

Matthews K. (2016) 'Balancing Profitability and Sustainability'. Triple Pundit (www.triplepundit.com/2016/02/balancing-profitability-sustainability/). Accessed September 2016.

Mearian L. (2011) 'Impact of Hard Drive Shortage to Linger Through 2013'. *Computer World* (www.computerworld.com/article/2500090/data-center/impact-of-hard-drive-shortage-to-linger-through-2013.html?page=2). Accessed September 2016.

Meehan R. (2012) 'Thailand Floods 2011: Causes and Prospects from an Insurance Perspective'. Stanford University (http://web.stanford.edu/~meehan/floodthai2011/FloodNotes17.pdf). Accessed September 2016.

Miller B. (2016) '2015 Is Warmest Year On Record, NOAA and NASA say'. *CNN* (www.cnn.com/2016/01/20/us/noaa-2015-warmest-year/). Accessed September 2016.

Morrison J., Morikawa M., Murphy M. and Schulte P. (2009) *Water Scarcity and Climate Change: Growing Risks for Businesses and Investors*. Ceres and Pacific Institute (www.ceres.org/resources/reports/water-scarcity-climate-change-risks-for-investors-2009). Accessed September 2016.

Munich RE (2016) 'Flood Facts: The Biggest Floods 2005–2015' (https://www.munichre.com/australia/australia-natural-hazards/australia-flood/economic-impacts/biggest-floods/index.html). Accessed February 2016.

Nagourney A. (2015) 'California Imposes First Mandatory Water Restrictions to Deal With Drought'. *New York Times* (www.nytimes.com/2015/04/02/us/california-imposes-first-ever-water-restrictions-to-deal-with-drought.html). Accessed September 2016.

Nature Conservancy (2012) 'Irapuato Water Stewardship Assessment. General Mills'. (www.nature.org/about-us/working-with-companies/companies-we-work-with/irapuato-water-stewardship-assessment.pdf). Accessed September 2016.

Pabi S., Amamath A., Goldstein R. and Reekie L. (2013) *Electricity Use and Management in the Municipal Water Supply and Wastewater Industries. Electric Power Research Institute and Water Research Foundation* (www.waterrf.org/PublicReportLibrary/4454.pdf). Accessed September 2016.

Peace J., Crawford M. and Seidel S. (2013) *Weathering the Storm: Building Business Resilience to Climate Change. Center for Climate and Energy Solutions* (www.c2es.org/docUploads/business-resilience-report-07-2013-final.pdf). Accessed September 2016.

Pechet T. (2015) 'Turning Water Problems into Business Opportunities'. TechCrunch (http://techcrunch.com/2015/06/22/turning-water-problems-into-business-opportunities/). Accessed September 2016.

PepsiCo India (2013) 'Replenishing Water' (www.pepsicoindia.co.in/purpose/environmental-sustainability/replenishing-water.html). Accessed September 2016.

Roy D. (2011) 'Texas Cotton Farmers May Abandon Record Acres Because Of Drought'. *Bloomberg* (www.bloomberg.com/news/articles/2011-06-30/texas-cotton-farmers-may-abandon-record-acres-because-of-drought). Accessed September 2016.

Schaper D. (2014) 'As Infrastructure Crumbles, Trillions of Gallons of Water Lost'. NPR (www.npr.org/2014/10/29/359875321/as-infrastructure-crumbles-trillions-of-gallons-of-water-lost). Accessed September 2016.

Shiao T. (2015) '3 Maps Explain India's Growing Water Risks'. World Resources Institute (www.wri.org/blog/2015/02/3-maps-explain-india%E2%80%99s-growing-water-risks). Accessed September 2016.

Solomon S., Qin D., Manning M., Marquis M., Avery K., Tignor M.B., LeRoy Miller Jr. H., and Zhenlin Chen (eds.) (2007) 'Climate Change 2007: The Physical Science Basis. Contribution of Working Group to the Fourth Assessment Report of the Intergovernmental Panel on Climate Change'. Cambridge and New York: Cambridge University Press (www.ipcc.ch/pdf/assessment-report/ar4/wg1/ar4-wg1-frontmatter.pdf). Accessed September 2016.

Tibken S. (2011) 'Thai Floods Hit PC Supply Chain'. *Wall Street Journal* (www.wsj.com/articles/SB10001424052970203658804576636951367373290). Accessed September 2016.

UNESCO (2003) *Water for People, Water for Life*. United Nations World Water Development Report (www.un.org/esa/sustdev/publications/WWDR_english_129556e.pdf). Accessed September 2016.

UNGC (2016) 'Physical Risks' (http://lucasx.webfactional.com/business-case/water-related-business-risks/physical-risks/). Accessed February 2016. Accessed September 2016.

USGS (2016) 'Where Is Earth's Water?' (http://water.usgs.gov/edu/earthwherewater.html). Accessed January 2016.

Van de Voorde J. (2012) 'Emerson Sales Delayed Due to Flooding'. Osher Van de Voord (www.oshervandevoorde.com/blog/500-emerson-sales-delayed-due-to-flooding.html). Accessed September 2016.

Wadi R. (2014) 'Chilean Farmers and Foreign Mining Firms Face Off Over Andes Gold'. *MintpressNews* (www.mintpressnews.com/chilean-farmers-and-foreign-mining-firms-face-off-over-andes-gold/199434/). Accessed September 2016.

Whipp L. (2011) 'Thai Floods Erode Toyota's Profits'. *Financial Times* (www.ft.com/cms/s/0/74941cfa-09e4-11e1-85ca-00144feabdc0.html). Accessed September 2016.

World Economic Forum (2015) *Global Risks 2015 – 10th Edition* (http://www3.weforum.org/docs/WEF_Global_Risks_2015_Report15.pdf). Accessed October 18, 2016.

Xylem (2015) *Powering the Wastewater Renaissance: Energy Efficiency and Emissions Reduction in Wastewater Management* (http://poweringwastewater.xyleminc.com/images/Xylem_Wastewater_Renaissance_2015_Report.pdf). Accessed September 2016.

Zabarenko D. (2015) 'Water Use Rising Faster Than World Population'. Reuters (www.reuters.com/article/us-population-water-idUSTRE79O3WO20111025). Accessed September 2016.

Chapter 10b

'Bottom-up' strategy

BlueSky Investment Management

Bud Sturmak

Introduction

The best investors in the world have always deeply examined everything that public companies disclose. While traditional sources of data such as financial statements remain important, today there is a new trove to mine. Increasing corporate transparency and disclosure, combined with a growing research field that quantifies and measures corporate environmental, social and governance (ESG) data, provides investors with the opportunity to evaluate companies across a more complete set of information to more fully reveal corporate risks and opportunities. ESG research measures non-financial factors such as corporate governance, resource efficiency, pollution and waste management, product safety, workplace quality, supply chain management and community impact. While investors have struggled with how to use this information, a methodical and well-executed ESG integration strategy can reveal both corporate risks and competitive advantages that may otherwise remain invisible to portfolio managers who rely solely on traditional financial analysis. As history has shown, a common attribute of highly successful investors like Warren Buffett lies in the ability to evolve great investment ideas as new information comes to light. Today, ESG presents a clear opportunity for forward-thinking investors and portfolio managers to drive alpha and better manage risk in the twenty-first century.

ESG and performance: the academic research

Hundreds of independent studies show that companies performing well on ESG measures also produce superior financial returns.[1,2] The phenomenon is well-documented in two meta-studies. Both concluded that companies with strong ESG performance enjoy a lower cost of capital, are more profitable, and that their stocks outperform. *From the Stockholder to the Stakeholder*, a 2015 meta-study by Arabesque Partners and the University of Oxford, analyzed more than 200 different ESG studies and found:

- 90 percent of studies show that firms with strong ESG performance experience a lower cost of capital;
- 88 percent of studies show a positive correlation between sustainability and operational performance;
- 80 percent of studies show a positive correlation between sustainability and stock performance.

Sustainable Investing, a 2012 Deutsche Bank meta-study that was reviewed by Harvard Business School professor George Serafeim, drew similar conclusions, and added:

- ESG factors are correlated with superior risk-adjusted returns at the securities level.
- Superior risk-adjusted returns are possible if investors choose capable managers who integrate ESG into otherwise well-executed strategies.
- Unlike ESG factors, socially responsible investing (SRI) approaches, which rely on exclusionary screens instead of seeking superior performance, add little upside.

A key takeaway of the Deutsche Bank meta-study is the importance of distinguishing modern ESG integrated approaches from traditional SRI approaches. There is a common misperception that incorporating ESG factors will negatively impact performance, which stems from the misguided view that ESG and SRI are one and the same. As the academic research shows, SRI has indeed struggled with performance as a result of employing restrictive screening designed to align the portfolio with certain ethical, moral or religious beliefs. By contrast, ESG can be integrated into the investment process to identify companies with strong competitive advantages to *enhance* investment performance. SRI tells a manager what to leave out. ESG says what to put in.

Unlocking the value of ESG

In practice, it is difficult to successfully integrate ESG factors into the investment process in order to capture the alpha clearly demonstrated by the academic research. There is a virtual sea of corporate ESG data, which to the typical observer may appear as 'noise' that can mask its potential value. Methodologies for measuring and quantifying a company's ESG performance vary widely, as does the quality of existing ESG research. These issues of quantity and quality feed Wall Street's misguided view that ESG has no value and that incorporating this information may negatively impact performance. This may explain the lack of existing products that integrate ESG to enhance performance and drive alpha.

Parsing through ESG data to identify what is useful is a crucial step to any successful integration strategy. The most successful investors in the world understand that information is imperfect and often distorted, resulting in the need to scrub financial data. This process can reveal nuggets of information that can more accurately convey a company's overall health in order to identify businesses that appear well-positioned for the future. Warren Buffett learned to focus on certain financial factors like ROE and owner earnings which can help identify companies generating superior returns. ESG data is no different. A thoughtful and well-executed ESG integration strategy should recognize the need to analyze each unique ESG data point to determine its value, and that each industry has its own unique set of material ESG factors.

Our research indicates that many of today's myriad ESG factors show little value or correlation to performance and risk. However, through a rigorous academic analysis and scientific approach, our research has clearly identified material ESG factors that are highly correlated with increased ROIC and increased alpha, presenting the opportunity to enhance investment performance. Our ESG optimization process has unlocked the potential value that ESG can provide, leading to the development of our multi-factor ESG model designed to drive alpha and better manage risk.

Abundant research shows that certain ESG factors are financially material and positively correlated with investment performance, yet few investors recognize their value. The fact that markets and investment managers ignore material information is nothing new. As Warren Buffett explains,

> I'm convinced that there is much inefficiency in the market. These Graham-and-Doddsville investors have successfully exploited gaps between price and value. When the price of a stock can be influenced by a 'herd' on Wall Street with prices set at the margin by the most emotional person, or the greediest person, or the most depressed person, it is hard to argue that the market always prices rationally. In fact, market prices are frequently nonsensical.
>
> (Buffett, 1984)

Evolving great investment approaches: the emergence of Warren Buffett

Integrating ESG into the investment process does not require that we reinvent the field of investing; rather it simply presents the opportunity to improve upon some of today's greatest approaches. This is not a new concept, as illustrated by Warren Buffett's evolution of Graham and Dodd, which led to him becoming one of the greatest investors of all time.

Value investing was pioneered by Benjamin Graham to address the growing need to better manage risk and enhance investment returns following the stock market crash of 1929. In their seminal 1934 book *Securities Analysis*, Graham and fellow finance professor David Dodd clearly described their approach, which focused on buying businesses trading well below their intrinsic value. This margin of safety provided downside protection in times of market distress, while allowing one to eventually capture rewarding upside. As a professor at Columbia, Graham mentored generations of successful value investors who would finesse his methodology, none more famous than Warren Buffett.

Warren Buffett and his partner Charlie Munger continued to evolve Graham and Dodd's value approach, recognizing that an over-emphasis on price was far less important than investing in a great company. In his 1990 letter to shareholders of Berkshire Hathaway, Buffett noted:

> I could give you other personal examples of 'bargain-purchase' folly but I'm sure you get the picture: It's far better to buy a wonderful company at a fair price than a fair company at a wonderful price. Charlie understood this early; I was a slow learner. But now, when buying companies or common stocks, we look for first-class businesses accompanied by first-class managements.
>
> (Buffett, 1990)

When a company develops an economic advantage, the basic principal of capitalism is that competition will erode this advantage over time. Buffett's focus on wonderful companies with high quality businesses is grounded in his recognition that some companies are uniquely positioned with distinct competitive advantages that are long-term in nature. In the 1996 letter to shareholders of Berkshire Hathaway, Buffett famously stated, 'In business, I look for economic castles protected by unbreachable moats' (Buffett, 1996). Further, Robert Hagstrom's book *The Warren Buffett Way* notes, 'The key to investing, is determining the competitive advantage of any given company and, above all, the durability of the advantage. The products or services that have wide, sustainable moats around them are the ones that deliver rewards to investors' (Hagstrom, 2014).

Buffett recognized that companies with wide moats were able to generate returns on invested capital (ROIC) that were higher than their competitors, and a wide moat allowed these companies to continue to produce high ROIC over the long term. This concept is illustrated in Figure 10b.1 below.

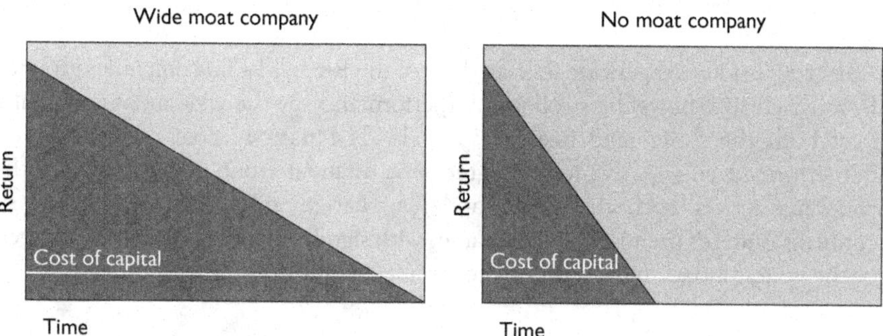

Figure 10b.1 ROIC with and without moats.
Source: BlueSky Investment Management.

'We like stocks that generate high returns on invested capital where there is strong likelihood that they will continue to do so' (Lowe, 2007). Buffett recognized that companies that are able to generate returns on capital that are higher than their cost of capital and sustain this for long periods of time are more valuable than companies without this advantage. By focusing on investing in this type of company, Buffett has been able to repeatedly capture value and drive superior investment returns.

> If Buffett correctly identifies a company with above-average economic returns, the value of the stock over the long term will steadily march upward as the share price mimics the return of the business. If a company consistently earns 15 percent on equity, its share price will advance more each year than that of a company that earns 10 percent on equity.
>
> (Hagstrom, 2014)

Joe Mansueto, founder of investment research giant Morningstar, was so compelled by Buffett's moat concept that he made moats a foundation of the firm's stock research. We conducted a performance analysis of Morningstar's moat ratings, to test the premise that moat companies with competitive advantages outperform companies with no moat.

Here is a summary of our findings:

Table 10b.1 Performance of Morningstar companies with and without moats (as of March 31, 2016)

	3-year performance	*5-year performance*
No moat	8.13	9.16
Narrow moat	12.00	12.09
Wide moat	12.72	13.53
Russell 1,000	11.52	11.35

Source: BlueSky Investment Management.

This straightforward performance analysis of the Russell 1,000 companies grouped by moat clearly shows the strongest outperformance by the wide moat companies over both the three- and five-year periods. The narrow moat companies also outperformed, though to a lesser degree. The no moat group underperformed the benchmark over both the three- and five-year periods. This simple analysis confirms Buffett's premise that companies with significant competitive advantages, or the widest moats, have powerful economic advantages.

The twenty-first-century business landscape: the need for ESG

While Buffett's value approach to investing remains quite relevant, the business landscape is changing in ways perhaps investors have not anticipated. Companies today must adapt to modern twenty-first-century forces including population growth, resource constraints, climate change, rapidly changing technology, changing regulations, changing consumer demands, the power of social media, and demands for greater transparency. These forces may have been insignificant in the twentieth century, but today the above-mentioned issues are financially material and companies must adapt and evolve to ensure their long-term viability.

The term most commonly used to describe today's global challenges is corporate sustainability, and companies have responded to sustainability in varying degrees. ESG is the modern tool that investors can incorporate into their investment process to assess how companies are responding to today's sustainability challenges. A 2013 Accenture study found that, 'Some 63 percent of CEOs expect sustainability to transform their industry within five years – and 76 percent believe that embedding sustainability into their core business will drive revenue growth and new opportunities' (Accenture, 2013).

One might ask, what are the differences between companies that are becoming sustainable, versus more traditional companies? Robert Eccles, Kathleen Miller Perkins and George Serafeim described the mechanisms in a 2012 *MIT Sloan Management Review* article titled 'How to Become a Sustainable Company'. They wrote:

> In contrast to the vast majority of traditional companies, sustainable companies are willing and able to engage in the kind of ongoing transformational change that is required as social expectations evolve. They aggressively create new processes, products and business models that improve environmental, social and governance performance – all of which conspire to boost financial performance through cost savings, new revenues, brand enhancement and better risk management.
>
> (Eccles et al., 2012)

Sustainable companies, or companies with strong ESG performance, can create shareholder value and increase return on invested capital in the following ways:

- *Growth through innovation* – New products and services designed to address today's sustainability challenges can win new customers and create significant growth.
- *Resource management and efficiency* – Companies can increase profitability through effective resource management, waste reduction and adoption of sustainable processes.

- *Risk management* – Sound governance practices can create a culture of transparency and accountability. Prudent management of the supply chain can ensure fair treatment of the workforce and suppliers and ensure that materials come from ethical sources. The resulting improvement in reputation can boost demand for products.
- *Human capital* – Companies can increase employee productivity and retention when sustainability is part of the culture and broader corporate mission. Attracting and retaining top talent produces a significant competitive advantage.

At BlueSky, we developed a proprietary multi-factor ESG model designed to identify companies exhibiting the above characteristics that can create shareholder value and drive returns. Our model incorporates many material ESG factors that are supported by a wide body of academic research and are proven to be financially material through our rigorous academic testing. Conceptually, our model is based in part on sound concepts such as the SASB Materiality Map created by the Sustainability Accounting Standards Board, which illustrates how industries have their own unique set of material ESG issues. Our model has enabled us to create proprietary ESG scores to quantify and rank companies by industry. We scored all of the companies in the Russell 1,000, and divided the group between High ESG (strong ESG performance) and Low ESG (weak ESG performance). Our research shows a direct correlation between ESG and ROIC, as companies with strong ESG exhibit significantly higher ROIC:

- Companies in the High ESG group exhibited 54 percent higher ROIC than the Low ESG group.
- There is a high correlation between material ESG factors and ROIC, confirming the significant financial impact of ESG and importance of inclusion in investment process.
- ESG drove higher ROIC across different industries, showing positive correlation in 8 of 10 GICS sectors.

Integrating ESG into Buffett's value approach – a powerful combination

Becoming a sustainable company and achieving strong ESG performance may not in itself provide enduring competitive advantages, nor translate into a wonderful company or winning investment idea. However, it should be noted that becoming a sustainable company and gaining the trust of customers, workers, and suppliers takes many years and represents a complicated process that requires significant long-term commitment. Superficial attempts at greenwashing, without a substantial commitment from management and buy-in from the workforce, will do little to raise ESG performance. The integration of ESG analysis into the investment process begins to make the intangible factors tangible, revealing the underlying elements that can provide the foundation for a durable franchise with above-average ROIC. ESG by itself can reveal important and financially material information about a company, but it only tells part of the story.

Likewise, some of Buffett's wide moat companies may appear far less attractive when viewed through an ESG lens. For example, long-time Buffett darling Walmart may have achieved good results in the past, but a closer look at Walmart's ESG performance reveals significant risks that may threaten its future outlook. Walmart has been credited for its environmental initiatives and management has demonstrated the business case for sustainability by becoming more energy efficient. However, a deeper dive into Walmart's ESG reveals significant risks stemming from a long track record of poor governance and poor social performance. Walmart has faced a never-ending list of complaints and accusations regarding treatment of workers, including poor pay, excessive use of part-time workers, and use of sweatshops. Walmart has also been dogged by poor governance, including a recent high-profile bribery case in Mexico and subsequent attempts at a cover up. Additionally, Walmart's business faces headwinds from changing consumer preferences toward online shopping from rivals such as Amazon. When viewed through a wider ESG/value lens, the long-term case for Walmart appears questionable, illustrating how the Buffett value approach can be significantly improved through the integration of ESG.

To further explore the relationship and the potential benefits of integrating ESG with a Buffett economic moat approach, we performed an ESG/moat analysis for all the companies in the Russell 1,000 Index. Using Morningstar's moat rating for each company, we divided the companies into three groups consisting of no moat, narrow moat, and wide moat. Using our proprietary ESG scoring methodology based on material ESG factors described previously, we further divided the moat groups into high ESG and low ESG. The results of the ESG/moat analysis for the Russell 1,000 companies are shown in Table 10b.2 below.

One of our key findings is that the strongest investment performance over the three- and five-year periods is exhibited by companies with both a moat and high ESG. The implication is that high ESG amplifies competitive advantages that are present in narrow- and wide-moat companies. In short, the combination of ESG integrated with Buffett's economic moats provides a powerful way to identify companies with enduring competitive advantages in today's modern business landscape. While each discipline may separately demonstrate value, the integration

Table 10b.2 Performance of Russell 1,000 companies with and without moats

Russell 1000	*3-Year Performance*		*5-Year Performance*	
	Low ESG†	*High ESG†*	*Low ESG†*	*High ESG†*
No Moat	7.64	10.22	8.83	10.49
Narrow Moat	11.10	14.06	10.86	14.93
Wide Moat	12.09	13.77	13.17	14.15

Source: BlueSky Investment Management.

of ESG with Buffett's moats significantly increases alpha when used together in the investment process.

An example of company with a wide moat and strong ESG, and one of BlueSky's top holdings, is Alphabet (Google). Charlie Munger recently said, 'Google has a huge new moat. In fact I've probably never seen such a wide moat.'[3] Google's dominance in the internet search arena provides it with a wide economic moat against competitors and allows it to command approximately 25 percent of the display advertising spending market. Beyond search, Google's YouTube is the top video website and continues to grow rapidly with more than a billion users, and Google is now a significant player in the cloud/enterprise business space. Google has been innovating aggressively and now provides quarterly updates on their 'Other bets' category which includes Google Fiber, Nest, Calico, Verily, Google Ventures, Google Capital, and the self-driving car unit, Google X.

From an ESG perspective, Google is proven leader with one of the lowest emissions profiles, resulting from one of most efficient data centers in the industry, and is well-known for creating a great work environment with fantastic benefits. A combination of initiatives that include a huge commitment to renewables, sustainable commuting, and investments in clean energy projects has resulted in Google being carbon neutral for several years.

Multinational consumer goods giant Unilever is another example of a company with a wide moat and strong ESG. With a big portfolio of globally recognized brands, Unilever has significant competitive advantages stemming from its position as a large supplier of sticky consumer products that command substantial retail shelf space. Unilever's size also allows it to produce its products at a low cost, making it difficult to compete with. As a result, Unilever has demonstrated a long track record of delivering high ROIC.

Unilever was an early mover in recognizing the business case for sustainability, having launched its 'Sustainable living plan' in 2010 which detailed ambitious plans for a 50 percent reduction its greenhouse gas, water and waste footprint by 2020. Unilever coupled this plan with a goal of doubling its sales, anchored by the company's core belief that sustainability drives growth. The company noted that its sustainable brands, which include such well-known names as Dove, Lifebuoy, Ben & Jerry's and Comfort, 'accounted for half the company's growth in 2014 and grew at twice the rate of the rest of the business'.[4]

As good as it is at picking winners, ESG may be equally adept at avoiding losers. Buffett minimizes risk by purchasing well-managed, wide-moat companies at attractive prices. By investing in great companies with strong ESG performance, portfolio managers can avoid some catastrophic losses. Volkswagen AG had poor governance ratings from several high-profile ESG monitors, including MSCI Inc. and International Shareholder Services, before December, when the company admitted that it had installed software in some car models to cheat emissions tests. That governance mea culpa lopped $17.6 billion off the carmaker's market capitalization in a single trading day. As shown below, Volkswagen's MSCI ESG rating was significantly lower than peers BMW and Daimler.

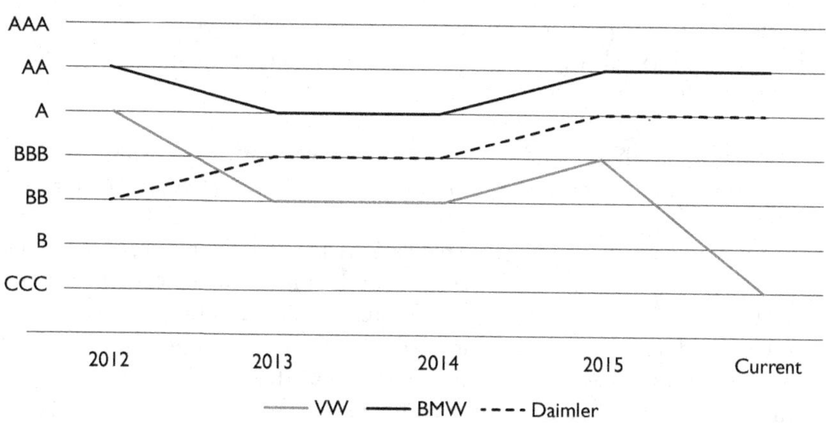

Figure 10b.2 MSCI ESG rating comparison.
Source: BlueSky Investment Management.

The performance impact of Volkswagen's emissions scandal, versus peers BMW and Daimler, is shown below:

Figure 10b.3 VW performance during emissions scandal.
Source: BlueSky Investment Management.

Fiduciary duty and ESG integration

Asset owners, fiduciaries, and investment managers should be aware that ESG issues have been widely proven in academic research to be financially material, and there is widespread acceptance globally of the financial benefits of integrating ESG into the investment process. The U.S. lags behind the rest of the world in terms of recognition, acceptance, and integration of ESG into the investment process, largely due to the misperception that ESG and SRI are one and the same.

A recent UN Principles for Responsible Investment (PRI) report, *Fiduciary Duty in the 21st Century*, clearly defines how fiduciary duty must be viewed today, drawing the following conclusions:[5]

- Failing to consider long-term investment value drivers, which include environmental, social and governance issues, in investment practice is a failure of fiduciary duty.
- Many countries have introduced regulations and codes requiring institutional investors to take account of ESG issues in their investment decision-making.
- In the U.S., there is a common misperception that ESG issues are purely ethical and without financial materiality, that a focus on ESG issues involves compromising investment performance, and that it is difficult to add investment value through a focus on ESG issues.

Globally, there is a clear trend toward increased investment in ESG-integrated strategies, including a large number of European institutional investors and pension funds. While progress has been slower in the U.S., there is evidence of improvement as large pensions, including CalSTRS and the New York State Common Retirement Fund, have moved billions of dollars into ESG-integrated investments. As this continues, fiduciaries who do not incorporate ESG will find it difficult to defend their omission of financially material information that has direct correlation with investment performance.

We anticipate that the recent landmark climate accord signed by 195 nations in December 2015 will accelerate the need for companies to address ESG risks, and for asset owners to integrate ESG into the investment process.

Conclusion

ESG data is a beneficial byproduct of the information age, creating greater transparency and an opportunity to analyze companies through a wider lens that more fully reveals corporate risks, competitive advantages, and future opportunities. A wide body of academic research has demonstrated the undeniable link between corporate ESG performance and superior financial returns. Throughout history, the most successful investors adapt and evolve great investment approaches over time as business landscapes change and new trends emerge. ESG presents a clear opportunity for investors to enhance performance and better manage risk in the twenty-first century. This can be achieved by allocating capital to thoughtfully constructed approaches, utilizing asset managers who have demonstrated a rigorous process that separates the signal from the noise in order to capture the alpha clearly demonstrated by the academic research.

Disclosures

†BlueSky's proprietary ESG ranking is a composite score based on over 100 factors sourced from corporate disclosures, specialized datasets, and other publicly filed information. The High ESG group is composed of companies that score above their GICS sector mean on material ESG factors. The Low ESG group is composed of companies that score below their GICS sector mean on material ESG factors.

BlueSky Investment Management, LLC is a Registered Investment Adviser. This chapter is solely for informational purposes. Advisory services are only offered to clients or prospective clients where BlueSky Investment Management, LLC and its representatives are properly licensed or exempt from licensure. Past performance is no guarantee of future returns. Investing involves risk and possible loss of principal capital. No advice may be rendered by BlueSky Investment Management, LLC unless a client service agreement is in place.

Notes

1 Clark, G. L., Feiner, A. and Viehs, M., 2014. *From the Stockholder to the Stakeholder*, Oxford University and Arabesque Partners study. Oxford: Oxford University Press. http://papers.ssrn.com/sol3/papers.cfm?abstract_id=2508281. Accessed September 8, 2016.
2 Fulton, M. and Kahn, B., 2012. *Sustainable Investing: Stablishing Long-term Value and Performance*. Climate Change Advisors report, Deutsche Bank, June. http://papers.ssrn.com/sol3/papers.cfm?abstract_id=2222740. Accessed September 8, 2016.
3 CBS Market Watch, May 2009. 'Buffett, Munger Praise Google's "Moat"'. www.marketwatch.com/story/buffett-munger-praise-googles-moat. Accessed September 8, 2016.
4 Unilever Press Release, 2015. 'Unilever Sees Sustainability Supporting Growth'. May 5. www.unilever.com/news/press-releases/2015/Unilever-sees-sustainability-supporting-growth.html. Accessed September 8, 2016.
5 UN PRI report, *Fiduciary Duty in the 21st Century*. www.unepfi.org/fileadmin/documents/fiduciary_duty_21st_century.pdf. Accessed September 8, 2016.

References

Accenture and UN Global Compact, 2013. 'The UN Global Compact–Accenture CEO Study on Sustainability 2013'. s.l.: s.n.

Buffett, W., 1984. 'The Superinvestors of Graham-and-Doddsville'. *Hermes, the Columbia Business School Magazine*, p. 11.

Buffett, W., 1990. Berkshire Hathaway Inc. Letter to shareholders, s.l.: s.n.

Buffett, W., 1996. Berkshire Hathaway Inc. Letter to shareholders, s.l.: s.n.

Deutsche Bank Group, 2012. 'Sustainable Investing: Establishing Long-Term Value and Performance'. https://institutional.deutscheam.com/content/_media/Sustainable_Investing_2012.pdf. Accessed October 18, 2016.

Eccles, R., Perkins, K.M. and Serafeim, G., 2012. 'How to Become a Sustainable Company'. *MIT Sloan Management Review*, 53, 4, pp. 43–50.

Hagstrom, R., 2014. *The Warren Buffett Way*. 3rd ed. Hoboken, NJ: Wiley.

Lowe, J., 2007. *Warren Buffett Speaks*. Hoboken, NJ: Wiley.

Chapter 10c

'Bottom-up' strategy

Mirova and Carbon Impact Analytics: an innovative methodology to measure the climate change impact of an investment portfolio

Mirova

For an investor, measuring financial assets' climate change impact is a necessary step in building portfolios which contribute to the shift to a low-carbon economy, both for limiting carbon risks and seizing low-carbon opportunities. Hence Carbone 4, in collaboration with Mirova, has developed an innovative methodology that goes beyond carbon footprinting. Carbon Impact Analytics provides asset managers with an in-depth, 'bottom-up' analysis of the carbon impact of a portfolio and its underlying firms, as illustrated in Figure 10c.1 below.

In its first version, Carbon Impact Analytics is designed to cover stocks and bonds of any listed company (even those not reporting their carbon footprint). It will be extended to other financial assets in future versions.

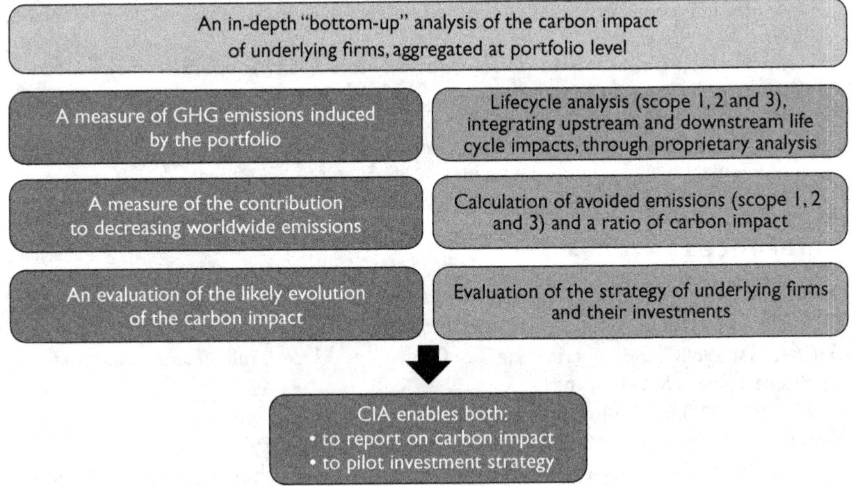

Figure 10c.1 Carbon impact analysis process.

Source: Mirova.

Core methodological principles of Carbon Impact Analytics

'Bottom-up' analysis

The analysis of the carbon impact of a portfolio begins with an in-depth assessment of each underlying firm, followed by aggregation at the portfolio level. This allows for differentiation between companies in the same business sector, and enables recognition of companies' efforts in integrating climate- and energy-related issues in their strategic decisions and reporting.

Sectorial approach with specific insights for 'high stakes' sectors

Challenges regarding the low-carbon transition vary depending on the characteristics of each economic sector. Therefore, Carbon Impact Analytics differentiates 'high stakes' and 'low stakes' sectors, and provides specific insights for 'high stakes' sectors with tailored calculation principles for each sector.

'High stakes' sectors for which a detailed Carbon Impact Analysis is performed are detailed in Figure 10c.2 below.

Aggregation at portfolio level eliminates emissions double-counting

Double-counting of GHG emissions arises when the same ton of GHG emissions is counted more than once within a portfolio due to the aggregation of companies' indirect emissions within the same value chain. While consolidating the carbon impact of a portfolio, Carbon Impact Analytics reprocesses results (both induced and avoided emissions) to eliminate most double-counting.

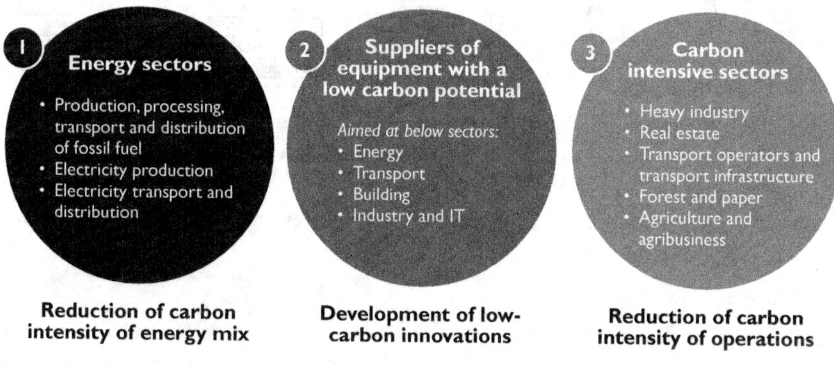

Figure 10c.2 High stakes sectors.

Source: Mirova.

Key outputs of Carbon Impact Analytics evaluation

Results of Carbon Impact Analytics evaluation are provided to asset managers at portfolio level as well as for each underlying firm, thereby enabling both reporting and piloting of investments.

Below (Figure 10c.3) is an example (illustrative only, without accurate figures) of key outputs, as provided at portfolio level.

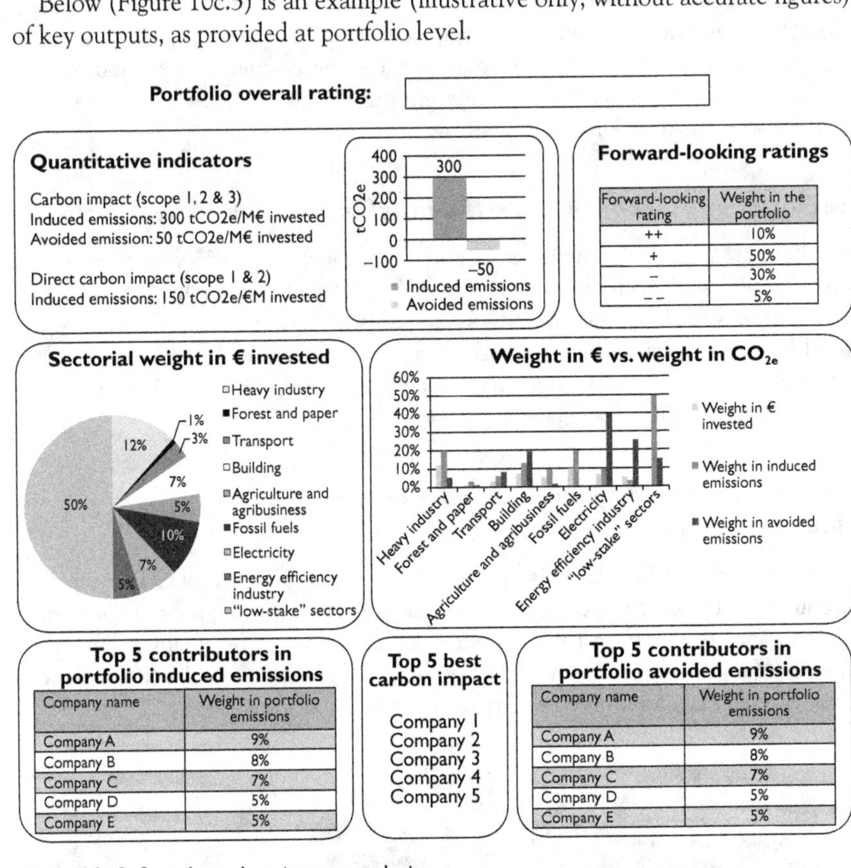

Figure 10c.3 Sample carbon impact analysis.

Source: Mirova.

Figure 10c.4 is an example (illustrative only) of key outputs provided for each underlying company.

Comments on the analysis:

X realizes 30% of its turnover from products linked to the low-carbon transition. The strategy of X is to increase strongly its turnover related to the low-carbon transition, however no information is available on CAPEX and R&D expenditures related to the low-carbon transition. The scope 1 and 2 emissions reporting is reliable.

Overall rating: **Significant contribution to the climate transition**

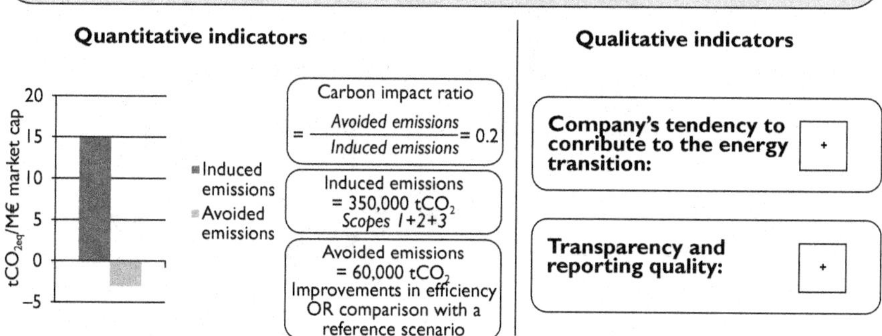

Figure 10c.4 Sample key outputs.

Source: Mirova.

Part III

The next frontier

Chapter 11

The main segments of global commerce and what's needed

Cary Krosinsky

As we saw earlier, there are four main segments of fossil fuel consumption that directly lead to the ongoing carbon emissions that we can no longer avoid to send into the atmosphere.

Those four are:

- transportation
- industrial processes
- buildings
- electricity generation.

Add a fifth area, mainly but not solely due to methane emissions, as involves:

- agriculture, deforestation and land use (or AFOLU)

and you have the five main areas of global commerce which create the ongoing greenhouse gas challenge.

The only way to move us into safety is to reduce the emissions coming out of these areas. They aren't each 20 percent of the problem, but each area is significant enough to present reduction opportunities which need further analysis to see how far and how rapidly these can be implemented, and what risks and opportunities are emerging for investors to consider.

Examples follow of what we can do about each area, including low-carbon transportation options, energy storage, industrial ecology, scaling lower-cost renewables, distributed energy, green infrastructure, energy efficiency and new financing options and standards for deforestation and land use, among much more.

This is where finance can really supercharge the low-carbon transition we require.

One of the great joys of teaching at institutions such as Yale and Brown is having a chance to work with some truly amazing undergraduate students. The chapters that follow are from a mix of leading investment institutions such as Norges Bank, Low Carbon and L&G Investment Management as well as leading students from Yale (Reichenbach, Childress), Brown (Kortenhorst, Kortenhorst Jr., and Bracy), and Tufts (Edelstein), who have themselves worked with leading firms and experts such as the Rocky Mountain Institute, Vision Ridge, Trillium Investment Management and Breckenridge, as they now describe the changes that are rapidly coming across the sector and throughout every asset class.

The section that follows also benefits from combining the views of financial experts such as London-based Hedge Fund GLG Partners (Mitchell) and students from Yale (Rutland, Smiley), along with some work from my occasional teaching colleague Gabriel Thoumi and some of his other partners. We hope you enjoy this blended global perspective.

Chapter 11a

Financing the renewables revolution

Winston Kortenhorst and Jules Kortenhorst

There is an energy revolution brewing. The way in which we power our homes, fuel our cars, and light our cities is evolving rapidly. Renewable energy has brought a low-carbon economy within our reach. Technological developments in renewable power generation, energy storage, and grid management services have made a complex, smart power system technologically feasible, while business models and regulatory advances have created the necessary economic milieu. As a result, renewable generation capacity has proliferated dramatically across power grids. As volumes have scaled up, costs have continued on a steady downward march. This is seen in the experience curve of solar, batteries, and wind (Figure 11a.1). As cumulative production increases, prices drop proportionally. Thus decreasing costs will incentivize further deployment, in turn decreasing costs in a self-perpetuating cycle.

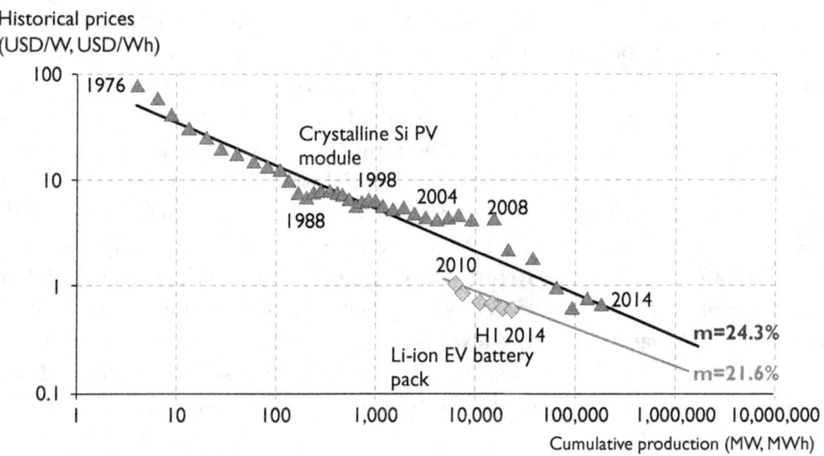

Figure 11a.1 The experience curve.
Source: Bloomberg New Energy Finance.

Capital to match the experience curve

Key to the progress of renewable generation technologies has been the deployment of capital to match their development and deployment. At each stage of the experience curve, different forms of capital have been called for. In the early stages, renewable technologies face considerable technical and commercial risk; there is no assurance that the technologies will work, and even if they do, that they will be commercially viable. At this stage, high-return, equity capital is needed to match the comparatively high risk. Given that most ventures will fail, investors require an outsized return from successful investments in order to offset their inevitable losses. As renewable technologies, especially wind and solar, have proven their technical and commercial viability, the type of financing also changes. We are entering the stage where deployment, not development, is the key challenge. To meet this challenge, low-risk, low-return debt financing is needed en masse. Investors are willing to accept a lower return for development capital, since the technological and commercial risks have largely been mitigated.

Six phases, six forms of capital

Broadly speaking, there are six phases of financing and development that play an important role in bringing renewable technologies to scale. Across these six phases, the risk appetite, expected return, and scale vary significantly.

1. Government-funded early stage R&D

In the earliest stages, government funding into researching new technologies is needed. Fundamental research and early-stage technological innovation faces immense risk and uncertain outcomes; many paths and hypotheses will be tested, but only a few will succeed. The reason that governments are willing to fund research into renewable technologies stems from their potential for immense societal benefit. At this point, there is no formal expectation of financial returns.

Organizations such as the Advanced Research Projects Agency-Energy (ARPA-E) and the National Renewable Energy Laboratory (NREL) play a key role in early stage R&D. Unlike their private (and sometimes even public) counterparts, these organizations do not promise to turn a profit for their 'investors', and can therefore undertake projects that are 'too early for private sector investment'.[1] Since their function is to advance society as a whole, not to provide an immediate return on invested capital, these organizations often share the results of their research broadly, allowing later-stage players to capture the economic value of the knowledge generated.

Within the energy sector, government R&D agencies play a salient part by bridging the 'valley of death' which stretches between very early stage laboratory research and full-size field testing. This space is characterized by a dearth of capital, as it is neither 'fundamental' enough to attract funding for university-like research, nor 'applied' enough to attract private sources of capital. Government organizations have made a valuable contribution in the form of pilot programs which take the first step in translating laboratory learnings to real-world applications.

2. *Venture capital*

Once technologies have demonstrated some degree of technological viability, investment moves into the private sector. Venture capital has a tradition of financing the commercialization of breakthrough technologies. This has particularly been seen in the tech sector, where many of today's technologies were nurtured in their early stages.

However, the energy sector provides unique challenges to venture capital financing. Unlike much tech innovation, which centers around small, consumer products with relatively short lifespans (e.g. telephones, PCs), energy innovations often target large institutional products, like power generation assets. Moreover, energy innovations do not emerge into an unconstrained environment, but rather must find their way in the highly regulated power sector. This adds an extra financial and strategic burden that startup ventures in other markets do not face.

As a result of these challenges, venture capital does not have a great track record in the renewable energy field. The high degree of risk, psychologically amplified by a number of high-profile bankruptcies (Solyndra, Fisker Automotive), means that limited partners demand an exceptionally high return. Nonetheless, there have been important success stories, which are revolutionizing the markets in which they operate. Companies such as Tesla, Nest, and Solar City have delivered the high returns commensurate with the associated risk. Interestingly, many of these success stories scale down clean power assets and place them in the hands of consumers, as if they were traditional tech devices.

3. *Private equity*

Once renewable technologies have made it through the earliest stages of commercialization, private equity provides the next stage of financing. At this point, energy companies are generally expected to have proved their ability to generate steady revenue and even positive earnings. Private equity investors need confidence in Earnings Before Interest, Taxes, Depreciation and Amortization (EBITDA), as these cash flows will be leveraged to pay off the debt taken on to acquire the business in the first place (this follows the leveraged buyout model of private equity).

Historically, private equity has not been a major player in the renewable energy space. Although the risks are smaller compared to venture capital financing, renewable power projects have not yet demonstrated the degree of degree of revenue and EBITDA stability required by private equity investors. Moreover, the relatively complex regulatory and grid environment in which power assets operate, even when at scale, adds a considerable risk component. Because of this, private equity investors still expect relatively high returns when investing in renewable power generation.

4. Public equities

Once a renewable energy technology has a proven track record of delivering positive earnings, it can turn to the public markets for financing. This requires an initial public offering (IPO), through which its shares become listed on public exchanges such as the New York Stock Exchange or Nasdaq, where 'average' investors can purchase stakes in the company. In the wake of the 2008 financial crisis, the Sarbanes-Oxley reforms mean that companies looking to go public are generally more mature in their life cycle and less risky. In this later stage of investing, the returns to buying public equities are much lower, around 5–10 percent.

While public markets provide cheaper capital than venture or private equity, they present their own troubles too. Once a company is publicly listed, its fortune becomes tied to market sentiments, which do not always accurately track underlying economic realities. For example, YieldCos are publicly listed companies which own operational power assets. Since such assets operate under PPAs and therefore generate consistent, predictable revenue, their share prices should be fairly constant. However, in the late summer of 2015, YieldCo share prices dropped precipitously without obvious reason, which hurt the YieldCos' ability to access the cheap public financing needed to acquire new assets and deliver on their business model. This kind of risk is particularly pronounced for renewable power companies, whose viability might shift rapidly in the public's eye as a result of intense political scrutiny and debate.

5. Project finance

Once a technology is fully proven to be commercially and financially viable, project finance is the lowest-risk and most attractive form of financing. As the name suggests, this tranche allows investors to allocate capital to specific projects, such as an individual wind farm or set of solar panels. At this far-advanced point on the experience curve, there is far less risk and the form of financing is typically debt. Given the lower risk profile, the yield on the debt – and hence return on the investment – is lower, hovering between 3 and 7 percent.

Nonetheless, project finance does bring with it some nuances. The structuring of project finance requires a high level of sophistication. Key issues revolve around questions of counter-party risk and policy risk – for example, changes to the Investment Tax Credit could have serious adverse effects on solar projects' free cash flows. Additionally, investing in project finance abroad incurs extra risks. For example, India has declared a significant commitment to installing solar capacities. Yet investing in solar projects in India bears currency and other country-specific risks for a foreign investor.

6. Alternative project debt financing structures

In recent years there have been many innovations around reducing the cost of capital to finance renewable energy projects. This is significant, as a lower cost of capital has immense consequences for reducing the levelized cost of electricity (LCOE) – a measure which compares the costs of generating power from fundamentally different power sources. Many strides forward have already been made here. Real estate investment trusts (REITs) and YieldCos are asset classes which provide investors with a steady and growing dividend stream at relatively low risk. Tax equity investment structures have allowed renewable power companies without significant tax burdens to capture some of the value of their tax credits, enhancing the overall attractiveness of their business. Financial engineering will surely continue to innovate in this space and continue to bring an expanding menu of asset classes for investors to access.

Conclusion

As scaling up renewables from 10 percent to 80 percent of the electricity grid continues, there will be immense demand for additional capital to finance this transition. Renewable technologies, certainly wind, solar, and battery storage, are now proven to be technologically, and moreover commercially, viable. Therefore, the bulk of the additional capital will be needed in the latter three stages. Here continued financial ingenuity is needed to continually lower the cost of capital, allowing renewable projects to reach their full commercial potential. Nonetheless, further research and funding is always welcome in the early stages of renewable energy as well: the next major breakthrough could yet be brewing in a lab.

Note

1 http://arpa-e.energy.gov/?q=arpa-e-site-page/about. Accessed September 8, 2016.

Chapter 11b

The driverless car

Mimi Reichenbach

Transportation is no small contributor to anthropogenic greenhouse gases (GHGs). In 2010, passenger and freight vehicles were responsible for 23 percent of global GHGs emitted.[1] Of the 7 gigatons of carbon dioxide released worldwide due to transport in 2010, 72 percent was attributable to road transport. Non-road-based carbon dioxide emissions, such as rail, shipping, and aviation, accounted for under 30 percent of transport-related carbon dioxide emissions.[2] In the future, the implementation of driverless cars and electric vehicles, as well as a system transformation towards a shared transportation economy, should go a long way to reducing future transport-related GHG emissions.

The Rocky Mountain Institute stated in 2015 that if the United States modified road transport to a shared, electric and autonomous transport system, it would result in annual savings of $1 trillion and 1 gigaton of carbon dioxide.[3] Unlike conventional gas and diesel engine driven vehicles, electric vehicles do not have any direct emissions. However, although an electric vehicle does not directly emit any greenhouse gases, it does cause significant indirect GHG emissions. An electric vehicle's carbon intensity traces back to the power generation source of the electricity grid supplying its charging station. When electric vehicles are sourced from a natural gas powered grid, or a grid supplied with high percentages of hydropower, wind or solar energy, they become much cleaner forms of transport compared to their fossil fuel powered counterparts.[4] Conversely, when coal is an electricity grid's primary generation source, electric vehicles have a higher carbon intensity than conventional internal combustion engines.

A shared autonomous transport system reduces carbon dioxide emissions by changing the transportation system rather than by changing energy sourcing. As seen today with ride-sharing platforms such as Uber and Lyft, ride sharing increases the use of a particular vehicle and decreases the need for personal vehicle ownership. Autonomous, or driverless vehicles, will increase the efficiency of vehicle transport through precise vehicle-to-vehicle communication to improve traffic flow, and reduce driver input errors, currently impossible with human drivers. This will lead to a reduction in automobile accidents caused by human error, as well as stop-and-go driving and idling.[5] When combined with traffic flow automation and optimal speed maintenance, future fuel savings are estimated to surpass 30 percent.[6] An MIT study projected that driverless cars will use slot-based intersections devoid of traffic lights, reducing delays and doubling road capacity.[7] Additionally, a driverless vehicle will automatically calculate routes around traffic, leading to fuel savings of 5 percent, as well as enabling a vehicle to act as a 'virtual valet' and park itself.[8] If driverless vehicles succeed in increasing safety, it is likely car weights will decrease as well, allowing for greater mileage per unit of energy. With freight transport, responsible for 25 percent of the United States' transportation greenhouse gas emissions, driverless cars will allow for safe platooning.[9] Similar to a peloton of cyclists, platooning permits semi-trucks to travel in links at a constant spacing and speed, reducing drag and leading to fuel savings of 4.5 percent for the lead truck and 10 percent or more for those following. With fuel accounting for 40 percent of a freight truck's operating costs, it is likely automated freight vehicles will form chains, similar to freight trains, on highways to maximize efficiencies.[10]

In a future of automated driving, car handling, acceleration and other factors that currently sway car purchasers will become irrelevant, as all cars will drive in an efficient manner from point A to B; this transition will lead to two potential scenarios: people will give up car ownership entirely, relying on autonomous ride-sharing fleets, or rather people will personalize their driverless vehicles to become an extension of the home or office. Given these two possibilities, and the reduced opportunity cost associated with driverless vehicle travel, it is unknown whether miles driven per capita annually will increase or decrease.

Investment examples

In the race toward an autonomous ride sharing fleet, there are three players: traditional car manufacturers, driverless car technology developers, and ride-sharing platforms. The year 2016 has seen a surge in partnerships across all three categories.

Google was the first to bring a driverless vehicle from fantasy to reality with the Google Self-Driving Car project. Since 2009, Google's (now Alphabet Inc.) self-driving cars have been traveling on California's roads, and the company announced in 2015 that its self-driving car will be ready for market in 2020.[11] In May 2016, Google revealed it would be opening a 53,000 ft^2 self-driving technology development center in Novi, Michigan, just outside of Detroit. As Detroit has been and is currently home to many car manufacturers – including Ford and General Motors – Google's decision to move to Novi makes it likely it is anticipating a future of partnerships with established vehicle manufacturers. The same month, Google also announced a partnership with Fiat Chrysler Automobiles to construct 100 self-driving Chrysler Pacifica hybrid minivans.[12] Fiat Chrysler Automobiles is parent corporation to Chrysler, Fiat Automobiles, Maserati, and Alfa Romeo. If a long-term partnership were to form further down the line between Google and Fiat Chrysler Automobiles, Google would be poised to enter a range of car manufacturing and distribution markets, allowing for rapid introduction of driverless car technology to compact, family, luxury and sports cars.

Tesla has approached the driverless car market differently. Rather than develop a completely driverless car prior to selling it to consumers, Tesla has designed its cars with remote software download capabilities, allowing for updates as Tesla enhances the vehicle control software. In October 2015, Tesla updated previously sold Model S cars (2014 and later models) with an 'autopilot' feature. Tesla's autopilot is not fully autonomous, but allows the Model S to steer, change lanes and park without human assistance.[13] Since 2014, Tesla Model S cars have been standardized with a forward radar, front-facing camera, ultrasonic sensor and GPS navigation reliant on high-precision digital maps, all of which are essential for their autopilot capability.

Daimler (Mercedes), Audi and Volvo have also been active in driverless vehicle development. Daimler demonstrated a successful platoon of three Mercedes big-rig trucks on the autobahn in March 2016; the vehicles communicated via wifi to maintain a spacing of 50 ft in order to reduce aerodynamic drag. The potential for efficiency gains and cost savings in freight transport has led Daimler to announce the company will invest $563 million in self-driving vehicles by 2020.[14] Additionally, Daimler's concept car, the Mercedes-Benz F 015, is a sleek vehicle without steering wheel or pedals: this car may be used in future for the shared vehicle economy, as Daimler owns car2go (car pooling and rental app), and MyTaxi (an Uber competitor), and also has partial ownership of HERE (a mapping service).[15] Audi currently has a fully autonomous vehicle under testing in China, with scheduled release of the A8 sedan in 2017.[16,17] In 2016, Volvo began operating a DriveMe project involving autonomous vehicles, and is also looking to deliver autonomous cars to market by 2017.[18]

General Motors, Ford, Volkswagen, and Toyota have followed suit, with all car companies investing in various ride-sharing efforts in 2016. In March 2016, General Motors acquired Cruise, a San Francisco based autonomous driving technology startup, for $1 billion.[19] Additionally, in January 2016, GM invested $500 million in Lyft, a ride-share company and Uber competitor.[20] GM's president Dan Ammann has said that he envisions the future of personal transport to be 'connected, seamless and autonomous'. A future autonomous Lyft fleet, manufactured by General Motors with Cruise operating systems, may become a future powerhouse in ride sharing. Ford on the other hand, has been developing its own autonomous technology and established a subsidiary, Ford Smart Mobility, to deal with mobility services, launching a FordPass mobile app in April 2016 which could be used for ride sharing in the future.[21] Looking to rebrand itself after their diesel scandal in the fall of 2015, Volkswagen has invested in electric vehicles as well as ride sharing, putting $300 million into the ride-sharing app, Gett, in May 2016.[22] Toyota has worked to develop fully autonomous cars as well as a ride-sharing fleet, creating R&D teams at MIT and Stanford, as well as investing in the ride-sharing app Uber in May 2016; Uber itself is also working to develop driverless technology.[23]

Not to be left out, Apple has similarly made moves in the ride-sharing and autonomous vehicle space. Apple is working on developing its own driverless vehicle, and in May 2016 the technology giant invested $1 billion in DidiChuxing, formerly DidiKuaidi, a strong competitor of Uber in China.[24]

Challenges, outlook and uncertainty

Regarding driverless cars, the time it will take to change from human-controlled vehicles to fully autonomous roads is largely uncertain. For example, human drivers require visible traffic lights at intersections, whereas autonomous vehicles may not. As the proportion of human drivers goes down, increased efficiencies due to coordination among driverless vehicles is more easily captured. The National Highway Transportation Safety Administration has defined five levels of car automation, with a Level 0 vehicle requiring total human engagement, to a Level 4 vehicle characterized as a completely driverless vehicle.[25] Today some vehicles operate at Level 3, such as the Google car, with primarily automated driving, yet still require an alert human driver.[26] A road comprised completely of Level 4 vehicles will be devoid of human error, leading to a projected 82 percent fewer accidents and increased efficiency due to computerized vehicle-to-vehicle communication.[27] This would allow for road system changes, such as the slot-based intersection, which would not be possible with human drivers still on the road.[28] In some cases, this will require banning human-driven vehicles on certain roadways, a scenario that will lead to further uncertainty in terms of social resistance and regulatory approval.

This transition time is also linked to how rapidly the cost of autonomous vehicles declines. The Victoria Transport Policy Institute predicts that at some point between 2020 and 2030 driverless cars will be available to affluent non-drivers. Yet energy conservation and pollution reduction will occur later, in the 2040s or 2060s when driverless cars become 'common and affordable', either through personal ownership or ride-sharing platforms.[29]

Pollution reduction and energy conservation are also dependent on a switch to electric vehicles, and establishing programs to ensure that driving demands remain stable as opposed to increasing. Driverless cars are not innately electric vehicles, yet there is likely to be synergy between the two technologies in the future, as seen with electric vehicle manufacturer Tesla and its already released autopilot feature. Electric vehicles face a substantial number of uncertainties as well, including advances in battery power density ratios, potential implementation of a carbon tax, fluctuating gasoline prices, and charging infrastructure availability. Additionally, driverless vehicles are not destined to reduce energy use; driverless cars will reduce the opportunity cost of driving and may lead to an increase in urban sprawl and per capita mileage.[30] The technology will also allow non-drivers such as children, the disabled and the elderly, as well as those without licenses, to travel more easily.

Another unknown variable is how driverless vehicles will affect other road users – pedestrians and cyclists. Whether roads remain a shared (but safer) resource, or become separate infrastructure, isolated from cyclists and jaywalkers to maximize safety and efficiency, is yet to be determined.[31]

Notes

1 Sims and Schaeffer, 2014 (https://www.ipcc.ch/pdf/assessment-report/ar5/wg3/ipcc_wg3_ar5_chapter8.pdf). Accessed 30 May 2016.
2 Sims and Schaeffer, 2014 (https://www.ipcc.ch/pdf/assessment-report/ar5/wg3/ipcc_wg3_ar5_chapter8.pdf). Accessed 30 May 2016.
3 Walker, Rucks and Weiland, 2015 (http://blog.rmi.org/blog_2015_03_12_how_the_us_transportation_system_can_save_big). Accessed 30 May 2016.
4 Holland, Mansur, Muller and Yates, 2015 (www.nber.org/papers/w21291.pdf). Accessed 30 May 2016.
5 Brown, Gonder and Repac, 2014 (http://link.springer.com/chapter/10.1007 percent2F978-3-319-05990-7_13). Accessed 30 May 2016.
6 Gonder, Earleywine and Sparks, 2012 (http://papers.sae.org/2012-01-0494/). Accessed 30 May 2016.
7 Tachet, Santi, Sobolevsky, Reyes-Castro, Frazzoli, Helbing, and Ratti, 2016 (http://journals.plos.org/plosone/article?id=10.1371/journal.pone.0149607). Accessed 30 May 2016 .
8 Wang, 2015 (http://ensia.com/features/are-self-driving-vehicles-good-for-the-environment/). Accessed 30 May 2016.
9 The White House Office of the Press Secretary, 2014 (https://www.whitehouse.gov/the-press-office/2014/02/18/fact-sheet-opportunity-all-improving-fuel-efficiency-american-trucks-bol). Accessed 30 May 2016 .
10 Wang, 2015 (http://ensia.com/features/are-self-driving-vehicles-good-for-the-environment/). Accessed 30 May 2016.
11 Google Self-Driving Car Project (https://www.google.com/selfdrivingcar/where/). Accessed 30 May 2016.
12 Kelly, 2016 (http://money.cnn.com/2016/05/25/technology/google-self-driving-cars-detroit/). Accessed 30 May 2016.
13 Truong, 2015 (http://qz.com/524400/tesla-just-transformed-the-model-s-into-a-nearly-driverless-car/). Accessed 30 May 2016.
14 Sorokanich, 2016 (www.roadandtrack.com/new-cars/car-technology/news/a28548/daimler-tests-autonomous-big-rig-convoy-on/). Accessed 30 May 2016.
15 Parkinson, 2015 (https://www.theguardian.com/technology/2015/sep/15/mercedes-benz-eyes-luxury-driverless-cars-uber-self-driving-autonomous-vehicles). Accessed 30 May 2016.
16 Dowling, 2015 (www.carsguide.com.au/car-news/first-self-driving-audi-due-in-two-years-32886). Accessed 30 May 2016.
17 Lingeman, 2015 (http://autoweek.com/article/technology/driverless-audi-rs7-logs-2-minute-1-second-lap-sonoma-raceway). Accessed 30 May 2016.
18 Muoio, 2015 (www.techinsider.io/these-5-companies-will-dominate-driverless-cars-2015-12). Accessed 30 May 2016.
19 Wright, 2016 (www.ft.com/intl/cms/s/0/16b55fe8-e79f-11e5-bc31-138df2ae9ee6.html#axzz49nkkyRt8). Accessed 30 May 2016.
20 Iyer and Bryson, 2016 (http://media.gm.com/media/us/en/gm/home.detail.html/content/Pages/news/us/en/2016/Jan/0104-lyft.html). Accessed 30 May 2016.
21 Thompson, 2016 (www.techinsider.io/ford-ceo-our-first-driverless-car-will-be-for-everyone-2016-3). Accessed 30 May 2016.
22 Miller and Rauwald, 2016 (www.bloomberg.com/news/articles/2016-06-01/vw-ceo-looks-toward-taxi-apps-to-move-past-diesel-scandal). Accessed 30 May 2016.
23 Bhuiyan, 2016 (www.recode.net/2016/5/24/11762436/toyota-uber-investment). Accessed 30 May 2016.
24 Love, 2016 (www.reuters.com/article/us-apple-china-idUSKCN0Y404W). Accessed 30 May 2016.

25 Silberg (KPMG), 2013 (https://www.kpmg.com/US/en/IssuesAndInsights/Articles Publications/Documents/self-driving-cars-are-we-ready.pdf). Accessed 30 May 2016.
26 Aldana, 2013 (www.nhtsa.gov/About+NHTSA/Press+Releases/U.S.+Department+of+Transportation+Releases+Policy+on+Automated+Vehicle+Development). Accessed 30 May 2016.
27 McMahon, 2015 (www.forbes.com/sites/jeffmcmahon/2015/09/28/autonomous-vehicles-arrive-in-3-years-in-3-stages/3/#6a0b98ca240f). Accessed 30 May 2016.
28 Ackerman, 2016 (http://spectrum.ieee.org/cars-that-think/transportation/self-driving/the-scary-efficiency-of-autonomous-intersections). Accessed 30 May 2016.
29 Litman, 2015 (www.vtpi.org/avip.pdf). Accessed 30 May 2016.
30 McDonald, 2016 (http://blog.nature.org/science/2016/04/20/why-driverless-cars-cities-sprawl-urban-suburban-development/). Accessed 30 May 2016.
31 Reid, 2013 (www.theguardian.com/environment/bike-blog/2013/oct/11/driver-less-cars-coming-bike-blog). Accessed 30 May 2016.

References

Ackerman, E., 2016 (http://spectrum.ieee.org/cars-that-think/transportation/self-driving/the-scary-efficiency-of-autonomous-intersections). Accessed 30 May 2016.

Aldana, K., 2013 (www.nhtsa.gov/About+NHTSA/Press+Releases/U.S.+Department+of+Transportation+Releases+Policy+on+Automated+Vehicle+Development). Accessed 30 May 2016.

Bhuiyan, J., 2016 (www.recode.net/2016/5/24/11762436/toyota-uber-investment). Accessed 30 May 2016.

Brown, A., Gonder, J. and Repac, B., 2014 (http://link.springer.com/chapter/10.1007%2F978-3-319-05990-7_13). Accessed 30 May 2016.

Dowling, J., 2015 (www.carsguide.com.au/car-news/first-self-driving-audi-due-in-two-years-32886). Accessed 30 May 2016.

Gonder, J., Earleywine, M. and Sparks, W., 2012 (http://papers.sae.org/2012-01-0494/). Accessed 30 May 2016.

Google Self-Driving Car Project (www.google.com/selfdrivingcar/where/). Accessed 30 May 2016.

Holland, S.P., Mansur, E.T., Muller, N.Z. and Yates, A.J., 2015 (www.nber.org/papers/w21291.pdf). Accessed 30 May 2016.

Iyer, V. and Bryson, S., 2016 (http://media.gm.com/media/us/en/gm/home.detail.html/content/Pages/news/us/en/2016/Jan/0104-lyft.html). Accessed 30 May 2016.

Kelly, H., 2016 (http://money.cnn.com/2016/05/25/technology/google-self-driving-cars-detroit/). Accessed 30 May 2016.

Lingeman, J., 2015 (http://autoweek.com/article/technology/driverless-audi-rs7-logs-2-minute-1-second-lap-sonoma-raceway). Accessed 30 May 2016.

Litman, T., 2015 (www.vtpi.org/avip.pdf). Accessed 30 May 2016.

Love, J., 2016 (www.reuters.com/article/us-apple-china-idUSKCN0Y404W). Accessed 30 May 2016.

McDonald, R., 2016 (http://blog.nature.org/science/2016/04/20/why-driverless-cars-cities-sprawl-urban-suburban-development/). Accessed 30 May 2016.

McMahon, J., 2015 (www.forbes.com/sites/jeffmcmahon/2015/09/28/autonomous-vehicles-arrive-in-3-years-in-3-stages/3/#6a0b98ca240f). Accessed 30 May 2016.

Miller, M. and Rauwald, C., 2016 (www.bloomberg.com/news/articles/2016-06-01/vw-ceo-looks-toward-taxi-apps-to-move-past-diesel-scandal). Accessed 30 May 2016.

Muoio, D., 2015 (www.techinsider.io/these-5-companies-will-dominate-driverless-cars-2015-12). Accessed 30 May 2016.

Parkinson, H.J., 2015 (www.theguardian.com/technology/2015/sep/15/mercedes-benz-eyes-luxury-driverless-cars-uber-self-driving-autonomous-vehicles). Accessed 30 May 2016.

Reid, C., 2013 (www.theguardian.com/environment/bike-blog/2013/oct/11/driver-less-cars-coming-bike-blog). Accessed 30 May 2016.

Silberg, G. (KPMG), 2013 (www.kpmg.com/US/en/IssuesAndInsights/ArticlesPublications/Documents/self-driving-cars-are-we-ready.pdf). Accessed 30 May 2016.

Sims, R. and Schaeffer, R., 2014 (www.ipcc.ch/pdf/assessment-report/ar5/wg3/ipcc_wg3_ar5_chapter8.pdf). Accessed 30 May 2016.

Sorokanich, B., 2016 (www.roadandtrack.com/new-cars/car-technology/news/a28548/daimler-tests-autonomous-big-rig-convoy-on/). Accessed 30 May 2016.

Tachet, R., Santi, P., Sobolevsky, S., Reyes-Castro, L.I., Frazzoli, E., Helbing, D. and Ratti, C., 2016 (http://journals.plos.org/plosone/article?id=10.1371/journal.pone.0149607). Accessed 30 May 2016.

Thompson, C., 2016 (www.techinsider.io/ford-ceo-our-first-driverless-car-will-be-for-everyone-2016-3). Accessed 30 May 2016.

Truong, A., 2015 (http://qz.com/524400/tesla-just-transformed-the-model-s-into-a-nearly-driverless-car/). Accessed 30 May 2016.

Walker, J., Rucks, G. and Weiland, J., 2015 (http://blog.rmi.org/blog_2015_03_12_how_the_us_transportation_system_can_save_big). Accessed 30 May 2016.

Wang, U., 2015 (http://ensia.com/features/are-self-driving-vehicles-good-for-the-environment/). Accessed 30 May 2016.

The White House Office of the Press Secretary, 2014 (https://www.whitehouse.gov/the-press-office/2014/02/18/fact-sheet-opportunity-all-improving-fuel-efficiency-american-trucks-bol). Accessed 30 May 2016.

Wright, R., 2016 (www.ft.com/intl/cms/s/0/16b55fe8-e79f-11e5-bc31-138df2ae9ee6.html#axzz49nkkyRt8). Accessed 30 May 2016.

Chapter 11c

Industrial ecology

Lillian Childress

In 1989, the international community learned that a cluster of factories in Kalundborg, Denmark were arranged in a network unlike anything the world had ever seen (Chertow, 2007). Instead of adhering to the traditional form of production and waste discharge, these factories were arranged in such a way that the wastes from one factory were used as inputs for another, and infrastructure such as steam generation was shared between multiple firms. Cooling water from an oil refinery was used as input water for a desulfurization process, which in turn produced industrial gypsum, which replaced use of natural gypsum at a co-located plasterboard factory (Jacobson, 2008). Each factory was linked in a complex network of energy, solid waste, and material flows.

Within the past three decades, a new paradigm has emerged for the organization of factories within an industrial park. This type of organization is known as industrial symbiosis. The arrangement takes a fundamental ecological process as its guiding metaphor: symbiosis, or the mutually beneficial relationship between two organisms or groups in close physical association. In this ideal arrangement, the effluents of one process serve as the inputs for another, and waste for the whole industrial park is minimal or nonexistent. Energy consumption is also minimal, and the factories act to support their surrounding communities and environment rather than being detrimental.

In order to better understand industrial symbiosis, it is helpful to examine the field of industrial ecology, which gave rise to it.

Industrial ecology

Traditionally, we think of ecology and industry as in opposition. Yet within the past few decades a new field of study has emerged called 'industrial ecology'. This field operates at the intersection of industry, environment, economics, policy, and engineering. In an endeavor to both stimulate economic growth and prioritize environmental protection, industrial ecology draws on the ecological system as a tool to optimize and better understand material and energy flows, and ultimately acts as a guide to designing industrial activity and crafting public policy (Ehrenfeld and Gertler, 1997; Daly, 1991).

The idea of industrial ecology was first proposed in 1989 by Robert Frosch and Nicholas Gallopoulos, two researchers at the General Motors Research Laboratory, in their seminal paper 'Strategies for Manufacturing'. In order to combat growing resource depletion and waste accumulation, Frosch and Gallopoulous suggested industrial activity should be transformed into a more integrated model called the industrial ecosystem. 'In such a system the consumption of energy and materials is optimized, waste generation is minimized, and the effluents of one process … serve as the raw material for another', they wrote.

The field of industrial ecology expanded rapidly in the 1990s. In 1995 Thomas Graedel and Braden Allenby published *Industrial Ecology*, the first textbook on the subject. The first scholarly journal devoted exclusively to the subject, the *Journal of Industrial Ecology*, was founded in 1997 at Yale University. The International Society for Industrial Ecology was founded in 2001. While numerous formal definitions of industrial ecology were proposed during this time, one of the most enduring is from Graedel and Allenby's 1995 textbook:

> Industrial ecology is the means by which humanity can deliberately and rationally approach and maintain sustainability, given continued economic, cultural, and technological evolution. The concept requires that an industrial system be viewed not in isolation from its surrounding systems, but in concert with them. It is a systems view in which one seeks to optimize the total materials cycle from virgin material, to finished material, to component, to product, to obsolete product, and to ultimate disposal. Factors to be optimized include resources, energy, and capital.

Numerous subfields have developed in conjunction with and as a result of the development of industrial ecology as a formal field of study. Chief among these are life cycle assessment (LCA) methodology, material flow analysis (MFA), socioeconomic metabolism, input–output analysis (IOA), design for environment, and industrial symbiosis (Graedel and Lifset, 2016). While all of these fields of study inform each other, they have developed their own distinct bodies of research and methodology over time.

Industrial ecology can operate at the facility/firm, inter-firm, or regional/global level (Chertow, 2000; Lifset and Graedel, 2002). The firm level includes activities such as pollution prevention, design for environment, and ecologically focused efficiency improvements. The inter-firm level is the level at which most activities we typically think of as under the umbrella of industrial ecology level take place. This includes industrial symbiosis and LCAs. Finally, the regional/global level encompasses MFAs, IOAs, and socioeconomic metabolism. These different levels form an important structure for developing different methodologies and ways of thinking about industrial ecology.

Table 11c.1 Subfields and related fields to industrial ecology

Related field/ subfield	*Description/definition*	*Source*
Life cycle assessment (LCA)	A *life cycle* is the combination of production, use and waste-processing systems describing the creation, existence and removal of a tradeable good, i.e. its life 'from cradle to grave'. A *life cycle assessment* can be used to support a decision about a purchase, innovation of production processes or product approval in the widest sense of the word. Such a decision may be based on environmental, social or economic aspects or other considerations.	Heijungs et al., 1992
Material flow analysis (MFA)	*Material flow analysis* is the analysis of the throughput of process chains comprising extraction or harvest, chemical transformation, manufacturing, consumption, recycling and disposal of materials. It is based on accounts in physical units (usually in terms of tons) quantifying the inputs and outputs of those processes. The subjects of the accounting are chemically defined substances (for example, carbon or carbon dioxide) on the one hand and natural or technical compounds or 'bulk' materials (for example, coal, wood) on the other hand.	Bringezu and Moriguchi, 2002
Industrial symbiosis	*Industrial symbiosis* engages traditionally separate industries in a collective approach to competitive advantage involving physical exchange of materials,energy, water, and/or by-products. The keys to industrial symbiosis are collaboration and the synergistic possibilities offered by geographic proximity.	Chertow, 2000
Design for environment	*Design for environment* takes place when firms explicitly incorporate environmental issues in their product design and manufacturing decisions.	Fiksel, 2009
Socioeconomic metabolism	*Socioeconomic metabolism* constitutes the self-reproduction and evolution of the biophysical structures of human society. It comprises those biophysical transformation processes, distribution processes, and flows that are controlled by humans for their purposes. The biophysical structures of society ('in use stocks') and socioeconomic metabolism together form the biophysical basis of society.	Pauliuk and Hertwich, 2015
Input-output analysis (IOA)	*Input–output tables* (IOT) in economics quantify the transactions that occur between different industrial sectors in an economy. They are expressed as flows from one sector to another, measured in either monetary or mixed units.	Graedel and Lifset, 2016

Source: Chapter author.

Ultimately, the study of industrial ecology is a stepping stone to a circular economy. Features of the circular economy include energy and resource efficiency through multiple phases (Yuan et al., 2008; Tukker, 2015), internalization of unpriced or undervalued services into the economy (Andersen, 2006), and the closure of industrial loops by transforming waste at one point in a value chain into input at another point (Mathews and Tan, 2011). This model differs from the economic model that Mathews and Tan (2011) call 'the mainstream linear "raw materials in" at one end and "waste out" at the other – a model that still implicitly dominates mainstream economics, as if natural limits simply did not exist'. While the term 'circular economy' is used widely throughout the literature, it still lacks precise definition and criteria. Yet interest in the concept is rapidly growing, with the establishment in 2010 of the Ellen MacArthur Foundation, an organization dedicated to advancing the study of the circular economy, and a report on the subject in 2012 by McKinsey & Company, a global consulting firm. By recognizing natural limits to economic growth and resource consumption, the circular economy has the potential to revolutionize traditional, deregulated capitalism.

Industrial symbiosis

Industrial symbiosis is a practical example of how an ecological metaphor can be implemented in the real world. The study of industrial symbiosis draws on a variety of classic ecological behavioral patterns, such as loop closing and energy cascades (Ehrenfeld and Gertler, 1997). Additionally, geographical proximity – a prerequisite for symbiotic exchanges in the environment – is also observed in most cases of industrial symbiosis (Chertow, 2000). Many symbiotic exchanges occur within eco-industrial parks (EIPs), which are co-located communities of factories or businesses seeking enhanced environmental and economic performance through co-managing environmental and resource issues (Lowe et al., 1995).

Generally, there are three categories of exchange that can occur within industrial symbiosis (Chertow et al., 2008). The first is by-product reuse, in which the effluent materials from one firm are used by another firm as substitutes for raw materials or commercial products. The second is utility or infrastructure sharing, where common resources like energy and water are jointly used and managed. The third is joint provision of services, where common needs such as food provision or transportation are met for a cluster of firms. Any cluster of at least three entities – none of which rely on recycling as their primary business – exchanging at least two different resources, is generally recognized as an example of industrial symbiosis (Chertow, 2007).

While some industrial parks have been founded and modified on the principles laid out by scholarship in the field, many of the most prominent examples of industrial symbiosis, like Kalundborg, arose spontaneously. There are certain precursors, or 'kernels', to industrial symbiosis, which if nurtured can begin the development process toward complex networks of exchanges. Common precursors of symbiotic exchanges are intra-firm synergies based in co-generation, landfill gas mining, and wastewater reuse (Chertow, 2007). Additionally, a key driver in the development of many EIPs, both planned and spontaneously arising, is the presence of an anchor tenant: a core, stable business that encourages the development of symbiotic exchanges (Gingrich, 2012). Anchor tenants are often large utility providers (Martin and Eklund, 2011).

While many existing examples of successful industrial symbiosis are, or at least originally were, self-organized, government policies can also influence the development of EIPs (Costa et al., 2010). But shaping conducive policy is difficult because, as many researchers have pointed out, it is hard to mandate cooperation. The opportunity to exchange secondary materials is often not enough of an incentive for firms to relocate (Gibbs and Deutz, 2007). Generally, the opportunity for byproduct exchange is only a major factor if the material is the most important input for a firm (Gibbs and Deutz, 2007). Some types of policy have been identified as helpful in encouraging nascent symbiosis (Chertow, 2007): identifying and mapping promising industrial areas; providing either technical or financial assistance to pre-existing factories and industrial parks with precursor features of industrial symbiosis; and encouraging firms to pursue locations where common symbiotic precursors are already in place. While there is no set policy formula for the creation of a successful EIP, governments should be aware of both the advantages and potential pitfalls in crafting policy conducive to industrial symbiosis.

Researchers have only begun in recent years to quantify the economic benefits of industrial symbiosis. Sources of economic benefit arising from industrial symbiosis include efficient removal of byproducts, which can capture revenue streams and cut disposal costs, and receipt of byproducts, which can avoid transportation fees and reduce raw material costs (Chertow and Lombardi, 2005). Additionally, less quantifiable benefits can come through working cooperatively with neighbors, facilitating the permitting process, and tapping into government subsidies and incentive programs (Chertow and Lombardi, 2005). However, the economic gains due to symbiotic exchanges are difficult to evaluate because (1) it is hard to compare existing EIPs to a base scenario where no symbiotic exchanges occur; (2) the complex structure and high cost of EIPs requires large amounts of data; and (3) it is difficult to determine which cost-saving and clean-production measures would have been taken regardless of the firm entering into industrial symbiosis (Karlsson and Wolf, 2008).

Economic analysis of EIPs is often best suited to computer modeling. Process analysis and chemical process simulation (CPS) have been used by many researchers, as well as mixed integer linear programming (MILP), which is becoming widely used because of its ability to examine a variety of different factors simultaneously (Karlsson and Wolf, 2008). Rigorous analysis of the economic benefits of industrial symbiosis has the potential to both illustrate the success of past EIP projects and provide evidence for the economic gains to be had from projects in the future.

Industrial symbiosis has the potential to transform how goods are manufactured worldwide. As the number of connections between firms in an EIP increases, circularity of flows both within the EIP and in the larger economy is enhanced. Currently, only around 6 percent of all materials processed by the global economy are recycled in a way that contributes to closing the global resource loop (Haas et al., 2015). There is much room for improvement. Ultimately, a mix of conducive policy and private sector awareness and willingness can guide our economy in the direction of a truly circular economy, where waste is minimized and natural resources are conserved.

Kalundborg case study

One of the most striking features of Kalundborg lies within its mottled history: Kalundborg was not planned. It was only after it attracted the attention of the worldwide media, which in turn attracted international academics, that Kalundborg was retroactively deemed a prime example of industrial symbiosis. When viewed interactively, the development of the Kalundborg looks almost like the development of a city like London or New York – from open land, to small clusters of 'settlements' (each individual firm), to a large, interconnected mass of firms, each inextricably linked to the other in a network.

The seedlings of Kalundborg appeared in 1959 in the municipality of Kalundborg, Denmark, as the lone factory of the Asneaes Power Station, an oil refinery which used freshwater from the nearby Lake Tisso because of the limited supply of groundwater (UNEP 2002). In 1972, plasterboard manufacturer Gyproc constructed a plasterboard plant. A pipeline was constructed between the refinery and the Gyproc facility to provide the plasterboard plant with excess gas from the refinery. A year later, in 1973, the Asneas power station expanded, and a connection was built to the Lake Tisso–Statoil pipeline. It was during the 1980s that the park began to rapidly expand. Novo Nordisk, a multinational biotechnology company that is a prominent global producer of insulin and industrial enzymes, as well as Bioteknisk Jordrens, a soil remediation and fertilizer production company, joined the party. Additionally, the municipality of Kalundborg receives excess heat from Asnaes for its residential district heating system. The park has added many other factories and other enterprises over the years, making it one of the largest, most intricately connected examples of industrial symbiosis in the world.

By acting in an economically self-interested manner, these firms were actually able to achieve a highly complex level of cooperation. Kalundborg's unplanned nature, however, does not make it inherently better or more achievable than EIPs that are shaped through government and private planning. Rather, Kalundborg serves as a model among the international community for the development of a successful EIP.

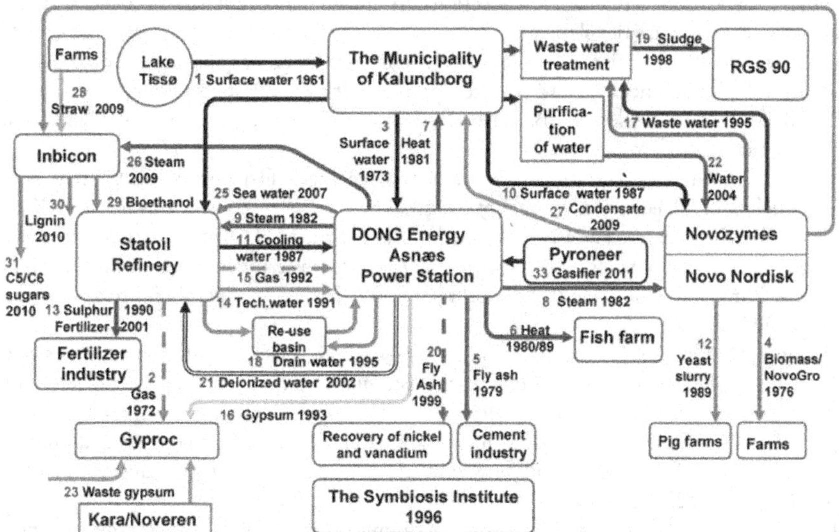

Figure 11c.1 Symbiosis at Kalundborg.

Source: www.kalundborg.dk.

Refereneces

Andersen, M. (2006). An introductory note on the environmental economics of the circular economy. *Sustainability Science*, 2(1), pp. 133–140.

Bringezu, S. and Moriguchi, Y. (2002). Material flow analysis. In Ayres, R. and Ayres, L. (eds.) *Handbook of Industrial Ecology*. Cheltenham: Edward Elgar, pp. 3–15.

Chertow, M. (2000). Industrial symbiosis: literature and taxonomy. *Annual Review of Energy and the Environment*, 25, pp. 313–337.

Chertow, M. (2007). 'Uncovering' industrial symbiosis. *Journal of Industrial Ecology*, 11(1), pp. 11–30.

Chertow, M. and Lombardi, D. (2005). Quantifying economic and environmental benefits of co-located firms. *Environmental Science and Technology*, 39(17), pp. 6535–6541.

Chertow, M., Ashton, W. and Espinosa, J. (2008). Industrial symbiosis in Puerto Rico: environmentally related agglomeration economies. *Regional Studies*, 42(10), pp. 1299–1312.

Costa, I., Massard, G. and Agarwal, A. (2010). Waste management policies for industrial symbiosis development: case studies in European countries. *Journal of Cleaner Production*, 18(8), pp. 815–822.

Daly, H. (1991). *Steady-state Economics*. 2nd ed. Washington, DC: Island Press.

Ehrenfeld, J. and Gertler, N. (1997). Industrial ecology in practice: the evolution of interdependence at Kalundborg. *Journal of Industrial Ecology*, 1(1), pp. 67–79.

Fiksel, J. (2009). *Design for Environment*. New York: McGraw-Hill.

Frosch, R.A. and Gallopoulos, N. (1989). Strategies for manufacturing. *Scientific American*, 261(3), pp. 144–152.

Gibbs, D. and Deutz, P. (2007). Reflections on implementing industrial ecology through eco-industrial park development. *Journal of Cleaner Production*, 15(17), pp. 1683–1695.

Gingrich, C. (2012). Industrial symbiosis: current understandings and needed ecology and economics influences. Ontario Center for Engineering and Publication. pp. 44–46.

Graedel, T. and Allenby, B. (1995). *Industrial Ecology*. Englewood Cliffs, NJ: Prentice-Hall.

Graedel, T.E. and Lifset, R.J. (2016). Industrial ecology's first decade. In Clift, R. and Druckman, A., eds., *Taking Stock of Industrial Ecology*. New York: Springer, pp. 3–20.

Haas, W., Krausmann, F., Wiedenhofer, D. and Heinz, M. (2015). How circular is the global economy? An assessment of material flows, waste production, and recycling in the European Union and the world in 2005. *Journal of Industrial Ecology*, 19(5), pp. 765–777.

Heijungs, R., Guinée, J.B., Huppes, G., Lankreijer, R.R., Haes, H.A.U. and de Sleeswijk, A.W. (1992). *Environmental Life Cycle Assessment of Products*. Report. Leiden, The Netherlands: CML.

Jacobsen, N. (2008). Industrial symbiosis in Kalundborg, Denmark: a quantitative assessment of economic and environmental aspects. *Journal of Industrial Ecology*, 10(1–2), pp. 239–255.

Karlsson, M. and Wolf, A. (2008). Using an optimization model to evaluate the economic benefits of industrial symbiosis in the forest industry. *Journal of Cleaner Production*, 16(14), pp. 1536–1544.

Lifset, R.J. and Graedel, T.E. (2002). Industrial ecology: goals and definitions. In Ayres, R. and Ayres. L., eds., *Handbook of Industrial Ecology*. Cheltenham: Edward Elgar, pp. 3–15.

Lowe, E., Moran, S.R. and Holmes, D. (1995). *A Fieldbook for the Development of Eco-Industrial Parks*. Prepared for the U.S. Environmental Protection Agency. Oakland, CA: Indigo Development.

Martin, M. and Eklund, M. (2011). Improving the environmental performance of biofuels with industrial symbiosis. *Biomass and Bioenergy*, 35(5), pp. 1747–1755.

Mathews, J. and Tan, H. (2011). Progress toward a circular economy in China. *Journal of Industrial Ecology*, 15(3), pp. 435–457.

Pauliuk, S. and Hertwich, E. (2015). Socioeconomic metabolism as paradigm for studying the biophysical basis of human societies. *Ecological Economics*, 119, pp. 83–93.

UNEP (2002). *The Industrial Symbiosis in Kalundborg, Denmark*. Report prepared for UNEP Environmental Management for Industrial Estates: Information and Training Resources (www.unep.org/publications/search/pub_details_s.asp?ID=132). At www.iisbe.org/iisbe/gbpn/documents/policies/instruments/UNEP-green-ind-zones/UNEP-GIZ-ppt-kalundborg%20case.pdf. Accessed September 8, 2016.

Tukker, A. (2015). Product services for a resource-efficient and circular economy: a review. *Journal of Cleaner Production*, 97, pp. 76–91.

Yuan, Z., Bi, J. and Moriguichi, Y. (2008). The circular economy: a new development strategy in China. *Journal of Industrial Ecology*, 10(1–2), pp. 4–8.

Chapter 11d1

Sustainable investing in real estate

Christopher Wright

Introduction

On December 3, 2015, a 'Green Building Day' was organised in Paris as part of the official programme of the Paris Climate Summit. It was the first time the built environment was so prominently featured at a conference of the parties (COP) to the United Nations Framework Convention on Climate Change (UNFCCC). The event signified the growing importance that governments and other stakeholders attribute to the built environment in reaching climate mitigation targets.

Buildings account for over one-third of final energy consumption globally, making it an important driver of global carbon dioxide (CO_2) emissions. According to the International Energy Agency (IEA), achieving the goal of limiting global temperature rise to 2°C – agreed in Paris – would require an estimated 77 per cent reduction in total CO_2 emissions in the buildings sector by 2050 compared to today's level. This is equivalent to the current combined total electricity consumption of South America, Africa, and the Middle East (IEA 2013). This daunting challenge presents both opportunities and risks for real estate investors.

This chapter has two objectives. The first section provides an overview of the growth of the green building industry, focusing on office markets in developed economies. The second section describes the sustainable investment approach of one major real estate investor – Norges Bank Real Estate Management (NBREM), the real estate division within the asset management arm of the Central Bank of Norway – Norges Bank – which manages the Norwegian Government Pension Fund – Global.

The growth of the green building industry

Few industries have developed such a strong and thriving green business constituency as the global real estate industry (Fedrizzi 2015). The green building industry brings together manufacturers of green materials and technologies, architects and developers promoting sustainable design, owners and occupiers seeking green space to buy and lease, and investors seeking 'green premiums' on real estate investments. It is supported by industry standards and regulations that set minimum requirements, provide financial incentives, and encourage greater transparency, which in combination significantly shape how buildings are designed, built, transacted, and operated.

There are five principle drivers that encourage growth in green building design and operation; tenant demand, green building certification, green building regulation, extreme weather risk, and green building technology (NBIM 2015).

Tenant demand for green office buildings

Commercial tenants are increasingly seeking office space with a variety of 'green' features. For property owners, this can positively impact the financial value and performance of buildings. Research analysing the relationship between 'green' features and common metrics of financial performance suggests that commercial office buildings with higher levels of energy efficiency or sustainability indeed achieve higher rents, occupancy rates and sales prices (Lyons et al. 2013; Jackson 2009; Pivo and Fisher 2010; Fuerst and McAllister 2011; Eichholtz et al. 2010; 2013; Devine and Kok 2015).

The 'sustainability premium' has a variety of explanations. First, more efficient and sustainable buildings generally have lower operating costs. For building owners, this reduces operational expenses associated with managing building services in common areas, and associated service charges passed on to tenants. For tenants, it can lower their total cost of occupancy, either directly if they pay for their own utility expenses, or indirectly through lower service charges. As an example, a survey conducted by the European Commission in 2006–2009 found that the average energy savings from sustainability-oriented improvements in existing buildings were 41 per cent per year, and a similar study in the US found average whole-building energy savings of 15 per cent (Mills et al. 2004). Demand for green office space has been found to be higher among tenants in energy-intensive services sectors, for example financial services firms with data centres, which stand to gain more from leasing energy-efficient spaces (Eichholtz et al. 2013; 2015; Wiencke 2013).

Second, many tenants lease office space in green buildings to fulfil a commitment to operate responsibly, and not just to realise cost savings (Bansal and Roth 2000; Malkani and Starik 2013; Mehdizadeh et al. 2013). Companies use their offices, especially corporate headquarters, in their public relations and branding activities. Many tenants carefully select offices in ways that reflect the public image they wish to project to employees, clients and other stakeholders. Many also report publicly on how their business operations impact the environment, including the carbon footprint of their offices (Devine and Kok 2015; Eichholtz et al. 2015). In such cases, green buildings can help tenants reach their own sustainability targets.

And third, many corporate tenants favour green buildings because research suggests they provide better indoor air quality for their employees (WGBC 2014). A European survey of motivations behind workplace strategy programmes at large companies found that attracting and retaining talented employees was the most common, followed by increasing employee productivity and achieving cost savings (CBRE 2014/15). The focus on employees makes sense given that employee costs – including salaries and benefits – often account for as much as 90 per cent of business operating costs. Hence, only a modest improvement in employee health and productivity could have a significant financial benefit for employers. Research has found the demand for sustainable office space to be particularly high in the financial services sector, where staff costs account for a large share of overall expenditure (Wiencke 2013).

Green building certification and benchmarking

Lack of transparency is an important impediment to sustainable investing. If individual investors are unable to differentiate between 'sustainable' and unsustainable' real estate companies, projects, or financial instruments, the market as a whole is unlikely to allocate capital efficiently. Similarly, tenants will only pay a premium for leases in 'green' buildings if information about the relative 'greenness' of buildings is accessible and credible. In real estate, a wide variety of green building certification schemes for new and existing buildings has played an important role in promoting transparency. Certification schemes often set both prescriptive standards, which identify green building practices that need to be followed, and performance-based standards, which identify goals that need to be met. They are entirely voluntary, but have come to define what constitutes green building design and operation, and the process by which building owners can obtain the right to market their buildings as 'green'.

There are different certification schemes across countries. The most widely recognised are LEED and BREEAM, developed by the US Green Building Council and BRE Group in the United Kingdom, respectively. LEED rates buildings as Certified, Silver, Gold or Platinum, while BREEAM has five ratings – Pass, Good, Very Good, Excellent and Outstanding – based on documented environmental performance in the nine categories of management; health and well-being; energy; transport; water; materials; waste; land use and ecology; and pollution. Others include Green Mark (Singapore), CASBEE (Japan), Green Star (Australia), DGNB (Germany), and HQE (France). Furthermore, there are more narrower building rating schemes, such as the Energy Star programme developed by the US Environmental Protection Agency (EPA) for energy and water performance, and the National Australian Built Environment Rating System (NABERS) rating for energy, water, and waste.

It is fair to say that growth of the green building industry preceded the significant uptake in investor interest in sustainable real estate. Historically, it has been difficult for real estate investors to identify what share of buildings in a real estate portfolio has obtained a green building certification, much less whether buildings are operated efficiently. This situation has improved since the establishment of the Global Real Estate Sustainability Benchmark (GRESB) in 2009. It is an investor-driven organisation that has developed an analytical tool to promote transparency and best practices in sustainable management of real estate. Each investment portfolio reporting to GRESB is scored in two dimensions: Management and Policy looks mainly at the manager's policies and processes relating to sustainability, while Implementation and Measurement focuses on sustainability actions and results associated with individual investment portfolios. GRESB ranks participating portfolios, managers and companies in an annual survey. While the GRESB survey does not allow readers to benchmark buildings against each other, it provides portfolio-level results that reflect buildings' underlying age, construction and condition, as well as different practices and expectations across global real estate markets. In 2015, 707 real estate companies and funds participated in the survey, representing $6.1 trillion in institutional capital, covering more than 61,000 buildings across different property sectors (GRESB website, www.gresb.com).

Green building regulations

Many national governments and municipalities have introduced regulations that require or encourage building owners to integrate sustainability considerations into building design, operations, renovations and marketing. The buildings sector has been identified as an important priority in international efforts to combat climate change. Regulations related to sustainability are very dynamic, and more restrictive laws are frequently called for to accelerate the rate of efficiency upgrades in the existing building stock (IEA 2013). Given that most developed economies have building codes that are up for revision within the next three to five years and likely to raise sustainability standards, this creates a significant risk of higher compliance costs for less sustainable properties.

Current laws addressing the environmental performance of buildings can take many forms. First, governments are increasingly requiring building owners to collect and report on energy performance. For example, several municipal governments in the US require the submission of energy data to a public registry for benchmarking purposes (Kontokosta 2013). In Europe, the Energy Performance of Buildings Directive (EPBD) has led a requirement on building owners to obtain and disclose an Energy Performance Certificate (EPC) when selling or leasing a building in most EU member states. In turn, disclosed energy data is often made publicly accessible through web-based registries, allowing the market to benchmark individual buildings with peer buildings. Such information-based regulation can be a powerful driver of better sustainability performance, and more capital allocation to green buildings.

Secondly, some governments are setting prescriptive requirements for building design and operations (IEA, 2013, 77). For example, Singapore requires building owners to periodically perform energy audits, and meet requirements with regards to thermal envelope performance, heating, ventilation and air conditioning (HVAC) efficiency, lighting, air-tightness and sub-metering. Similarly, New York City requires commercial building owners to perform energy audits and install sub-meters in individual tenant spaces. Perhaps a precursor of how buildings will be regulated in the future, a provision in the UK Energy Act 2011 makes it unlawful to lease properties after 2018 that fail to achieve a prescribed minimum energy performance standard. This means buildings that underperform on energy efficiency are at risk of becoming obsolescent.

Third, a relatively new regulatory trend is to encourage owners and tenants to integrate sustainability considerations into lease contracts. Although such clauses exist in a number of countries, they are currently mandatory only for certain leases in France (CMS 2013). A green clause may include requirements for tenants to share information such as energy consumption data, fit out office spaces in accordance with green criteria, or share in the up-front costs of energy efficiency improvements. The latter addresses the split-incentive problem that often inhibits investments in energy efficiency upgrades in buildings. Many upgrades in the areas of heating, cooling, ventilation and lighting offer positive returns on investment and relatively short payback periods. However, in accordance with most lease agreements, building owners do not recover the benefits resulting from lower energy costs themselves, but instead pass them on to tenants in the form of lower service charges. When building owners are unable to directly recoup capital spent on upgrades, they will typically not pursue them. At an aggregate level, this has led to underinvestment in energy-efficiency upgrades in buildings.

Extreme weather risk

An increasingly important driver in promoting green building design is the physical risks that climate change presents to the built environment. The exposure of an individual building to climate change risk – in particular extreme weather events – is a function of its exact location, physical resilience and contingency plans. The high damage costs associated with recent extreme weather events suggest that many buildings were not originally built to withstand storms and floods of the intensity and frequency we see today. Building owners can perform risk assessments, perform building upgrades that make them more resilient, and purchase insurance against associated damage. Greater weather volatility is affecting the ability of investors in particularly exposed areas to insure their assets at a reasonable cost (Bienert 2014). While the financial consequences of physical damage to a building are most evident for owners, they equally affect the occupiers, who may face interruptions of their operations or unanticipated hikes in insurance premiums. Moreover, from the tenants' perspective, extreme weather can also inflict costs indirectly by harming the energy, water and transport infrastructure upon which buildings and their occupiers depend. While some direct costs can be addressed and reduced through building upgrades, indirect impacts are more difficult to prevent and are often addressed through contingency planning.

Green building technology

Technology has an important multiplier effect in the green building industry, as it enables greater efficiency gains at lower cost, thereby increasing both the supply of and demand for 'green' features. The most notable technological innovations are occurring in three inter-related areas. First, innovations in building materials and equipment are allowing building owners to provide building services at the same or higher quality, at lower cost. For example, the replacement of traditional lighting systems with light-emitting diodes (LED), the most efficient and rapidly diffusing lighting technology, together with automated sensor technology, can improve lighting quality while reducing costs, as measured in energy savings, and repair and maintenance. Similar technological breakthroughs are occurring in building thermal envelopes, heating and cooling systems, and equipment and appliances.

Second, innovations in building management technology are providing opportunities for building owners and tenants to better manage utility expenditures. A notable overall trend in the building sector is increased automation. A new generation of building management systems (BMSs) allows building owners to centrally monitor and manage technical services such as heating, cooling, ventilation, hot water, lighting, and other energy loads in real time through a data terminal. In some cases, portfolios of buildings and associated equipment can be networked in a centralised monitoring and management system. A BMS can allow building owners to adjust energy usage in accordance with shifts in energy prices, and take advantage of financial incentives from utilities to reduce energy use during periods of supply shortages. It recognises that buildings are best managed as dynamic systems defined by fluctuations in weather, occupancy and energy prices.

And finally, a new generation of utility meters – known as 'smart meters' – is providing more transparent and accurate readings of energy usage. Since smart meters provide detailed billing per tenant space at short intervals, they can be used by building owners to help tenants reduce their costs related to energy and water consumption, and waste generation. Since tenants are billed for actual energy use, rather than a fixed share of overall energy use in buildings, they have a much greater financial incentive to control their own consumption and ability to control costs. Smart meters are replacing conventional meters that need to be read manually and which typically produce less frequent and more error-prone readings.

Case study: Norges Bank Real Estate Management (NBREM)

The Norwegian Government Pension Fund – Global turns petroleum revenue into financial wealth. When the Fund was established in 1990, the Norwegian Ministry of Finance gave Norges Bank, the central bank of Norway, the task of managing the Fund on the behalf of the Norwegian people. The role of Norges Bank, through its asset management division Norges Bank Investment Management (NBIM), is to provide long-term and professional management of the Fund so that Norway's oil wealth benefits both current and future generations. The overarching objective is to achieve the highest possible international purchasing power over time with an acceptable level of risk.

In 2010, the Ministry of Finance issued a mandate to invest up to 5 per cent of the Fund in unlisted real estate, adding to the existing investment mandates in listed equities and bonds. In 2014, the real estate operation was reorganised as Norges Bank Real Estate Management (NBREM), a separate organization within NBIM with its own leader group (NBIM 2016, 11). By the end of 2015, it consisted of more than 100 employees spread across six offices in five time zones. NBREM has built up a global portfolio of unlisted real estate investments of 837 properties totalling 17 million square metres, valued at 180 billion Norwegian kroner at the end of 2015. It invests in unlisted real estate predominately through joint ventures where both sides invest similar amounts and have a similar investment horizon and philosophy, but also directly as a 100 percent owner.

Sustainability strategy

Unlisted real estate investments differ from listed equities and bonds when it comes to the execution of investment decisions, the management framework, oversight, and control. This is also reflected in how real estate investors apply responsible investment principles. Sustainable investing in real estate – commonly referred to as 'responsible property investing' – is an emerging field of practice in global real estate markets. In broad terms, it captures practices aimed at 'maximizing the positive effects, and minimizing the negative, of property ownership, management and development upon society and the natural environment in a way that is consistent with investor goals and fiduciary responsibilities' (Pivo and McNamara 2008, 117). NBREM's strategic approach is to focus on the intersection between the sustainability mandate for unlisted real estate set by the Ministry of Finance, which calls for a focus on energy efficiency, water consumption, and waste management, and its overarching goal to generate a good long-term financial return with acceptable risk. Underlying this strategy is a belief, supported by empirical research, that sustainably managed buildings are likely to generate financial value in the long term (Eichholtz et al. 2015; Fuerst and van den Wetering 2015).

NBREM's sustainability strategy covers four main areas: due diligence, benchmarking, sustainability upgrades, and certification.

Perform environmental due diligence

Before a real estate investment is made, NBREM undertakes a thorough review of environmental risks associated with the building or buildings considered for acquisition. It uses external experts to identify any materials that could cause harm to the environment or adverse health effects. The land is mainly examined to assess whether there is contamination, either from current or previous use of the site, that may result in environmental liabilities. Due diligence typically includes an inspection of the building, a review of any outstanding violations of building codes and regulations, and an assessment of the physical state of building systems and materials and associated repair and replacement costs. Material findings may influence the financial value attributed to the building.

Benchmark sustainability performance

NBREM uses the GRESB survey to benchmark the sustainability of its real estate investment portfolio (NBIM 2016, 44). It became a member of GRESB in 2011, and more recently joined its Board to promote greater transparency around sustainability in capital markets. It uses the framework to gather information about the sustainability performance of different joint venture partnerships and direct investments, and compare its work on sustainable real estate management with that of other funds. Each year NBREM discusses the strengths and weaknesses of each investment portfolio with the respective joint venture partners and asset managers. The purpose is to identify sustainability measures that can be incorporated into annual operating plans and budgets. NBREM also publicly discloses the overall GRESB scores of unlisted real estate portfolio as a measure of its own aggregate sustainability performance (NBIM 2016, 46).

NBREM seeks to supplement the portfolio-level benchmarking offered by GRESB with building-level benchmarking. While GRESB has increased market transparency at the portfolio level, transparency around building performance on sustainability metrics remains varied. Four trends are likely to make it easier and more compelling for investors to access building-level sustainability data. First, the diffusion of smart meters is making utility data more accessible and shareable in centralised databases. Second, energy disclosure laws are putting pressure on building owners to make this information public, and ensure that their buildings outperform peer buildings. Third, a number of new startups are using big data strategies to estimate the energy performance of buildings using publicly available information, putting pressure on building owners to disclose actual data. And fourth, another set of startups are pursuing business models that integrate energy management services with a variety of advisory and reporting services, which is expected to reduce the cost and increase the benefits of collecting and reporting building-level benchmarking.

Sustainability upgrades

Upgrading buildings to use best available technologies is central to good asset management, and an important aspect of improving operational efficiency and reducing costs. As part of its approach to asset management, NBREM works with its partners to include environmental initiatives in all operating plans and budgets (NBIM 2016, 45). In addition to environmental certification and reporting, its work with partners in 2015 included setting up building management systems (BMS) for monitoring energy, water, and waste performance at buildings across its portfolio, and installing automatic electricity meters to make it possible to analyse energy consumption continuously and identify potential improvements. Together with its partners, NBREM also invested in energy management systems that allow for better utility cost tracking across buildings over time. Measures to reduce water consumption and improve waste management are also routinely part of operating plans.

Certify building design and operations

NBREM's long-term goal is for all its office and retail buildings to be certified. Obtaining green building certifications was an important aspect of its sustainablity strategy in 2015. During the year, the share of its office and retail buildings above 2,000 square meters that had obtained certification increased from 42 per cent to 55 per cent (NBIM 2016, 45). The number of certified buildings in the portfolio increased by 12, of which eight were certified under NBREM's ownership and four were acquired during the year and already certified. In addition, it purchased 12 buildings that were not certified. NBREM expects a higher certification rate over time to increase the quality of its portfolio, reduce overall operating costs, and make its buildings more attractive to tenants.

The notion that certification builds financial value is backed by research, and is accepted by a growing number of building owners, particularly those that predominately own commercial office buildings in developed markets. A survey of building owners in the United States who have pursued LEED certification found that 80 per cent expected to attract more tenants. One study found that rental premiums for LEED ranged from 4 to 27 per cent, and from 2 to 13 per cent for Energy Star (Eichholtz et al. 2013). Certified buildings are also attractive due to the reputational benefits they provide both owners and tenants. Some international companies globally, and many government agencies in the US, have adopted sustainability policies that commit them to only lease office space in certified buildings. Finally, evidence suggests that tenants favour certified buildings because they provide higher-quality building services (Devine and Kok 2015).

References

Bansal, P. and Roth, K. (2000). Why companies go green: A model of ecological responsiveness. *Academy of Management Journal*, 43(4), 717–737.

Bienert, S. (2014). *Extreme weather events and property values: Assessing new investment frameworks for the decades ahead*. London: Urban Land Institute.

CBRE (2014/15). *European occupier survey 2014/15: Creating interconnected value: People, place and property*. Available at https://researchgateway.cbre.com. Accessed 9 September 2016.

CMS (2013). *Green lease clauses in Europe*. Available at www.cmslegal.com. Accessed 9 September 2016.

Devine, A. and Kok, N. (2015). Green certification and building performance: Implications for tangibles and intangibles. *Journal of Portfolio Management*, 41(5), 151–163.

Eichholtz, P. M., Kok, N., and Quigley, J. M. (2010). Doing well by doing good? Green office buildings. *American Economic Review*, 100(5), 2492–2509.

Eichholtz, P. M., Kok, N. and Quigley, J. M. (2013). The economics of green building. *Review of Economics and Statistics*, 95(1), 50–63.

Eichholtz, P. M., Kok, N., and Quigley, J. M. (2015). Ecological responsiveness and corporate real estate. *Business and Society*, March.

Fedrizzi, R. (2015). *Green think: How profits can save the planet*. New York City: Disruption Books.

Fuerst, F. and McAllister, P. (2011). Green noise or green value? Measuring the effects of environmental certification on office values. *Real Estate Economics*, 39(1), 45–69.

Fuerst, F. and van de Wetering, J. (2015). How does environmental efficiency impact on the rents of commercial offices in the UK? *Journal of Property Research*, June. doi: /10.1080/09599916.2015.1047399.

IEA (2013). *Policy Pathways: Modernising building energy codes*. International Energy Agency. www.iea.org/publications/freepublications/publication/policy-pathways-modernising-building-energy-codes.html. Accessed 14 September, 2016.

Jackson, J. (2009). How risky are sustainable real estate projects? An evaluation of LEED and Energy Star development options. *Journal of Sustainable Real Estate*, 1(1), 91–106.

Kontokosta, C. E. (2013). Energy disclosure, market behavior, and the building data ecosystem. *Annals of the New York Academy of Sciences*, 1295(1), 34–43.

Lyons, R., Bio Intelligence Service and IEEP (2013). *Energy performance certificates in buildings and their impact on transaction prices and rents in selected EU countries*. Final report prepared for European Commission (DG Energy). https://ec.europa.eu/energy/sites/ener/files/documents/20130619-energy_performance_certificates_in_buildings.pdf. Accessed 9 September, 2016.

Malkani, A. and Starik, M. (2013). The green building technology model: An approach to understanding the adoption of green office buildings. *Journal of Sustainable Real Estate*, 5(1), 131–148.

Mehdizadeh, R., Fischer, M. and Celoza, A. (2013). LEED and energy efficiency: Do owners game the system? *Journal of Sustainable Real Estate*, 5(1), 23–34.

Mills, E., Friedman, H., Powell, T., Bourassa, N., Claridge, D., Haasl, T. and Piette, M. A. (2004). *The cost-effectiveness of commercial-buildings commissioning: A meta-analysis of energy and non-energy impacts in existing buildings and new construction in the United States*. Lawrence Berkeley National Laboratory Report no. 56637. Available at http://evanmills.lbl.gov/pubs/pdf/cx-costs-benefits.pdf. Accessed October 18, 2016.

NBIM (2015). Global trends in real estate. NBIM Discussion note 02/15. Available at www.nbim.no/contentassets/c199863ae8374916ac15e780662db960/nbim_discussion notes_2-15.pdf. Accessed 9 September, 2016.

NBIM (2016), *Real Estate Investments*, Norges Bank Investment Management, April 2016. Available at www.e-pages.dk/nbim/145/. Accessed 14 September, 2016.

Pivo, G. and Fisher, J. (2010). Income, value, and returns in socially responsible office properties. *Journal of Real Estate Research*, 32(3), 243–270.

Pivo, G. and McNamara, P. (2008). Sustainable and responsible property investing. In *Sustainable investing: The art of long-term performance*, ed. C. Krosinsky and N. Robins. London: Earthscan.

WGBC (2014). *Health, wellbeing and productivity in offices: The next chapter for green building*. World Green Building Council. Available at www.worldgbc.org/activities/health-wellbeing-productivity-offices/. Accessed 9 September, 2016.

Wiencke, A. (2013). Willingness to pay for green buildings: Empirical evidence from Switzerland. *Journal of Sustainable Real Estate*, 5(1), 111–130.

Chapter 11d2

LGP

A case study in sustainable real estate

Harold Bracy

Legal and General Property (LGP) owns over 760 properties in the UK, all with a path towards sustainability (2016). Sustainable property development protects long-term value for a wide variety of stakeholders (tenants and communities as well as investors.)

Recent research published by the Royal Society has shown that modest property refurbishment can dramatically reduce energy consumption (Qomi et al. 2016). It found that targeting the lowest performing buildings in Cambridge, Mass (a mere 16 per cent) can cut 40 per cent of the natural gas usage of the entire city. LGP has already recognized the value in these types of targeted improvements, becoming a leader in sustainable real estate and adding to the value of its investments while consistently meeting ambitious sustainability targets.

Success

Compared to 2010 levels, LGP plans to cut carbon, water, and energy consumption by 20 per cent across all of its properties by 2020. So far, it has seen remarkable success:

- Electricity use and carbon emissions have been cut by 17 per cent.
- Fuel use was cut by 23 per cent.
- Water use was cut by 7 per cent.

Additionally, 87 per cent of total waste is recycled and LGP measures 95 per cent of its suppliers' carbon emissions. 96 per cent of LGP's buildings boast an Energy Performance Certificate (EPC) over F and G.

On top of all of this, LGP's largest property fund, the UK Property Fund, has consistently outperformed indexes, seeing its value increase by 22 per cent over a period of 9 months in 2015, even as it improved all its assets to at least a C-rating.

Strategy

LGP's success appears to reflect a combination of stakeholder engagement and efficient design, with clear benchmarks to facilitate both. Approximately 95 per cent of LGP's emissions are under the direct control of tenants, meaning that tenant engagement is the first priority for LGP. While LGP ensures that at least 80 per cent of its tenants are surveyed by its managing agents, it has been moving from questionnaires to one-to-one conversations with tenants, learning how best to provide sustainable living spaces. Likewise, LGP has integrated sustainability criteria into managing agent contracts, ensuring that an Asset Sustainability Plan (ASP) is executed for all properties. Additionally, LGP measures the carbon emissions of almost all suppliers, allowing it to assess both the embedded and operational carbon emissions of its buildings. On the design front, LGP is targeting the lowest hanging fruit, with plans to refurbish the lowest performing assets, while also ensuring all new properties have an EPC rating of at least B. LGP boasts three properties with solar panels, one that recycles 99 per cent of waste, another that obtains 80 per cent of its energy from hydroelectricity, and improved HVAC systems that have resulted in energy savings of up to 22 per cent.

With the National Energy Foundation, LGP has created 'VolDecs' to guide and measure its substantial progress. VolDecs are an innovative sustainability benchmark that looks at operational data, as opposed to the more theoretical EPCs, which rely on inspections. It is clear that LGP's small steps in engaging with tenants, suppliers and designers with clear benchmarks have boosted the long-term value of these properties for all involved. By staying ahead of the curve, LGP is attracting environmentally conscious tenants and investors by discounting the regulatory and environmental costs to come.

References

Legal and General Investment Management (2016). *Legal and General Property Sustainability Review 2015*. Available at www.lgim.com/library/property/lgp_sustainability_review.pdf. Accessed 9 September, 2016.

Qomi, M. J. A., Noshadravan A., Sobstyl, J. M., Toole, J., Ferreira, J., Pellenq, R. J.-M., Ulm, F-J. and Gonzalez, M. C. (2016). Data analytics for simplifying thermal efficiency planning in cities. *Journal of the Royal Society Interface* (online), vol. 13 (117). Available at http://rsif.royalsocietypublishing.org/content/13/117/20150971. Accessed 9 September, 2016.

Chapter 11e

Infrastructure

Helene Winch

Definition of renewable energy infrastructure

Infrastructure as an asset class is generally defined as having the following attractive investment characteristics:

1 real asset exposure i.e. tangible assets;
2 stable, inflation-linked cashflows, often government backed;
3 long asset life of twenty years or more;
4 uncorrelated to the equity markets and GDP and immune from systemic risk;
5 direct investment can lead to low fees due to low maintenance costs.

Renewable energy is more difficult to define, with solar photovoltaic (PV) and wind energy attracting the vast majority of investment that is currently taking place. This is driven by the investible nature of these proven technologies and their scalability. Additionally, bioenergy (including anaerobic digestion), hydropower, geothermal and marine (wave/tidal) are all included in the definition of renewable energy. One source of 'classification' for low-carbon energy assets is the Global Investor Coalition's Low Carbon Investment registry.[1]

The installed OECD[2] countries capacity for 2015 highlights the dominance of wind and solar PV in the renewable energy mix as well as the historical existence of hydro as a mature technology (Figure 11e.1) with 9.0 per cent and 6.3 per cent share respectively.

Using these definitions, it is possible to see that direct ownership of an unlisted wind or solar PV asset that produces and sells electricity via a PPA (Power Purchase Agreement[3]) at an inflation-linked price has all the characteristics that fulfil the definition of infrastructure. It's worth noting that energy-generating assets that are fossil-fuel based have significant oil price risk as input costs and may not fulfil the core infrastructure criteria due to the lack of inflation-linked, stable cashflows.

Renewable energy generation is a function of solar intensity or wind speed, and income is hence uncorrelated to financial markets or GDP. Historically, short-term weather patterns are mean-reverting, and over medium-term holding periods (of a few years) generation income is stable.

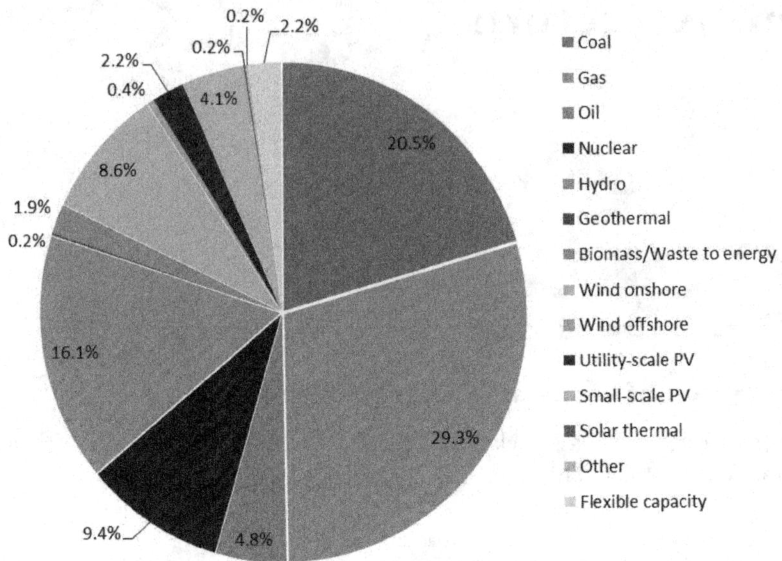

Figure 11e.1 OECD countries' cumulative installed capacity by technology, 2015.
Source: Bloomberg New Energy Finance, www.bnef.com/core/new-energy-outlook.

In some projects, the investor may have some exposure to power (electricity) prices. However in most countries domestic power prices are part of the inflation basket and, with energy price increases, a major cause of unexpected inflation, which can negatively impact an investment portfolio, energy price risk is an inflation hedging, diversifying risk to hold. Renewable infrastructure is also a hedge for carbon price risk (via the power price which will include the cost of carbon) which may exist elsewhere in the portfolio, for example in the listed equity allocation.

In recent years many countries have encouraged the development and construction of renewable energy capacity by offering inflation-linked government subsidies to improve the 'bankability' of the future cashflows – this action, whether deliberately or otherwise, has led to the creation of a huge pool of attractive infrastructure assets.

A note on the importance of assets with inflation linked cashflows: much of the world's wealth is managed or invested with an implicit or explicit domestic inflation reference – whether a sovereign wealth fund such as NZ Super, a corporate pension scheme such as the BT Pension Scheme, or a university endowment such as Harvard.

Market returns and correlation

Historic risk-adjusted returns are difficult to calculate in renewable infrastructure for two reasons: lack of public transparency in the market and the fact that renewable energy is new and developing rapidly as an asset class.

The more transparent, listed infrastructure indices are often used as a proxy to represent the unlisted market. Data series such as the Dow Jones Brookfield Global Infrastructure Index are often quoted. Over ten years this index has returned 8.93 per cent p.a. with volatility of 13.81 per cent and a positive relationship with inflation.[4]

UK yieldcos (listed vehicles comprising of diversified operational assets across wind and solar) are currently targeting a dividend of 6 per cent with inflation-linkage. However, a lack of transparency on tax assumptions, power price assumptions and leverage levels are potential risks to investors.

Indicative long-term unlevered pre-tax returns for different UK operational technologies are described below (OECD countries will have similar returns with variations dependent on local tariff structures):

- UK offshore wind circa 9–11 per cent return. Offshore wind is usually strong and constant, has little physical obstruction and has low volatility compared to onshore wind. Operational costs are higher compared with onshore wind.
- UK onshore wind circa 8 per cent return. Onshore wind is more volatile.
- UK solar PV circa 7 per cent return. Solar PV has very low volatility as solar intensity is generally predictable but seasonal. There are no moving parts so operational costs are low.

In the UK, wind and solar PV are uncorrelated natural resources over a 12 month plus horizon, although over a shorter time period, the uncorrelation is less reliable.[5]

With historic returns unavailable to predict the future under climate change, Mercer's study in 2015[6] entitled 'Investing in the time of climate change' utilised forward-looking scenarios. The summary charts below suggest that renewables as a sector and infrastructure as an asset class would outperform other investments by 0.73 per cent and 0.5 per cent to 3.5 per cent p.a. respectively (Figures 11e.2 and 11e.3).

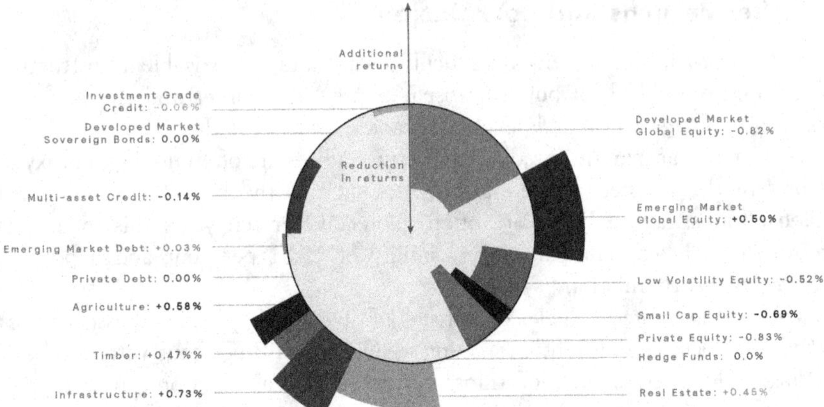

Figure 11e.2 Impact on future returns by asset class.

Source: Mercer, www.mercer.com/our-thinking/investing-in-a-time-of-climate-change.html.

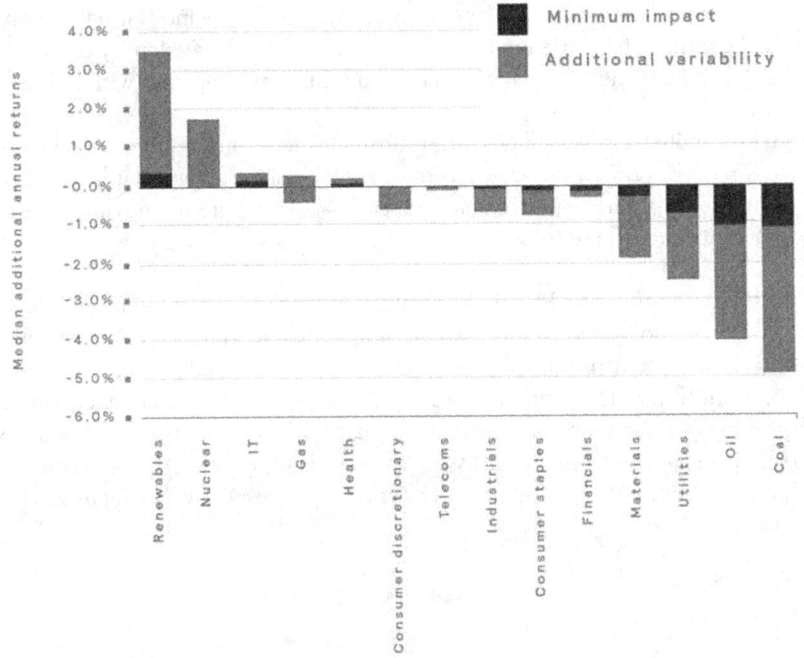

Figure 11e.3 Impact on future returns by sector.

Source: Mercer, www.mercer.com/our-thinking/investing-in-a-time-of-climate-change.html.

Policy risk

Investors generally prefer assets where subsidised income is small and where a project's electricity costs are close to grid parity[7] as a lower risk of default, over a project where the government subsidy provision is a large portion of cashflow.

Competition with fossil fuels

With input costs for many renewable generation technologies zero or minimal, renewable energy generation is able to provide long-term, low-cost electricity, and hence is able to compete with fossil fuel generation regardless of global oil and gas prices.

Operational management

Operational day-to-day management of the assets can be outsourced to a third party who will optimise the operation and efficiency of equipment as well as the sales of the power into the market. Operational costs such as lease costs, rates, insurance and network charges as well as equipment maintenance costs are generally small. At the end of design life, extensions to land leases and planning permission can generally be negotiated and assets will continue to generate, although some assets such as wind may require repowering. Generally, an annual accrual is factored into the operational management costs for replacement parts or decommissioning costs where required.

Financial structuring

While the assets provide the right characteristics, financial structuring can have an impact. Too much leverage can significantly increase risk such as the sensitivity to changes in income due to seasonality, as well as reduce the inflation sensitivity and introduce new risks such as managing the loan covenant terms. Investing in the debt of renewable energy assets fails to deliver the real asset exposure that direct equity ownership provides but includes the same risks. An allocation to direct asset equity can be very concentrated, with one technology or one subsidy regime which, if taken in isolation rather than within an entire asset portfolio, can increase risk.

How much investment in renewable energy is required?

It is generally agreed that in the developed world we need investment to replace the old, inefficient infrastructure as well as to switch from fossil-fuel-based generation to zero-carbon generation. The historical correlation between GDP and electricity demand has recently ended, driven by energy efficiency, meaning that in OECD countries, energy demand is no longer expected to increase with

GDP growth. In the developing world, however, investment is required to build generation to increase people's access to affordable energy (BNEF estimates non-OECD countries energy capacity is forecast to grow from 3,000GW to 10,000GW by 2040.)

The Paris Agreement[8] included commitments on peaking GHG emissions by 2030 (at approximately 40GT CO_2) and reaching net zero emissions by 2050. With infrastructure asset life at a minimum of 25 years (many solar assets are guaranteed for 25 years and will last 40 years plus with no significant additional capital expenditure), we need to start building exclusively renewable energy assets today to avoid building carbon emitting assets that in 20–30 years will become stranded.

BNEF New Energy Outlook 2015 forecasts[9]

BNEF predicts that about 60GW per year of new renewable capacity will be added in the OECD countries for the next 25 years under an assumption of a low demand growth scenario. An estimated $12.2 trillion will be invested globally in electricity power generation to 2040 with over 60 per cent in renewables, mostly solar. BNEF also predicts that renewables will increase from 35 per cent of energy generation in 2015 to 64 per cent in 2040. The transition has begun, with Denmark already achieving 60 per cent electricity from renewables and the UK achieving 25 per cent in 2015 and the EU potentially targeting 30 per cent electricity by renewable by 2030 under the Renewable Energy Directive II.

IEA World Energy Outlook 2015 forecasts[10]

The IEA forecasts that by 2030 we will need to be investing $400 billion per year to have a chance of limiting warming to 2 degrees (IEA World Energy Outlook 2015). The IEA also highlights that investment requirements also include electricity distribution and transmission such as inter-country interconnectors and upgrades to create smart grids that can cope with an increase in small, local generation. IEA estimates new investment requirements in OECD European countries between 2015 and 2040 by technology as follows: $852 billion wind; $357 billion solar; $143 billion hydro; $126 billion bioenergy; $98 billion other.

How to succeed in the provision of affordable, renewable energy at scale?

Estimates vary across every organisation, although everyone agrees that a large amount of investment is needed to switch our energy sources. Some investment can be diverted from existing fossil fuels, which is a subject investors are exploring within the divestment debate. The IIGCC's *Climate Change Investment Solutions* report[11] suggests that to achieve a 2-degree scenario investors need to invest 25 per cent of their assets in climate opportunities. Looking at infrastructure allocations by institutional investors, allocations are currently small varying from 0 per cent to 10 per cent of total portfolios with an average 3 per cent across the larger pension schemes. Using an OECD-estimated value for the total global investment market value of $100 trillion, and assuming that all future infrastructure is indeed renewable under a climate opportunities allocation, the potentially available investment for long-term renewable infrastructure could be circa $3 trillion. However, this investment needs to be encouraged and facilitated to flow into 'investment grade' infrastructure by policy makers and regulators, and with financial innovation to assist investors with delivering their commitments to reduce portfolio carbon footprints and to reallocate to climate opportunities.

In the UK, the Climate Change Act (facilitated by the Committee on Climate Change (CCC)) provides a decarbonisation framework with five-year carbon budgets to be met and requiring a supportive government strategy and associated legislation. Additionally, the UK's recent renewable energy strategy successfully illustrating that government subsidies do work to motivate investment, with solar PV deployment exponentially increasing from 3GW to nearly 10GW in the two-year period 2014–2016 (Figure 11e.4).

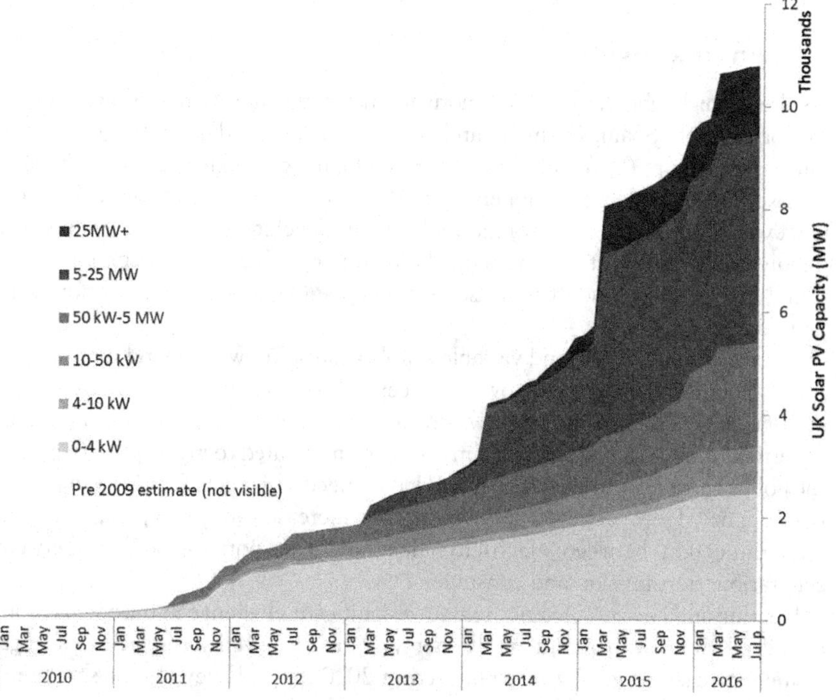

Figure 11e.4 UK solar deployment by capacity, October 2016.

Source: UK Department of Energy and Climate Change, www.gov.uk/government/organisations/department-of-energy-climate-change.

Examples of institutional investors' participation in renewable energy

During 2010–2015 many leading investors invested in 'clean tech' companies including evolving technology developers, and solar and wind manufacturers. Unfortunately, although many of the investment themes became reality, the Chinese government's alignment and support for the same themes and technology brought about unit price reductions through scale which then undermined commercial and investment returns.

More recently, investors such as the BT Pension Scheme, PGGM and the Danish pension schemes (via Copenhagen Infrastructure Partners) have started to invest directly in renewable assets as part of their infrastructure portfolios. These investments all include long-term, inflation-linked cashflows ideal for matching liabilities. Most investors have started in their domestic markets and it is hoped that once they become comfortable with the technology, they will consider global opportunities. Many investors work closely with industry partners to share construction and operational risks and power price management, such as BT Pension Scheme with EDF on onshore wind, PGGM with Triodos, and Copenhagen Infrastructure Partners with Dong.[12]

Known unknowns

As already highlighted, we need to motivate the energy transition – either by subsidy (as for example Spain, Germany and the UK), tax (e.g. the USA), government direct expenditure (Denmark, China), or by a higher carbon tax (Europe, China).

Best practice preference is for energy subsidies to be auctioned to drive efficiency and ever lower pricing for new renewable energy development keeping in line with rapidly falling unit costs. A focus on the technology that gives the best outcome from local available resources is also best practice (e.g. the UK and offshore wind and tidal energy).

Uncertainties exist around variable supply against known demand patterns and the potential role of storage. How will decentralised energy, including off-grid and mini-grids generation, operate? Where does the investment come from – does government have the money? Can investors be motivated to invest prior to getting the policy certainty they feel they need? Do we need a higher CO_2 price to motivate investment? How do we deal with the increase and complexity of the interconnection between electricity, heat and transport, as well as between generation, transmission and consumers?

Heating and energy efficiency remain a significant challenge in Europe. Heating in the UK uses 40 per cent of all energy. When the McKinsey greenhouse gas abatement cost curves[13] were published in 2010 it was believed that short-term paybacks from energy-efficiency projects would ensure that investment flowed, but unfortunately human behaviour and the reluctance to change has proved a barrier to the funding of these projects.

Obstacles to delivering a zero-carbon economy by 2050

Solar and wind 'experience' curves show that the technology costs and hence generation costs continue to fall, efficiencies and load factors are improving, and average site capacities are growing. Solar equipment costs are expected to halve again between 2015 and 2030. Technological innovation in storage is happening quicker than expected. Additionally, renewable energy is fast and easy to construct, with a wind farm taking 9 months and a solar farm 3–6 months – both significantly shorter than other energy generation technologies. Despite falling oil prices, fossil fuels are increasingly uncompetitive compared to renewable generation costs, and this may be exaggerated as higher carbon pricing and supporting legislation develops with time.

However, a problem that remains for investors is the lack of transparency in private markets and in historic data which, if analysed, could show strong investment returns and attract significant investment. The key factors to make markets investible are good wind/solar resources to support cashflows; supportive long-term policy/subsides and a long term 'bankable' energy offtake. One outstanding unknown is the financial modelling assumptions, with renewable assets having high upfront capital expenditure and then delivering long-term, bond-like cashflows with minimal operational or input costs – the question remains: What is the required investment return for these stable and predictable, often government-guaranteed cashflows?

Notes

1 Global Investor Coalition on Climate Change (GIC) Low Carbon Investment (LCI) registry taxonomy published at http://globalinvestorcoalition.org/wp-content/uploads/2015/10/LCI-Registry-Taxonomy_3rd-Release_211015.pdf (accessed 6 June 2016).
2 OECD (Organisation for Economic Cooperation and Development).
3 Google is leading on market practice on developing the green PPAs market, see https://static.googleusercontent.com/external_content/untrusted_dlcp/www.google.com/en/us/green/pdfs/renewable-energy.pdf (accessed 6 June 2016).
4 Cheng, T. and Srivastava, V. (2015) 'Approaches to benchmarking listed infrastructure', S&P Dow Jones Indices published October 2015. (https://us.spindices.com/documents/research/research-approaches-to-benchmarking-listed-infrastructure.pdf (accessed 6 June 2016).
5 Bett, P. E. and Thornton, H. E. (2016) 'The climatological relationships between wind and solar energy supply in Britain'. *Renewable Energy*, 87, 1–14.
6 www.mercer.com/our-thinking/investing-in-a-time-of-climate-change.html (accessed 29 September 2016).
7 Grid parity is when a renewable energy source electricity generation cost is the same as the cost of buying electricity from the market via the electricity grid.
8 The Paris Agreement was agreed on 12 December 2015 at the COP21 by 195 countries; see the agreement at http://unfccc.int/resource/docs/2015/cop21/eng/l09r01.pdf. Accessed September 8, 2016.
9 Source: Bloomberg New Energy Finance, www.bnef.com/core/new-energy-outlook. Accessed April 2016.

10 International Energy Agency. (2015) 'World energy outlook 2015'. www.worldenergyoutlook.org/weo2015/. Accessed September 8, 2016.
11 Institutional Investors Group on Climate change (IIGCC), www.iigcc.org. Accessed September 8, 2016.
12 Further reading is available in the following reports: IIGCC's *Climate Change Investment Solutions*, OECD's *Mapping Channels* and UNEP-FI's *From Disclosure to Action.*
13 Example of the costs curves at www.mckinsey.com/business-functions/sustainability-and-resource-productivity/our-insights/impact-of-the-financial-crisis-on-carbon-economics-version-21. Accessed September 8, 2016.

Chapter 11f

Developments in sustainable fixed income

Ali Edelstein

Sustainable, Responsible, and Impact (SRI) investing was more common in public equities in the industry's nascent years (Roy and Gitman 2012). In 2012, Mercer reported that only 20 percent of SRI strategies were used in fixed income (Ambachtsheer and Burstein 2012); however, that figure has since grown. With approximately $25 billion in assets under management, Boston-based Breckinridge Capital Advisors (BCA) is one of the largest fixed income advisors to focus on SRI strategies. It has integrated environmental, social, and governance (ESG) factors into traditional credit analyses and pursued engagement calls with holdings since 2011. In December 2015, the firm surpassed $1 billion in sustainable strategy assets, signaling a growing interest in SRI fixed income advisors. This interest is due to proliferating global risks, client demand, the increasing materiality of ESG factors, and the rise of green bonds, which reached a record-breaking $41 billion issuance in 2015 (Shankleman 2016). This section explores developments in SRI fixed income investing and delves deeper into green bonds to show progress achieved and improvements that remain. Fixed income refers specifically to corporate, municipal, and national and supranational bonds.

In this asset class, risk mitigation fueled the shift from negative screens or values-based investing to best-in-class and ESG integration, where the market is moving into today. Investors holding 10- and 20-year bonds seek to understand the impacts long-term risks like climate change will have on issuers' assets, revenues, and credit quality in coming years, incorporating findings into credit analyses to assess bonds' relative value. Indeed, when comparing the net income volatility of the 100 top ESG rated S&P 500 companies, BCA (2015) found that its higher-rated ESG corporate credits had less variable earnings. In this way, the long-term nature of sustainability issues meshes well with the fixed income market's longer maturities and holding patterns. Fixed income investors increasingly believe that ESG factors impact credit quality and are asking rating agencies to incorporate ESG considerations into bond credit ratings more systematically through an engagement initiative with the United Nations Principles for Responsible Investment (UN PRI). As of May 2016, the group secured commitments from S&P Global Ratings, Moody's, Dagong, Scope, RAM Ratings and Liberum Ratings (UN PRI 2016), suggesting that ESG may be able to directly affect a borrower's cost of capital in the future. This is a foundational development since ESG data historically did not focus on the fixed income market – which outsizes equities. Client demand for ESG within fixed income strategies is growing, making more comprehensive credit ratings a useful tool for new arrivals to the space.

Client demand itself is also attributable to several factors. First, it is an inevitable result of the sheer size of the fixed income market, which realized $6.4 trillion in new issuance and an average daily trading volume of about $700 billion in 2015, compared to an equity market with a $200 billion average daily trading volume (SIFMA 2016). Low returns are increasing client demand, as well. At the 2016 annual US SIF Conference, Jeffrey MacDonagh, a principal at Grandfield & Dodd, LLC emphasized that 'Having a story to tell behind fixed income investments is a real plus in an environment of low yields.' Indeed, ESG stories are a differentiating factor for some clients deciding amongst a sea of high-grade, low-yield bonds. For others, ESG factors are a more central part of the investment process, playing a key role in investment advisors' fiduciary duties – a viewpoint supported by recent work from the Sustainability Accounting Standards Board (SASB), Professor George Serafeim, and the United States Department of Labor (DOL). SASB's work highlights industry-specific ESG factors that can bear material effects. Serafeim (Mozaffar et al. 2015) traces companies' progress against those factors to show that companies who outperform on material ESG issues outperform others who perform poorly against the same material factors. Finally, in October 2015, DOL reissued its guidance on economically targeted investments by retirement plans under the Employee Retirement Income Security Act to acknowledge that ESG factors may serve as 'tiebreakers' and 'proper components of the fiduciary's analysis of the economic and financial merits of competing investment choices'. Now that employees' retirement plans can integrate ESG factors into credit analyses, many investors' clients are making this request.

Therefore, risk mitigation and client demand led SRI fixed income to where it is today, and material ESG outperformance and impact investments will move it forward. Investors now realize fixed income is one of the most impactful asset classes because unlike equities, whose bulk activity stems from secondary trades, fixed income allows investors to allocate capital to sustainable issuers more directly. Additionally, fixed income instruments provide more insight into what capital is funding through 'use of proceeds' documents, allowing investors to target impact investments like green bonds, whose proceeds go to fund environmentally beneficial investments in projects like transportation and utility infrastructure. Green bonds will continue to grow in importance as their structure and benefits are more clearly defined, and as issuers like companies, municipalities, countries, and supranational entities work together to finance the transition to a greener economy that limits global warming to below 2° Celsius in the long term, as agreed upon in Paris at the 21st Conference of the Parties (COP21) in 2015.

Green bonds

Green bonds are therefore a sub-section of SRI fixed income commonly issued by companies, municipalities, countries, and supranational entities to finance environmentally beneficial projects. The European Investment Bank and World Bank issued the first green bonds in 2007. Five years later in 2013, the Commonwealth of Massachusetts and Bank of America issued the first municipal and corporate green bonds in the United States at $100 million and $500 million respectively. Between then and 2014, the green bond market more than tripled in size from $11 billion to $36.6 billion (CBI 2014) – setting high expectations for $100 billion issuance in 2015. Unfortunately, the market saw only $41 billion issuance in 2015, leaving investors to question why.

After all, strong COP21 commitments and a growing infrastructure require green financing, and current green bonds have performed well to-date. In 2016, emerging markets have already issued $10 billion green bonds – more than double what they borrowed last year (Hughes et al. 2016). Examples include $5 billion in two deals from Shanghai Pudong Development Bank (China), $1.5 billion from Industrial Bank (China), $600 million from Bank of Qingdao (China), and $500 million from India's Axis Bank as recently as May 2016. Markets are absorbing the issuance well, with most green bond deals largely oversubscribed. While the Climate Bonds Initiative suggests that this market is based on flat pricing – where the bond is priced similarly to ordinary bonds or vanilla bonds from the same issuer – leading research from Barclays (2015) shows investors currently pay a premium to acquire green bonds in the secondary market, suggesting primary market trends may change. In the secondary market, Barclays' research (2015) highlights green bonds trading 17 basis points tighter than conventional bonds after accounting for credit risk, duration, and other characteristics. Finally, Barclays (2015) demonstrates green bond investor premiums increasing steadily as the market grows, astutely noting, 'If that spread divergence continues, investors and their sponsors will need to consider exactly how much they are willing to pay to be green.'

And *that tension* over green bonds' definition, benefits, and cost burden is perhaps one of the largest inhibitors to market growth that groups like the Climate Bonds Initiative (CBI) and Green Bond Principles (GBP) are trying to change. These groups seek to more clearly define what green bonds are and to delineate the benefits to both investor and issuer. According to ICMA (2015), green bonds must (1) fund projects identified as environmentally sustainable (2) according to the project evaluation and selection process of the issuer, and potentially a third party reviewer such as Sustainalytics or Vigeo. (3) The 'use of proceeds' is a key identifying factor of a green bond that must be traceable within the issuer's organization, often through a ring-fenced sub-account, and (4) be reported on annually to promote effective use and disclosure. Green bonds that fit this definition help investors increase ESG exposure in their portfolios with minimal risk, fulfill their commitments as UN PRI signatories, and provide impact reporting to end asset owners (CBI 2016), usually at the expense of the issuer since additional costs like third-party assurance and impact reporting aren't transferred to investors in the primary issuance. The issuer therefore currently lacks clear incentives to issue green bonds instead of traditional bonds, hampering investments in climate change progress. However, these principles are voluntary, and a lack of compliance standards means that investors often have no recourse if green bond proceeds are not used appropriately – leaving doubts in investors' minds, as well.

What's next?

Challenges to innovative forms of SRI fixed income investing remain, but that won't stop green bonds and other forms of impact investments from growing. For example, in May 2016, Starbucks issued the first 'sustainability bond' – a 10-year, $500 million offering of 2.45 percent Senior Notes that closely reflect the structure of a green bond, funding ESG projects and issuing annual reports. Starbucks (2016) announced that proceeds would fund purchases from suppliers meeting ethical sourcing practices, the development and operation of farmer support centers in coffee growing regions, and short- and long-term loans made through the Starbucks Global Farmer Fund. These projects aren't new for Starbucks and – while the company commits to reporting on use of proceeds throughout the life of the bond – its SEC filing states it 'expects to allocate the majority of the net proceeds from the sale of the 2026 notes to Eligible Sustainability Projects within one year of the date of issuance'. These factors – combined with Starbucks' great care to avoid the term 'green bond' – leads some investors to question whether the initiative is a sustainability marketing scheme instead of a true commitment to the impact investing movement. Starbucks' executive vice president for Global Coffee, Craig Russell, simply responds by saying, 'This new sustainability bond offers a way for investors to better understand the work we are doing to help ensure that there is a future for farmers and our industry', emphasizing transparency and education. Scott Maw, the company's chief financial officer, adds: 'Issuing a bond focused on sustainable sourcing demonstrates that sustainability is not just an add-on, but an integral part of Starbucks, including our strategy and finances.' Starbucks' sustainability bond closely mimics the green bond structure, but is the first of its kind in name, so its true nature remains to be seen.

In future, the SRI fixed income market will seek scale, standardization, and a clearer delineation of risks and rewards between issuers and investors. Scale in the green bond market will allow green-bond specific portfolios to develop. Standardization will allow for greater end asset owner education, bond comparison, and risk mitigation in the SRI fixed income market – aided by Morningstar's sustainability fund ratings and green bond indices such as Solactive Green Bond Index, S&P's Green Project Bond Index, the Bank of America Merrill Lynch Green Bond Index, and Barclays MSCI Green Bond Indices right now. Finally, a clearer system will develop to reward both issuers and investors for participating in the sustainable finance market. For example, a green bond premium in primary offerings would reward issuers with a lower cost of capital and potentially empower them to pursue environmental projects that would otherwise go unrealized. On the other hand, more innovative uses of bond covenants – namely those that promise to deliver specific environmental or social impacts in exchange for certain premiums – would provide more assurance and less risk to investors, and empower them to more clearly manage their impact as bondholders.

References

Ambachtsheer, J. and Burstein, K. (2012) 'Mercer's ESG Ratings Update: 5,000 and Counting'. Mercer.com Insight, February 13, 2012.

Barclays (2015) 'The Cost of Being Green'. US Credit Alpha, September 17, 2015.

BCA (Breckinridge Capital Advisors) (2015) 'ESG Integration in Corporate Fixed Income'. www.breckinridge.com/insights/whitepapers/esg-integration-in-corporate-esg/. Accessed September 9, 2016.

CBI (Climate Bonds Initiative) (2014) 'Explaining Green Bonds: History'. Webpage. https://www.climatebonds.net/market/history. Accessed September 9, 2016.

CBI (Climate Bonds Initiative) (2016) 'Investor Appetite'. Webpage. www.climatebonds.net/market/investor-appetite. Accessed September 9, 2016.

Hughes, J., Jackson, G., and Hale, T. (2016) 'Chinese Banks Lead "Green" Bond Boom'. *Financial Times*. www.ft.com/cms/s/0/9ee1a5f4-20d2-11e6-aa98-db1e01fabc0c.html#axzz4AGU1PF36. Accessed September 9, 2016.

ICMA (International Capital Market Association) (2015) 'Green Bond Principles'. www.icmagroup.org/Regulatory-Policy-and-Market-Practice/green-bonds/green-bond-principles/. Accessed October 18, 2016.

MacDonagh, J. (2016) 'Fundamentals of Sustainable Investing Workshop'. Personal Presentation at the 2016 Annual US SIF Conference in Washington, D.C.

Mozaffar, K., Serafeim, G., and Yoon, A. (2015) 'Corporate Sustainability: First Evidence on Materiality'. Harvard Business School Working Paper 15-073.

Roy, H. and Gitman, L. (2012) *Trends in ESG Integration in Investments*. BSR Report. www.bsr.org/reports/BSR_Trends_in_ESG_Integration.pdf. Accessed September 9, 2016.

Shankleman, J. (2016) 'Green Bond Market Will Grow to $158 Billion in 2016, HSBC Says'. www.bloomberg.com/news/articles/2016-01-26/green-bond-market-will-grow-to-158-billion-in-2016-hsbc-says. Accessed September 9, 2016.

SIFMA (Securities Industry and Financial Markets Association) (2016) 'Statistics'. Excel sheets. www.sifma.org/research/statistics.aspx. Accessed September 9, 2016.

Starbucks (2016) 'Starbucks Issues the First U.S. Corporate Sustainability Bond'. Press release. https://news.starbucks.com/news/starbucks-issues-the-first-u.s.-corporate-sustainability-bond. Accessed September 9, 2016.

UN PRI (2016) 'Credit Ratings Agencies Embrace More Systematic Consideration of ESG'. www.unpri.org/press-releases/credit-ratings-agencies-embrace-more-systematic-consideration-of-esg. Accessed September 9, 2016.

U.S. Department of Labor (2015) 'New Guidance on Economically Targeted Investments in Retirement Plans from US Labor Department'. Press release 15-2045-NAT, www.dol.gov/opa/media/press/ebsa/ebsa20152045.htm. Accessed September 9, 2016.

Chapter 11g

Financing climate-smart landscapes

Gabriel Thoumi, Brian McFarland and Winnie Lau

Introduction

Financing climate-smart landscapes and seascapes requires capital market participants to recognize the financial implications of the interlocks between landscape- and seascape-level ecologies and the capital markets. Investors and analysts need to have clear understanding of these discrete and specific interlocks if global markets participants want to demonstrate their commitment to mitigate and adapt to climate change. Beyond demonstrating such a commitment, understanding how landscapes impact investment decision-making is a required skill for twenty-first-century financial analysts.

Managing landscapes and seascapes for a 2 degree Celsius warmer planet, which is the temperature increase range that underpins the consensus framework within the Paris Agreement, requires financial analysts to incorporate landscape- and seascape-level criteria into their financial decision-making. For example, to meet the Paris Agreement goals, the agriculture sector globally needs to reduce its emissions by 1 gigaton a year, but a recent study found that the global agriculture sector is three to four times below reaching this goal that is required to keep the planet well below 2 degrees Celsius.[1]

Financial analysts need to incorporate climate change-related variability associated with raw material production – alongside 2 degree Celsius target carbon sequestration goals – into financial modeling. Both chronic and acute risks and opportunities must be included in financial models if these models are to be effective. In other words, global supply chains are rapidly migrating to a 'produce and protect' framework that is focused on jurisdictional-level carbon sequestration and landscape/seascape conservation, alongside the agricultural production required to feed 9 billion people by 2050.[2]

Financing climate-smart landscapes requires investment decision-makers to apply a consistent understanding of how climate change-impacted risk and return models are a function of financial model outliers. At its most basic level, climate change – in itself – is a statistical outlier when examining human existence on Earth.[3] For example, the last time the Earth had atmospheric carbon dioxide concentrations in the range they are today, at 400 ppm, was about 3.6 million years ago in the middle of the Pliocene.

In other words, in the existence of the history of our functioning capital markets – since 1602 and the development of the world's first stock exchange in Amsterdam[4] – markets have rarely experienced both the systemic and idiosyncratic risks now present as a result of climate change. Systemic risks are associated with the collapse of a financial system while idiosyncratic risks are associated with the collapse of a single firm and/or a financial asset. In fact, some data now demonstrate that both climate change systemic and idiosyncratic risks are, at times, driving asset valuations.

Essentially, climate change risk is a statistical outlier – whether occurring only once since 1602 when modern markets began in Amsterdam or once since 3.6 million years ago when the Earth was last at 400 ppm – a 'tail risk' or a 'black swan risk'. But these systemic and idiosyncratic tail risks are now actively impacting markets today.

For example, the $18 billion California water and sewer sector municipal bond market is in the process of seeing its credit spreads widen as investors realize that climate change-impacted drought is causing cash flow constraints and increasing risks that principal will not be repaid.[5] This financial sector's median credit rating is AA– from Standard & Poor's and Aa3 from Moody's. Credit analysts reviewing this sector of the California bond market now require a basic scientific understanding of the natural hydrological cycles – and how climate change is impacting these same hydrological cycles – that 'systematically' underpin the California water and sewer market.

To actualize financing climate-smart landscapes in public and private finance, whether through capital and money markets or through government and public sector mechanisms, the following seven frameworks need to be addressed.

Responsibility

Fiduciaries need to integrate material climate change impacts into the duties, responsibilities, and financial products, goods, and services provided by all financial institutions.

Risk management

Investment decision-makers in the public and private sectors need to incorporate climate change's systemic and idiosyncratic risks into their financial models.

Return enhancement

Analysts must adjust their financial models for opportunities that may drive financial performance. The business case of why financing climate-smart landscapes is prudent and a fiduciary responsibility while mitigating financial risk and enhancing financial returns must be described.

Requirements to invest

Once investment decision-makers understand how climate change-impacted risk and return frameworks are affected, they need to address requirements. Requirements are constraints on financial products. These constraints include: legal/regulatory, taxes, time horizons, liquidity, and unique aspects. In common practice, many social and environmental components of climate-smart landscapes, financial products, goods, and services fall into the unique category. These five requirements will further adjust the risk and return aspects of a climate-smart landscape financial product.

Reallocation of funds

Next, investment policies by these actors need to address frameworks that support moving capital to more efficient risk and return models where climate change's idiosyncratic and systemic risks can be attempted to be addressed. After taking responsibility, addressing risk and return concerns and opportunities, an effective investment decision-maker will reallocate their portfolio to address these risks, opportunities, and constraints. In practice, reallocation is driven by adjustments to investment policy statements (IPS) that describe investors' approaches to risk mitigation and obtaining desired returns within a discrete set of investor constraints.[6] Other policy level tools also exist through capital market regulations and policies.

Reporting of results

Next to last, it is critical that tools that support financing climate-smart landscapes report their results consistently in a manner that enables capital markets and public sector finance support and engagement. Only through consistent reporting can best practices develop over time.

Roadmap expansion

Finally, reporting can drive global roadmaps that further expand climate-smart landscape financing, whether through strategies that enable green bond expansion and independent certification of agriculture products as deforestation free, or through frameworks that implement Intended National Determined Contributions and Sustainable Development Goals.

In summary, climate risk is both a systemic risk and an idiosyncratic risk that is currently impacting global capital markets and public sector finance. Investment decision-makers have tools that they can apply today – the 'seven Rs' of responsibility, risk management, return enhancement, requirements to invest, reallocation of funds, reporting of results, and roadmap expansion– to enable financing climate-smart landscapes. Case studies follow below.

Case study: jurisdictional level programs

Jurisdictional-level programs are national or subnational programs designed to reduce emissions from forests (known as REDD+ for Reducing Emissions from Deforestation and forest Degradation) and other landscapes. Other landscapes include agriculture-dependent landscapes, coastal landscapes, seascapes, and other relevant ecologies. Proposed criteria for 'produce and protect' landscapes include:

- a functional system to measure greenhouse gas emissions and sequestration within the jurisdiction;
- a commitment to adhere to financial, social (e.g. labor), and environmental safeguards;
- an operative policy environment whose timeframe exceeds investment and risk management cycles and supports program-level objectives;
- mechanisms for stakeholder engagement in the development and implementation with stakeholders including investors, regulators, forest-dependent communities, indigenous peoples, and representatives associated with relevant supply chains;
- an overall strategy to reduce emissions, increase food production, provide for financial stability for investors, and improve workers' livelihoods.

Currently, jurisdictional-level programs are globally being financed and funded by various governments, NGOs, funds, supply chains, communities, and philanthropic organizations. These global financiers of jurisdictional-level programs include a US$1 billion commitment from the Norwegian federal government (via the Ministry of Foreign Affairs of Norway) to the Brazilian Amazon Fund (managed by the Brazilian Development Bank), along with additional commitments from Petrobras, the Federal Republic of Germany's KfW Development Bank, the Climate and Land Use Alliance, the Readiness Fund of the World Bank's Forest Carbon Partnership Facility (FCPF), and the UN-REDD Programme.

Case study: palm oil supply chain

As analyzed by Chain Reaction Research in 2016, IOI Corporation, a large Malaysian palm oil producer, was temporarily suspended from the Roundtable on Sustainable Palm Oil (RSPO) after its failure to resolve issues related to deforestation and land grabbing in violation of RSPO's policies. IOI had multiple opportunities to resolve these two climate change related issues – as direct deforestation and deforestation linked to land grabbing release significant carbon emissions – starting in 2010, but it did not pursue this path.

In response to its temporary suspension, IOI sued RSPO. As a direct result of this, 27 major global corporations including Unilever, Mars, Nestlé, Kellogg, and Ferrero have stopped buying from IOI. In the same period IOI's share price fell by 15 percent, and Moody's has placed IOI 'on review for downgrade' from Baa2 to Baa3. Baa3 is one notch above 'speculative'. Baa3 is the lowest possible rating for a company to maintain and still be labeled 'investment-grade'. If IOI were to be rated 'speculative-grade', many global institutional investors would be prevented from investing in IOI, as these same investors' investment policy statements may prohibit investing in equity and debt positions from 'speculative-grade' companies.[7]

Case study: US land trusts[8]

In the US, there are an estimated 1,700 land trusts with 4 million financial supporters and 12,000 full-time staff. Since 1950 these land trusts have conserved over 47 million acres. Their annual operating budgets are estimated at US$1.7 billion. Primary conservation finance instruments include purchasing land and/or purchasing conservation easements placed on property deeds. The Land Trust Alliance, a US association of over 1,100 US land trusts, has supported the creation of Terrafirma, a charitable risk pool that now is insuring 7.2 million acres across 24,000 parcels from 476 land trusts for members against the legal costs to defend conservation and their conservation easements. Finally, many high net worth individuals sit on the boards of these local land trusts.

A possible discrete conservation finance opportunity within the US land trust industry is for financial institutions to provide simple, replicable, and scalable financial instruments to service this sector. Some of these financial products might be existing financial products that have a conservation finance component, such as local credit cards where a percentage of credit card spend finances local conservation outcomes managed by the local land trust, or providing discounted cash management and payroll services to the land trust.

Stand-alone financial instruments might include developing conservation easement asset-backed securities where the financial return might come from the sale of conservation easement encumbered properties whose ecosystem services have improved, resulting in sale to a private high net worth individual. In summary, the US land trust segment may be underbanked due to institutional finance silos. By offering these land trusts integrated financial products that meet their needs, financial institutions can learn to bank these land trusts and provide them with the funding and financial tools they need to expand their operations.

Other market innovations to watch include those seen among: carbon markets (Pope Francis' concerns notwithstanding, growth in carbon markets is being seen in China, California and elsewhere, as well as encompassing new landscapes, such as coastal mangroves and sea-grass beds) and/or establishing a price on carbon through taxation; evolving definitions of fiduciary duty and the establishment of investment beliefs; the possibility of future increased litigation against investors on climate and other forms of societal damage; ongoing innovations in index construction through forms of Environmental Smart Beta, incentives which align strategy and environmental results, as well as changes to perception on asset allocation scenarios and standards across all asset classes.

Increased participation in financial market innovation and further scaling of such recent innovations can bring about the sort of gradual societal performance that is called for by the likes of PwC[9] and others who estimate an annual 3–5 percent reduction in carbon emissions can help avoid the sort of longer-term damage which will otherwise negatively affect future financial returns.

Watching for gaps as to whether such reductions are annually achieved or not in the US is a key metric to measure and watch to understand the ongoing distance from target of what strategies need to be scaled accordingly.

Part of what is also needed to achieve this scaling is a shift in culture on Wall Street toward understanding the shared problem that is being faced, alongside what can be done individually, collaboratively and through advocating for the right policies.

Case study: Brazilian jurisdictional REDD+

Brazil – with the world's largest intact rainforest and the world's largest supply of freshwater, along with being the world's seventh largest economy and the fifth most populated country – is a pivotal country when it comes to financing climate-smart landscapes. On the federal level, Brazil has been able to successfully increase agricultural productivity (particularly within the soy and cattle sectors), while reducing tropical deforestation and mitigating the release of greenhouse gas emissions. These actions were accomplished by a variety of measures including improved forest monitoring, tougher enforcement of environmental legislation, ongoing campaigns against deforestation (e.g. Greenpeace's 'Slaughtering the Amazon' campaign[10]), and incentives for commodity producers, such as the soy moratoria.[11]

On the jurisdictional-level, the State of Acre, which is located in northwestern Brazil bordering Peru and Bolivia, has one of the world's most advanced jurisdictional approaches to climate-smart landscapes. In June 2007, the State of Acre passed Law 1.904/2007 known as the State Ecological-Economic Zoning (ZEE in Portuguese) Law. This law provided the foundation for spatial land-use planning and land-use management throughout the state.[12] Complementing the ZEE, the State of Acre then enacted Law 2.308/2010, known as the State System of Incentives for Environmental Services (SISA in Portuguese), in October 2010.[13] Among numerous measures related to valuing ecosystem services, SISA also established the Institute of Climate Change and Environmental Services Regulation (IMC in Portuguese). The State of Acre, through the ZEE, SISA and IMC, is actively promoting sustainable economic development including improved forest management, cattle pasture intensification, and sustainable fish farming. In addition, Acre is ensuring its actions are open and transparent through numerous public forums, and is promoting social and environmental co-benefits via its independent assessment against the REDD+ Social and Environmental Standards.[14] Due to these accomplishments, it is now posititoned to possibly become the first jurisdiction in the world to sell compliance-grade emission reduction credits from tropical forest conservation activities into the California Cap-and-Trade Program starting in January 2018.

Case study: sustainable fisheries

With half of the world's fisheries at capacity and another 30 percent over capacity, the long-term sustainability of global fisheries is in question, especially with climate change impacts in the ocean and increasing global demand for seafood. In particular, many species of tuna, a high-value fish, are severely overfished. The financial markets are responding to the long-term viability of global fisheries. In 2014, China Tuna Industry Group, the largest supplier of sushi-grade tuna to the Japanese market from 2011 to 2013, failed in its IPO to raise over $100 million to expand its operation in Japan.[15] In its draft IPO documents, China Tuna, rather than addressing the long-term sustainability of tuna catches, stated that a lack of enforcement by the international regulatory bodies (regional fisheries management organizations) would ensure tuna supply – 'there is no sanction for non-compliance with Bigeye [tuna] catch limits'. As a result, the Hong Kong Stock Exchange ordered China Tuna to suspend its IPO.

On the other hand, sustainable fisheries and fishing practices reduce risks for both the industry and its investors. Certification, such as from the Marine Stewardship Council (MSC), can vastly increase the value of the fisheries. In 2016, parties to the Nauru Agreement (a group of eight Pacific small island developing nations) achieved MSC certification for yellowfin tuna. The practices certified under the MSC standards are expected not only to increase the long-term supply of yellowfin, but also to yield a premium product that will increase demand from the European market.[16]

Notes

1 http://thinkprogress.org/climate/2016/05/19/3779777/agriculture-emission-mitigation-gap/. Accessed June 2, 2016.
2 https://blogs.state.gov/stories/2015/12/02/produce-and-protect-sustainable-solutions-paris. Accessed June 2, 2016.
3 www.scientificamerican.com/article/ice-free-arctic-in-pliocene-last-time-co2-levels-above-400ppm/. Accessed June 2, 2016.
4 http://dare.uva.nl/document/2/85961. Accessed June 2, 2016.
5 https://blogs.wf.com/advantagevoice/2016/01/drought-proofing-your-municipal-bond-portfolio/. Accessed June 2, 2016.
6 www.etfrn.org/publications/etfrn_news_54_-_individual_articles. Accessed June 2, 2016.

7 https://chainreactionresearch.com/2016/05/18/the-chain-ioi-threatened-by-possible-moodys-downgrade/. Accessed June 2, 2016.
8 www.unepinquiry.org. Accessed June 2, 2016.
9 www.pwc.co.uk/assets/pdf/low-carbon-economy-index-2014.pdf. Accessed June 2, 2016.
10 www.greenpeace.org/international/en/publications/reports/slaughtering-the-amazon/. Accessed June 2, 2016.
11 www.nature.com/news/stopping-deforestation-battle-for-the-amazon-1.17223. Accessed June 2, 2016; and http://science.sciencemag.org/content/344/6188/1118.full. Accessed June 2, 2016.
12 www.cifor.org/redd-case-book/case-reports/brazil/acres-state-system-incentives-environmental-services-sisa-brazil/. Accessed June 2, 2016.
13 www.gcftaskforce.org/documents/Unofficial%20English%20Translation%20of%20Acre%20State%20Law%20on%20Environmental%20Services.pdf. Accessed June 2, 2016.
14 www.redd-standards.org/countries/latin-america/state-of-acre-brazil. Accessed June 2, 2016.
15 www.theguardian.com/sustainable-business/2014/oct/27/toyo-reizo-shell-companies-fisheries-china-tuna-overfishing-oceans-ipo?CMP=share_btn_fb. Accessed June 2, 2016.
16 http://finance.yahoo.com/news/pacifical-pna-secure-msc-certification-180000172.html. Accessed June 2, 2016.

Chapter 12

Regional differences

Difficult risks, big opportunities

Cary Krosinsky

The world looks very different depending on where you stand, especially when it comes to climate change, but also from a social dimension.

Western nations such as the US and UK have a developed world perspective on climate change, coming from legacy positions of relative economic strength. Here the opportunity is to innovate into the future to maintain positions of global leadership, and even while some worry about what might be being conceded, the diversified nature of their economies remains a source of baseline strength. Culturally similar countries such as Canada and Australia are resource-rich nations already being impacted by a lower-carbon future where the need to diversify their economies is clear. Other resource-rich nations have been financially decimated by a lower price of oil, such as Russia and Venezuela. The European Union runs the risk of breaking apart on the back of the UK's June 2016 decision to leave. Low-lying nations are rightly concerned about sea level rise. African nations are rising up economically, with the mobile phone giving many a chance to start a business, arguably the most positive sustainability development on the continent in centuries.

There are roughly 200 countries in the world and each has a different stance on climate change, largely dependent on where they stand on resources, their economies and the likelihood of their being affected by severe climate change effects.

It is no wonder that negotiations requiring a consensus or even a majority of countries, especially when under the auspices of the UN, are such a struggle to conclude as there are so many issues, and the future of each country's economy is at direct stake.

All of this made the Paris Agreement a real achievement, even if it remains insufficient at what are present-day voluntary levels of commitment, and its ratification, implementation and enforcement remains a separate and ongoing challenge.

What arguably has the best chance to succeed is a vision for every nation on where it needs to get to by a certain date, to stretch those goals to the limit, to line up all of the many parallel efforts that need to come together in concert to give the necessary low-carbon future we require a fighting chance of success.

Here's a glance at three regional perspectives and some of the tougher but critical areas requiring major focus: China (and the work of the UNEP Inquiry into the Design of a Sustainable Financial System), India and the significance of state-owned enterprises and what can be done about them.

We also look at Japan and how a focus on governance and quality seems to lead to financial outperformance, exactly the sort of outcome we seek. We must remain laser-focused on solutions, even in the light of the major challenges we all face in these and many other areas of the world, to finding that right blend of sustainability benefit combined with better financial returns.

Chapter 12a

Climate finance and greening China's finance

Gabriel Thoumi and John Waugh

Taking a step back, it is useful to further understand what climate finance means.

Climate finance is public sector and private sector financing channeled through national, regional, and international governments, non-profits, and private sector institutions and individuals focusing on financial risk mitigation, return enhancement, and structural support for discrete projects related to climate change mitigation, adaptation, and resiliency projects and programs.

What is climate change mitigation, adaptation, and resilience?

Climate change mitigation, adaptation, and resilience definitions do overlap at times yet generally are separated into three categories. Climate change mitigation efforts refer to activities to reduce or prevent greenhouse gas emissions. Mitigation includes using energy efficient technologies and increasing renewable energy investment, and changing management practices and consumer behavior. Climate change adaptation seeks to lower the risks posed by current and forecasted consequences of climate change. Climate change resilience is the capacity of the socio-ecological system to absorb climate change stresses while maintaining its ability to function, adapt, and evolve better functioning systems in the face of ongoing climate change.

Financial risk, return, and underlying structures

Finance is both the study of financial flows and associated movements and the ability to provide funding for a discrete set of activities by an institution or individual. Analyzing financial mechanisms to provide funding generally follows a risk and return model, or in similar economic terms, a cost–benefit model. Funding will be deployed through financial mechanisms if risks per unit return meet investors' objectives. Because of this, climate finance mechanisms overall are focused on (1) decreasing risk per unit return, (2) increasing return for similar amounts of risk, and (3) providing underlying structural support to increase supply and/or demand for specific climate finance instruments.

For example, decreasing risk per unit return can occur through public sector loan guarantees, tax breaks and incentives, and policy changes, and through private sector scaling-up financial mechanisms to benefit from economies of scale, improving analysis to map climate change impacts on physical and financial risks, and launching and expanding new product sets to meet growing demand. Likewise, increasing return for similar amounts of risk for the public sector can occur through revenue guarantees, tax breaks and incentives, and for the private sector through innovative product development and other pathways. Finally, both public sector and private sector mechanisms can provide and benefit from underlying structural support. This occurs through direct and indirect government policies and private sector actions to support broader climate finance sectoral investments.

Financial risk, return, and underlying structures in underlying frameworks

To actualize financing climate change mitigation, adaptation, and resilience, whether through capital and money markets or through government and public sector mechanisms, the following seven frameworks need to be addressed. These frameworks can be thought of thematically:

1. *Responsibility*: Fiduciaries need to integrate climate change impacts into the financial products, goods, and services provided by all financial institutions.
2. *Risk management*: Investment decision makers in the public and private sectors need to incorporate climate change's systemic and idiosyncratic risks into their financial models.
3. *Return enhancement*: Analysts must adjust their financial models for opportunities that may drive financial performance.
4. *Requirements to invest*: Once investment decision-makers understand how climate change can impact on risk and return frameworks, they need to address requirements to achieve these outcomes. Requirements are constraints on financial products. These constraints include:
   a. legal/regulatory,
   b. liquidity,
   c. taxes,
   d. time horizons, and
   e. unique aspects.

   In common practice, many social and environmental components of climate-smart landscapes, financial products, goods, and services fall into the unique category. These five requirements will further adjust the risk and return aspects of a climate-smart landscape financial product.
5. *Reallocation of funds*: Next, investment policies by these actors need to address frameworks that support moving capital to more efficient risk and return

models where climate change's idiosyncratic and systemic risks can be attempted to be addressed.

6 *Reporting of results*: Next to last, it is critical that consistent reporting develop over time, in a manner that can be easily attested, audited, validated, and verified.

7 *Roadmap expansion*: Finally, expanding roadmaps for all relevant financial activities is required to further industries' progress.

Many aspects of these seven steps overlap. Table 12a.1 below describes some examples. Many other examples could also be described.

Table 12a.1 Examples of risk return frameworks

	Public sector	*Private sector*
Decreasing risk per unit return	*Responsibility*: green procurement programs, EU directive on ESG listing standards for publicly traded companies, UK law on reporting carbon emissions by UK entities, improving disclosure/reporting *Reallocation of funds*: public pension funds and sovereign wealth funds, mandatory climate change considerations	*Responsibility*: incorporating climate risk into fiduciary responsibility for all asset management activities *Reallocation of funds*: choosing to invest in low-carbon emissions technology given its decreasing risk per unit return *Return enhancement*: securitization, green bonds
Increasing return per unit risk	*Requirements to invest*: incorporating climate risk into fiduciary responsibility for public finance activities	*Requirements to invest*: incorporating climate risk into fiduciary responsibility for all asset management activities *Risk management*: accurately modeling supply chain risk (e.g. palm oil, soy, timber, cattle, etc.)
Structural support	*Reporting of results*: policy structures: government emissions accounting *Roadmap expansion*: carbon markets, RINs, conservation finance tools, financing resilience and adaptation activities	*Reporting of results*: exchange level listing standards *Roadmap expansion*: climate-smart landscape incentives

Source: Chapter authors.

Measuring climate finance cash flows

Climate finance activities can be broken down into renewable energy, energy efficiency, transport, land-use, adaptation, and disaster risk reduction. Global tracking of total sums invested each year in each of the six categories by the private sector, public sector DFI and international finance, and public domestic budgets is not complete. Yet, data that do exist demonstrate that some sectors are receiving more funding than others. Research suggests that in 2015 total climate finance was around $391 billion,[1] excluding categories that have data collection problems. This means that data do contain selection bias that may lead to undercounting of totals by subgroup.

The majority of this $391 billion of invested capital has been delivered to renewable energy projects and programs globally. Roughly 50 percent of financing has been delivered in the East Asian, Pacific and Western European regions. Many significant territories and population centers have received very little climate finance capital, including much of Latin America, parts of North America, Africa, the Middle East, and Sub-continental Asia.

China's green economy transition

China has made switching its economy to a low-pollution model a key strategy.[2] Key priorities include clean energy, industrial energy conservation, building energy conservation, transport energy conservation, improvement of energy efficiency, and environmental pollution control. China needs to invest $460 billion annually from 2015 to 2020 to achieve this goal. Of this capital, 70 percent needs to come from private sector capital market financial instruments.

Meanwhile, China's financial system is evolving, so that alignment of financial system evolution and green economy demands and constraints needs to be considered in a manner such that greening China's economy enables the financial system to develop. Constraints do exist for China. Price signals are not well-aligned. A focus on short-term investment prohibits long-term climate change mitigation, adaptation, and resilience. Frameworks are uncertain and may be confusing. This is complicated by divergent institutional interests.

Yet consensus is emerging regarding the requirement to report information, the responsibility to improve the financial system, the need for return enhancement and risk mitigation so that assets are appropriately priced and do not become stranded, clear understanding of the requirements to invest to enable market growth in green bonds and other instruments, and finally, the desire to expand the roadmap to broader, economy-wide concerns and constraints such as public health.

This work has been championed at length by the UNEP Inquiry into the Design of a Sustainable Financial System,[3] whose *Greening China's Finance* report is a must-read among the dozens of reports available on its website.[4] The recommendations of *Greening China's Finance* can be summarized in the framework shown in Box 12a.1 below.

Box 12a.1 Greening China's finance: framework for action

a Establish and strengthen legal frameworks – including environmental and law enforcement legislation – that contribute to the demand for green finance.

b Improve coordination and information sharing between environmental, financial and industrial regulators and with third-party institutions.

c Develop comprehensive policy support for green finance.

 i Align monetary policy with sustainable development goals.

 ii Continue to strengthen green credit policies in banking.

 iii Provide incentives to expand the market for green securities, including green bonds.

 iv Expand the scope of green insurance and strengthen environmental liability insurance regulations.

 v Use fiscal incentives to accelerate the development of green finance markets.

d Foster the development of the information infrastructure with information on environmental costs and a green credit rating system.

e Green the policy banks as leaders in establishing markets and best practices for commercial banks.

The UNEP Inquiry has been influential in changing the dialogue, establishing gaps in regional markets that need filling by both public and private means, and through directly working with central bankers and others on implementable solutions. We won't go into great detail about the work of the Inquiry as it would simply repeat what you can find on their website, but suffice to say it is a treasure trove of useful information and analysis on what is needed to fix global and regional financial systems and what gaps remain.

Climate finance gaps

In other regions, and in general, it can be difficult to disaggregate climate financing from financing for development more broadly, because there is overlap between climate resilience, food security, and disaster risk reduction.

This may explain some undercounting, for example, for sub-Saharan Africa, which has very low greenhouse gas emissions, and where energy investment is still relatively low. Because Africa is home to some of the most vulnerable populations, and has relatively low levels of resilience, the focus has been on adaptation support from public sources. A development-first approach to climate adaptation provides an opportunity for a less reactive, more strategic approach to climate finance in Africa. Such an approach can increase options and improve the resilience of communities, businesses, and governments. For example, the Power Africa initiative seeks to double the access to electricity in sub-Saharan Africa, where two out of three people presently lack access. Universal access, which would require approximately $300 billion in investments over the next 15 years, has the potential to transform land use and livelihood options in ways that can substantially reduce greenhouse gas emissions through sustainable land use while enhancing the capacity to withstand climate shocks.

The UN International Strategy for Disaster Risk Reduction reports that the $1 trillion in losses from natural disasters in the past decade may have been underestimated by at least 50 percent. Investment in disaster response outpaces investment in disaster prevention by nearly 10:1, according to the Overseas Development Institute. However, as evidence of climate-related risk mounts, disaster risk reduction is increasingly viewed as a climate-smart investment rather than an external cost.

Climate finance should therefore be expected to be a growth sector in the coming decade, especially as the urgent necessity to fill such gaps becomes even clearer.

Notes

1 http://climatepolicyinitiative.org/publication/global-landscape-of-climate-finance-2015/. Accessed September 7, 2016.
2 www.unep.org/newscentre/default.aspx?DocumentID=26802&ArticleID=34981. Accessed September 7, 2016.
3 http://unepinquiry.org/. Accessed September 7, 2016.
4 http://unepinquiry.org/?s=&post_type=publication. Accessed September 7, 2016.

Chapter 12b

India's energy future

Emily Rutland

Growing economies like India's are projected to contribute over half of the global increase in carbon emissions over the next 25 years as a result of population increase and industrial development. With a population of around 1.3 billion people, India is the world's third largest energy consumer. Despite this, however, a staggering 300 million citizens lack energy access, a number that is projected to increase along with electricity generation and consumption.

Under Prime Minister Narendra Modi's government, which took office in 2014, the subcontinent is beginning to see robust economic and developmental growth. In order to accommodate India's economic and population growth, India's energy production and consumption is predicted to increase significantly. By 2040, the International Energy Agency projects that India's energy consumption will be more than OECD Europe combined, and approaching that of the US.[1]

In order for India to be internationally competitive as an economic and industrial power, access to low-cost, reliable electricity will be fundamental. India currently faces the challenge of balancing the energy needs of its growing population and economy with the global effort and commitment to reduce carbon emissions.[2]

The Paris talks

The Paris conference in late 2015 was an unprecedented and historic deal to address climate change. Led by Prime Minister Modi, India signed a final agreement that safeguards the principle of 'common but differentiated responsibility'[3] – the principle that puts responsibility on developed nations to drastically cut their carbon emissions and develop economic and technological methods to mitigate and adapt to climate change.

In his opening speech at the Paris negotiations, Modi urged that the amount of carbon that can be further emitted before breaching the average temperature threshold must be equally and fairly distributed.[4]

India is taking a more active stance in ensuring carbon reductions, pushing for greater financing and capacity building for its transition to renewable energy. Developed nations pledged to raise 100 billion dollars annually by 2020 (with a commitment for further financing afterwards) while India sought 2.5 trillion dollars to achieve its INDC by 2030. While the agreement is not legally binding, India signed in a spirit of compromise. Modi tweeted after the conference that the result was 'a win for climate justice'.[5]

Rising temperatures present a direct threat to the lives and livelihood of Indian citizens. Achieving the 1.5-degrees target will prevent jeopardizing the lives of millions of people along the coastline and those dependent on agricultural yields who are at risk.[6]

India's low-carbon transition promises not only environmental rewards, but economic gains too. Climate Policy Initiative (CPI) analysis indicates that, with the right policies – those that encourage innovation and reduce demand such as taxes or terminating fossil fuel subsidies – India's low-carbon transition would free up significant financial capacity – an estimated investment capacity increase of $600 billion – over the next 20 years to in turn invest in better economic and development growth. While India is attempting to meet ambitious energy and developmental goals with limited financial resources, there is evidence that the country could actually maximize its financial capacity to meet these goals while transitioning to a low-carbon economy. Renewable energy sources have reduced operational cost compared to coal – high and volatile costs for coal and gas extraction and transportation – and these savings can in turn provide financial capacity to fuel economic and developmental progress.[7]

Policy decisions will be critical, not only for India, but for nations around the world:

> with the right policy choices, over the next twenty years India and the rest of the world can achieve the emissions reductions necessary for a safer, more stable climate and still free up billions for investment in development and other parts of the economy.[8]
>
> (David Nelson, senior director, Climate Policy Initiative)

Coal

India's renewable energy goals are ambitious, with the aim to increase the installed capacity of renewable technologies to 175 gigawatts in 2022, up from around 65 gigawatts in early 2015 (distribution: 100 GW of solar power, 60 GW wind energy, 10 GW small hydro power, and 5 GW biomass-based power projects operational). Recently, Piyush Goyal, India's energy minister, shortened this timeframe by two years, aiming to achieve the total target of 175 GW of renewable energy capacity – over seven times more renewable energy capacity than is currently used in the UK – by 2020.[9]

While India is working toward these renewable energy targets, the country is simultaneously expanding its coal-fired electricity generation capacity. While it is true that many OECD countries have already delivered on commitments to reduce their use of coal and oil, this rate has been more than offset by higher consumption in highly populated emerging countries such as India, China, and those in

Southeast Asia. In India, thermal coal imports have increased from almost zero in the 1990s to overtaking Japan as the world's second largest coal importer by 2013. In 2012, coal-fired electricity accounted for 60 percent of India's installed capacity and 71 percent of its electricity generation.[10]

While coal will remain an inevitable energy source in the short term, Goyal believes that India can still follow a less polluting path to development, despite expanding the coal sector, and claims that India will be a 'renewables superpower' while also experiencing rapid coal expansion.[11]

This reliance on coal is projected to continue for the foreseeable future, with the goal of boosting domestic production and reducing reliance on foreign imports. Coal India Ltd. – reportedly the world's largest coal producer, accounting for more than 80 percent of coal production in India – has been increasing production volumes. Modi estimates that Coal India's production will rise to 1 billion tons per year by 2020.[12]

The former head of climate negotiations at the UNFCCC and current director-general at the Global Green Growth Institute in South Korea, Yvo de Boer, has an interesting perspective on coal. He calls for continued use of coal in India, so long as it is used more efficiently. Declining to back the growing fossil fuel divestment movement, de Boer argued that 'a proper price on carbon' would be a better way of tracking climate change rather than to 'declare war' on a particular technology or fuel category. Until this price on carbon is put in place, however, coal will be necessary in emerging economies like India's.[13]

Coal, de Boer asserts, will be a 'necessary part of the energy mix for decades to come' for emerging economies: 'You really have to be able to offer these countries an economically viable alternative before you begin to rule out coal'.[14]

This approach to coal is controversial in the realm of climate finance. In 2014, the OECD Finance Inventory indicated that wealthy nations had mobilized \$62 billion of investment to help poor nations mitigate the impacts of climate change; however, while both Japan and Australia believe that funding for high efficiency coal plants should be considered as climate finance, the \$3.2 billion that Japan provided to the coal sector was discounted from this total.[15]

De Boer agrees that new coal projects should be considered climate finance. However, it will be necessary that these new coal plants are built to be as efficient as possible.[16] In fact, from 2017, all new coal-fired projects developed in India are required to use supercritical technology or better (supercritical technology is far more efficient than subcritical plants, using less coal and generating fewer emissions).[17]

India currently includes highly efficient coal plans in its recent national climate change strategy, recognizing that coal will continue to play a major role in India's energy mix:

> it's a question of ideology … If I look at the Indian national plan, India has very clear goals on renewables, but it has also openly said 'we are going to rely very significantly on coal, we are going to focus specifically on domestic coal', which is not exactly the best quality coal in the world.[18]

Thus, it could actually be counter-productive for international entities to ignore the implications of India's plan, the consequence being that India may not opt for ultra-supercritical coal-fired generation, instead going for something that results in higher pollution. Ultimately, de Boer insists, the political question is how much money is being mobilized to help developing countries in the context of their specific climate action plans.[19]

This coal expansion is not without its own constraints, however. While India has plans to almost double its coal production to 1 billion tons by 2020, this growth is likely to be constrained by limited land access, lengthy approval processes, inadequate transportation systems and poor productivity as a result of outdated production techniques. The increased use of advanced coal-fired generation technologies will require high quality coal that is not available in large quantities in India, thus resulting in continued reliance on imports.[20]

In order to accelerate the transition to renewable energy and meet these goals, however, the Indian government must address the huge financial debt – several billion dollars worth – accrued by state power utilities, which has prevented it from increasing the share of renewable energy in the electricity mix, despite mandatory renewable energy procurement targets. The government has recently announced a comprehensive financial package to restructure this debt.[21]

In addition to India's internal attempts to manage its debt, the subcontinent is receiving investments worth over 100 billion US dollars, driving an unprecedented shift to renewable energy in India. As of October 2015, there were more than a dozen major deals in the renewable energy sector.[22]

Reliance Power, one of the main private electricity generators in India, is reported to be abandoning almost its entire coal- and gas-fired generation plant expansion plans, focusing instead on profitable growth which, in India, almost entirely revolves around solar and hydroelectric expansion plans:[23]

> Smart money is backing renewable energy ... India is executing one of the most radical energy sector transformations ever undertaken and this year has shown that the flow of finance is matching the ambition.[24]

How can India accelerate its transition to low-carbon?

In order for India to deliver on its ambitious renewable energy targets, implementation and delivery are critical. The complexity of India's energy sector, characterized by a complicated institutional structure, makes policy development difficult, resulting in continued weakness in energy policy. Significant electricity storage and flexible generation capacity are necessary before renewable energy sources may be used as direct substitutes for fossil fuels.[25]

Notes

1. 'World Energy Outlook 2015'. *Springer Reference* (n.d.): n. pag. International Energy Agency, 2015. Web.
2. 'Coal in India 2015'. *Coal Information* (2015): n. pag. Industry.gov. Australian Government Department of Industry and Science, June 2015. Web.
3. Clark, Pilita. 'COP21 Paris Climate Talks: Modi Tells Rich Nations to Do Their Duty – FT.com'. *Financial Times*, 29 November 2015. Web. 8 June 2016.
4. Shankleman, Jessica. 'Former UN Climate Chief: Why Efficient New Coal Plants Should Qualify for "Climate Finance"' www.businessgreen.com. *Business Green*, 13 October 2015. Web. 8 June 2016.
5. See note 4 above.
6. See note 4 above.
7. 'A Low-Carbon Energy Transition in India Can Free Up More Than $600 billion in Investment Capacity to Support Economic Development – CPI'. Climate Policy Initiative, 29 October 2014. Web. 8 June 2016.
8. See note 7 above.
9. See note 2 above.
10. See note 2 above.
11. Carrington, Damian. 'India Will Be Renewables Superpower, Says Energy Minister'. *Guardian*, 1 October 2014. Web. 8 June 2016.
12. Swarup, Anil. 'Indonesia Investments'. *India Boosts Domestic Coal Production: Pressure on Coal Prices*. Indonesia-Investments, 9 February 2016. Web. 8 June 2016.
13. Darby, Megan. 'Former UN Climate Chief Yvo De Boer Defends Coal Finance'. *Climate Home*, 11 April 2015. Web. 8 June 2016.
14. See note 13 above.
15. See note 4 above.
16. See note 4 above.
17. See note 2 above.
18. See note 4 above.
19. See note 4 above.
20. See note 2 above.
21. Mittal, Smiti. 'India Aims to Achieve Colossal Renewable Energy Targets 2 Years in Advance'. *Clean Technica*, 9 November 2015. Web. 8 June 2016.
22. 'US$100 Billion in New Renewable Investments Power Indian Energy Transition'. *Blue & Green Tomorrow*, 12 November 2015. Web. 8 June 2016.
23. See note 22 above.
24. See note 22 above.
25. See note 2 above.

Chapter 12c

The need for sustainable action by state-owned enterprises

Morgan Smiley

Introduction

As a group, state-owned enterprises (SOEs) have not emerged as leaders in the response to global climate change concerns. Institutional investors, fully publicly traded companies, investment banks, non-governmental organizations, concerned government actors, and activist groups have all played a role in the global efforts to mitigate climate change. SOEs, for the most part, are nowhere to be found. This chapter argues that SOEs have an important role to play in these efforts. SOEs uniquely have the capability to help solve two significant problems plaguing the global energy landscape, i.e., the risk of stranded assets and the deficit of green financing. This chapter will explain the significance of these two problems, introduce some of the actions already taken by other groups, justify the argument that SOEs should act now, and outline what actions SOEs could and should be taking.

Why is action needed? The dual problems of the financial risk of stranded assets and a deficit of green financing

Stranded assets

The stated goal of the nations represented at COP21 to not exceed the 2°C warming limit would leave much of the world's fossil fuel reserves unburnable, which would render much of the capital expenditures of international oil companies (IOCs) and national oil companies (NOCs) unnecessary and wasted. Using just the reserves listed on the world's stock markets in the next forty years would take us beyond the 2°C warming limit. The situation is even more pressing considering that SOEs or private companies hold two-thirds of the world's fossil fuels. Moreover, there is still expected discovery of new reserves built into companies' capital expenditure plans (CTI 2011, 8–9).

According to UN IPCC, under the 2°C warming limit it is projected that the world can use up only about one-third of its proven reserves by 2050 (Dumaine

2015). The International Energy Agency (IEA) also concluded that 'no more than one-third of proved reserves of fossil fuels can be consumed prior to 2050 if the world is to achieve the 2°C goal, unless carbon capture and storage (CCS) technology is widely deployed' (Heede and Oreskes 2015, 12). Fifty percent of the financial value of oil companies comes from their reserves. As a result, stranded assets and unburnable carbon have the potential to lead to huge impairment charges and very significant financial losses for affected companies (CTI 2011, 2,19).

Kepler Cheuvreux projected that the fossil fuels industry would lose $28 trillion in cumulative gross revenues between 2013 and 2035 under the IEA's 2°C warming compatible scenario when compared with the IEA's New Policies Scenario, its base-case scenario (Lewis 2014; Baron and Fischer 2015, 9–10). Citigroup projected that the level of stranded assets in the fossil fuels industry between now and 2050 under the 2°C scenario is just over $100 trillion (Parkinson 2015). It used McGlade and Ekins's analysis that found that worldwide a third of oil reserves, half of gas reserves, and between 82 and 88 percent of all coal reserves would need to remain unused from 2010 to 2050 in order to meet the 2°C target (McGlade and Ekins 2015, 187, 189). These projections highlight the damage that stranded assets and the ensuing carbon bubbles would cause to financial markets (Heede and Oreskes 2015, 13).

Deficit of green financing

According to Bloomberg New Energy Finance, in 2014 there was new investment of $310 billion globally into clean energy. This amount may seem like an impressive sum of money, but the current financing for green projects, provided by mostly private equity, is not sufficient to enable the transitions that are needed. According to the IEA, we need to invest $1 trillion a year if we are to decarbonize fast enough to mitigate the worst effects of climate change. This investment requirement is known as the 'clean trillion' target (Mills 2015; Dumaine 2015).

Why must state-owned enterprises act?

SOEs are not among the groups responding to the concerns about stranded assets and the deficit of green financing. Many of the oil SOEs are at least partially publicly traded. As a result, they have an ethical responsibility to the global citizens whose pension and retirement money is vulnerable to their negligently managed assets. Second, SOEs have heavy risk exposure to write-offs due to stranded assets. As such, action to minimize this risk would be in the SOEs' self-interest. This chapter will explain how the actions we propose could serve to do so. Third, oil SOEs will eventually need to do something to keep up with some of their competitors, notably Thai Oil and PTT PCL, which continue to take their sustainability efforts very seriously. Fourth, the scope of SOEs gives their actions a potentially huge impact. SOEs possess the dominant control over global oil, gas, and coal reserves. They constitute some of the largest private and semi-public companies in the world, and their controlling shareholders, i.e., national governments, have the power to play significant and unique roles, as this chapter will further discuss.

Visibly not 'e pluribus unum'

Institutional investors have acted via the Principles for Responsible Investment (PRI), as have investment banks via the Equator Principles, Carbon Principles, and the Green Bond Principles (Ceres 2014; Equator Principles 2013; PRI 2015). We acknowledge that many of the big partially publicly traded oil SOEs are participants in the UN Global Compact, but this participation does not amount to a sufficient response to the two problems that this chapter presents (UN Global Compact 2015).

SOEs' financial decisions impact the lives of ordinary citizens

Many of the largest oil SOEs are listed on stock exchanges. While to be appropriately called a SOE, 50 percent or more of the shares must be owned by the home country's national government or an associated governmental body, some percentage of these shares is held in the pension funds and the mutual funds in which ordinary citizens invest and upon which some of them rely for their retirement income. Table 12c.1 below shows the extent to which some of the largest oil SOEs are owned by entities other than their controlling governments.

These are also not small companies. In the Fortune Global 2,000 for 2015, Sinopec ranked number 24, Gazprom 27, Rosneft 59, CNOOC Limited and Statoil 103, and PTT PCL 225 (Forbes 2015).

Table 12c.1 SOEs and government ownership

SOE	*Percentage of shares not owned by SOE's government*
Gazprom (Russia)	49.8
Rosneft (Russia)	30.5
Sinopec (China)	24.2
Statoil (Norway)	33
CNOOC Ltd (China)	35.6
PTT PCL (Thailand)	48.9

Sources: CNOOC Ltd 2015; Gazprom 2015; PTT PCL 2015; Rosneft 2015; Sinopec 2015; Statoil 2013.

Dominant control of global reserves

When it comes to stranded assets, SOEs are particularly at risk. According to Wood Mackenzie, as of 2009 NOCs owned 73 percent of world oil reserves and 68 percent of world gas reserves (Thurber 2012). Heede and Oreskes found that SOEs control 75 percent of global reserves of oil and NGLs, and the World Bank found that 90 percent of global reserves is under some form of government control (Heede and Oreskes 2015, 15). According to data from Wood Mackenzie, as of 2009 the ranking of global oil companies with the greatest reserves, including unlisted companies, is Saudi Aramco, Gazprom, PDVSA (Venezuela), NIOC (Iran), Qatar Petroleum, Iraqi Oil Ministry, ADNOC (Abu Dhabi), ExxonMobil, Rosneft, Petrobras, and PetroChina. It is noteworthy that the only non-SOE on this list is ExxonMobil (Thurber 2012). Heede and Oreskes show that the majority of potential emissions from proved reserves are in the hands of SOEs and nation states. In their analysis, reported proved reserves were declared by 78 of the largest fossil fuel producers, 70 of which are incorporated entities, with 42 of those 70 investor-owned and the remaining 28 state-owned. This analysis found that 440 GtC total emissions of CO2 and methane would result from production of proved reserves reported by the world's largest producers of oil, natural gas, and coal. Of the 440 GtC, the investor-owned oil, gas, and coal companies hold reserves with potential emissions of 44 GtC, only 16 percent of the IPCC's remaining carbon budget (RCB), while the SOEs possess reserves of 210 GtC, 76 percent of the RCB. Oil reserves dominate this 210 GtC sum, making up 131 GtC (Heede and Oreskes 2015, 12, 15–17).

While SOEs as a group of oil companies are most at risk for stranded assets write-offs, they have the capability to hedge themselves against this risk. They can even profit while playing a major role in the solution to the problems of stranded assets and the deficit of green financing. This unique position is due to governments' potential ability to redirect the vast funds being used for oil and fuel subsidies to green project financing, to align regulatory policies with national financial objectives, and to issue heavily subscribed bonds, in this case green bonds for which demand is rapidly growing.

Thaioil Group and its financial partners, for example, issued domestic debentures amounting to 15 billion baht in 2014, which were 4.29 times oversubscribed and rated AA– by Fitch Ratings (Thailand) (TOP Annual Report 2014, 28). An important similarity can be drawn between this issuance and Thaioil Group's debenture issuance in 2006. In 2006 the demand from institutional investors more than doubled the value of the securities, which were given AA– ratings largely because of Thaioil Group's importance to PTT, which is a state-owned oil company (Kate 2006). If Thaioil Group is able to issue unsecured debentures that become so largely oversubscribed by institutional investors, it could also presumably issue green bonds specifically to finance renewable energy projects.

Unique ability of SOEs to solve both problems simultaneously

In addition to green bond issuance and the leveraging of debt capital markets, we could also see SOEs reallocate unneeded capital expenditures to green projects. According to stranded assets research recently released by Carbon Tracker Initiative, under the 2°C pathway there is a 'danger zone' of projects which would put $2 trillion at risk if they were to proceed. Moreover, oil represents about two-thirds of the financial risk, but only one-fifth of the carbon risk. Carbon Tracker Initiative suggests that a substitute for contracting or returning capital to shareholders could be the development of alternative business models, which could include diversification into renewables or green financing (CTI 2015, 4). Clearly, the unneeded capital expenditures associated with stranded oil assets would be substantial, but the newly available source of funds could be put to other uses, including green project financing.

Normally an oil company presented with the chance of doing so would balk, as renewables projects are rarely cost competitive with production or processing of crude petroleum products. SOEs, however, are in a uniquely favorable position to diversify into renewables. In addition to issuing potentially very oversubscribed green bonds, SOEs can ensure that their majority shareholders, i.e., governments, are able to align countries' regulatory frameworks and incentive regimes to the effect that the SOEs' green projects are profitable. Some examples of these regulatory frameworks are tax incentives, renewable producer credits, renewable fuel standards, and renewable fuel and feedstock subsidies.

SOEs could emerge as players in corporate green bond issuance, leverage debt capital markets, and reallocate capital expenditures to simultaneously finance green projects and hedge against the risk of stranded assets.

What kind of action do oil SOEs need to take?

First and foremost, SOEs need to act now to protect themselves and their investors against the impending risk of stranded assets. In the process of doing so they can and should play a role in the achievement of the 'clean trillion' and the solution to the problem of the green financing deficit. SOEs should face stranded assets risk management and green financing requirements. They should also have reporting and disclosure requirements, and labor, corporate governance, and safety standards. All corporations, especially SOEs, that hope to list on exchanges for the first time must be required to report their fossil fuel reserves and the potential CO_2 emissions of these reserves. If oil companies were to start reporting on the carbon stocks represented by their fossil fuel reserves, material climate change risk would no longer remain hidden from corporate reports. Carbon Tracker Initiative notes that currently this risk remains hidden. What we need, explains Carbon Tracker Initiative, is integrated, rather than standalone, reporting with a mandatory requirement for oil companies to conduct forward-looking analyses and reporting to cover the future emissions embedded in their reserves (CTI 2011, 3, 22, 27).

Conclusion

SOEs can uniquely solve one problem with the solution to another. They can hedge themselves against the very tangible risk of stranded assets, namely the huge loss to company value due to asset impairment, either via green bond issuance or shifting of capital expenditures. The unique ability of SOEs – to maximize return on investment in green projects through manipulation of regulatory regimes and issuance of green bonds that are likely to be heavily oversubscribed – also has the potential to be extraordinarily beneficial. Redirecting capital expenditures no longer needed and investing in green projects as a hedge present at least the start of a solution to the SOEs' stranded assets problem while also helping to green our planet. It is time to engage with SOEs and to see how far they can go toward protecting themselves and the countries led by their largest shareholders.

References

Baron, R. and Fischer, D. (2015) 'Divestment and Stranded Assets in the Low-carbon Transition'. Background paper, OECD 32nd Round Table on Sustainable Development, 1–25 (www.oecd.org/sd-roundtable/papersandpublications/Divestment%20and%20Stranded%20Assets%20in%20the%20Low-carbon%20Economy%2032nd%20OECD%20RTSD.pdf). Accessed September 2016.

CTI (Carbon Tracker Initiative) (2011) *Unburnable Carbon: Are the World's Financial Markets Carrying A Carbon Bubble?* 1–33 (www.carbontracker.org/report/carbon-bubble/). Accessed September 2016.

CTI (Carbon Tracker Initiative) (2015) *The $2 Trillion Stranded Assets Danger Zone: How Fossil Fuel Firms Risk Destroying Investor Returns*, 1–27 (www.carbontracker.org/report/stranded-assets-danger-zone/). Accessed September 2016.

Ceres (2014) 'Green Bond Principles Created to Help Issuers and Investors Deploy Capital for Green Projects' (www.ceres.org/press/press-releases/green-bond-principles-created-to-help-issuers-and-investors-deploy-capital-for-green-projects). Accessed September 2016.

CNOOC Limited (2015) 2016 Company Profile (www.cnoocltd.com/col/col7871/index.html). Accessed November 2015.

Dumaine, B. (2015) 'Billionaires Versus Big Oil'. *Fortune* (http://fortune.com/2015/04/25/billionaires-versus-big-oil/). Accessed September 2016.

Equator Principles (2013) 'About the Equator Principles' (www.equator-principles.com/index.php/about-ep). Accessed November 2015.

Forbes (2015) 'The World's Biggest Public Companies' (www.forbes.com/global2000/list/#header:assets_sortreverse:true). Accessed November 2015.

Gazprom (2015) 'Equity Capital Structure' (www.gazprom.com/investors/structure/). Accessed November 2015.

Heede, R. and Oreskes, N. (2015) 'Potential Emissions of CO_2 and Methane from Proved Reserves of Fossil Fuels: An Alternative Analysis'. *Global Environmental Change*, 6, 12–20.

Kate, D. T. (2006) 'Demand Soars for Thai Oil Debentures'. *ICIS News* (www.icis.com/resources/news/2006/10/31/1102398/demand-soars-for-thai-oil-debentures/). Accessed September 2016.

Lewis, M. (2014) 'Stranded Assets, Fossilized Revenues'. ESG sustainability report, Kepler Cheuvreux, 1–32 (www.keplercheuvreux.com/pdf/research/EG_EG_253208.pdf). Accessed September 2016.

McGlade, C. and Ekins, P. (2015) 'The Geographical Distribution of Fossil Fuels Unused When Limiting Global Warming to 2°C'. *Nature*, 517, 187–190.

Mills, L. (2015) 'Global Trends in Clean Energy Investment'. Bloomberg New Energy Finance (http://about.bnef.com/presentations/clean-energy-investment-q4-2014-fact-pack/content/uploads/sites/4/2015/01/Q4-investment-fact-pack.pdf). Accessed September 2016.

Parkinson, G. (2015) 'Citigroup Sees $100 trillion of Stranded Assets if Paris Succeeds'. *Renew Economy* (http://reneweconomy.com.au/2015/citigroup-sees-100-trillion-of-stranded-assets-if-paris-succeeds-13431). Accessed September 2016.

PRI (Principles for Responsible Investment) (2015) 'About the PRI' (www.unpri.org/about-pri/about-pri/). Accessed November 2015.

PTT PCL (2015) 'Major Shareholders' (www.pttplc.com/EN/IR/index.aspx). Accessed November 2015.

Rosneft (2015) 'Shareholder Structure' (www.rosneft.com/Investors/structure/share_capital/). Accessed November 2015.

Sinopec (2015) 'Our Company' (http://english.sinopec.com/about_sinopec/our_company/20100328/8532.shtml). Accessed November 2015.

Statoil (2013) 'The Norwegian State' (www.statoil.com/en/InvestorCentre/Share/Shareholders/Pages/StateOwnership.aspx). Accessed November 2015.

Thurber, M. (2012) 'NOCs and the Global Oil Market: Should We Worry?' Program on Energy and Sustainable Development, Stanford University (https://energy.stanford.edu/events/national-oil-companies-and-world-oil-market-should-we-be-worried). Accessed September 2016.

TOP (Thai Oil Public Company Limited) (2014) *Thai Oil Public Company Limited Annual Report*, 1–157.

UN Global Compact (2015) 'What Is UN Global Compact?' (www.unglobalcompact.org/what-is-gc/mission). Accessed November 2015.

Chapter 12d

Japan and governance

Jason Mitchell

Japan's great experiment in Abenomics remains as divided now as several years ago when Shinzo Abe won re-election in late 2012. Gains in the Topix since then have been impressive but less so when adjusted for the weaker Yen. Central bank measures – either easing or rhetoric – have clearly supported a US and European market recovery, but Japan by comparison has struggled to get the reflation narrative right and, ultimately, hit the Bank of Japan's inflation targets.

The loss in momentum behind structural reforms, the third arrow of Abenomics, hasn't helped. Efforts to join the Trans-Pacific Partnership have stalled partly due to shifting US trade preferences. Corporate tax reform ran a gauntlet of embedded interests and remains only half solved. Even indecision over a wider nuclear restart has delayed liberalization of the power market.

Signs of progress

While labour, tax and deregulation reforms suffered from high expectations at the start of Abenomics, corporate governance reform expectations began modestly. Early sceptics pointed to the DPJ's (Democratic Party of Japan) poorly executed policy agenda that touched on corporate governance, and a decision by the Japan Exchange Group to disregard recommendations by the Financial Service Agency for greater corporate disclosure.

There's been significant change since Abe's election, so much so that corporate governance reform has to be considered one of his chief legacies. Headlines over the past several years note the improvement in independent board representation, a rise in Western-style shareholder activism and the adoption of normative codes like Japan's Stewardship Code and Corporate Governance Code. These clearly played an integral role in recalibrating corporate governance norms, reinforced by large asset owners like the Government Pension Investment Fund (GPIF), whose adoption of the Stewardship Code provided a strong precedent for wider adoption and more active ownership.

What is often overlooked, however, are Japan's wider efforts to address corporate governance and capital efficiency as constituents of the same problem set relating to poor return on equity (ROE). This became prominent in 2014 for several reasons. The Japan Exchange Group launched the Nikkei 400, an ROE and profitability-driven index that includes a governance component. With nearly two thirds of the Nikkei 225 benchmark not qualifying on its debut, the Nikkei 400 raised awareness about Japan's serial underperformance in these areas. Companies reacted in kind by their exclusion. Amada announced plans for a 100 per cent payout ratio over the next two years via share buy-backs and dividend hikes to make its ROE more competitive.[1] The market's reaction to Amada's announcement – the stock finished up 16 per cent on the day – provoked speculation for the 'next Amada' into the Nikkei 400's August rebalancing.[2]

Asset owners also acknowledged the turn to capital efficiency. The GPIF signalled that it would reallocate from passive Topix investments to indices and strategies that target high-yielding companies like the Nikkei 400. International proxy advisory firms like Institutional Investor Services (ISS) began considering how to include ROE among their voting policy criteria for Japan.

At the same time, the government also worked on conflating the notion of governance and the cost of capital into a unified talking point. In April, Japan's Ministry of Economy, Trade and Industry (METI) published the *ITO Review of Competitiveness and Incentives for Sustainable Growth*, which addresses capital efficiency and governance as an interlinked problem.[3] Return ratios, it concludes, are either applied with too little management accountability or ignored altogether, contributing to the market's chronic short-termism. Better governance, the logic goes, leads to improved long-term capital allocation.

Addressing the cost of capital

In retrospect, Japan's renewed emphasis on ROE is not entirely surprising. A trend of declining corporate profitability, excess capacity and low reinvestment all formed the productivity gap that Abenomic reflation was supposed to close. On this measure, Japan stood out as the anomaly among developed countries. For almost fifty years, Europe and the US generated consistent returns across business cycles while Japan's have conspicuously lagged (Figure 12d.1). Europe and the US, already producing cross-cycle returns at or above their cost of capital, faced little urgency to undergo a similarly self-reflective examination. For Japan, Abenomic reflation simply offered a multi-pronged means which included governance reform, to cure this ROE underperformance.

While the focus on returns had undergone previous periods of popularity, it has had to negotiate the near-perpetual headwinds of deflation and the lack of nominal GDP growth. Japan's persistent deflation removed the pressure on managements to put corporate balance sheets to work, which explains why so many highly regarded companies sat on cash piles unable to earn their cost of capital. At the start of Abenomics in 2013, almost half of Topix companies operated with net cash positions, up from 35 per cent a decade ago.[4] By comparison, less than 30 per cent of US and European companies maintained net cash positions.[5]

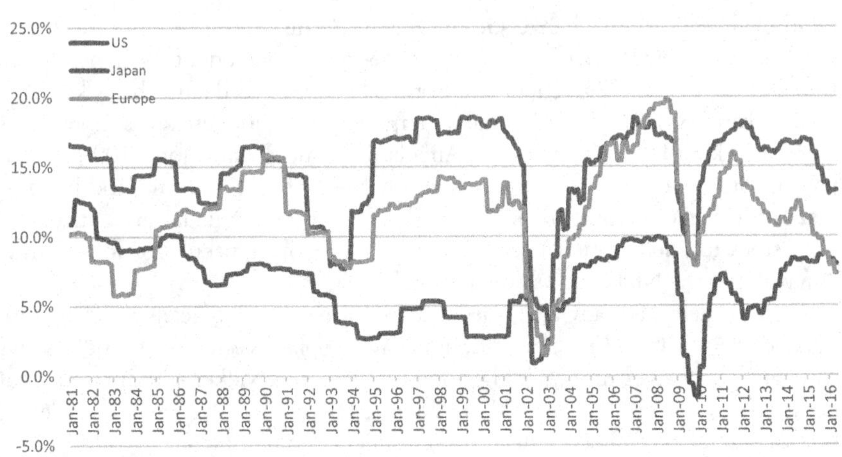

Figure 12d.1 Historic ROE for US, Europe and Japan.
Source: Credit Suisse, 2016.

But a singular focus on financial returns misses the larger case for corporate governance reform, which is to say that ROE is an imperfect measure by itself. A company generating high returns may simply reflect a profitable business faced with little reinvestment pressure rather than rigorous efforts around more efficient capital allocation. Equally, a company operating at low returns may be burdened by excess capital reserves or a temporary period of high capital intensity. If the *ITO Review* was accurate about the general lack of understanding around capital efficiency, Abenomic reform marked the ideal opportunity to reinforce the business case for improved governance and greater awareness of Japan's low returns.

The sudden focus on financial returns illustrates how managements began to respond to changing shareholder preferences. With monetary policy and fiscal stimulus priming a 2 per cent inflation target, investors – particularly domestic pension funds like the GPIF that was struggling to offset inflating liabilities – began to demand higher payout ratios and, implicitly, to expect greater accountability for a company's capital structure. Higher return-generating companies simply matter more in a reflationary environment. This led to reframing the need for shareholder distributions in the larger context of being a social good that could alleviate Japan's societal pressures.[6]

Capital efficiency targets as commitment devices

If the Nikkei 400 Index marked a passive turn toward capital efficiency and a wider awareness for corporate governance, the *ITO Review* represented more active measures, many that concentrated on elevating corporate understanding of the cost of capital through better, long-term disclosure.

How did investors position themselves around this theme? Attempts to correlate broadly-defined governance criteria with share performance yielded mixed results at best.[7] Moreover, Japanese studies even demonstrated significant outperformance by companies with low governance scores relative to better governed firms.[8] The same applied to returns like ROE where backtesting showed that companies with high ROE historically underperformed the Topix.[9] Companies with rising ROEs fared slightly better, but the relative outperformance appeared to apply only to the top quintile.[10]

In our approach to testing the *ITO Review*'s recommendations, we viewed companies' capital efficiency targets as a commitment signal that produced an audience cost, or the risk to a company's credibility. Developed as a game theory approach to determine the credibility of political threats during international crises, the theory of domestic audience costs proposes that politicians are more likely to fulfil their promise if they face a risk of being penalized in the next election cycle.[11] In other words, politicians generally don't make empty promises. Like the electoral pledges that politicians make, companies are similarly constrained by – and incentivized to fulfil – their commitments to their domestic audience, in their case the investor community. Like politicians, corporates are incentivized to try to achieve their ROE commitments to the market or lose credibility.

Despite the dismal ROE performance of Japan's corporate sector, we found that few companies issued medium-to-long-term ROE and return on assets (ROA) targets to investors. Most investors simply conformed with the Nikkei consensus in issuing sales, operating profit and net income guidance that set an expectations baseline. After all, companies are under no obligation to publish these forecasts, much less offer additional guidance around financial returns. Indeed, managements risk losing their credibility by offering additional targets which they could potentially miss. We viewed these guidance targets as providing an important distinction – a signal – to the market, differentiating companies that formally present guidance to investors from those that do not or only informally share their internal targets.

What does a group of companies that publicly commits to capital efficiency targets tell us? What does greater accountability to formalized return targets say about share performance across economic cycles? When we first began asking these questions in 2013 at the start of Abenomics, we identified eighty-six companies that had committed to ROE or ROA targets.[12,13] Now, several years later, groups like the Life Insurance Association of Japan regularly compile survey data. On its most recent figures, it estimates that more than 240 companies now formally issue ROE targets.[14]

The persistent, equal-weighted outperformance of the group of eighty-six companies we found relative to the Topix (Figures 12d.2 and 12d.3) over more than twelve years suggests several messages. First, the market appears to reward companies with higher relative valuations if they publicly commit to return targets. Although the group's five- and ten-year median earnings growth lag behind the Topix, the group realizes a significant rerating on a price-to-earnings and

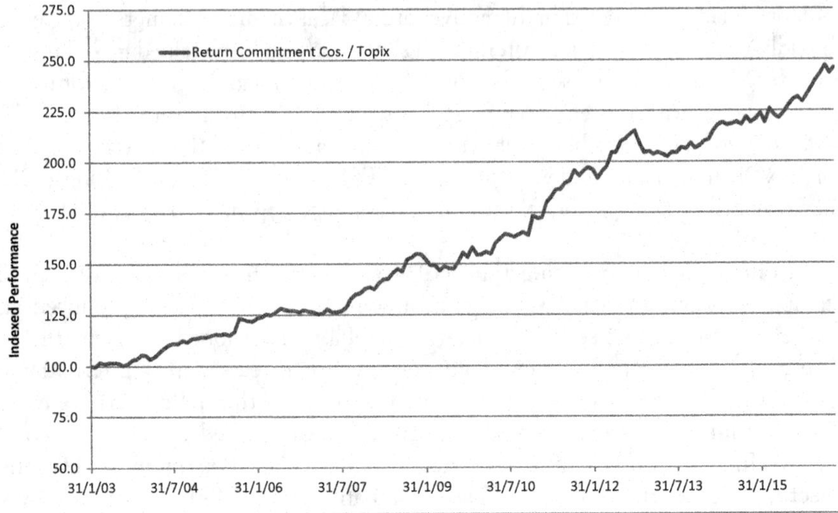

Figure 12d.2 ROE/ROA Commitment Group relative to Topix.

Source: GLG Partners, Bloomberg, 2016.

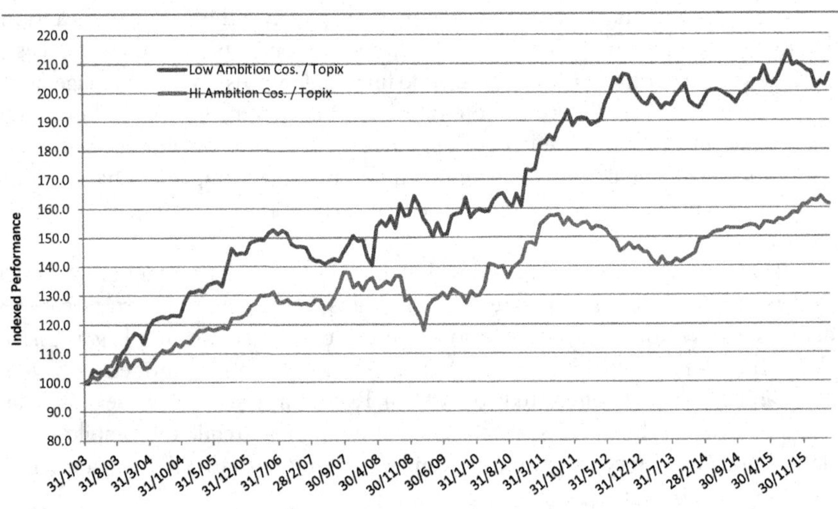

Figure 12d.3 High- and low-ambition target groups relative to Topix.[1]

Source: GLG partners, Bloomberg, 2016.

Note: [1] We defined high-ambition companies as though targeted greater than 100 bps of return improvement relative to their long-term average, and low-ambition companies as less than 100 bps improvement. Fifty-six companies qualified as high-ambition and 30 companies as low ambition.

price-to-book basis which drives the majority of share outperformance.[15] In raw valuation multiples, the group of commitment companies goes from trading at a 15 per cent to 20 per cent discount to the Topix ultimately to a premium on both metrics (Figure 12d.4).

Second, the governance signal – defined here by companies committing to ROE or ROA targets – modulates over time and across different market regimes. That is, the group's performance lags during periods of economic reflation like Koizumi's 2006 reform agenda, the global economic recovery in 2009 and the start of Abe's term in 2013. This is consistent with the notion that better governed companies lose their premium during reflationary periods, underperforming as markets become less discriminating in quality.

Third, the act of formally committing to a financial return target matters more than the target itself. The 35 percent of companies that set unambitious targets – defined as a 100 basis points (bps) or less of improvement relative to their long-term average – outperformed both the Topix as well as the group of companies issuing ambitious targets, particularly during reflationary periods. Overall, the share outperformance suggests that investors tend to prioritize transparency around capital efficiency objectives above specific expectations targeting.

Last, leadership appears to drive broader adoption within several sectors. In the food, heavy industry and machinery groups, one company historically led by example, establishing a practice of return targets which was later adopted by sector peers.[16] These moves often outlined transformational change to their capital structures. Like Amada's announcement, Ajinomoto's decision in 2009 to address ROE said more about better asset allocation and addressing its capital reserves via higher shareholder returns than any fundamental change to its sales or margin profile.

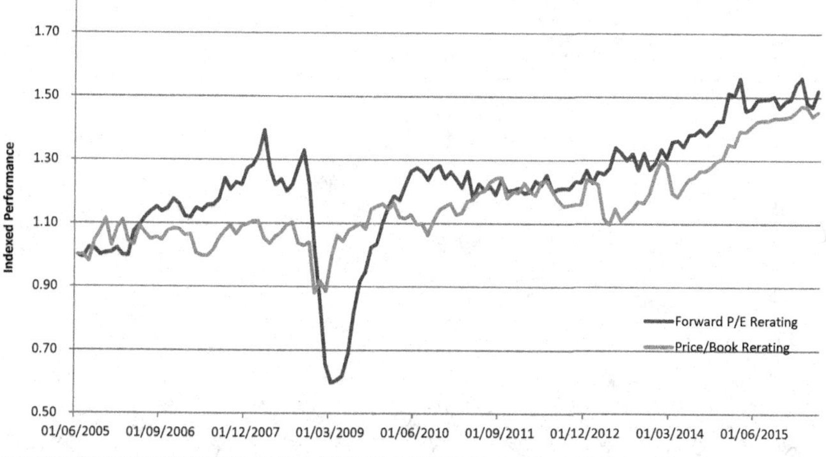

Figure 12d.4 Indexed rerating of the Commitment Group vs. Topix.
Source: GLG partners; Bloomberg, 2016.

Opportunity amid the challenges

Japan's problems have been exhaustively defined: an ageing demographic, a dependency on energy imports, geopolitical pressure from China, weak corporate governance, embedded interests slowing reform, a deflation-conditioned national psyche and an unprecedented monetary expansion programme. Yet, important signs indicating a shift in corporate behaviour have already emerged from the subtleties of Abenomic reform.

Efforts to tie capital efficiency to governance represented (and still do) a unique opportunity to reform and reframe corporate and investor norms. In the process, we expect correlations between persistent share outperformance and companies who formally commit to returns targets to continue driving greater discussion and transparency around the cost of capital in Japan.

Since 2013, we have viewed the correlation between outperformance and Japanese corporate governance reform as a strong enough factor to develop an investment strategy specifically around this type of screening. It has also afforded us, as asset managers and a UNPRI signatory, the opportunity to present this empirical data to Japanese managements and engage in capital allocation and shareholder returns, and move to long-termist forecasting and governance issues. The strategy is of a low-volatility, factor-neutral basket of companies structured around companies that formally commit to ROE targets or companies that focus on it as an important operational metric but do not yet disclose targets. On an equal-weighted basis, the strategy (Figure 12d.5) has outperformed the Topix by roughly 700 basis points annually.

More broadly, though, conflating financial profitability and better governance carried important advantages for Japan. It helped reinforce the integrity of Abenomic reform and arguably helped rerate Japan. On the outset of Abenomics,

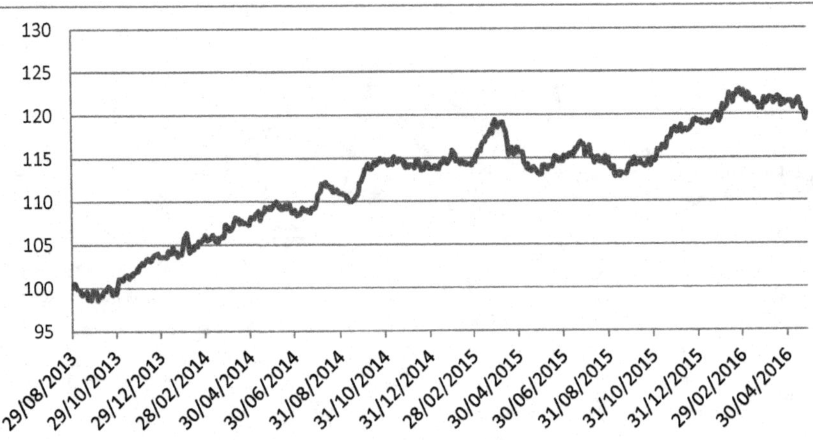

Figure 12d.5 'Quality' strategy vs. Topix.

Japan's low return on equity during our study implied a 7.5 per cent equity risk premium, well above that of the US and Europe at 4–5 per cent. As Japan improved its ROE to Europe's level, its risk premium gradually narrowed over the last several years. That alone offers a compelling reason to adopt the *ITO Review*'s recommendations in pushing corporates to commit to formal targets and to define how they will achieve them.

Notes

1 Santazono, Tetsuji. 'Looking for the next Amada'. *Nikkei Asian Review* (28 May 2014). http://asia.nikkei.com/Markets/Equities/Looking-for-next-Amada. Accessed 7 September, 2016.
2 Tamura, Hiromichi. 'JPX-Nikkei Index 400: Our views on the next Amada'. *Nomura* (9 June 2014).
3 Japan Ministry of Economy, Trade and Industry. *ITO Review of Competitiveness and Incentives for Sustainable Growth*. 25 April 2014. www.meti.go.jp/english/press/2014/0425_02.html. Accessed 7 September, 2016.
4 Rial, Patrick. 'Japan dividend trade ideas'. J. P. Morgan (20 March 2014); Bloomberg, 2014.
5 *Morgan Stanley Research* (20 May 2014).
6 Kamiyama, Naoki. 'Japan investment strategy: new dawn for growth'. BofA Merrill Lynch (8 April 2014).
7 There is a plethora of studies supporting this. For the most recent, see Vintila, Georgeta and Stefan Christian Gherghina (2013) 'An empirical investigation of the relationship between corporate governance mechanisms, CEO characteristics and listed companies' performance'. *International Business Research*, 5(10), 175–191.
8 Aman, Hiroyuki and Pascal Nguyen. (2008). 'Do stock prices reflect the corporate governance quality of Japanese firms?' *Journal of the Japanese and International Economies*, 22(4), 647–662.
9 Naito, Michiro. 'Equity derivatives review: what works in Japan – factors backtested'. J. P. Morgan (2 June 2014). Abe, Kenji. 'Japan equity strategist: investment strategy for high ROE stocks'. *Citigroup Research* (15 October 2013).
10 Bennett, Jason and Kenji Abe. *Citigroup Research* (16 June 2014).
11 Fearon, James D. (1994). 'Domestic political audiences and the escalation of international disputes'. *American Political Science Review*, 88(3), 577–592.
12 Companies compiled as of 30 April 2014 using the investment research of Barclays, BofA Merrill Lynch, Citigroup Global Markets, CLSA Japan, Credit Suisse, Goldman Sachs, J. P. Morgan, Macquarie Securities, Mizuho Securities and Morgan Stanley MUFG Securities.
13 In defining our scope, we focused on companies formally issuing ROE and/or ROA targets, excluding companies that issued ROIC, ROI and other return variants. Factor exposure analysis by Nomura Securities (22 April 2014) revealed quality exposure to be zero. Within this, there is a higher than average exposure to financial gearing, value (via dividend yield) with minimal exposure to deep value, momentum and growth. Average and median market cap for the group are ¥1.12 trillion and ¥800 billion, respectively.
14 Life Insurance Association of Japan. 23 March 2016. www.seiho.or.jp/info/news/2015/pdf/20160323_3.pdf. Accessed October 18, 2016.
15 GLG Partners, Bloomberg. 2016.
16 Komatsu first established return targets in 2000 in the industrial machinery and equipment sector; Mitsubishi Heavy in 2007 in the heavy machinery sector; and Ajinomoto was the first to introduce targets in the food sector in 2009.

Chapter 13

Fiduciary duty[1]

Rory Sullivan, Will Martindale and Elodie Feller

Introduction

'Fiduciary duty' may well be the most important phrase in the language of finance. Yet, too often it is misunderstood and misinterpreted, in particular when it comes to making the case for taking account of environmental, social and governance (ESG) or sustainability issues in investment practice.

Why is it so important? It is because fiduciary duties exist at the very top of the investment chain to ensure that those who manage other people's money act in the interests of beneficiaries. The manner in which fiduciary duty is defined and interpreted affects the entire investment chain, from asset owners to companies (Martindale *et al.* 2016). It informs the manner in which asset owners select, appoint and monitor investment managers. It influences investment decision-making processes and ownership practices. Ultimately, it affects the way in which companies are managed.

This chapter focuses on how fiduciary duty shapes and influences investment practice, and on how changes in investment practice are changing our understanding of fiduciary duty. It also looks at the wider relationship between investment and society, and discusses how the concept of fiduciary duty needs to evolve to reflect the social and environmental challenges faced by investors today.

Fiduciary duty and responsible investment: a brief history

In 2005, the United Nations Environment Programme Finance Initiative (UNEPFI) together with the law firm Freshfields Bruckhaus Deringer published a ground-breaking report titled *A Legal Framework for the Integration of Environmental, Social and Governance Issues into Institutional Investment* (commonly referred to as the 'Freshfields Report'). The report, in what was seen as a radical conclusion at the time, argued that 'integrating ESG [environmental, social and governance] considerations into an investment analysis so as to more reliably predict financial performance is clearly permissible and is arguably required in all jurisdictions' (Freshfields Bruckhaus Deringer 2005).

The case for investors and policymakers to be concerned about these issues has strengthened significantly over the past decade. The global financial crisis has shown how failures within the financial system can have major negative effects on investors, on society and on the global economy as a whole. Events such as the *Deepwater Horizon* oil spill show how billions of dollars can be knocked off the market capitalisation of companies as a result of weaknesses in corporate management systems and controls.

Since the Freshfields report was published in 2005, the investment landscape has changed dramatically. Many investment organisations (e.g. the over 300 asset owners and almost 1,000 investment managers who have signed the Principles for Responsible Investment[2]) have committed to take account of environmental, social and governance issues in their investment processes and to encourage higher standards of corporate governance and corporate responsibility in the companies in which they are invested. The policy landscape has also changed. Voluntary codes that encourage asset managers and asset owners to actively engage with the companies in which they are invested have been established in the United Kingdom, Japan and South Africa, with other countries likely to follow suit. Many regulatory agencies now require asset owners and other institutional investors to disclose their policies on responsible investment and to report on how these policies have been implemented.

Box 13.1 *The Fiduciary Duty in the 21st Century* project

In September 2015, the Principles for Responsible Investment (PRI) UNEPFI, the UNEP Inquiry into the Design of a Sustainable Financial System and the UN Global Compact launched a major report on fiduciary duty. The report – *Fiduciary Duty in the 21st Century* – analysed investment practice and fiduciary duty in eight countries: Australia, Brazil, Canada, Germany, Japan, South Africa, the UK and the US.

It was based on interviews with over fifty asset owners, asset managers, lawyers and regulators across the eight countries, a comprehensive review of law and policy on fiduciary duty in each of these eight countries, and a series of roundtables, conferences and webinars where the findings were discussed with institutional investors and global experts on fiduciary duty and responsible investment.

What is fiduciary duty?

In the modern investment system, organisations or individuals (fiduciaries) often manage money or other assets on the behalf of beneficiaries and savers. Many of these relationships are based on trust and confidence. That is, beneficiaries and savers rely on the fiduciary to act in their best interests, where these best interests are usually defined exclusively in financial terms.

In practice, investment decision-makers have varying degrees of discretion as to how they invest the funds they control. The scope of that discretion varies. It may be narrow, for example, in the case of tailored mutual funds where the beneficiary specifies the asset profile and only the day-to-day stock selection and other management tasks are left to the investment decision-maker. It may be wide, as with many occupational pension funds. Further, some public funds are subject to considerable state control and the discretion afforded to these decision-makers may be further narrowed by parameters set by government.

Within the scope of discretion left to the investment decision-maker, fiduciary duties – and equivalent obligations in civil law jurisdictions – exist to ensure that those who manage other people's money act responsibly in the interests of savers (clients or beneficiaries), rather than serving their own interests. These duties are of particular importance in asymmetrical relationships, i.e. those situations where there are imbalances in expertise and where the ability of the beneficiary to monitor or oversee the actions of the person or entity acting in their interests is limited.

The manner in which these duties are framed differs between countries and between common law (where these duties are articulated in statute and in decisions of the courts) and civil law jurisdictions (where the rules tend to be code or statute-based). In common law jurisdictions, the most important fiduciary duties are the duty to act prudently and the duty to act in accordance with the purpose for which investment powers are granted (also known as the duty of loyalty).

Box 13.2 Fiduciary duties

Fiduciary duties (or equivalent obligations) exist to ensure that those who manage other people's money act in the interests of beneficiaries, rather than serving their own interests. The most important of these duties are:

- Loyalty: Fiduciaries should act in good faith in the interests of their beneficiaries, should impartially balance the conflicting interests of different beneficiaries, should avoid conflicts of interest and should not act for the benefit of themselves or a third party.
- Prudence: Fiduciaries should act with due care, skill and diligence, investing as an 'ordinary prudent person' would do.

In civil law jurisdictions, while the term 'fiduciary duty' may not be used, similar obligations are often imposed in investors. These generally include a duty to act conscientiously in the interests of beneficiaries – this duty is expressed in different terms, with jurisdictions using terms such as 'good and conscientious manager' (Japan) or 'professionally' (Germany) – and a duty to seek profitable investments.

How does fiduciary duty relate to ESG issues?

From a legal perspective, fiduciary duties are widely considered to be procedural and purposive requirements, rather than obligations to achieve particular beneficial outcomes. That is, when evaluating whether or not an institutional investor has delivered on its fiduciary duties, courts will distinguish between the decision-making process and the resulting decision (i.e. outcome of the decision-making process). In general, the law is reluctant to second-guess judgments that inherently involve a balance of commercial risks, so long as the fiduciaries can demonstrate that they applied an appropriate degree of diligence in their good-faith pursuit of beneficiaries' interests.

To date, no jurisdiction or regulator has sought to exhaustively prescribe how decision-makers should go about integrating ESG considerations into their decisions. In most cases, it is left to decision-makers to determine the approach that will enable them to meet their legal obligations in the particular circumstances. In practice, conduct must be directed towards beneficiaries' best interests, and due process and competence must be applied in decision-making.

The discussions with regulatory authorities that informed the *Fiduciary Duty in the 21st Century* report suggested that – acknowledging the inevitable differences in the structure of financial systems, regulatory mandates, legal environments and cultures – regulators generally give asset owners wide freedom to decide how they wish to take account of ESG opportunities and risks in their investment practices and processes, and on the timeframes over which they define their investment goals. While regulatory authorities generally do not take a view on whether or not asset owners should invest in particular sectors or activities, they do expect asset owners to be aware of and to manage ESG-related risks, and to pay close attention to decisions that lead to skews in portfolios. Regulatory authorities will, however, tend to look closely at investment decisions that expose funds to particular risks (e.g. a high-carbon portfolio, a portfolio with a weighting to renewable energy) and will expect them to explicitly assess the implications for the overall risk profile of the fund.

Conceptually at least, this suggests that asset owners may take account of wider ESG issues, so long as there is a clear focus on beneficiaries' interests. In that context, for example, a decision not to invest in coal mines (e.g. because of concerns about these assets being stranded as a result of climate change policy) is likely to be seen as consistent with fiduciary duties so long as this decision is based on credible investment assumptions and a robust investment decision-making process. This requires trustees to have the discipline to set out their investment beliefs, to be prepared to review the investment outcomes achieved and to have the willingness to change if the data change or if it is clear that the decision is causing significant damage to the beneficiaries' financial interests.

The changing landscape of responsible investment

Fiduciary Duty in the 21st Century concluded that taking account of ESG issues should be seen as an integral part of investors' fiduciary duties. The report pointed to the many examples of ESG issues affecting investment value and investment performance, and the growth in the quality and quantity of sell-side research on the investment implications of ESG issues as evidence that the investment relevance of these issues is accepted within the investment industry. The report also pointed to normative change in investment practice, noting the increasing number of institutional investors that have committed to integrating ESG issues into their investment processes and to engaging with companies on ESG issues (see, for example, the results of recent PRI signatory surveys (PRI 2015a; 2015b)).

These changes have been reinforced by law and policy changes in many jurisdictions. While there has been little change in the formal definitions of fiduciary duty over the past decade, there has been a significant increase in ESG-related policy instruments. For example, voluntary stewardship codes (where signatories to these codes commit to engaging with the companies in which they are invested) have been developed by or in conjunction with the investment industry in the UK, Japan and South Africa. An increasing number of countries have adopted disclosure requirements, requiring investors to publish details of their policies on and approaches to responsible investment. To present just one example, Ontario's pension standards legislation (PBA909) requires pension funds to disclose information about whether ESG factors are incorporated into their investment policies and procedures.

Despite these changes, many investors have yet to integrate ESG issues into their investment processes or to engage with the companies in which they are invested. In some cases, this is an issue of capacity, with smaller funds often lacking the resources, expertise or awareness to focus much attention on ESG issues. But this is also an issue for larger organisations, even those that have made explicit commitments to responsible investment or to ESG. Many have yet to extend their commitments to all asset classes and, even where implementation has commenced, it is not uncommon to observe that there are often weaknesses in their implementation of these commitments (see, for example, Martindale *et al.* 2016; PRI 2015a). For example, while it is now reasonably common for large asset owners to ask questions about responsible investment in requests for proposals, it is often unclear whether any weight is assigned to responsible investment when appointing, reappointing or monitoring investment managers.

Fiduciary duty: a rhetorical or a real obstacle?

From the interviews that underpinned the *Fiduciary Duty in the 21st Century* report, two distinct perspectives emerged. The first was that, for those asset owners who have taken a proactive approach to responsible investment, fiduciary duty is not seen as a particular obstacle to action. This was a consistent message, across all eight of the countries studied. Many of the asset owners interviewed described fiduciary duty as a practical and pragmatic requirement that informs investment and management practice in a similar manner to aspects such as cost, investment returns, etc. Some went further, arguing that fiduciary duty created a positive duty on them to take ESG issues into account in their investment practices, and suggesting that a failure to take account of ESG issues could be seen as a breach of their fiduciary duties.

However, those who had yet to make significant progress often pointed to fiduciary duty as the reason why they cannot integrate ESG issues into their investment processes or engage with companies on these issues. When we dug into these arguments, we found that they could be summarised as: concerns about investment returns, concerns about legal implications, and the advice being given by investment consultants.

In relation to investment returns, many of these interviewees held the view that a focus on ESG issues would involve compromising investment performance and/or that it would be difficult to add investment value through a focus on ESG issues. These concerns were compounded by what interviewees saw as a lack of robust evidence on the relationship between environmental and social issues and investment performance. A number commented that this contrasts with corporate governance, where there is good academic research on the investment relevance of these issues (e.g. issues such as bad governance and aggressive accounting are widely understood as having negative implications for investment performance), there has been legal clarification of governance expectations, and there are broadly accepted principles on the characteristics of good governance.

Interviewees also pointed to the lack of legal clarity in all of the jurisdictions about the relationship between ESG and fiduciary duty. Interviewees raised different issues: the absence of clarity on the extent to which the duty to maximise benefits for beneficiaries may be viewed as consistent with analysis of ESG issues, the limited guidance from regulatory bodies on how responsible investment should be applied in practice (and the associated concern that long-term responsible investment may run counter to trustees' fiduciary duties) and the lack of formal obligations on investors to take account of ESG issues in their investment processes or to engage with companies.

The important policy issue raised by interviewees was the weaknesses in the implementation and oversight of existing policies (e.g. stewardship codes, ESG and responsible investment-related disclosure requirements). Interviewees commented that many of the stewardship codes and asset owner disclosure requirements are not effectively implemented. This is partly because many of these requirements are relatively new and the relevant policymakers have concentrated on encouraging their adoption and uptake. But it also reflects the fact that there is limited assessment of the quality of implementation of these commitments. While most of these codes and disclosure requirements do require some sort of public reporting on the number of signatories to a code or the number that have complied with the code, there has been limited analysis of the actions that have been taken or of how the actions taken have affected investor or corporate practice.

Finally, the views held by investment consultants (actuaries) are particularly important. The reason is that obtaining advice from such consultants is a legal requirement in many – but not all – countries. Many jurisdictions allow asset owners to use the fact that they followed the advice given by investment consultants as a defence in court. The practical consequence is that the views held by investment consultants are often a key influence on the actions taken by asset owners. A recurring theme in the interviews was that the advice being given by these consultants– particularly in the US but also in other jurisdictions – is often based on a very narrow interpretation of fiduciary duty. This advice generally stresses that delivering short-term, financial performance is the key expectation of fiduciaries, and that fiduciaries should have an exclusive focus on financial returns. This narrowly drawn advice, often underpinned by the belief that taking account of ESG issues will have a negative impact on investment returns, has acted as a brake on asset owners' willingness to adopt long-term, responsible investment.

How do we make progress?

The *Fiduciary Duty in the 21st Century* report concluded that many of the barriers identified above are not insurmountable. It offered a series of practical suggestions on the actions that could be taken by institutional investors, by intermediaries and advisers, and by policymakers to address these barriers.

For institutional investors (in particular asset owners), the key recommendation was that they needed to make commitments to ESG integration and to long-term responsible investment, including explanations of how these commitments align with their fiduciary duties, and then ensure these commitments are implemented. Implementation mechanisms include incorporating these commitments into investment mandates, monitoring how investment managers (internal and external) are implementing these commitments, reporting to beneficiaries on how these commitments have been implemented and the outcomes that have resulted, and ensuring that trustees, boards and executives have the resources and knowledge to hold investment managers and advisers to account on ESG integration (see, further, Martindale *et al.* 2016). It was also argued that these institutions should look to influence and support change in the wider market, through encouraging better corporate disclosures on ESG issues and through playing a supportive role in policy discussions on responsible investment.

Intermediaries, particularly investment consultants, were an explicit focus. The report recommended that they publish commitments to ESG integration and to long-term responsible investment, and ensure that these commitments are implemented effectively in the research and advice they provide to their fiduciary clients. It was also recommended that they report to their fiduciary clients on how these commitments have been implemented and the implications for the research and advice they provide to these clients. In a similar manner to asset owners, it was also suggested that they contribute to change in the wider market by supporting research on the relationship between ESG issues and investment performance, and on the relationship between engagement and corporate performance. They were also encouraged to support efforts to change wider market views on ESG issues through ensuring that these issues are an integral part of professional training.

Finally, the report recommended that policymakers in each country should clarify that fiduciaries must analyse and take account of ESG issues in their investment processes, in their active ownership and voting activities, and in their public policy engagement. They should support this through the development of guidance on implementation processes, specifically on how investment beliefs, investment mandates, monitoring and reporting should be structured to encourage a greater focus on ESG issues. Transparency was another important area of focus, with policymakers encouraged to require much greater transparency on all aspects of ESG integration and investment practice. Regulators were also encouraged to strengthen the implementation of existing legislation and policy instruments on long-term responsible investment (e.g. stewardship codes, asset owner disclosure requirements).

Future challenges

If the core recommendations of the *Fiduciary Duty in the 21st Century* report were fully implemented, they would have a transformative effect on current investment practice. They would result in investors paying much greater attention to ESG issues in their investment processes and in their engagement. In turn, this would result in greater amounts of capital being invested in socially and environmentally positive activities, and would significantly increase the pressure on companies and issuers to have high standards of corporate governance, of social and environmental issue management, and to ensure that these issues are properly integrated into corporate strategy and capital investment decisions. In fact, following the launch of the report, the PRI, UNEPFI and the Generation Foundation announced that they would be launching a three-year programme of work to implement the report's recommendations and to extend the work to a further six jurisdictions (China, Hong Kong, India, Malaysia, Singapore and South Korea) (PRI *et al.* 2016).

However, the report cautioned that delivering all of the recommendations in the report would not address all of the sustainability and other challenges presented by the financial system. Two issues were identified as being of particular concern. The first is the move in many countries from defined benefit (DB) to defined contribution (DC) schemes. This raises questions about whether fiduciary duty concepts will also apply (or be applied) to these types of scheme. In some cases it has been clarified that fiduciary duties will continue to apply; for example, in South Africa funds continue to be liable for outsourced activities, and need to ensure that appropriate contracts are in place and that the fund has a right of recourse against the service provider. In other markets, the nature of the duties owed by insurance companies, asset managers, and sponsoring organisations in contract-based schemes (i.e. where the pension provider does not have fiduciary or equivalent obligations to the beneficiary in the way that a trustee would in a trust-based scheme) are not yet fully defined. A number of interviewees expressed concern that a reliance on contract law could weaken the duties owed to the beneficiaries of these schemes, pointing to the potential accountability gap that might arise with the absence of trustees and to the risk that pension savers might receive different levels of protection depending on the form of their pension arrangements.

The second relates to wider social and environmental impacts such as climate change. Investors can make an important contribution by building consideration of the risks and opportunities presented by these issues into their investment processes, by analysing these risks and opportunities over the longer term and by encouraging companies to adopt higher standards and better practices on these issues. These actions are all likely to be consistent with their fiduciary duties. However, the specific actions taken will ultimately be driven by the incentives provided. That is, wider public policy measures such as trading schemes, taxes and other regulations will be the key determinant of the rate at which investors will take action (e.g. to reduce portfolio-related emissions, to invest in clean technologies). Interviewees suggested that, as an integral part of their fiduciary duties, investors need to engage with governments to encourage the adoption of policy measures to correct market failures.

Clearly, both of these issues represent significant challenges to prevailing conceptions of fiduciary duty. Even the complete implementation of the recommendations proposed in the *Fiduciary Duty in the 21st Century* report will only go part of the way to delivering a socially, environmentally and economically sustainable financial system. We see the enlightened approach to fiduciary duty described in the *Fiduciary Duty in the 21st Century* report as a necessary but not sufficient condition for the delivery of this wider objective.

As such, the report represents a staging post rather than a final destination. We see fiduciary duty as a dynamic concept, not one that is set in stone. As noted by Paul Watchman, the lead author of the 2005 Freshfields report: 'The concept of fiduciary duty … will continue to evolve as society changes, not least in response to the urgent need for us to move towards an environmentally, economically and socially sustainable financial system' (as quoted in Sullivan *et al.* 2015).

Notes

1 This chapter is an abridged version of Rory Sullivan, Will Martindale, Elodie Feller and Anna Bordon (2015) *Fiduciary Duty in the 21st Century* (London: UN Global Compact, UNEPFI, Principles for Responsible Investment and UNEP Inquiry into the Design of a Sustainable Financial System).

2 www.unpri.org/directory/, last viewed 17 May 2016.

References

Freshfields Bruckhaus Deringer (2005) *A Legal Framework for the Integration of Environmental, Social and Governance Issues into Institutional Investment*. Geneva: UNEP.

Martindale, W., Sullivan, R. and Fabian, N. (2016) *How Asset Owners Can Drive Responsible Investment: Beliefs, Strategies and Mandates*. London: Principles for Responsible Investment.

PRI (2015a) *Report on Progress 2015*. London: PRI.

PRI (2015b) *Annual Report 2015: From Awareness to Impact*. London: PRI.

PRI, UNEPFI and Generation Foundation (2016) 'Fiduciary Duty in the 21st Century: Scoping Paper 2016–2018'. London and Geneva: PRI, UNEPFI and Generation Foundation.

Sullivan, R., Martindale, W., Feller, E. and Bordon, A. (2015) *Fiduciary Duty in the 21st Century*. London: UN Global Compact, UNEPFI, Principles for Responsible Investment and UNEP Inquiry into the Design of a Sustainable Financial System.

Chapter 14

The risk management opportunity

Cary Krosinsky

Scientific research has found that a series of new, fully expected outcomes are extremely likely to manifest fully over the next decades, resulting in categories of risk and a 'new normal' fully expected to abruptly affect financial value, such as an expected acceleration in global average temperature that will increasingly impact human and natural systems on all continents and across the oceans.[1]

The US and other countries and their militaries also see such risks specifically emerging, with strategic planning well underway, in the US case as can be partly seen within the latest Quadrennial Defense Review (QDR).[2]

Scientific risk categorization has also matured, as have traditional financial definitions, yet attempts to bring these classifications together has lagged to date, hence we here attempt to do just that, bring categories of risk together in a single frame, so that Risk Management systems can start to be built with such features, which right now are sorely lacking.

Categories of risk, emerging from scientific and military analysis, expand and inform traditional areas of financial risk, and include:

- *Emergent risk* – for example, climate change or sea level rise: these would be new risks not currently in financial models that are most used within investment decision making.
- *Persistent risk* – Here there are additional factors to add to more traditional persistent risks that are already within investors' grasp. For example, ongoing and careful consideration of expectations surrounding future price/earnings ratios among any other financial metrics combined with qualitative considerations as to the ongoing expected quality of a business. Managing for weaknesses in potential future value at risk would be forms of avoidable and persistent risk, such as has evolved during the history of BARRA and through more recent developments such as 'smart beta' and factor-based investing.
- *Single event risk* – such as a catastrophic and unexpected earthquake in Los Angeles.
- *Cascading or triggered risk* – such as displaced people from fresh water shortages, as some argue the Syrian refugee crisis was one such example.

- *Time-specific risk* – such as risks not likely to affect short-term investors such as day traders, but which are fully expected to affect long-term buy-and-hold investors.
- *Systemic risk* – as is most commonly expressed by the example of the 'tragedy of the commons'. For example, assume there is a single pasture and a group of farmers and the extra value for all farmers of adding one head of cattle is +1. Eventually, the pasture becomes overcrowded, and the ongoing success of the system is doomed to failure unless balancing mechanisms are established. The danger in such a scenario is the observation of the system and financial outcomes which may result for those unprepared.
- *Material risk* – where risks are either likely to be financially material to an investor or not.
- *Avoidable risk* – such as those risks which could potentially be hedged for.

Examples of observed impacts to date and how they fit in the above categories include:

- Changes in precipitation or melting snow and ice, which alter hydrological systems, affecting water quantity and quality. Academics at the Earth Institute, especially within the Columbia Water Center, are extremely alarmed by the nexus of water quality and availability and the near-term outcomes that their analysis is projecting. This would be an example of a new Emergent Risk.
- Shifts in ranges and changes in algal, plankton, and fish abundance as well as changes in ice cover, salinity, oxygen levels, and circulation have been associated with rising water temperatures in some marine and freshwater systems.[3] These are both Cascading and Emergent categories of risk.
- Increases in warm temperature extremes and reductions in cold temperature extremes. There is also higher surface temperature expected under all possible future scenarios, with oceans having absorbed much of the heat, especially in the Southern Ocean, that would have otherwise affected temperatures further already. Surface temperatures are expected to accelerate on a decadal basis throughout the twenty-first century under all assessed emission scenarios. It is very likely that heatwaves will occur more often and last longer, and that more extreme precipitation events will become intense and frequent in many regions. The ocean will continue to warm and acidify, and global mean sea level is fully expected to rise, affecting some areas more strongly than others at first. Here we have both Emergent and possibly Single Event Risk as well.[4] These are also Time-Specific Risks as well as Systemic Risks.[5]
- Further examples of Systemic Risk include future changes which become of potential financial concern if they 'expose people, societies, economic sectors, and ecosystems to risk'. For just one simple example, endangered ecosystems may be recognized to include old growth forests determined to require conservation.

Traditional measures of financial risk go back primarily to the likes of Barr Rosenberg and his colleagues whose research at Berkeley helped lead to the risk management industry we know today.

Well-developed concepts such as 'value at risk' have become accepted and standard practice, yet such assessments do not factor in sustainability risks such as the above, let alone other concepts such as:

- business as usual in a changing world of dwindling resources;
- geopolitical and other supply chain risks;
- reputational risk;
- employee quality/turnover risk;
- customer loyalty risk;
- other regulatory risks;
- innovation opportunities not taken, as have been seized by industry disruptors from Airbnb (hotels) to Tesla (energy technology) to Uber (taxis) to Warby Parker (eyeglasses) to Zipcar (rental cars).

Value at risk calculations and the entire field of risk management stands to improve with consideration of risk categories such as the above. These fields developed at a different time and age, and investors using such arguably antiquated and incomplete measures increasingly look to ESG data to supplement what is missing. Yet as we saw previously, ESG data is also insufficient.

Credit agencies have taken notice, with many traditional names recently pledging to factor in ESG considerations.[6]

One recent estimate shows the risk management industry bringing in over $13 billion in annual revenue in 2016, with 100 percent growth anticipated by 2020.[7] This would be a factor of roughly one hundred times the revenue of ESG data providers.

All of this work is clearly nascent but also essential to coalesce and come together. The concept of risk is clearly evolving, or at least it should be increasingly treated that way.

Notes

1 www.ipcc.ch/pdf/assessment-report/ar5/syr/AR5_SYR_FINAL_SPM.pdf. Accessed 7 September, 2016.
2 www.defense.gov/News/Special-Reports/QDR. Accessed 7 September, 2016.
3 http://ar5-syr.ipcc.ch/resources/htmlpdf/WGIIAR5-Chap18_FINAL/#pf22. Accessed 7 September, 2016.
4 http://ar5-syr.ipcc.ch/topic_summary.php#node149. Accessed 7 September, 2016.
5 www.ipcc.ch/pdf/assessment-report/ar5/syr/AR5_SYR_FINAL_SPM.pdf. Accessed 7 September, 2016.
6 www.unpri.org/press-releases/credit-ratings-agencies-embrace-more-systematic-consideration-of-esg. Accessed 7 September, 2016.
7 www.prnewswire.com/news-releases/risk-analytics-market-worth-usd-2632-billion-by-2020-520607292.html. Accessed 7 September, 2016.

Chapter 15

Shareholder engagement and advocacy

Cary Krosinsky

As mentioned earlier, one of the most popular 'tribes' of sustainable investing is shareholder engagement and advocacy, which after decades of activity has reached something of a fever pitch of activity, especially on climate change.[1] An all-time-high 94 shareholder resolutions on climate were filed on US companies in 2016 according to As You Sow, up from what were record levels in 2015.

Some of the many filed initiatives can be seen at the shareholder resolutions page of Ceres,[2] many of which would have already been withdrawn before any vote after direct investor conversations with the company, such as those with AES Energy, a major US utility on so-called proxy access, and with Akamai Technologies to set goals on increasing use of renewable energy.

Many such proposals are withdrawn before any shareholder vote. One reason you don't hear that much about shareholder advocacy and engagement is that it often happens behind closed doors, a tradition born both out of UK practices of the likes of Hermes as well as four decades of religious investors in the US.

Proxy access is an increasingly important issue, giving minority shareholders an opportunity to place someone on the board of a company, and the vote on this issue at ExxonMobil in May 2016 received over 60 percent support, the first time a shareholder proposal of any kind had been approved over the last ten years of the company.[3] The culture of many organizations, US universities included, can be skewed towards a small number of voices who take turns sitting on each other's boards, harboring views which can become quickly outdated; hence fresh voices help, not to mention diverse views (see subsequent chapter on diversity and financial value for another example).

This ExxonMobil vote marks a watershed moment as a statement by a majority of investors (and a much larger percentage of those who actually vote) of unhappiness with the governance of the firm in an age of increasing concern about climate change.

Companies sometimes face multiple resolutions, for example AES settled with investors on proxy access while a request for the company to assess its business model from a 2-degree-Celsius-temperature-increase perspective remained unresolved and went on to receive over 42 percent approval of shareholders. Again, keep in mind that many individual investors don't vote on their proxy statements, so these votes are a sizeable majority of those who actually choose to vote. Many mutual funds continue to vote with management by default, which is unfortunate and arguably an abdication of their responsibilities as members of society. More individual shareholders should take notice of this disconnect and insist that this changes. When that happens, everything could change, or so the theory goes.

Other withdrawn resolutions per Ceres include that on American Electric Power, another large US utility, which has agreed to provide a report on its exposure to stranded assets that must stay in the ground for the world to remain a safe and prosperous place, as we first championed publicly at the Carbon Tracker Initiative in the landmark *Unburnable Carbon* report of 2011.[4]

Additional excellent websites on shareholder resolutions include those maintained by As You Sow,[5] who themselves filed almost 100 resolutions in 2016, and by the ICCR.[6]

The ICCR (the Interfaith Center on Corporate Responsibility) arguably began the entire field of shareholder engagement[7] and tracks shareholder resolutions over time, finding 257 filings in 2016, up from a previous record of 227 in 2015, and which was 160 in both 2011 and 2012. Lobbying is the primary issue for which ICCR members, whose resolutions at times can be joined by trillions of dollars in assets, file the most resolutions.

Shareholder engagement might appear to be a negative activity to some but these are typically intended to be positive requests for improved business practices which will be both financially and societally beneficial. Ceres, for example, only files resolutions on this mutually positive basis.

This positive strand of activism stands in contrast with the more negative approaches of the likes of Nelson Peltz, Paul Singer and Carl Icahn, where the financial performance of these latter approaches has not been so positive. Icahn Enterprises was found by Forbes to be 'down 45 percent in the past year',[8] and a review of the aggressive targeting of Nelson Peltz has not resulted in significant positive financial performance success after his arguably vicious attacks have occurred. These negative activist requests, asking for companies to break up and scale down, can cause long-term damage to sustainability-related plans of companies such as Dupont, who had been seeking to expand their sustainability enhanced and advantaged revenue as headlined in the value driver model work they performed over the past decade plus – such efforts can be simply cast to the side due to such negative shareholder activism. Hence we see short-term, destructive activism as a negative and long-term activism for necessary change as a positive activity.

Unabated, climate change could destroy shareholder value, as much as 45 percent of economic value according to the University of Cambridge in their *Unhedgeable Risk* report of late 2015,[9] hence we suggest that positive shareholder activism around the nexus of sustainability and financial value is ultimately an important tool in the box for investors to also consider in future.

A major strand of ongoing shareholder engagement activity surrounds so-called Carbon Asset Risk. As mentioned, the main concern of the Carbon Tracker Initiative remains that up to 80 percent of the remaining coal, oil and gas, as potential carbon emissions, needs to stay in the ground and that trillions of investment dollars are at significant risk, which could otherwise cause a future financial crisis or bubble.

Hence, the carbon asset risk strand of shareholder engagement calls for companies to return cash to shareholders rather than spend it on capital expenditure for fossil fuel extraction which would otherwise be wasted on high-cost projects that no longer make economic sense. Fortunately, there is a correlation between high cost and high carbon.

Most importantly, countries such as Saudi Arabia, Iraq, Iran and Kuwait have the least expensive resources remaining on the oil side of the equation. Qatar has some of the cheapest gas reserves.

More expensive resources and reserves, such as those in Alberta and in the Arctic are also the most environmentally polluting, in addition to being the most costly.

These figures are likely to put a squeeze on companies such as ExxonMobil, BP and Shell, all of whom are moving towards becoming gas companies rather than oil producers.

Saudi Arabia is likely to become the world's largest investor as it starts spinning off state owned enterprises in its plans for a post-oil era, as we have discussed earlier.

Coal remains under severe threat and figures to continue to come under pressure, as most of the remaining carbon in the ground is in the form of coal.

Oil companies have been doing all they can to maintain dividends, including rounds of layoffs, selling assets and increasing debt levels.[10] They know shareholders won't be happy if these dividends disappear.

The Carbon Asset Risk strands of engagement suggest another way to maintain those levels – by returning cash to shareholders rather than wasting it on projects doomed to fail financially.

Another strand of activity involves companies such as ExxonMobil funding disinformation campaigns even while fully understanding the dangers of climate change.[11] The New York State Attorney General's Office led the charge on the potential financial liability for ExxonMobil on this basis, now being championed by many other states and jurisdictions.[12]

This litigation risk adds another category of financial consideration for investors to keep in mind when they consider whether oil companies have room to financially rebound in a future world of lower oil demand, even if enhanced available resources are at hand through improvements in oil production technology.

This all also adds fuel to shareholders who have been filing shareholder resolutions on lobbying, among other disinformation campaigns over the years, most recently by Yale's Dwight Hall, using the famous book *The Ethical Investor*.[13]

The head of Yale's ACIR committee (which makes recommendations to the Yale Endowment), Jonathan Macey, said recently that 'the ACIR is committed to voting for resolutions that are consistent with the reality of climate change'. Macey also said that he would 'encourage the ACIR to support Dwight Hall's shareholder proposal'.

While the proposal did not go through, such pressure builds up over time and these longer-term engagement techniques have been useful for building awareness of issues which eventually have significant financial impact.

As *The Ethical Investor* says, Yale will 'sell its stock in a company if it is unlikely that shareholder engagement will successfully improve a company's activity'.

This is also the stance of the world's largest investor, Norges Bank, whose entire investment strategy and positions are transparent and available at their website,[14] including the companies they have sold over time after shareholder engagement failed to bring about a positive result.

Academic research also finds that poorly performing companies with whom shareholder engagement is performed go on to outperform.[15] Wilshire Associates somewhat famously wrote on the so-called 'CalPERS effect'[16] where companies, first found to be the poorest on governance, after shareholder engagement efforts ensue, go on to outperform the rest of the market.

There is also the somewhat British concept of stewardship to consider. Basically, this calls for being a responsible investor if you choose to own shares in any particular company. It would be very interesting indeed if this were applied to not only public but private companies as well, and there are signs of that starting to happen.

For example, Aviva Investors, whom we profiled in our first two books, lays out seven clear principles for other investors to consider in their 'Stewardship Statement'[17] and follows this by disclosing its own stewardship policy, avoiding conflicts of interest, committing to monitor companies it owns, establishing clear guidelines, committing to collaborate with other investors, having a clear and informed policy on shareholder resolution voting, and reporting on these activities.

Some call for more 'forceful' forms of stewardship[18] in the light of the rapidly approaching effects of climate change, which makes sense as an additional step given the likelihood of degraded shareholder value unless meaningful steps are taken quickly.

But again, many large fund managers simply vote with management. Particularly puzzling is the position of BlackRock, the world's largest investor, who published a climate stewardship guide with Ceres in 2015,[19] and a separate 'Price on Climate Change on Portfolios' piece in October 2015,[20] yet they continue to vote with management on climate change, a position they are not believed to have moved from,[21] and which will likely become increasingly untenable.

Many companies have come to appreciate the value of multi-stakeholder dialogues and arguably now take proactive positions on environmental and social issues, anticipating what investors might otherwise do.

Many NGOs also take a more positive stance in their conversations with corporates, seeking to find common ground and positive solutions as opposed to always finger pointing, even if there is a spectrum of 'light to dark green' NGOs to always consider. Nothing like a 'good cop, bad cop' dynamic to make things happen: therein the power and appeal of shareholder engagement.

Notes

1 https://next.ft.com/content/01e2bfb6-f1d1-11e5-aff5-19b4e253664a. Accessed 7 September, 2016.
2 www.ceres.org/investor-network/resolutions. Accessed 7 September, 2016.
3 www.reuters.com/article/us-oil-climatechange-idUSKCN0YG2I6. Accessed 7 September, 2016.
4 www.carbontracker.org/wp-content/uploads/2014/09/Unburnable-Carbon-Full-rev2-1.pdf. Accessed 7 September, 2016.
5 www.asyousow.org/our-work/current-resolutions/. Accessed 7 September, 2016.
6 www.iccr.org/corporate-engagements. Accessed 7 September, 2016.
7 www.iccr.org/about-iccr/history-iccr. Accessed 7 September, 2016.
8 www.forbes.com/profile/carl-icahn/. Accessed 7 September, 2016.
9 www.cisl.cam.ac.uk/publications/publication-pdfs/unhedgeable-risk.pdf. Accessed 7 September, 2016.
10 http://money.cnn.com/2016/02/04/investing/oil-prices-dividends-conocophillips-exxonmobil/. Accessed 7 September, 2016.
11 www.newyorker.com/news/daily-comment/what-exxon-knew-about-climate-change. Accessed 7 September, 2016.
12 www.huffingtonpost.com/entry/attorneys-exxon-probe_us_56fab959e4b0a372181b113d. Accessed 7 September, 2016.
13 http://acir.yale.edu/pdf/EthicalInvestor.pdf. Accessed 7 September, 2016.
14 www.nbim.no/. Accessed 7 September, 2016.
15 www.kempen.nl/uploadedFiles/Kempen/01_Asset_Management/Producten_en_diensten/VerantwoordBeleggen/Research percent20paper percent20ECCE.pdf. Accessed 7 September, 2016.
16 www.calpers.ca.gov/page/newsroom/calpers-news/2014/company-performance. Accessed 7 September, 2016.
17 https://uk.avivainvestors.com/gb/en/individual/about-us/responsible-investment/stewardship-and-active-ownership.html, Accessed 7 September, 2016.
18 https://preventablesurprises.com/programmes/climate-change/. Accessed 7 September, 2016.
19 www.blackrock.com/corporate/en-us/literature/publication/blk-ceres-engagement guide2015.pdf. Accessed 7 September, 2016.
20 www.blackrock.com/corporate/en-mx/literature/whitepaper/bii-pricing-climate-risk-international.pdf. Accessed 7 September, 2016.
21 http://socialinvesting.about.com/od/Sustainable-Investing/fl/BlackRock-Fidelity-and-Vanguard-Exposed-on-Climate-Change.htm. Accessed 7 September, 2016.

Chapter 15a

Thoughts on filing a shareholder resolution at ExxonMobil

Shareholder Engagement Team of the Dwight Hall SRI Fund at Yale University

Our story begins in August of 2014, when the Yale Corporation Committee on Investor Responsibility announced that the Yale Endowment would adopt a special proxy voting directive for the issue of climate change:

> Yale will generally support reasonable and well-constructed shareholder resolutions seeking company disclosure of greenhouse gas emissions, analyses of the impact of climate change on a company's business activities, strategies designed to reduce the company's long-term impact on the global climate, and company support of sound and effective governmental policies on climate change.

As a student-run socially responsible investment fund, we at Dwight Hall SRI sought to file a shareholder resolution that the Yale Endowment might be able to vote for in an application of the new directive.

Moreover, the adoption of the proxy voting directive represented a decision by the Yale Corporation against pursuing fossil fuel divestment. Indeed, Yale's decades-old guidelines for ethical investment, set forth in *The Ethical Investor* (1972), prescribe exercise of shareholder voice as the 'firstline' approach for mitigating corporate social injuries to which the University is exposed via its investments. Nevertheless, the guidelines hold that when the exercise of shareholder voice seems unlikely to eliminate a grave social injury within a reasonable timeframe, the University should divest.

We therefore recognized that filing a resolution would be a valuable opportunity to gauge the efficacy of shareholder engagement in this specific context. In filing a shareholder resolution, we sought to make an evidentiary contribution to the ongoing debate on divestment, climate change, and fossil fuel companies.

After some deliberation, we chose ExxonMobil over other possible companies, partly because of its status as the largest publicly traded international oil and gas company in the world. Early in December of 2014, we purchased stock in ExxonMobil. The SEC requires that shareholders must continuously hold a minimum of $2,000 in a company's stock for at least one year in order to file a resolution.

It then fell to us to choose a climate-related issue on which to file a shareholder resolution. An oil and gas company such as ExxonMobil faces resolutions around diverse climate-related issues, including but not limited to: GHG emissions reductions, executive compensation, board membership with independent expertise, reporting of ESG information, extractive practices, disclosure of regulatory risk and the possibility of increased dividends, and, lastly, the one we picked – public policy, political spending and disclosure thereof.

As we researched these possibilities, we looked at various criteria for our consideration, such as the broader significance of the issue to climate change mitigation, relevance of the issue to the conversation at Yale, its accordance with the University's new proxy voting directive, the presence of other shareholder advocates previously in the space, and the likelihood of being included on the ballot. We benefited from the good advice of numerous experts, practitioners, and climate-focused shareholder advocates.

Another deciding factor was how, in the months leading up to the filing deadline, Exxon came under unprecedented media scrutiny for having been aware of the science behind climate change for decades, at least as early as 1977; despite this, however, Exxon for many years worked to undermine public certainty about the science. As a result of these revelations, a number of state attorneys began investigating Exxon for having possibly intentionally misled the public and company shareholders; the Department of Justice sent a request for a probe to the FBI; Exxon's public policy and political spending was therefore quite a topical issue.

One thing we kept coming back to was how Yale's new proxy voting directive placed special emphasis on the critical role governments must play in efforts to reduce emissions:

> [T]he formidable problem of climate change, which rightly deserves the attention and involvement of all, is heavily dependent on government policy interventions, both nationally and internationally.

Although Exxon purports to no longer support climate denial and to support a revenue neutral carbon tax, the company continues to financially support, among others, the American Legislative Exchange Council (ALEC); ALEC is one of the primary forces obstructing sound government climate policy in the United States. Yale expects 'company support of sound and effective governmental policies on climate change', and yet Exxon in this case contributes to efforts that undermine such policies.

Ultimately, we chose public policy and political spending as our issue. We co-filed our resolution in December 2015 with the United Steel Workers, the largest labor union in North America, itself partly comprising over 5,000 Exxon workers. Other co-filers of the resolution included AP7, the Swedish national pension fund, and Walden Asset Management, the oldest institutional investment manager in the SRI industry.

After filing the resolution, we had the opportunity to interact with Exxon's investor relations team on several occasions. During these discussions, Exxon's management was obliged to justify its position. They maintained that Exxon endorsed some but not all the actions of ALEC; they claimed to support ALEC due to its advocacy for STEM education. Ultimately, our resolution made it to the proxy statement, and Exxon's management recommended that shareholders oppose our resolution.

In the weeks and months preceding the vote, we sought to do what we could to confirm investor support of our resolution. Most importantly, perhaps, we obtained an official public statement from Yale University backing our resolution.

Exxon's Annual General Meeting of the shareholders took place in Irving, Texas, on the morning of May 25, 2016. Fortunately, we were able to make it there and represent ourselves in person.

At the meeting, our resolution was presented by an amiable man named Hughes who worked at Exxon's Baton Rouge Refinery; he spoke on behalf of the United Steel Workers union. Once all resolutions had been presented, one of our senior members, Gabe Rissman, stood up to make an official comment. Addressing the company's CEO Rex Tillerson, Gabe emphasized the contradiction between Exxon's public position on climate change and ALEC's record of climate denial and policy obstructionism.

Tillerson, however, disagreed; he defended Exxon's contributions to ALEC, saying that company management 'found our engagement with them to be very productive', and said, 'whether we agree or not we find it very useful'. When asked what Exxon might do to counteract ALEC's negative impacts, Tillerson made clear that the company did not care if it was supporting climate denial and policy obstruction; in his own words, 'we will never withdraw our support for people to express their free speech opinions on any matter whatsoever'.

For equating support of climate denial to the defense of free speech, Tillerson was met with robust applause from the Dallas audience. It was not the only instance in which the audience exposed the nature of its views. Rather than applauding any of the climate-focused resolutions, the audience applauded a shareholder who claimed that the world had experienced global cooling and that climate change was caused by volcanoes. Tillerson, who had previously ostensibly acknowledged the reality of climate change, did nothing to rebut this man's views, despite the contradiction with stated company policy. Instead, in an act of tacit approval, Tillerson thanked the man and moved on. By contrast, Tillerson took considerable time to dispute the claims of an actual climate scientist who spoke at the meeting.

Our resolution garnered 25.7 percent of the vote. This figure was considered by shareholder advocates to be a respectable sum. On one level, the resolution had succeeded; it had garnered increased votes from the previous year and encouraged media scrutiny of Exxon's current practices. On another level, the resolution failed; it had not changed the company's policy for the better. Indeed, only one of the eleven shareholder resolutions filed at Exxon for the 2016 proxy season actually succeeded in winning a majority of the vote – namely, the one calling for proxy access bylaws, which would allow certain shareholders to nominate candidates for election to the company's board of directors.

We believe our experience with Exxon raises a host of important questions. Are shareholder resolutions an effective form of engagement? Can shareholder engagement be expected to move Exxon in the foreseeable future? How many more years of failed engagement are needed to reach the conclusion that Exxon is as unmovable as Mr. Tillerson would have us believe? And, if this conclusion is reached, should investors divest shares in the company?

At a time when climate change threatens to destabilize the world as we know it, at least one thing is clear—none should continue to countenance the funding of climate denial and policy obstructionism.

Chapter 16

Emerging new paradigms

Cary Krosinsky

In addition to the New Frontier perspectives of what's going to be required by sector of the economy, and by region, there also are emerging new ways of thinking about business that investors need to keep in mind.

Shifting business models are leading to disruption in many sectors, through the sharing economies being fostered by companies from Airbnb to Uber and well beyond. We take a brief further look at this in the chapters that follow, including a look at the roots of the concepts of shared ownership as played out even before what came to be known as Islamic finance.

There are also, importantly, new value constructs emerging, tying financial value generation directly to sustainability efforts, which include new ways for investors to identify value as it is being generated. This is also increasingly useful for recognizing the potential for innovation ahead of its deployment.

There is also a 'holy grail' being sought, that of being able to measure the positive impact businesses can have on society through investment. One prime example would be the work of KPMG on Safaricom,[1] which demonstrates how a company can create almost ten times the economic benefit in societal terms than is demonstrated by their financial profit alone (their recent accounting scandal[2] notwithstanding).

We end this section of the book with a review of the work of the Principles for Responsible Investment, with questions remaining of what is enough, who can drive the necessary change, who can best identify the necessary pace of change, how to accelerate change while maintaining healthy financial returns, and whether investors themselves can do what is necessary for the sake of the system and all of us.

We also cover diversity within, as it has clearly emerged as a key ingredient of business success, and the right thing to do besides.

Business as usual never was ideal anyway, was it? These can be the good old days.

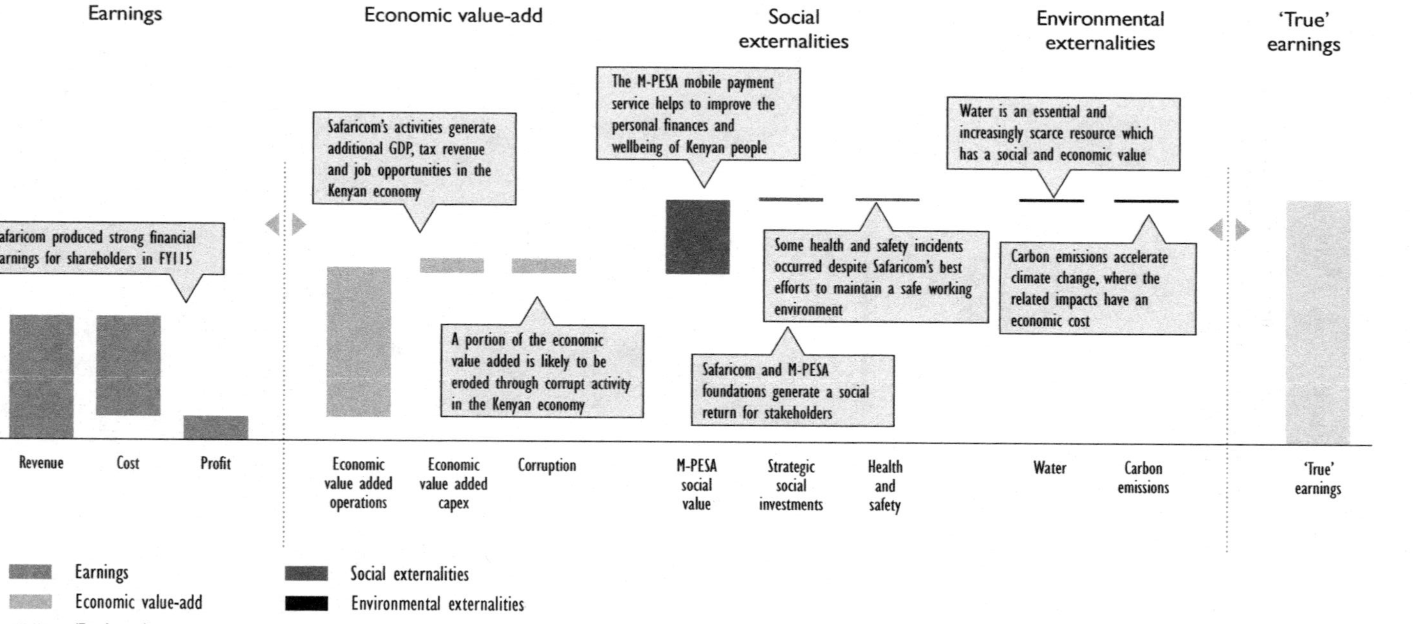

Figure 16.1 Safaricom true value.

Source: KPMG.

Note

1 https://www.home.kpmg.com/content/dam/kpmg/pdf/2016/01/case-study-safaricom-limited.pdf. Accessed October 18, 2016.
2 See *Business Daily Africa* at www.businessdailyafrica.com/Corporate-News/Senior-Safaricom-executives-billion-shillings-procurement-scam/-/539550/3206682/-/4jgwqn/-/index.html. Accessed 7 September, 2016.

Chapter 16a

Value drivers

David Lubin

Investors who wish to align their investment strategies with sustainability risks and opportunities have many challenges to overcome. First and foremost is the reality that reliable data needed to evaluate how companies are performing on sustainability related factors is still a work in progress.

While there have been notable advances from organizations such as SASB, as they attempt to bring a 'materiality focus' to the typical KPI model, and CDP's work to provide in-depth disclosure on key climate and environmental impacts, gaps remain in what is arguably required, as discussed earlier. Current efforts seek to improve the taxonomies that underlie the sustainability data models. They start with a theory of sustainability – the issues, the measures, and the metrics. They intend to provide a standardized basis for comparing companies on any of a broad array of variables that are deemed important to many different categories of sustainability-oriented stakeholder.

Negative screens require broad taxonomies

The primary use case for sustainability data was to enable values investors, analysts, and other stakeholders to create negative screens that could identify companies for engagement or investor actions (e.g. tilts, divestiture) due to exposure to any of myriad factors, such as GMO sales, diversity issues, ethics controversies, or carbon intensity, that range across the environmental, social or governance pillars of the ESG data model. Being responsive to the wide range of issues under the SRI umbrella required an exhaustive data scheme. The taxonomies are well suited to this purpose.

We are now in the midst of another substantial expansion in use cases for sustainability data.

The biggest single change is the proliferation of positive strategies that attempt to identify companies who score highly on one or more of the ESG factors. Once these are identified as leaders or movers, investors are developing strategies to both achieve market rate returns with more sustainable portfolios and/or beat the market by finding sustainability factors that drive financial outperformance.

Companies have taken note of this shift, and in many cases are expanding their reporting in ways that highlight their leadership in creating material benefits.

Implications of the positive perspective

For those investors and analysts focused on the potential 'upside' opportunity from sustainability, the issue is value creation. The question for analysts becomes 'How do sustainability initiatives contribute to the firm's strategy for creating value? And how is it working?' Given that each company's strategy is the unique formulation of how a firm intends to create competitive advantage, effectively analyzing performance requires an open framework centered on strategy that tells the company's story, rather than a closed taxonomy designed to enable sustainability comparisons.

For the purpose of identifying companies deriving meaningful and durable competitive advantage from successful integration of sustainability drivers into their business model, the metrics chosen must describe the strategy, *directly* link it to value creation, and provide for both lead and lag indicators of business results. The implications of a strategy-centered approach to external sustainability reporting that makes the business value visible, and directly supports managing the execution of sustainability strategy internally, suggests a significant change in direction on metrics for most companies.

Back to basics – what's old is new

The author and his colleagues have previously made the case for such an open framework in which companies can describe and report on the business impact of *their* unique sustainability strategy (Lubin and Esty, 2014; Lubin and Krosinsky, 2013), and we believe the framework already exists. It's a 'back to basics' approach, and it argues for measuring sustainability strategies' direct impact on *revenue growth*, *productivity*, and *risk*. Through this strategy-focused lens, we believe investors and analysts should more clearly see the elements of competitive advantage, and the potential for a 'sustainability premium', i.e., a meaningful increase in shareholder value from the successful execution of sustainability strategy.

Our model is based upon the earlier work of Porter and van der Linde (1995) as adapted by Esty and Winston (2009), who proposed that the materiality of sustainability strategies could be found by examining impacts on four fundamental factors – brand value, revenue growth, eco-efficiencies, and risk exposure.

We combined this perspective with the work of my colleagues Kaplan and Norton (1992 through 2008) who posit that all business strategies have in common objectives to drive revenue growth, enhance productivity, and reduce risk. Furthermore, performance on each element of a company's strategy can best be measured and managed by defining both lead and lag indicators of performance. So, in a simplified example, a company seeking sales growth must satisfy customer demands, which in turn rests upon internal company processes such as product development and sales management, which themselves requires key enablers such as IT systems and skilled employees to ultimately produce the desired business benefit. Defining, measuring and reporting specific indicators along this line of 'cause and effect' gives an observer a deep and predictive view about how a company is performing or the likelihood of achieving future results. This approach was first introduced to the sustainability field in a 2013 UNGC/UNPRI report developed by Lubin and Krosinsky and dubbed the 'Value Driver Model'.

The value driver framework assumes that improving visibility into how a firm's sustainability strategy drives new revenue growth, improves productivity and reduces risks, is the most direct means of gaining mainstream investing involvement in sustainability. Rather than ask analysts to integrate sustainability data into their financial models, we argue that measures should be designed to show the impacts on sustainability on these generally accepted core business performance indicators. Moreover, the value driver approach has the added benefit of helping firms gain alignment internally and within their supply chains to achieve the results they seek.

At the highest level, the framework holds that firms can define the business value of sustainability by measuring lead and lag indicators of:

1 revenue growth from sales of internally or externally designated sustainable products and services;
2 total annual cost savings (and cost avoidance) from sustainability related initiatives; and
3 reduced risk exposure from sustainability – related factors that could materially impair a company's performance.

Generating a firm-level value driver analysis poses its own challenges. Few firms today know or report on how their product mix is shifting toward sustainability-advantaged products – even those companies actively promoting and branding such innovations. Only a handful of companies today report on the aggregate total cost saving from their portfolio of sustainability initiatives – even those companies who have robust programs saving meaningful dollars. And while many companies report on risks, few highlight the sustainability-related risks that could impair the firm's strategic objectives.

But the value driver leaders are making great progress both in garnering business benefits from sustainability strategy and more effectively communicating these results to stakeholders. In these cases, growth and value investors in search of opportunity are getting important signals in a familiar framework they understand that enable them to see sustainability strategy as an increasingly important aspect of business strategy.

Pirelli's green performance strategy[1]

In 2009, amidst the economic turbulence of the financial crisis, Pirelli took a bold step toward transforming itself from a generalist to a specialist in the highly competitive tire business. The Pirelli team, led by chairman Marco Provera, briefed government ministers, industry analysts and other stakeholders on their new 'Green Performance Strategy'. Pirelli saw the introduction of the EU's tire rating system, scheduled to take effect in 2013, as an opportunity to differentiate itself from competitors, not a threat. The new EU rules called for labeling all new tires from A to G, based on a set of critical factors like rolling resistance, stopping power on wet surfaces, and rolling noise. Comparing 'A' (Green) to 'G' (Red) rated tires, a buyer would find a 7.5 percent boost to fuel efficiency, a reduced stopping distance by 45 ft at 50 mph, and much less road noise.

Meeting the EU standards was not easy. Many believed that it was not possible to make tires that both reduced rolling resistance to gain mileage and stopping distance for safety.

Pirelli presented its strategy of employing newly developed 'green' materials that would allow it to meet or even exceed the new top tier standards before the competition. What's more, it would do so with a set of engineering innovations, including development of environmentally advantaged sources of silica – one of the most important raw materials of low rolling resistance tire compounds. This advance would play a big role in meeting the EU performance criteria. Pirelli's engineers had discovered that they could use rice husk ash, a waste product from rice production, as an economical, scalable and altogether superior source of the amorphous silica. Unlike ethanol, that takes agricultural land out of food production for energy, Pirelli's solution used only the non-edible scrap and therefore posed no societal issues.

Pirelli saw the chance to dominate the high end of the market, driving profitable growth and building its brand, and it has never looked back. In recent years, Pirelli has been widely recognized for its sustainability leadership, and is following our UN PRI/ Global Compact value driver model to report on the revenue growth, productivity, and risk mitigation business impacts of its sustainability strategy.

Pirelli's growth strategy

In 2010, Pirelli reported €1.75 billion or 36 percent of its €4.85 billion in total revenue from the 'green performance' product category. In 2013, it reported 45 percent or €2.84 billion of its €6.3 billion in total revenue, thereby demonstrating an impressive shift in the product mix. Computing the growth ratio, the 'green performance' revenue in comparison to revenue overall shows a value of 2.14, meaning that green performance products are growing at more than twice the rate of overall revenue.This is especially significant given Pirelli's strong baseline growth and the scale of the green performance revenues. With this simple metric, Pirelli can establish that sustainability strategy is a key driver of the business and that it is positioned to achieve its growth projections.

Pirelli's productivity strategy

Evaluating the impact of sustainability factors on Pirelli's productivity strategy highlights the need for an open model, reflecting the particulars of the firm. Pirelli has made significant strides in improving the natural resource intensity of its revenue. The results of those efforts have reduced energy costs by an estimated €6 million per year, certainly of interest to any analyst. However, the big story at Pirelli is the cost saving of approximately $1,000 per ton for rice husk silica in comparison to the purchase of traditional silica from the market. While the product performance logic and environmental rationale for this innovation are compelling, the business case makes it a game changer. Pirelli's unique use of this low-CO_2, renewable resource began in the rice-producing region of Brazil, and by 2016 is expected to supply significantly more than 30 percent of the total used in the Latin American market. While Pirelli cites the savings achieved and planned as proprietary, analysts in the industry can readily estimate the range of impact of this innovation of future unit costs and potential EPS improvement.

Pirelli's risk mitigation strategy

The assessment of sustainability-related risk mitigation for Pirelli is similarly impressive. The company will spend approximately €47 million in 2013 to support its '360 degree risk management' process. The system covers key external, strategic and operational risks, including many sustainability-related factors. While Pirelli, like other sustainability leaders, reports a wide variety of ESG data to various stakeholder groups, its '360' program is designed to focus attention on key issues which pose a threat to achieving the firm's strategic and financial goals. Several indicators are especially relevant to sustainability, including:

1 *Water intensity of revenue*, which has declined by 70 percent since 2009.
2 *The waste recovery index* is on track for a greater than 30 percent increase between 2010 and 2015.
3 *Accident frequency* from 2009 to 2012 has declined some 56 percent, saving €5 million through less injuries to the workforce.
4 *Uncovered spend at suppliers* (i.e. percentage of spend not covered by risk assessment or management, including ESG factors), is down from 29 percent in 2011 to 0 percent in 2013–15
5 *Manufacturing and operational process certification*: the percentage of processes not certified as meeting or exceeding independent standards is reported at near 0 percent for 2012.

In sum, the Pirelli metrics tell the story of a company that has deeply integrated sustainability into its business strategy – a company positioned for growth in its sustainability advantaged products, realizing significant productivity gains from sustainability initiatives, and effectively managing sustainability-related risks.

Pirelli's changing investor base

Pirelli's leadership team has made a special effort to attract sustainability-oriented mainstream investors and unlike many, they report significant success. In 2009, when the green performance strategy was launched, only 33 percent of Pirelli's free float was held by growth-oriented institutional investors. That figure now stands at 74 percent, with the biggest increase among Nordic institutional investors widely recognized for their interest in sustainability strategies that drive business results.

In speaking of the power of Pirelli's green performance reporting to close the gap with shareholders on sustainability, Filippo Bettini, head of Sustainability and Risk Governance, says this:

> We are at a turning point, globally, in understanding that an ESG approach pays off in monetary terms. At Pirelli, we are attentive to measuring return on capital, which we see clearly in operational efficiency, in human capital management and in economic power of our reputation. In other words, we want to gain by developing, producing, and selling tires that are 'safe for people' and 'safe for planet'– we want to gain from sustainability.

Note

1 For additional value driver model sample case studies, see Appendix C.

References

Esty and Winston 2009 is a reference to their book *Green to Gold* www.wiley.com/WileyCDA/WileyTitle/productCd-0470393742.html. Accessed September 7, 2016.

Kaplan and Norton 1992 through 2008 is a general reference to this body of work on balanced scorecards. http://balancedscorecard.org/Resources/About-the-Balanced-Scorecard. Accessed September 7, 2016.

Lubin and Esty 2014. http://sloanreview.mit.edu/article/bridging-the-sustainability-gap/

Lubin and Krosinsky 2013. www.unglobalcompact.org/docs/issues_doc/Financial_markets/Value_Driver_Model/VDM_Report.pdf. Accessed September 7, 2016.

Porter and van der Linde 1995. www.uvm.edu/~gflomenh/ENRG-POL-PA395/readings/Porter_Linde.pdf. Accessed September 7, 2016.

Chapter 17

New business models

'Conscious Capitalism'

Jeff Cherry

During January 2016, with one line in his State of the Union speech,[1] President Obama recognized a trend playing out in the business and investing realms which holds the promise of a more just, joyous, prosperous and sustainable economy for us all. Early in that speech the President said:

> And this year I plan to lift up the many businesses who've figured out that doing right by their workers, or their customers, or their communities, ends up being good for their shareholders.

I'll be a little nitpicky and suggest that he should have said 'and' not 'or' (workers *and* customers *and* communities ... etc.), but, with this single sentence, the president tapped deeply into the ideals of Conscious Capitalism® and perhaps opened the door to solving some of our most intractable economic debates.

'Conscious Capitalism'[2] is a term that has been used to describe companies that operate with this more holistic, inclusionary mindset. Remarkably, this mindset does not compromise shareholders' interests. In fact, shareholders often experience greater gains than shareholders in competing companies.

To demonstrate this you need look no further than the ground-breaking work done by my colleagues, Raj Sisodia and the late David B. Wolfe. In their book *Firms of Endearment: How World Class Companies Profit from Passion and Purpose*,[3] Raj, David and co-author Professor Jag Sheth found that publicly traded so-called 'firms of endearment' – companies that celebrate and promote purpose, meaning, appreciation, joy, and even love – returned 750 percent over 10 years, while the S&P overall provided a 128 percent return. In five years, these same companies provided their investors 205 percent return, while the S&P *lost* 13 percent.

Over my career as an entrepreneur, CEO, consultant, business advisor and now as an investor, two things have become plainly apparent to me. First: capitalism offers society the best hope of making life better for people all over the planet. This basic premise cannot be ignored in the face of overwhelming historical evidence. And second: although many don't like to admit it, capitalism is in a state of crisis. Look around, and you will find far too many examples of companies that seem to have lost their way. Capitalism as currently practiced, with its many hard edges born of a myopic focus on the shareholder, has given birth to unintended consequences. Most of us simply accept this as the price of 'doing business'. But as the president has discovered, a better way is emerging.

In an environment of increasing transparency fostered by social media, and a growing societal desire to find meaning in all we do, we are collectively rethinking our relationship with capitalism. We are considering new metrics as we choose whom we want to work for, buy from, and allow to operate within our communities. In response, the best-managed companies are creating work environments that inspire people to bring their whole self to the office, to give their best efforts and that cause them to take pride in their work and company.

These companies don't expect communities to simply be grateful for the jobs they bring in, regardless of what kind of neighbor they turn out to be. They don't seek to externalize environmental costs onto the rest of society in search of profits. They endeavor always to treat employees with respect and pay them a wage that allows them to care for their families. Simply put, they don't sacrifice the long-term health of their organization on the altar of short-term earnings. They are setting the example for how companies can smooth the hard edges of capitalism that prevent it from being universally viewed as a positive force for good.

In the investment world there are a number of us working on the front lines of these new business models. At the Conscious Venture Lab[4] we are working to train as many new businesses as possible in the practice of Conscious Capitalism®. We've recently created the Conscious Venture Fund to do seed stage investments to support this work, and are looking to locate in places like West Baltimore, MD, Cleveland, OH and Detroit MI, connecting these cities and their citizens to opportunities where they are most needed.

Rick Frazier and Peter Derby at Concinnity Advisors[5] have created an elegant model to identify and invest in the largest public corporations practicing this more holistic and humane stakeholder model. Sunny Vanderbeck and his team at Satori Capital[6] are another example of this work in the growth-stage private equity arena.

The abbreviation to keep in mind here is ESC, not ESG. E as in Employees and treating them well and fairly; S as in Suppliers, relationships with whom you want to nurture as a business; and C as in Customers, who you treat as family and who you want to do well by so that they become loyal and return for repeat business for generation after generation. Conscious Capitalism® ends up being about trust, integrity and building relationships that last.

The relationship between business and the rest of society is a fundamental component of life, liberty and the pursuit of happiness.

At the Conscious Venture Lab we exist to answer a simple question in that regard: What kind of world could we create if investors and entrepreneurs cared as much about people as they do about profit? Transforming the way business is practiced in America is perhaps one of the most important missions of our time. I'm happy the president has taken on this discussion and excited to continue supporting those extraordinary entrepreneurs making this dream a reality.

Notes

1 www.whitehouse.gov/the-press-office/2016/01/12/remarks-president-barack-obama-–-prepared-delivery-state-union-address. Accessed October 18, 2016.
2 Conscious Capitalism® is a registered trademark of Conscious Capitalism®, Inc.
3 www.firmsofendearment.com/. Accessed September 8, 2016.
4 www.consciousventurelab.com/. Accessed September 8, 2016.
5 www.eda.gov/news/blogs/2014/07/01/guest-column.htm. Accessed September 8, 2016.
6 www.satoricapital.com/. Accessed September 8, 2016.

Chapter 18

Sharia and shared ownership

Mujtaba Wani

In his book *Flash Boys*, Michael Lewis argues that certain parts of the market are literally rigged.

The 2008 financial crisis arguably resulted in large part from the irresponsible activities of big banks. The resulting recession has had a lasting effect. Long-term unemployment remains four times higher than it was before the recession; long-term damage could amount to more than a trillion dollars a year.[1] Moreover, income inequality in the United States is now at the highest level since 1928: 90 percent of the country receives less than half the national income.[2] Additionally, 77 million Americans are delinquent on their debt: one third of the United States population has debt in collections.[3] As global sea levels and ocean temperatures increase, the environment also suffers potentially irreversible damage because of corporate greed. In short, the economic system has severe problems.

Authorities, experts, and entrepreneurs are trying to fix these issues with many strategies. Some corporations are pivoting towards a focus on sustainability, such as producing less toxic waste. Some specialty firms are focusing on financing alternative energy generation, such as solar panels. Some businesses emphasize ethics-based economics. Individually, these ideas are making varying degrees of progress. Combining particular ideas could create a prosperous business and agent of change. Perhaps sustainable investing (SI) could coalesce with Islamic finance.

Basics of Islamic finance

In Islam, business and finance adhere to *sharia*, which is the divine way of life. The root of the word sharia, a controversial term in the West, is 'road' or 'path'. While interpreters often translate the term as 'Islamic law', it is actually a very broad phrase that includes all of God's commands and forbiddances to humankind. Praying and giving charity are examples of commands, while abstaining from the consumption of alcohol is an example of a forbiddance. Contrary to Western conceptions of the word, sharia actually connotes justice. This expanded definition explains the positive understanding of the word among Muslims. Sharia is much broader than the contemporary Western understanding of law.[4]

Fiqh, or Islamic jurisprudence, develops the human interpretation of sharia. In terms of grammar, fiqh means 'understanding' or 'knowledge'. In practice, the term encompasses the human process of determining God's law. Muslims call the process of reasoning and interpretation *ijtihad*, and it can be undertaken only by qualified scholars with an extensive understanding of theology, the sources of law, and Arabic grammar. The sources of law are the *Quran*, the Muslim holy book, the *Hadith*, the reported sayings and deeds of the Prophet Muhammad, *Ijma*, consensus among the scholars, and *Qiyas*, analogical reasoning. Today the terms fiqh and sharia are often used interchangeably.[5]

Jurisprudence usually occurs with the objective of producing a *fatwa*, a legal opinion. The term derives from a root that means 'explanation'. Typically, jurists give a fatwa in response to a specific question posed to a qualified scholar. Fatwas are given in the context of the particular issue and the surrounding circumstances; they are neither automatically transferrable nor binding. This question and answer system is a means of determining solutions to problems. And because Islam permits everything not explicitly forbidden by the Quran and Hadith, jurists have a lot of freedom in decision-making.[6]

Through fatwas and fiqh, Muslims attempt to adhere to sharia in every aspect of life, including finance. While the comprehensive nature of sharia may appear restrictive, Muslims believe that in reality sharia liberates its adherents from slavery to the personal ego. The purpose of sharia is to preserve religion, life, intellect, property, and honor. Moreover, Muslims believe that God is the almighty sovereign and creator of all humans – God best determines what is in the interest of creation. Seeking provision in this world is obligatory and considered beneficial; however, seeking provision for after death takes precedence. During the time of Umar ibn al-Khattab, the second caliph, merchants were not permitted to do business in the marketplace until they had learned the fiqh of business.[7]

Islamic finance is an economic system based on Islamic principles and in compliance with fiqh. Because the Islamic scholastic tradition does not discuss many of the issues in modern business, much of the rules are a result of contemporary ijtihad. The most basic principle is that trade must be based on mutual agreement and mutual benefit. Risk and profit should be shared. Those participating in transactions ought to avoid uncertainty; speculation is condemned. Muslims also may not conduct business involving forbidden items and activities. And most significantly in relation to modern finance, sharia prohibits interest, whether paid or charged.[8]

Although interest no longer carries a negative stigma, historically the concept has been perceived negatively because it creates inequality, debt, and exploitation. Hindu texts dating to 2,000 BCE and Buddhist texts dating to 600 BCE make negative comments regarding usury. Passages in the Hebrew Bible, specifically in Exodus, Leviticus, and Deuteronomy, scorn interest-based moneylending. Thomas Aquinas called the practice unjust and unequal. The philosophers Seneca, Cato, Cicero, Plato, and Aristotle stringently opposed usury: Aristotle thought it was unnatural and unjust while Cato compared it to murder. Even Adam Smith and

John Maynard Keynes, fathers of the modern economic ideology, thought interest rates ought to be capped.[9] Yet, today interest is ubiquitous. In the United States, 40 percent of people live paycheck to paycheck. Average payday lending rates are between 391 percent and 521 percent, and only 2 percent of payday borrowers are non-repeat customers. Interest rates create a vicious cycle of debt. Moreover, a 30-year loan of 1 million dollars at a 5 percent interest rate will come to a grand total of 1.9 million dollars.[10] Clearly, interest rates take from borrowers and give to lenders. Hence, Islamic finance forbids usury.

Muslim investors are free, however, to purchase equity because of the shared profit and loss structure. The investors, nonetheless, do not purchase equity in companies that earn a significant part of their income from forbidden transactions. Because of these requirements, not only can Muslims not deal with normal bonds, loans, or mortgages, but also they cannot deal with products and services such as pornography, alcohol, and casinos.[11] Moreover, Muslims do not buy equity in companies with a high debt ratio. These rules may seem overbearing, but they leave the vast majority of sectors viable.[12]

Core values of sustainable investing: ESG and ESC

Integrating environmental concerns comprises a key part of sustainable investing. Climate change poses a serious threat to the global economy. Yet, the vast majority of capital in the energy sector continues to flow into unsustainable, polluting, carbon-intensive practices.[13] Currently the planet is on track to see a temperature increase of 2 degrees Celsius, which scientists agree would result in disastrous consequences for human society and the environment.[14] The International Energy Agency estimates that around $36 billion more in clean energy investment is needed by 2050.[15] Preventing environmental and economic disaster requires a transition, and this transition needs to be accelerated with significantly more capital, the majority of which will need to come from private sources.[16] Hence, conscious and Islamic investors ought to shift funds away from carbon-intensive energy, and rather toward clean energy alternatives.

Social concerns constitute the second traditional focus of conscientious investing. Sadly, many of the products society consumes today are made at the expense of others. Verité, a labor consulting firm, recently found that about one third of all foreign workers in Malaysia's electronics industry are effectively in conditions of forced labor. About two thirds of workers interviewed for the report felt highly constrained in their movements; 88 percent said they did not have the option to insist on a different job arrangement. People in situations like these make products that wealthy residents of the developed world use without thinking. In comparison to the conditions of child cocoa harvesters in West Africa or clothing seamstresses in South Asia, some of the Malaysian workers seem to have tolerable circumstances. And these examples still do not include people lucky enough to work in decent conditions in the United States, and yet those workers do not make a living wage. Investors of all stripes should shift money away from companies engaging in poor social practices, and rather toward businesses operating mindfully of their supply chain, among many other social factors.[17]

Corporate governance is the third traditional, significant concern for socially responsible investors. Effective governance benefits not only companies themselves, but also the investors, the economy, and society. The UK Corporate Governance Code recognizes certain principles essential to an effective company. Public disclosure of policies, stringent policies regarding conflicts of interest, clear voting policies, monitoring investments, periodic reports – each is an important principle. In order to invest in companies that are run well as well as financially strong and ethical, a responsible investment firm ought to take principles of governance into account. Investors should make sure a company has genuine balance sheets, voting procedures free of corruption, and a diverse and well-organized leadership. These metrics reflect a company's responsibility as well as financial strength and are consistent with the premises of Islamic finance.[18]

Less traditional, conscientious investing practices consider stakeholders beyond shareholders, and employees are the first consideration. This concern overlaps somewhat with the social aspect of ESG, but it is much more specific. Working hours, maternity leave, pay structure, performance incentives – each presents an example of factors that concern a company's employees. Experts believe that people and attitudes are perhaps the most important determinants of a business's success. Thereupon, evaluating a company's treatment of its employees ought to be a significant interest in conscientious investing.

Suppliers compose the second less traditional factor of socially responsible investing. In many situations, companies face issues regarding sustainability and ethics not because of their own practices, but because of problems in the supply chain. Walmart itself may not have employed forced labor, but a contracted Louisiana seafood supplier down Walmart's supply chain did. If companies such as Walmart monitored supplier activities, such as those regarding workers and pollution, they could provide the pressure and/or resources necessary for suppliers to correct the problems. Not only would these corrections provide for more sustainable business, but also they would reduce corporate risk to public relations disasters. The relevance of suppliers affirms that investors should take this consideration into account during their investment processes.

Customers constitute the third stakeholder of conscientious investing. Many companies understand that long-term financial health requires caring for customers. Poor customer service and poor-quality products may result in short-term profit, but often such a strategy will fail in the long run. Listening to customers represents a learner's attitude and a good business strategy. Because these attitudes are crucial, investors should take into account how companies interact and care for customers, and both ESG and ESC as a result are consistent with Islamic finance as it can be practiced.

Convergence of Islamic finance and SI

Principles of Islamic finance cohere neatly with sustainable investing's environmental, social, and governance concerns. Regarding the environment, Muslims must care for the planet and prioritize such concerns over profit. Planting a tree and sowing seeds that could some day benefit an animal or person are considered forms of charity. The Prophet Muhammad said, 'If the Hour [the day of Resurrection] is about to be established and one of you was holding a palm shoot, let him take advantage of even one second before the Hour is established to plant it.'[19] Clearly, Islam emphasizes environmental concerns, which are also the first consideration of sustainable investing. Regarding social issues, Islamic finance emphasizes the rights and dignity of employees. Work is considered worship: workers should be treated with dignity. Clear contracts must be written and followed, and employees must be given what they are due.[20] The Prophet said, 'Give to the worker his wages before his sweat dries', and 'Do not give them work that will overburden them and if you give them such a task then provide them assistance.'[21] Islamic finance and sustainable investing both noticeably emphasize social consciousness.

Regarding governance, Islamic finance does not explicitly endorse specific items such as public reports or diverse boards, but the tradition does include principles that support such measures. The Quran emphasizes fairness and honesty in business. God says, in the holy book, 'Give full measure and do not be of those who cause loss [to others]. And weigh with an even [honest] balance.'[22] The Prophet said, 'Anyone who cheats us is not of us.'[23] Regarding diversity, the Quran reads, 'We have created you from male and female and made you peoples and tribes that you may know one another.'[24] Consequently, both Islam and conscientious investing emphasize fairness, honesty, and diversity.

Potential for success

Ethical investing, as a combination of sharia-compliance and social responsibility, has a large potential clientele. As of 2013, the global sharia-compliant sector held 1.6 trillion dollars in assets. Most of those assets are held overseas, though several billion are in the United States.[25] The Amana Mutual Funds, some of the largest sharia-compliant instruments in America, hold roughly $3 billion in assets. Most of the shareholders are actually not Muslims.[26] Attracted by the ethical values of the firm, conscientious people choose to buy the mutual fund. With the rise of sustainable investing assets increasing across all of its strategies, the potential market for sharia-compliant investing is likely to continue to grow.

Investing in a sharia-compliant and sustainable way, in combination with thorough financial analysis, can yield returns equivalent to or higher than market averages. Sustainability continues to increase its importance as a metric in financial evaluations every year. Leaders across multiple industries also are often leaders in sustainability. For example, Apple spearheads electronics companies in both financials and socially responsible business. Because more sustainable practices can result in reduced costs, risks, or waste, these practices can provide a competitive advantage. Externalities such as environmental change or public pressure emphasize more responsible practices; such changes can create brand value. This shift presents a business megatrend – companies should adapt or be pushed aside.[27] Furthermore, studies on the impact of 'values investing' on investment returns indicate that profit ought to be on par with the market averages. Some evidence even indicates that ESG may provide enhanced revenue.[28] The financial success of firms such as Jupiter Ecology and Generation Investment Management bolster these claims. Rather than be concerned that ethical investing may reduce returns, investors should see values as a potential advantage.

One well-run and thoughtful Muslim investment firm may not individually solve the injustices of the economic system; however, such a firm can have an impact and offer an alternative. Perhaps more importantly, financial success for any such organization could demonstrate to large institutional investors and the general public that profit does not require the sacrifice of morality, nor vice versa. Muslim investing, incorporating sharia and SI models, could drive positive change and create a true alternative.

Challenges

Islamic finance's broadest challenge is adhering to both the letter of the law and the spirit of the law. For example, a sharia-compliant commodity loan, often taken out by businesses, involves a bank selling commodities, in installments and at a premium, to a client. Because the commodities are easily convertible to currency, many traditional scholars perceive this as equal to an ordinary credit transaction.[29] Similarly, supposedly sharia-compliant hedge funds are replacing the speculative practice of short selling by drawing up contracts of sale months before the execution date.[30] Technically the transaction becomes permissible, but morally and economically it is almost the same. Firms ought to follow the stated vision of funding sustainability and presenting an alternative. Rather than create a bubble of technical legal permissibility within an ocean of impermissibility, investors ought to strictly stick to the noble goals. The Prophet Muhammad said,

> That which is lawful is clear and that which is unlawful is clear, and between the two of them are doubtful matters about which many people do not know. Thus he who avoids doubtful matters clears himself in regard to his religion and his honor, but he who falls into doubtful matters [eventually] falls into that which is unlawful.[31]

Muslims should heed the Messenger's advice.

Sharia-compliant investing faces another challenge regarding scholarship. Scholars of Islam hold a wide variety of diverse opinions. Jurists of the classical scholastic tradition agree that the fundamentals of the faith are universally true by consensus of the scholars, and they also agree that there are valid differences of opinion regarding many minutiae. Islam, as a faith of 1.6 billion people, incorporates a huge degree of pluralism. However, banking systems and international finance desire standardization and universal rules. With a subject as detailed, subtle, and complex as Islamic finance, such a standard is very hard to achieve.[32] Moreover, not enough scholars currently work in this field. A 2008 report suggested that perhaps only 20 people are fully qualified for such a task, which seriously puts into question the validity of current boards and supposedly sharia-compliant companies.[33] Companies engaging in sharia-compliant finance must pursue the expensive, expansive screening of investments, find qualified scholars who understand the complexity of the issues in all regards, and retain as well as finance the talent and the process.[34] In short, the modern state of Muslim scholarship poses unique, albeit surmountable, challenges.

Conclusion

Muslim investment strategies could work with sustainable investing to become an agent of important change. Ethical investing holds moral superiority over contemporary investing. Academic research and real-world businesses suggest that conscientious investing also holds financial superiority. Sharia and SI principles provide ethics and safety. These ideas would insulate against the unsustainability and immorality of the larger system, as well as provide a moral alternative.

Notes

1 Krugman, Paul. 'The Mutilated Economy'. *New York Times*. 7 November 2013. Web.
2 Desilver, Drew. 'U.S. Income Inequality, on the Rise for Decades, Is Now Highest since 1928'. Pew Research Center, 2013. Web.
3 Malcolm, Hadley. 'A Third of Americans Delinquent on Debt'. *USA Today*. 29 July 2014. Web.
4 Vikør, Knut S. 'Sharīah'. In *The Oxford Encyclopedia of Islam and Law*. Oxford Islamic Studies Online. 14 October 2014.
5 Rabb, Intisar. 'Fiqh'. In *The Oxford Encyclopedia of the Islamic World*. Oxford Islamic Studies Online. 14 October 2014.
6 Masud, Muhammad Khalid , Joseph A. Kéchichian, Brinkley Messick, Ahmad S. Dallal and Jocelyn Hendrickson. 'Fatwā'. In *The Oxford Encyclopedia of the Islamic World*. Oxford Islamic Studies Online. 14 October 2014.
7 Rabbani, Farraz. 'Money Matters'. 'Islamic Finance in Everyday Life. Seekers Guidance'. Web.
8 Ibid.
9 Visser, Wayne A.M., and Alastair MacIntosh. 'A Short Review of the Historical Critique of Usury'. *Accounting History Review* 8.2 (1998): 175–190.
10 'Fast Facts – Payday Loans'. Center for Responsible Lending. N.p., n.d. Web. 27 November 2014.
11 Bälz, Kilian. 'Islamic Finance'. In *The Oxford Encyclopedia of Islam and Politics*. Oxford Islamic Studies Online. 14 October 2014.

12 Rabbani, 'Money Matters'.
13 *Inquiry into the Design of a Sustainable Financial System: Policy Innovations for a Green Economy*. Report. United Nations Environment Programme, n.d. Web. 27 November 2014.
14 Fulton, Mark, and Reid Capalino. *Investing in the Clean Trillion: Closing the Clean Energy Investment Gap*. Report. Ceres, January 2014. Web. 27 November 2014.
15 Ibid.
16 *Inquiry into the Design of a Sustainable Financial System.*
17 *Forced Labor in the Production of Electronic Goods in Malaysia: A Comprehensive Study of Scope and Characteristics*. Report. Verité, 17 September 2014. Web. 28 November 2014.
18 *The UK Stewardship Code*. Report. Financial Reporting Council, September 2012. Web. 28 November 2014.
19 Siddiqi, Muzammil. 'Rights of Workers in Islam'. On Islam. N.p., 1 May 2014. Web. 28 November 2014.
20 Quran 51:56; Rabbani, 'Money Matters'.
21 Siddiqi, 'Rights of Workers in Islam'.
22 Quran 26:181–182.
23 Siddiqi, 'Rights of Workers in Islam'.
24 Quran 49:13.
25 Caulderwood, Kathleen. 'Could Sharia-Compliant Banking Change The Finance World This Year?' *International Business Times* N.p., 7 February 2014. Web. 29 November 2014.
26 Randall, David K. 'Islamic Fund Star'. *Forbes*. N.p., 21 January 2010. Web. 29 November 2014.
27 Krosinsky, Cary, Nick Robins, and Stephen Viederman (eds.) *Evolutions in Sustainable Investing Strategies, Funds and Thought Leadership*. Hoboken, NJ: Wiley, 2012. 1–8.
28 Ibid., 432.
29 Bälz, 'Islamic Finance'.
30 Burroughes, Tom. 'The Risks and Rewards from the Explosive Growth in Sharia Finance'. *The Business*, 1 February 2008. ABI/INFORM Trade and Industry. Web.
31 Nawawi. 'Hadith 6'. 40 Hadith. N.p.: n.p., n.d. N. pag. Sunnah. Web. 30 November 2014.
32 Ibid.
33 Rarick, Charles A., and Thaung Han. 'Islamic Finance: Panacea for the Global Financial System?' *Journal of Applied Business and Economics* 11.3 (2010): 27–32. ABI/INFORM Complete. Web.
34 Bhatti, Maya (ed.) *Sharia-Compliant Funds: A Whole New World of Investment*. Price Waterhouse Coopers. Web.

Bibliography

Bälz, Kilian. 'Islamic Finance'. In *The Oxford Encyclopedia of Islam and Politics*. Oxford Islamic Studies Online. 14 October 2014.

Bhatti, Maya (ed.) *Sharia-Compliant Funds: A Whole New World of Investment*. Price Waterhouse Coopers. Web.

Burroughes, Tom. 'The Risks and Rewards from the Explosive Growth in Sharia Finance'. *The Business*, 1 February 2008. ABI/INFORM Trade and Industry. Web.

Caulderwood, Kathleen. 'Could Sharia-Compliant Banking Change the Finance World This Year?' *International Business Times* N.p., 7 February 2014. Web. 29 November 2014.

Desilver, Drew. 'U.S. Income Inequality, on the Rise for Decades, Is Now Highest since 1928'. Pew Research Center, 2013. Web.
Erman, Michael. 'Five Years after Lehman, Americans Still Angry at Wall Street: Reuters/ Ipsos Poll'. *Reuters*. N.p., 15 September 2013. Web. 26 November 2014.
'Fast Facts – Payday Loans'. Center for Responsible Lending. N.p., n.d. Web. 27 November 2014.
Forced Labor in the Production of Electronic Goods in Malaysia: A Comprehensive Study of Scope and Characteristics. Report. Verité, 17 September 2014. Web. 28 November 2014.
Fulton, Mark, and Reid Capalino. *Investing in the Clean Trillion: Closing The Clean Gnergy Investment Gap*. Report. Ceres, January 2014. Web. 27 November 2014.
Graham, Benjamin, and Jason Zweig. *The Intelligent Investor*. New York: Collins Business Essentials, 2006.
Inquiry into the Design of a Sustainable Financial System: Policy Innovations for a Green Economy. Report. United Nations Environment Programme, n.d. Web. 27 November 2014.
Krosinsky, Cary, Nick Robins, and Stephen Viederman (eds.) *Evolutions in Sustainable Investing Strategies, Funds and Thought Leadership*. Hoboken, NJ: Wiley, 2012.
Krugman, Paul. 'The Mutilated Economy'. *New York Times*. 7 November 2013. Web.
Lewis, Michael. *Flash Boys: A Wall Street Revolt*. New York: Norton, 2014.
Malcolm, Hadley. 'A Third of Americans Delinquent on Debt'. *USA Today*. 29 July 2014. Web.
Malkiel, Burton G. A *Random Walk Down Wall Street*. 10th ed. New York: Norton, 2012.
Masud, Muhammad Khalid , Joseph A. Kéchichian, Brinkley Messick, Ahmad S. Dallal and Jocelyn Hendrickson. 'Fatwā'. In *The Oxford Encyclopedia of the Islamic World*. Oxford Islamic Studies Online. 14 October 2014.
'Meet The Managers'. Azzad Asset Management. N.p., n.d. Web. 29 November 2014.
Mozer, Paul. 'China Scrutinizes 2 Apple Suppliers in Pollution Probe'. *Wall Street Journal*. N.p., 4 August 2013. Web. 28 November 2014.
Nawawi. 'Hadith 6'. 40 Hadith. N.p.: n.p., n.d. N. pag. Sunnah. Web. 30 November 2014.
'Our Funds'. Saturna Capital. N.p., n.d. Web. 29 November 2014.
Rabb, Intisar. 'Fiqh'. In *The Oxford Encyclopedia of the Islamic World*. Oxford Islamic Studies Online. 14 October 2014.
Rabbani, Farraz. 'Money Matters'. 'Islamic Finance in Everyday Life. Seekers Guidance'. Web.
Randall, David K. 'Islamic Fund Star'. *Forbes*. N.p., 21 January 2010. Web. 29 November 2014.
Rarick, Charles A., and Thaung Han. 'Islamic Finance: Panacea for the Global Financial System?' *Journal of Applied Business and Economics* 11.3 (2010): 27–32. ABI/INFORM Complete. Web.
Seckan, Bakary. 'Confidence in Banks, Financial Institutions and Wall Street, 1971–2011'. *Journalist's Resource*. N.p., 27 March 2012. Web. 26 November 2014.
Siddiqi, Muzammil. 'Rights of Workers in Islam'. OnIslam. N.p., 1 May 2014. Web. 28 November 2014.
Swensen, David F. *Unconventional Success*. New York: Free Press, 2005.
The UK Stewardship Code. Report. Financial Reporting Council, September 2012. Web. 28 November 2014.
Vikør, Knut S. 'Sharīah'. In *The Oxford Encyclopedia of Islam and Law*. Oxford Islamic Studies Online. 14 October 2014.

Visser, Wayne A. M., and Alastair MacIntosh. 'A Short Review of the Historical Critique of Usury'. *Accounting History Review* 8.2 (1998): 175–190.

Woll, Lisa. *US Sustainable, Responsible and Impact Investing Trends*. Report. The Forum for Sustainable and Responsible Investment, 2014. Web. 30 November 2014.

Chapter 19

Gender diversity

Ella Warshauer

While the environmental component of investing along ESG guidelines (environment, social, and governance) has received significant attention from investors, many of the social and governance factors have received less attention. Another important area of opportunity for thematic consideration is in gender diversity. Gender diversity is valuable to businesses: a variety of social backgrounds provides a better foundation for generating innovative solutions, insulating the company from volatility in the macroeconomic sphere, and ultimately delivering higher returns for investors. Recently we have seen businesses and investors alike place a higher value on diversity in the workplace, which has led to developments such as the Bloomberg Financial Services Diversity Index, as well as thematic investments, such as the SHE ETF. Gender diversity, like climate change, is an issue that crosses economic, political, and social boundaries, and as investors gain interest, more comprehensive tools will be developed to quantify this field.

Making the business case for diversity

It is important to view gender diversity as not an exclusively social or moral issue, but instead as a critical economic challenge. According to a report released by the McKinsey Global Institute in September 2015, as much as $12 trillion could be added to global GDP by 2025 by advancing women's equality. From a global economic perspective, women represent a largely untapped portion of the market that when activated, would increase global productivity and innovation. Training and employing this workforce would unlock global economic potential, translating to a long-term investment opportunity.

Research from the fundamental and quantitative perspective further supports the macroeconomic case for including gender diversity in investment decisions. A recent study published by Morgan Stanley Global Quantitative Research outlines a comprehensive quantitative framework for analyzing the importance of different aspects of diversity, including representation, empowerment, equality in pay, policies, and work/life balance programs. The econometric analysis indicates that pay parity and empowerment are the most important characteristics in the framework, while policies are the least important, as they are not necessarily followed by measurable results. Quantifying this information is an extremely valuable tool for investors, as it allows them to develop investment strategies that align with data trends. The findings on the gender pay gap, unequal distribution of women's representation in the corporate hierarchy, disparities in women's representation by industry sector, as well as a lack of policy support, all further highlight gender diversity as a macroeconomic issue, and one that deserves more attention from the investment community.

The results of this quantitative analysis are exciting for investors, and show that gender diversity is a critical component of a successful business. Businesses that have higher gender diversity yield higher returns, compared to competitors. According to a recent report on diversity by Credit Suisse, companies with one or more women on the board have outperformed by 3.4 percent annually over the past 10 years. Since 2005, ROE for companies with a woman on the board averaged 14.1 percent vs 11.2 percent for all male boards. For companies with more than 15 percent women in senior management, ROE was 14.7 percent vs 9.7 percent for companies with less than 10 percent. Finally, where diversity in CEO and key operations is greater, profitability is 27 percent higher. Overall, 'companies that promote gender diversity are more likely to be long-term oriented and to carefully consider a diversity of viewpoints when making strategic decisions' (Parker et al., p. 25), and experience less volatility, making for strong, long-term investments.

Indicators of diversity

Given that a broad scope of characteristics can be used to define diversity, what specific aspects of a company contribute to viewing diversity as a competitive advantage? Research has identified the following four indicators that show high gender diversity as beneficial for businesses.

Businesses that promote diversity can attract and retain the best talent. Recruiting employees from a variety of social backgrounds allows a business to tap into a larger talent pool than competitors. Policies that support equality in the workplace, provide essential services and benefits, legal protection, and physical security all contribute to helping recruit and retain the best talent. This creates an inclusive work environment, which increases productivity of employees. Furthermore, better retention leads to lower hiring costs, fewer productivity losses, and a better culture in the workplace.

High levels of diversity are linked to higher rates of innovation. Teams comprised of a range of social backgrounds are able to develop innovative solutions to business challenges, while employees of similar backgrounds risk becoming subject to 'groupthink', which is an impediment to innovation. A more diverse company is able to understand the values of a broader consumer base, which allows it to cater to a larger segment of the market, and keeps it globally competitive.

Increased diversity enhances financial performance. Diversity allows a company to quickly adapt to changing market conditions, insulating it from macroeconomic volatility. Women play a key role here by managing downside risk, while men maximize upside returns, which can lead to underperformance.

Diversity in the workplace is critical to the success of a business and leads to increased financial returns. However, it is more difficult to quantify the mechanisms needed to accomplish increased diversity, and apply this to the investing world.

Investing in practice

Quantifying the impacts of diversity on a portfolio will be an important step for making diversity investments increasingly accessible. There is already demand for this type of analysis; in May 2016, Bloomberg released its Financial Services Gender Equality Index (GEI) in response to employers placing greater value on diversity in the workforce. Investors are increasingly seeking to incorporate measures of social capital in their investment decisions, but it remains challenging to quantify these characteristics. Bloomberg represents just one company that is addressing this discontinuity; the goal of the GEI is to identify appropriate indicators to use as metrics and provide investors with quantifiable information that can be acted upon. The GEI includes 53 data points on diversity and policies in the workplace, including number of women in the company, number of women on the board, length of parental leave, provided child care and adoption services, and perhaps most importantly, comparisons to the market as a while. The development of this index illustrates the increased value that investors are placing on diversity in the workplace. By providing the tools required to quantify diversity, Bloomberg is facilitating change, helping to make investing in diversity accessible, and enabling investors to efficiently allocate resources to businesses that align with investors' views.

Case studies

Bank of America provides a concrete example of a company embracing diversity from both the global economic perspective and the business perspective. Bank of America was identified by GEI as a global leader in gender equality and supporting women in the workplace. Of the bank's workforce, 52 percent are women (compared to 45 percent on average), and 38 percent of the executive team is female. The bank has partnered with the Tory Burch Foundation Capital program, and provides capital in the form of more than $10 million in affordable loans to over 450 women business owners since 2014. Additionally, Bank of America announced a $20 million expansion over the next 20 years, further indicating that the diversity landscape is expanding. To create economic opportunity for women entrepreneurs worldwide, the bank has partnered with Vital Voices and the Cherie Blair Foundation to connect nearly 2,000 women entrepreneurs from more than 80 countries with mentors – 200 of whom are mentored by Bank of America employees. These efforts are important and have placed Bank of America in the forefront of tackling gender diversity and equality; however, in addition to initiatives, widespread success will require shaping the corporate attitude to include diversity in its culture.

In addition to actions taken at the corporate level, there has been an emphasis at the fund level to invest in companies that are better than their peers in promoting women in leadership. Recently, the SPDR SSGA Gender Diversity Index ETF, better known as the SHE ETF, selects companies that are advancing women through gender diversity on their board of directors and women in management. This fund tracks the SSGA Gender Diversity index, and has a very low expense ratio of .20 percent. Barclay's offers a similar product called the Women in Leadership ETN, which has $28.6 million AUM, and was incepted in 2014. This ETN is comprised of companies only with female CEOs, and has an expense ratio of .45 percent, which is higher than its competitors. One of the main concerns with this ETN is liquidity, which serves as a barrier to entry for investors, and is an issue that pertains to many smaller funds. The rapid increase in gender diversity product offerings indicates investor interest, which is backed by the correlation between women in leadership and strong financial performance. It will be interesting to see how quantitative tools will influence the investing style in this niche.

Conclusion

Diversity in the workplace is an important component of a successful business model, which for investors, translates to increased financial returns. While there has been a surge in impact investing specifically targeting the environment and climate change mitigation, there are other social components, such as gender equality and diversity, which play critical roles in the global economy and present a significant economic opportunity for investors. Inclusive work environments and policies encourage innovative solutions, enabling businesses to more quickly adapt to changing macroeconomic trends, insulating them from volatility, and thereby making them a better investment. The success of gender diversity investment strategies hinges on successfully unlocking the potential of the female population, and harnessing this untapped productivity as an economic opportunity.

As definitions of 'socially responsible investing' and 'environmental, social, and governance' definitions develop, it is important that investors see gender diversity in the context of an issue that transcends economic, political, and social boundaries. As current political attitudes change, and as we witness what could be the election of the first female president of the United States, it is clear that society is placing a higher value than ever on gender equality and diversity. Gender equality, like climate change, is a multifaceted, convoluted issue, and will require the support and integration of both the public and private sectors. It is important to continue to quantify diversity metrics so that we can measure the changing landscape, and efficiently allocate resources to the areas that require the most attention. Gender diversity as an investment theme is on the rise, and as more information metrics become available, it will be interesting to see how this theme evolves.

Bibliography

Authers, John. 'Women in Investment Management'. Women in Investment Management. CFA Institute, 14 September 2016. Web. 29 May 2016.

Dieterich, Chris. 'SHE Power State Street Launches Gender Diversity ETF'. Focus on Funds RSS. Barron's, 8 March 2016. Web. 29 May 2016.

Evans, Akousa Barthwell, and Juila Dawson. *Diversity and Inclusion: Evidence on Corporate Performance*. Report. Credit Suisse, the Barthwell Group, April 2016. Web. 29 May 2016.

Bank of America 'Newsroom'. 'Bank of America Is a Leader in First-Ever Bloomberg Financial Services Gender-Equality Index'. Bank of America, 3 May 2016. Web. 29 May 2016.

Pacheco, Brad W. 'CalPERS Hears Report on the Financial Benefits of Diversity and Inclusion in the Global Corporate Market'. CalPERS, 28 April 2016. Web.

Parker, Adam S., Lin Lin, Charles Clavel, Chandrama Naha, Eva T. Zlotnicka, and Jessica Alsford. 'Putting Gender Diversity to Work: Better Fundamentals, Less Volatility'. Morgan Stanley Global Quantitative Research, 2 May 2016. Web. 23 May 2016.

Sullivan, Paul. 'In Fledgling Exchange-Traded Fund, Striking a Blow for Women'. *New York Times*, 4 March 2016. Web. 29 May 2016.

Woetzel, Jonathan, James Manyika, Richard Dobbs, Anu Madgavkar, Kweilin Ellingrud, Eric Labaye, Sandrine Devillard, Eric Kutcher, and Mekala Krishnan. *How Advancing Women's Equality Can Add $12 trillion to Global Growth*. Report. McKinsey & Company, September 2015. Web. 29 May 2016.

Zarya, Valentina. 'Bloomberg's New Gender Equality Index Shows Who's Investing In Women'. *Fortune*, 2 May 2016. Web. 29 May 2016.

Chapter 20a

The future of innovation

Cary Krosinsky and Will Martindale

The word innovation gets thrown around a lot these days, to the point where you start to wonder if you should not use it at all.

Regardless, innovation can lead the way to more efficient business through cloud computing, and more revenue through better product design, and so innovation remains mission critical.

One ranking quickly shows the danger of isolating on innovation alone. In 2013, *Strategy and Business* magazine's Innovation 1,000[1] had Volkswagen as the number 1 company in so far as future-oriented research and development spending is concerned. Of course, they got so much else wrong in the end.

Assuming such companies don't trip up on integrity, if there is ever a way to accelerate financial growth while reducing the global environmental footprint, innovation will lead the way, so we need to encourage, explore and accelerate such efforts and give this high priority.

Innovative forms of transportation, closed loop processes and renewable energy technologies all help the cause, as do new forms of finance across infrastructure, including public–private partnerships and much more.

Other forms of financial innovation are leading to the possibility of further dramatic change. So-called 'big data', for example, is all the rage, but whether systems can parse signal from noise remains a critical question. There certainly is a rush to invest in the possibility of finding asymmetrical information, always at a premium, especially in markets and systems where so much is assumed to be priced in to the value of assets.

This is also an age of ever-increasing transparency, whereby the definition of privacy starts to feel like whatever the powers that be decide not to share publicly on what it knows about all of us. There are myriad implications from this alone on what information markets have and when, and investment consumers also figure to increasingly be able to connect to the eventual net impacts of their investments, which hopefully can also someday create its own positive dynamic.

Separately, 'blockchain' technology and alternative currencies spark the following possible future thinking. Following this perspective, we have some final thoughts on the ability to measure and thereby further encourage and maximize innovation potential, and a review of the work of the Principles for Responsible Investment's first ten years feels like an appropriate place to finish.

Blockchain and bitcoin

For investors, cryptocurrency technology could affect the post-trade value chain, eliminating clearing, settlement and counterparty risk. Cryptocurrencies, such as bitcoin, are decentralized digital currencies, meaning that the databases used to record bitcoins are not centrally controlled.

These systems are built using a 'distributed ledger', or 'blockchain', which is a decentralized public database collectively maintained by a network of people, known as 'miners', who run the software. There is no bank or country responsible for issuing bitcoin, meaning there's no central point that can fail.

Bitcoin's elegance is that – unlike a normal banking system – it ties its money creation process to the process of validating payments. Bitcoin transactions are anonymous, yet transparent. Bitcoin addresses aren't linked to names or other personal identification. A single person may hold dozens of addresses and even transfer between them. However, the number of bitcoins per address is public. Transactions are secure, international, arrive within minutes and fees are miniscule.

Within the bitcoin business ecosystem some businesses have gained scale. These include merchant payments processor Bitpay, the wallet company and exchange Coinbase and Blockchain.info. The use of the distributed ledgers has gained scale too. Ripple's distributed financial technology allows banks to transact without the need for a central counterparty. The use of blockchains to issue shares ('cryptoequity') is already being tested by companies like Overstock. Recently NASDAQ piloted a blockchain clearing system for shares.

Ten years ago when the UN's Principles for Responsible Investment was set up, Facebook had just a few thousand users and the iPhone wasn't invented. Collectively bitcoin, its database system, blockchain, and other cryptocurrencies, are creating the future of electronic payments. They are a cornerstone of the emergent truly international, cashless society. Bitcoin is not yet a dominant force in financial reform or innovation right now, but it's certainly gaining credibility.

Recognizing and encouraging innovation potential

Energy efficiency investing is supposed to account for much of the additional $1 trillion per year of the new investment needed to keep us within a safe degree of climate change, according to the International Energy Agency,[2] yet the past 25 years has only yielded $5.7 trillion total, or about 22 percent of what is required annually.

Making buildings more efficient, for example, will likely only happen when there is a financial incentive and will to do so, which may make this missing trillion a challenge to achieve. Other efficiency wedges may be necessary to fulfill this need for lowering the carbon emissions of the status quo. Scaling innovation potential would appear to be one such possible and perhaps critical additional wedge.

Efficiency through shared resources such as cloud computing is just one such efficiency enhancing technique, as is the potential for shared data efficiency, but so is learning from nature's processes, or what has become known as biomimicry. Examples of efficiency through nature can be found at the website of the Biomimicry Institute.[3] For example, learning from the flipper design of humpback whales to generate more efficient wind power, or designing more energy efficient buildings through climate control techniques which termites use to build mound structures, or learning from prairies how to grow food in a more sustainable, resilient manner. There are thousands of such examples.

There is also innovation potential to be found in everything from new product design, to switching to the use of more efficient materials, and to lighter materials to lower the footprint of the transportation of goods. The implementation of newer forms of thin-film solar panels to allow buildings and technology devices to be self-sufficient on energy also would qualify, as would 3D printing, newer forms of energy storage and lighting being researched, and other methods to lower the resource use of the supply chain of businesses, and even methods of carbon capture and removal from the atmosphere.

Is this important to investors?

Disruption has already caused many companies or industries to shrink or disappear. Think of Eastman Kodak and the camera, replaced for the most part by the iPhone and Instagram. Xerox, long an innovative company, didn't fully implement their discoveries, and so there is also the risk of not benefiting from one's own innovation potential. IBM handing over the franchise for Windows to Microsoft when they could have reaped such benefits is just one more of many examples. The sharing economy is also disrupting many traditional businesses, from automobile rental to hotels.

The implementation of new technologies and ways of doing business can lead to increased revenue from product development and business model design which markets can at least try to foresee if not encourage. Activist investors have hounded companies such as Dupont and GE to increase efficiency, often without achieving a meaningful payback in terms of financial value.

What if we can at least try to predict the value that could be generated from innovation potential and other techniques that are possibly growth and productivity enhancing through sustainability? Will the activist investor of tomorrow push companies to be more efficient and innovative for the sake of financial value and societal benefit?

Sustainable investing, performed with a value first construct, attempts to isolate the winners of tomorrow while keeping a firm view on the bottom line and the culture of the companies that are owned in the portfolio.

While it can be difficult to predict the future, the effect innovation will have on financial value may well accelerate as a driver of better financial performance, while at the same time enabling badly needed additional environmental efficiencies that are not found today in the trillion-plus dollar wedge of efficiency we appear to require annually.

We won't always know who will emerge as the winner of tomorrow in the race to create the driverless car or truck, among other innovations which may go on to dominate the future of industry, but there is increasingly a diversification argument for being in this game to catch this potential future upside.

Perhaps in addition to innovating on products, companies can innovate on their own efficiency through innovation implementation as one more critical wedge that we can deploy as companies and investors.

Notes

1 http://digitaledition.strategy-business.com/publication/?i=183015&p=34. Accessed 8 September, 2016.

2 www.iea.org/publications/freepublications/publication/MediumTermEnergyefficiencyMarketReport2015.pdf. Accessed 8 September, 2016.

3 https://biomimicry.org/biomimicry-examples/#.V1gEEZErLNM. Accessed 8 September, 2016.

Chapter 20b

Industry-led change

The Principles for Responsible Investment

Sagarika Chatterjee

This chapter takes stock of institutional investor experience of the Principles for Responsible Investment on its ten-year anniversary, highlighting the importance of collaboration in driving future industry change, including on climate change.

Growth and spread of support for the Principles for Responsible Investment

Globally, the Principles for Responsible Investment (PRI), an investor initiative supported by the United Nations in 2006, has strong mainstream investor support. As of 2016, ten years on since the launch of the PRI, approximately 63 per cent of professionally managed assets globally are held by PRI signatory investment managers and 19 per cent by PRI signatory asset owners.[1] Within the G20, there are 1,330 PRI signatories as of March 2016.[2]

Becoming a PRI signatory requires investors to take a wider view, acknowledging the full spectrum of risks and opportunities facing them, in order to allocate capital in a manner that is aligned with the short- and long-term interests of their clients and beneficiaries.[3] The six principles embody incorporation of ESG issues across investment practices – in investment decisions, active ownership and disclosure.

The PRI[4] has seen consistent growth; from 100 signatories representing US$6.5 trillion in 2006 to 1,380 signatories representing US$59 trillion by 2015. This has included strong three-year growth[5] in North America (25 per cent), continental Europe (38 per cent), Africa (28 per cent) and Japan (28 per cent).[6]

There are geographic differences in the level of engagement on responsible investment across markets. The largest numbers of PRI signatories are in the US (256) and European Union (696), but there are a significant number of PRI signatories in other regions including Australia (118), Canada (76) Brazil (57), South Africa (52), Japan (39) and China (17).

1	We will incorporate ESG issues into investment analysis and decision-making processes.	4	We will promote acceptance and implementation of the Principles within the investment industry.
2	We will be active owners and incorporate ESG issues into our ownership policies and practices.	5	We will work together to enhance our effectiveness in implementing the principles.
3	We will seek appropriate disclosure on ESG issues by the entities in which we invest.	6	We will each report on our activities and progress towards implementing the principles.

Figure 20b.1 The six Principles for Responsible Investment.
Source: PRI, 2016.[7]

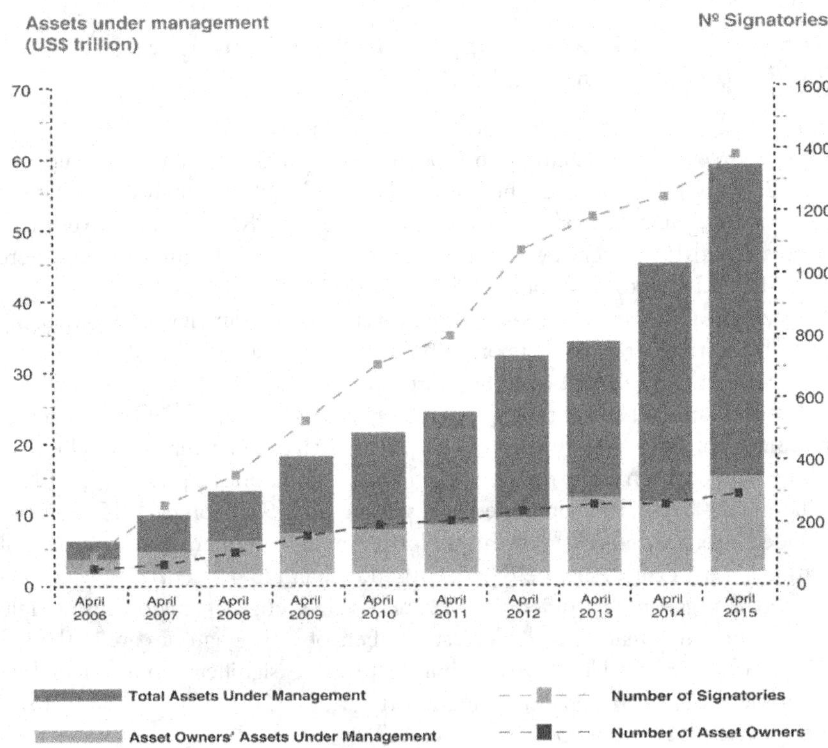

Figure 20b.2 Global PRI signatory growth 2006–2015.
Source: PRI, 2015.[8]

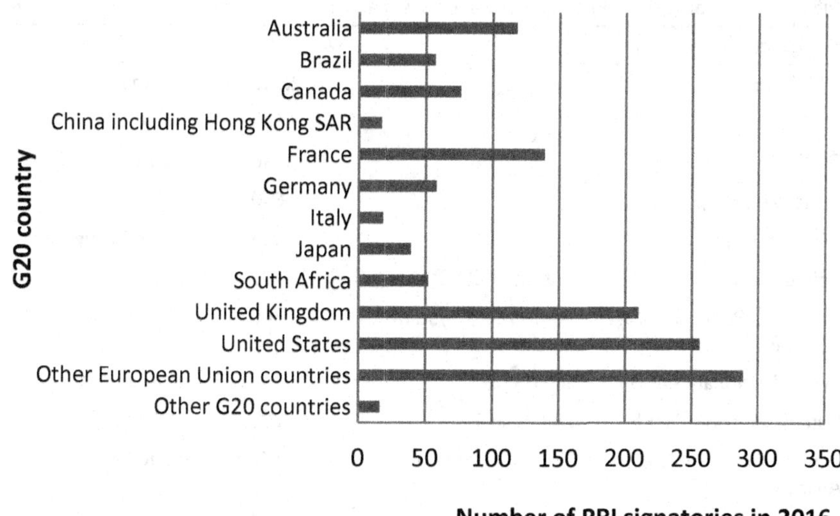

Figure 20b.3 Number of PRI signatories across countries.
Source: PRI Signatories, 2016.[9]

Year	Event
2006:	Principles for Responsible Investment launched Freshfields report on ESG and Fiduciary duty
2010:	*Universal Ownership: Why Environmental Externalities Matter to Institutional Investors*
2012:	$100 million in damages from Hurricane Sandy
2015:	*Fiduciary Duty in the 21st Century report*, PRI Sustainable Development Goals adopted
2016:	RI Blueprint consultation by the PRI on its future direction Paris Agreement enters into force

Figure 20b.4 Timeline of the Principles for Responsible Investment.
Source: Principles for Responsible Investment, 2016.[10]

Investor support across countries for the PRI

Some of the world's largest asset owners managers have become PRI signatories, including Allianz SE and Old Mutual plc. Investors with smaller assets under management are also signatories, such as Ak Asset Management in Turkey and Ainda, Energia & Infrastructura in Mexico.

Table 20b.1 Examples of PRI signatories across markets

PRI signatory asset owners	*AUM (US$bn)*	*Country*
Allianz SE	2,528	Germany
AXA Group	1,675	France
GPIF	1,146	Japan
Generali Group	630	Italy
Old Mutual plc	529	United Kingdom
Caisse des Dépôts et Consignations (CDC)	403	France
California Public Employees' Retirement System (CalPERS)	300	United States
Korea National Pension Service (NPS)	283	Korea, Republic of
Canada Pension Plan Investment Board	201	Canada
Government Employees Pension Fund of South Africa	148	South Africa
AustralianSuper	80	Australia
PREVI (Caixa de Previdência dos Funcionários do Banco do Brasil)	74	Brazil

Source: PRI, 2016.

Implementation of the six principles

Over 900 investors from forty-eight countries across six continents publish *RI Transparency Reports*[11] on how they govern and implement the PRI's six principles (see Figure 20b.1). Listed equity is the most commonly held asset class for PRI signatories. Within this asset class, the proportion of investment managers incorporating ESG into decision-making grew to 95 per cent in 2015, from 93 per cent the year before. Integrating ESG factors into company analysis remains the most common ESG incorporation strategy, with 84 per cent of PRI signatories reporting this for listed equity.[12] 63 per cent of investors engage policy makers or standard setters on ESG topics, with 50 per cent of investment managers doing so.

PRI signatories are building industry capacity to implement the six principles across asset classes, indicated in the *Corporate Bonds – Spotlight on ESG Risks* guide,[13] a new *Sustainable Real Estate Investment* guide,[14] *Limited Partners Responsible Investment Due Diligence Questionnaire*,[15] *and Responsible Investment in Farmland*.[16]

PRI signatories are also making public commitments to taking action on climate change.

Table 20b.2 PRI signatory leadership on climate change

Country	*PRI signatory*	*Action announced during/before Paris COP 21, December 2015*	*Total assets under management (US$)*
France	Caisse des Dépôts et Consignations	€55 billion to be decarbonized by 20% by 2020. No shares in companies with over 20% in coal.	$402.7 billion
Netherlands	ABP	€29 billion allocated to investments into a 'clean world', €4 billion into renewable energy by 2020, carbon budget for equities (€100 billion) and carbon footprinting.	$449.7 billion
USA	New York State Comptroller's Office	$5 billion allocated to sustainable investing strategies, of which US$2 billion for a new low carbon index that will reduce fund's carbon footprint, with tracking error of 25 basis points.Pure coal will be divested. Carbon footprint of fund will be 70% below that of FTSE Russell.	$146.5 billion
Germany	Allianz SE	€4 billion allocated to renewable energy, phase out of coal investments, ESG incorporation.	$2,528 billion
France	AXA Group	€3 billion allocated to green bonds, divesting from €0.5 billion from coal, ESG incorporation, active ownership and carbon footprinting.	$1,674.8 billion
South Africa	Old Mutual plc	Climate change position including carbon footprinting for portfolios.	$529.3 billion
United Kingdom	Aviva Investors	Climate change strategy including low carbon infrastructure, incorporation of ESG, active ownership, divestment and carbon footprinting.	$406.6 billion

Source: PRI, 2016.

Drivers for support for PRI

There has been long-standing investor interest in ESG topics but the last decade has seen deeper investor recognition of the materiality of ESG issues.The five key drivers of investor support for the PRI are: long-term value, risk mitigation, client demand, strategic policy signals and growing regulatory action.

Long-term value

There is growing and widespread belief among mainstream investors across markets that consideration of ESG factors is a source of long-term value creation.

Canada Pension Plan Investment Board states that: 'We believe that organizations that manage Environmental, Social and Governance (ESG) factors effectively are more likely to create sustainable value over the long-term than those that do not … we consider responsible investing simply as intelligent long-term investing'.[17]

Similarly, Japan's Government Pension Investment Fund states: 'It is our belief that considering Environmental, Social and Governance (ESG) issues properly will lead to increase in corporate value, foster sustainable growth of the investee companies, and enhanced the medium- to long-term investment return for the pension recipients.'[18]

There is also a body of academic evidence on enhanced investment returns. In 2016, Deutsche Asset and Wealth Management and the University of Hamburg analysed over 2,200 studies on the effect of ESG on corporate financial performance (CFP).[19] Overall, 62.6 per cent of meta-analyses find a positive correlation between ESG and corporate financial performance and 90 per cent of studies a non-negative relation, with a strong correlation between ESG and corporate financial performance in emerging markets.

Risk management

Risk is a driving factor for investors to consider green issues, including both reputation risk and portfolio-level risk.[20] Examples of inadequately managed green risks commonly cited by investors include the Volkswagen emissions scandal and BP's Deepwater Horizon accident in the Gulf of Mexico. Asset owners are actively seeking to encourage their portfolio managers to understand and mitigate such risks. CalPERS (US$300 billion in assets under management, ranked sixth globally[21]), for example, has developed 'investment beliefs' to manage investments and determine priorities in 2013. These state that 'strong governance, along with effective management of environmental and human capital factors, increases the likelihood that companies will perform over the long-term and manage risk effectively'.[22]

Large investment managers such as State Street Global Advisors (US$2.4 trillion in assets under management, ranked third globally by assets[23]) already place emphasis on the need for company directors to demonstrate strong risk oversight of material environmental issues.[24]

Box 20b.1 Investment belief 9

Risk to CalPERS is multi-faceted and not fully captured through measures such as volatility or tracking error

Sub-beliefs

- CalPERS shall develop a broad set of investment and actuarial risk measures and clear processes for managing risk.
- The path of returns matters, because highly volatile returns can have unexpected impacts on contribution rates and funding status.
- As a long-term investor, CalPERS must consider risk factors, for example climate change and natural resource availability, that emerge slowly over long time periods, but could have a material impact on company or portfolio returns.

Source: CalPERS Beliefs[25]

Client demand

Demand for ESG is growing and according to a YouGov survey, emerging markets investors are more engaged on green issues than their counterparts in developed countries.[26] This survey covered pension fund holders in the UK, USA, France, Japan, Australia, South Africa and Brazil, to identify attitudes to companies and ESG issues. 52 per cent of respondents in Brazil and 43 per cent in South Africa said it would be helpful if their fund manager sent them information on how companies in their funds deal with ESG issues such as climate change. In all countries except the UK, at least 23 per cent of respondents said they would like more consultation with their fund managers about issues that are meaningful to investors. Investors have indicated to the authors that pressure from civil society has also been a driver of growing beneficiary interest in ESG and green issues.

Growing regulatory action

This includes growing reporting requirements such as the Energy Transition Law and policy action to assist in SRI fund labelling in France, as well as stewardship codes. Globally, there are nearly 400 disclosure schemes relating to climate or sustainability developed by regulators, industry groups, NGOs and international organisations.[27] Within the G20, eight countries have pension fund regulation covering ESG disclosure, seven stock exchanges have a sustainability listing rule and sixteen countries have environmental regulation.

Investor governance: fiduciary duty, disclosure and stewardship codes

Fiduciary duties exist to ensure that those who manage other people's money act in the interests of beneficiaries, rather than servicing their own interests. The most important of these duties are:

- Loyalty: Fiduciaries should act in good faith in the interests of their beneficiaries, impartially balance the conflicting interests of different beneficiaries, avoid conflicts of interest and not act for the benefit of themselves or a third party.
- Prudence: Fiduciaries should act with due care, skill and diligence, investing as an 'ordinary prudent person' would do.

Legal context for fiduciary duty

Investors have varying degrees of discretion as to how they invest the funds they control. Within the discretion left to investors, certain legal rules define their ability to integrate green risks into decision-making. In both common law (e.g. Australia, Canada, South Africa, the UK and the US) and civil law jurisdictions (e.g. Brazil, Germany and Japan), the rules that affect investment decision-making take the form of both specific laws and general duties that must be fulfilled. Generally, the rules do not prescribe how investors should go about integrating ESG risks in their investment practices and processes, or the timeframe over which investors define their investment goals. In most cases, it is left to investors to determine the approach that will enable them to meet their legal obligations in the particular circumstances. When evaluating whether or not an institutional investor has delivered on its fiduciary duties, courts will look at the evaluation and integration process of ESG issues into the investment decision-making.

Over the past decade, there has been relatively little change in law relating to fiduciary duty. However, throughout the G20, there has been an increase in ESG disclosure requirements for investors, and in the use of soft law instruments such as stewardship codes that encourage investors to engage with the companies in which they are invested. Stewardship codes encouraging active ownership already exist in eight G20 countries: Japan, Germany, United Kingdom, Italy, South Korea, Indonesia, France, Belgium, the Netherlands and Portugal.

Box 20b.2 Fiduciary duty in the twenty-first century

Following on from a 2005 report on fiduciary duty commissioned by UNEP FI from Freshfields Bruckhaus Deringer, *Fiduciary Duty in the 21st Century* clarifies that failing to consider long-term investment value drivers including ESG issues in investment practice is a failure of fiduciary duty.

The report, published in 2015, covered eight countries: Australia, Brazil, Canada, Germany, Japan, South Africa, the UK and the USA.

It identifies that problems today include perceptions about fiduciary duty and responsible investment, a lack of clarity on prevailing definitions, lack of transparency, inconsistency in corporate reporting and weaknesses in implementation of legislation and industry codes.

The report's recommendations include that policy makers and regulators should:

- Clarify that fiduciary duty requires investors to take account of ESG issues in their investment processes, active ownership and public policy engagement.
- Strengthen implementation of legislation and codes clarifying these referring to ESG issues, and require investor transparency on ESG integration.
- Support efforts to harmonise legislation and policy instruments on responsible investment globally.

From 2016, the report has been developed into a three-year project by UNEP FI, PRI and the Generation Foundation to engage investors and policy makers to harmonise a global understanding of fiduciary duty. The project will include legal reviews of Asian markets and encourage a new international statement on fiduciary duty.

Source: PRI 2016.[28]

Strategic policy signals: the Paris Agreement and the Sustainable Development Goals

The Paris Agreement has been welcomed by investors as a clear signal of the long-term global policy trajectory on green issues and an important foundation for national policies.[29] The seventeen Sustainable Development Goals[30] (SDGs) were adopted by 193 countries at the UN Sustainable Development Summit in September 2015.

As an indicator of investor engagement, in a recent global investor survey[31] over 65 per cent of respondents agreed that acting on the goals aligned with their fiduciary duties. Over half of respondents believe that working towards achieving all seventeen goals would have high or medium potential to help meet their organisation's investment objectives. Investors already plan to take action on the Sustainable Development Goals, with 75 per cent of respondents already taking action on three or more goals. Of the top three goals investors are prioritising this year, two are green goals.

Collaboration: a key component of the PRI's success

Collaboration has played a key role in PRI's success. PRI facilitates industry collaboration through convening investor groups to focus on implementation of the six principles within specific asset classes, investor engagement with companies and with policy makers. Through collaboration through the PRI 'umbrella', investors are able to leverage their collective influence, in a resource-efficient manner, while allowing for different investment objectives and geographic diversity.

Collaborative investor engagement with companies

Active ownership refers to investors using their formal rights – proxy voting and filing shareholder resolutions – and their position as an investor to influence the activity or behaviour of companies or other entities. As an indicator of 2016 investor priorities, collaborative investor engagement with companies is underway not only on climate change but also on:

- *Palm oil:* Thirty-nine investors are engaging with palm oil buyers and growers to improve transparency of certified palm oil, encourage yield gains to minimise the need for further land-use, and policies prohibiting deforestation.
- *Water risks:* Forty-one investors are engaging on agricultural supply chain water risk in the food, beverage, food retail and apparel sectors to encourage strong risk management of water-related risks.[32]

Box 20b.3 Water and collaborative investor engagement with companies

To inform investor engagement with companies on water, PRI, the World Wildlife Fund (WWF) and PwC Germany collaborated on an in-depth research report.

The research found a strong correlation between individual company revenue and estimated water consumption in water scarce regions, and large differences between the average and median water consumption of companies researched. Companies in the food and soft drink, agricultural products and food retail sectors had greater supply chain water footprints than apparel, brewing, distilling and wine-producing companies. Overall performance in risk management by companies was poor.

The research findings have been used to inform investor engagement with high-risk companies, to encourage stronger transparency and risk management practices on water.

Source: PRI, WWF and PwC Germany, 2014.[33]

Box 20b.4 Collaborative investor engagement on natural capital

The Natural Capital Declaration Initiative seeks to assist the finance sector in integrating natural capital, including water and soft commodities, into loans, fixed income, accounting and insurance products, as well as in accounting, disclosure and reporting frameworks. Twenty-nine financial institutions have signed the Natural Capital Declaration, reaffirming the importance of natural capital in maintaining a sustainable global economy. Natural capital refers to soil, air, water, flora and fauna, and the ecosystem services resulting from them. Investors that have signed the Natural Capital Declaration include Caisse des Dépôts (France), Infraprev (Brazil) and VicSuper (Australia).

The initiative has developed a new water risk valuation tool with Bloomberg LP, enabling analysts to evaluate how water risk factors can be incorporated into valuations using a DCF model.

Source: The Natural Capital Initiative.[34]

Collaborative investor engagement with policy makers

Investors are already making interventions on ESG issues for better functioning markets and recognise that wider market shifts are needed to accelerate investor action. *The Case for Investor Engagement on Public Policy* highlights the growing importance of public policy to long-term investors and frameworks for this.[35] Reflecting investors' needs for clear incentives and policy stability, over 400 investors representing US$24 trillion have already called for governments to strengthen regulatory support for energy efficiency and renewable energy, where this is needed to facilitate deployment, and support innovation in and deployment of low-carbon technologies, including financing clean energy research and development.[36]

Stock exchanges

Stock exchanges play a critical role in raising capital for green flows through new issues, IPOs and green bonds. SRI indexes for companies with strong green practices can help raise the bar. Investors are actively encouraging action on green issues by stock exchanges. Eighteen stock exchanges within the G20 are already part of the Sustainable Stock Exchanges Initiative.[37] This is a collaborative initiative for enhancing corporate transparency on ESG issues and encouraging sustainable investment. The *SSEI Model Guidance*[38] encourages listed companies to provide strong disclosure on material environmental factors to investors.

In 2009, PRI launched investor collaboration with stock exchanges, led by Aviva Investors (UK), now known as the Sustainable Stock Exchanges' Investor

Working Group, comprising forty-three investors representing US$7.6 trillion in assets under management. In 2015, Allianz GI, one of the investor working group members, led a coalition of 100 investors representing US$10 trillion to encourage seventy-seven stock exchanges worldwide to produce or update ESG guidance for issuers by the end of 2016. Already, twenty exchanges have agreed to do this.

Credit rating agencies

Investors are actively encouraging integration of ESG within credit ratings, with 100 investors representing US$10 trillion in assets reporting their support for this.[39] In 2016, investors and credit rating agencies are agreeing a joint 'Statement on ESG in Credit Ratings'. This statement specifically covers, among other areas:

- formal integration of ESG factors into credit ratings, with the aim of enhancing systematic and transparent consideration of ESG factors in the assessment of creditworthiness;
- evaluating the extent to which E (green) factors are credit-relevant across different issuer types in the corporate sectors; and
- transparent publication on how such factors are considered in credit ratings.

Box 20b.5 Statement on ESG in credit ratings

In order to more fully address major market and idiosyncratic risk in debt capital markets, underwriters, credit rating agencies and investors should consider the potential financial materiality of ESG factors in a strategic and systematic way. Transparency on which ESG factors are considered, how these are integrated, and the extent to which they are deemed material in credit assessments will enable better alignment of key stakeholders. In doing this they should recognize that credit ratings reflect exclusively an assessment of an issuer's creditworthiness.

Source: PRI, 2016.[40]

Collaboration on climate change

Within one week of the Paris Agreement, over 100 investors signed the 'Paris Pledge', publicly declaring their support for implementation of the Agreement. Mainstream investors made commitments for COP 21 going beyond renewable energy and covering areas such as green bonds and low-carbon infrastructure, as outlined in the section above. Collaborative investor initiatives on climate change played an important role in signalling investor action on climate change and support for the Paris Agreement, including the Montreal Carbon Pledge and the

Portfolio Decarbonization Coalition, both of which achieved significant investor support. Both of these are initiatives are listed on an official UNFCCC platform for non-state actors, which is recognised and explicitly referenced in the text of the Paris Agreement.

In addition, investor collaboration has seen the creation of the Low Carbon Investment Registry,[41] a global public online database created by the Global Investor Coalition on Climate Change.[42] This aims to capture and share low-carbon and emissions-reducing investment examples, with over US$50 billion in entries. Investments registered include not only wind, solar and hydro, but also green buildings, energy efficiency, national rail and freight systems, and forestry. The registry was launched in 2015 and investors are still making entries.

The G20 Energy Efficiency Statement provides a further strong example of investors calling for supportive policy, while demonstrating that investors will also take action. Convened by UNEP FI, the statement is supported by 100 banks and investors representing approximately $4 trillion.

Investors have also created a new Green Infrastructure Coalition for closer collaboration with governments to scale-up green infrastructure investment by assisting investors in understanding the forward pipeline and addressing barriers to capital flows. In certain G20 countries such as France, policy makers have already supported evolution of SRI labels to assist investors in selecting green funds (Figure 20b.5).

Table 20b.3 Global collaborative investor initiatives on climate change (Portfolio Decarbonization Coalition[43] and Montreal Carbon Pledge)

Global initiative	*Investors involved*	*Objective*
Montreal Carbon Pledge	120 investors with US$10 trillion convened by PRI. Investors include Old Mutual plc, HSBC Global Asset Management, and CalPERS.	Investor commitment to undertake and disclose portfolio carbon footprint.[44]
Portfolio Decarbonization Coalition – global initiative	25 investors convened with decarbonization goal of $600 billion in AUM. Co-founded by UNEP FI. PRI is a supporting partner. Investors include AP4, Amundi, CDC, and BNP Paribas.	Systematic effort to align investment portfolios with a low-carbon economy. Includes but not limited to efforts to reduce the carbon footprint of investment portfolios, to increase investment in areas such as renewable energy, to withdraw capital from high energy consumption activities and to encourage companies and other entities to reduce their emissions and support the transition to a low-carbon economy.[45]

Source: Portfolio Decarbonization Coalition[46] and Montreal Carbon Pledge.

Box 20b.6 The G20 energy efficiency statement

As our contribution to the work of the G20 Energy Efficiency Finance Task Group, as managers and investors, we share a common understanding of the positive economic and societal benefits of energy efficiency. In order to ensure that our activities promote and support energy efficiency, and in consideration of our fiduciary responsibility: We recognize the need to fully embed energy efficiency into our investment process. We, the undersigned, undertake to:

1 Embed material energy efficiency considerations into the way in which we evaluate companies;
2 Include energy efficiency as an area of focus when we engage with companies;
3 Take into consideration energy efficiency performance, to the extent relevant to the proposal being considered, when we vote on shareholder proposals;
4 To the extent relevant, incorporate energy efficiency investment considerations when we select managers;
5 Assess our existing real estate assets and managers and monitor and report on their energy efficiency performance;
6 Seek appropriate opportunities to increase energy efficiency investments in our portfolios.

Source: The Energy Efficiency Finance Task Group (IPPEC) and UNEP FI, 2015.[47]

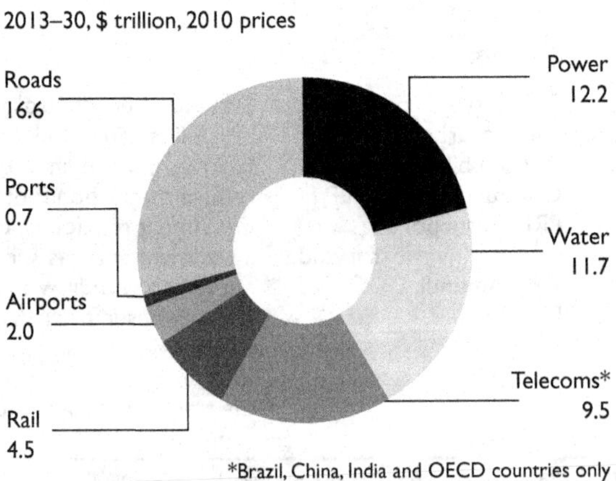

Figure 20b.5 Green infrastructure investment.
Source: Green Infrastructure Coalition, 2015.[48]

Conclusion

Collaboration has played a key role in the success of the PRI, providing a way for investors to work together to achieve tangible changes in investor, company and policy maker practices. The end-benefits of this industry collaboration are ultimately clients and beneficiaries, whose investments are better protected through strong investor implementation of the six principles.

In 2016, on its ten-year anniversary, the PRI has launched an industry-wide consultation on its future direction, which will result in an 'RI Blueprint' for the next ten years. An independent evaluation of PRI's impact by Steward Redqueen finds that overall the PRI is well-positioned for the future. For further progress and real-world change, the following three areas will be important: clarity and consensus about PRI's purpose and ambition, enhanced focus and added value for signatories, and an improved signatories accountability process.

As the PRI considers the next ten years – which will include the challenge of peaking of emissions by 2020 and delivering on the Sustainable Development Goals – we look forward to building on the PRI's strengths to deepen industry implementation of responsible investment.

Notes

1 https://www.unpri.org/download_report/9483. Accessed 18 October, 2016.
2 As of 28 February 2016. An updated, publicly available 2016 figure will be available from April 2016.
3 www.unpri.org/introducing-responsible-investment/. Accessed 8 September, 2016.
4 http://www.aspaonline.org/global/pdfs/Whatisresponsibleinvestment.pdf. Accessed 18 October, 2016.
5 Time period from April 2012 to April 2015.
6 www.unpri.org/news/pri-fact-sheet/. Accessed 8 September, 2016.
7 www.unpri.org/about-pri/the-six-principles/. Accessed 8 September, 2016.
8 www.unpri.org/news/pri-fact-sheet/. Accessed 8 September, 2016.
9 www.unpri.org/signatories/signatories/. Accessed 8 September, 2016.
10 www.unepfi.org/about/background/. Accessed 8 September, 2016.
11 www.unpri.org/areas-of-work/reporting-and-assessment/reporting-outputs/2014-15-public-ri-transparency-reports/. Accessed 8 September, 2016.
12 https://www.unpri.org/download_report/13718. Accessed 18 October, 2016.
13 www.kfw.de/Presse-Newsroom/Themen-Kompakt/PRI/PRI_CORPORATE_BONDS_SPOTLIGHT_ON_ESG_RISKS_2013.pdf. Accessed 8 September, 2016.
14 www.unepfi.org/fileadmin/documents/SustainableRealEstateInvestment.pdf
15 https://www.unpri.org/download_report/6385. Accessed 18 October, 2016.
16 http://2xjmlj8428u1a2k5o34l1m71.wpengine.netdna-cdn.com/wp-content/uploads/PRI_RI_IN-FARMLAND_REPORT-2014_2015.pdf. Accessed April 2016.
17 www.cppib.com/en/how-we-invest/sustainable-investing.html. Accessed 8 September, 2016.
18 www.gpif.go.jp/en/topics/pdf/20150928_signatory_UN_PRI.pdf. Accessed 8 September, 2016.
19 The academic paper 'ESG and Financial Performance: Aggregated Evidence from More Than 2,000 Empirical Studies', in the *Journal of Sustainable Finance and Investment* can be found here: www.tandfonline.com/doi/full/10.1080/20430795.2015.1118917.

The ESG white paper published by Deutsche Asset and Wealth Management and the University of Hamburg, including a Foreword from PRI managing director Fiona Reynolds, can be found here: https://institutional.deutscheawm.com/globalResearch/investment_strategy_3540.jsp. Accessed 8 September, 2016.

20 www.unpri.org/viewer/?file=wp-content/uploads/2014_report_on_progress.pdf. Accessed April 2016

21 www.towerswatson.com/en-GB/Insights/IC-Types/Survey-Research-Results/2015/09/The-worlds-300-largest-pension-funds-year-end-2014. Accessed 8 September, 2016.

22 www.calpers.ca.gov/docs/forms-publications/calpers-beliefs.pdf. Accessed 8 September, 2016.

23 www.towerswatson.com/en-GB/Insights/IC-Types/Survey-Research-Results/2015/11/The-worlds-500-largest-asset-managers-year-end-2014. Accessed 8 September, 2016.

24 www.ssga.com/investment-topics/environmental-social-governance/2016/Climate-Change-Risk-Oversight-Framework-For-Directors.pdf. Accessed 8 September, 2016.

25 www.calpers.ca.gov/docs/forms-publications/calpers-beliefs.pdf. Accessed 8 September, 2016.

26 www.unpri.org/wp-content/uploads/Consumer-Survey-Executive-Summary.pdf. Accessed April 2016

27 www.bankofengland.co.uk/publications/Documents/speeches/2016/speech873.pdf. Accessed 8 September, 2016.

28 www.unepfi.org/fileadmin/documents/fiduciary_duty_21st_century.pdf. Accessed 8 September, 2016.

29 www.parispledgeforaction.org/. Accessed 8 September, 2016.

30 United Nations (2015) *Transforming our World: the 2030 Agenda for Sustainable Development* A/RES/70/1 https://sustainabledevelopment.un.org/post2015/transformingourworld/publication. Accessed 8 September, 2016.

31 Responses to a survey from investment managers and asset owners across the globe, with US$5.9 trillion in assets under management, and interviews with twelve other stakeholders. Research conducted for a forthcoming 2016 PRI and ShareAction publication, *Transforming our World through Investment*.

32 www.unpri.org/areas-of-work/clearinghouse/coordinated-collaborative-engagements/. Accessed 8 September, 2016.

33 www.unpri.org/publications/#WATER-RISKS. Accessed 8 September, 2016.

34 www.naturalcapitaldeclaration.org/water-risk-valuation-tool/. Accessed 8 September, 2016.

35 https://www.unpri.org/download_report/3938. Accessed 18 October, 2016.

36 http://investorsonclimatechange.org/wp-content/uploads/2015/12/11DecemberGISCC.pdf. Accessed 8 September, 2016.

37 www.sseinitiative.org/. Accessed 8 September, 2016.

38 www.sseinitiative.org/wp-content/uploads/2015/09/SSE-Model-Guidance-on-Reporting-ESG.pdf. Accessed 8 September, 2016.

39 PRI investor survey on ESG and credit rating agencies, 2015.

40 Available on request from PRI. See: www.unpri.org/areas-of-work/implementation-support/fixed-income/. Accessed April 2016.

41 http://globalinvestorcoalition.org/low-carbon-investment-registry/. Accessed 8 September, 2016.

42 http://globalinvestorcoalition.org/. Accessed 8 September, 2016.

43 http://unepfi.org/pdc/ and http://montrealpledge.org/. Accessed 8 September, 2016.

44 http://montrealpledge.org/. Accessed 8 September, 2016.

45 www.unepfi.org/fileadmin/documents/FromDisclosureToAction.pdf. Accessed 8 September, 2016.

46 http://unepfi.org/pdc/ and http://montrealpledge.org/. Accessed 8 September, 2016.

47 www.unepfi.org/fileadmin/documents/EnergyEfficiencyStatement.pdf. Accessed 8 September, 2016.

48 www.unpri.org/whatsnew/green-infrastructure-investment-coalition-launched-at-cop21/. Accessed 8 September, 2016.

Conclusion

Climate and impact

Cary Krosinsky and Sophie Purdom

Climate change and workplace conditions emerge as two urgent issues which can be focused on through sustainable investing, not only within university endowments, but by any and all investors. This was the conclusion of our 2016 class at Brown University, and is also the main focus of many investors who choose to integrate ESG considerations. Creating a main focus on such issues, with a sense of scale through implemented investment strategy, can help drive change via a race for capital.

In effect, we need to solve for both climate change and the sorts of social issues impact investing tends to focus on, in a unified if not intertwined fashion, but whether we can achieve this success in time remains an open question. If we stick with the status quo of investment practices as things stand, this locks in business-as-usual, which climate science for starters finds to be distinctly unsustainable.

Something will give, and probably sooner than we think if we don't move quickly and dramatically. The value of everything, for example, will more or less stay as it is until systemic failure sets in from ignoring the consequences of environmental damage, especially on climate change and water as the perception of value shifts until systems eventually fail.

Cambridge's 'Unhedgeable Risk' suggests a high percentage of value at risk, much higher than the $2–2.5 trillion figures being considered on capital expenditure alone by the likes of the Carbon Tracker Initiative or Harvard Business School. Surely more value is at risk from climate change and water than just 2 percent?

But we choose to stay primarily optimistic in the face of all this.

We are closer to understanding the scale of investment that is required to keep us out of this danger – it is in the many trillions of dollars to be sure: a rough estimate we have used is 50 trillion USD. But this is only 10 percent or so of the value of everything. We have the opportunity to develop case studies of investment success, identify where these need to be scaled, and build public–private partnerships to scale such solutions across the areas of commerce we discussed earlier. Investors can kick in half, as mentioned, as can governments, and longer-term investment frameworks and payback schemes can ensure that longer-term beneficiaries are accounted for and sharing both the risk and the opportunity. We need to get those first case studies done and in hand, along with a global roadmap for achieving scale. Scaling a good idea is hard, but harder will be getting this wrong.

We also need to develop the education, awareness and understanding of not only what is possible, but what will happen if we get this wrong. Those consequences are too dire to think about, but we should keep in focus what failure looks like, as a reminder. Much more important, as systems thinking informs us, is to envision what success looks like and work backwards from the outcomes we seek and require.

The very good news is that the necessary transition will create tens if not hundreds of millions of badly needed jobs, which may be the key to unlocking any remaining political barriers, as jobs and livelihoods are and will remain a key variable in this equation.

Culture development also remains critically important.

The opportunity is to ensure that we have leaders who understand and champion a unified climate and impact vision, who make sure we ask the right questions as we form our strategies, who coordinate positively on shared goals on a global basis, who build the necessary capacity to execute on the transitions we require, and then build strategies for needed change. After implementing these strategies, including deep global public–private partnership investment collaborations, we can then measure and track our annual success or lack thereof, and cycle back annually through 2020 and every year beyond to 2025 and onward.

This is very likely going to take all global hands on deck or at least a majority to make this change happen. We all need to find our wedge where we can make a positive difference. There are many wedges both required and possible.

This is why in our teaching we encourage students to explore ESG risks and opportunities, isolate down to subtopics of their interest, and then explore these fully, seeking solutions to problems not yet fixed as their final presentations and papers.

A sampling of such final presentation categories follows, some of which became chapters in this book.

Yale 2014 and 2015: college seminar on business and sustainability

- How to do sharia investing through shared ownership and shared value;
- The potential for a carbon tax in the US to help fund clean energy;
- India's energy future;
- Revolutions in the American power grid;
- Transforming the cruise industry;
- Developments in solar financing;
- Fossil fuel and Yale's investment policy;
- The state of sustainability indexes and standards;
- The potential for bike sharing in Asia;

- Saving the world through the use of derivatives;
- On stopping deforestation in Borneo;
- The potential for a US waste tax – Europe as a case study;
- An analysis of industrial symbiosis;
- How to erase human trafficking from supply chains;
- The potential for sustainable state-owned enterprises;
- Smart microgrids: mapping America's future;
- Balancing economic development and soil pollution in China;
- Free market solutions to the energy transition;
- How to restore coral reefs;
- Hydropower in Canada – infrastructure investment potential;
- Integrating sustainable practices into healthcare supply chains;
- Natural gas in Africa;
- Improving the Latin American sugarcane industry through multi-stakeholder dialogue;
- The potential for benefit corporations in China;
- Removing obstacles to climate action.

Concordia 2016: sustainable financial management

- Embedding sustainability in business schools;
- Fiduciary duty in Canada;
- Strengths and weaknesses of microfinance;
- Sustainable real estate in Canada;
- Ethics and pharmaceutical industry: Gilead sciences and AIDS medicine affordability;
- Aquaponics as an agricultural solution for indigenous people in Quebec;
- GMOs as a problem and solution;
- Sustainable tourism in Chile;
- Analyzing energy innovation potential.

Finding your own wedge is very much the opportunity. We will need a wedge not just 15 deep as per Socolow, but hundreds if not thousands of solutions to occur in tandem alongside investment dollars to scale these good ideas.

Education and raising necessary awareness of the risks, but especially the opportunities, remains a critical part of what is still needed. A majority of the world's people won't insist on the right solutions unless they understand the predicament we are in, and how they can benefit. This requires close examination of tradeoffs and choices, and must include the developing world, or conflict and disagreement will continue.

My own (Cary) teaching began through the amazing Nancy Degnan of Columbia University asking me to teach when I'd never thought of it. She helped incubate my teaching to where it is now an important part of my life and what feels most rewarding. The power of multidisciplinary perspectives came through her leadership as played out during the RFK Sustainable Investing program, which successfully brought together students representing $15 trillion of assets, trying to take the next steps on their sustainability journey as organizations together, building a community, sharing learnings and teaching each other and us.

At Yale, this teaching has evolved into what will shortly be a look at innovation and sustainability and what is possible to implement, also keeping an eye on corporate and investor strategies.

At Brown, for Sophie and myself it was about embedding and empowering positive sustainable investing within a university endowment and how to do that well, with thorough analysis and with discipline.

This is how we have made an impact – it's hard to move assets, really hard, but this is where that journey starts, on the road to a sustainable financial system where all of its assets are sustainable because it is fully baked in.

Your own wedge of difference may well be something completely different, or learning and scaling what others have tried and succeeded with.

We are very positive that the future is bright, filled with opportunity, but the next five to ten years are everything. The field is already taking off like a rocket ship over the past year or two like never before. We need you to get on board, and let's ride the nexus of sustainability and financial value to the solutions we desperately need.

Let's make it happen!

Appendix A
Concise guides to climate change

The Intergovernmental Panel on Climate Change (IPCC),[1] established in 1988, and representing global climate scientists, has gone on to produce consensus research on climate change and its expected effects, leading up to the most recent *5th Synthesis Report*.

This Synthesis Report, while comprehensive in nature, isn't readily digestible to the average person, so it can be helpful to have a more concise guide to climate change.

Two such concise guides are available to the interested reader, one as part of the new *Climate Lens* report of Wilshire Associates,[2] as well as an excellent document entitled 'Climate Change: Warming to the Facts' authored by Black Bear Environmental Assets.[3]

Within this concise document, a clear case is made for how

> NASA and the National Oceanic and Atmospheric Administration (NOAA) have concluded that recent years have been the warmest on earth, and that 19 of the hottest years since 1880 have occurred in the past 20 years. The annual average temperature in 2014 was 0.69°C (1.24°F) above the average of the 20th century and this increase is likely to exceed 2°C (3.6°F) by the end of this century.
>
> Global ocean temperatures have also increased by 0.74°C since the late 19th century. Since over 90% of excess atmospheric heat is trapped in the ocean, at the current rate of greenhouse gas emissions, ocean temperatures could increase by 4.2°C (7.25°F), by the end of the 21st century.
>
> The majority of scientists believe that these increases in temperature are caused by increasing concentrations of greenhouse gas emissions and other human activities. Scientists predict that warming temperatures can have devastating consequences, resulting in changing global weather patterns, food and water scarcity, and displacing tens of millions of people.

Notes

For more details, please refer to one of these concise guides on climate change.

1 www.ipcc.ch/report/ar5/syr/. Accessed 8 September, 2016.
2 https://globenewswire.com/news-release/2016/05/18/841252/0/en/New-Wilshire-Consulting-Program-Assists-Clients-Concerned-With-Implications-of-Climate-Change.html. Accessed 8 September, 2016.
3 http://nebula.wsimg.com/edf5b696c3bde9a8952279d5ef53f2a1?AccessKeyId=D9D974DEC5F930B854CF&disposition=0&alloworigin=1. Accessed 8 September, 2016.

Appendix B
ESG issues

Cary Krosinsky

One attempt to clarify what all of the major environmental, social and corporate governance (ESG) issues are was recently performed by the Generation Foundation in 2015 in their piece 'Allocating Capital for Long-Term Returns',[1] which is worth a read for those wanting a starting-point taxonomy of ESG risks and opportunities to consider.

For example, environmental issues include those pertaining to:

- air quality;
- biodiversity;
- carbon emissions;
- climate change resiliency;
- energy consumption;
- environmental policy and regulation;
- water use and depletion;
- impacts on food supply;
- natural resource, waste and supply chain management;
- land use;
- ocean acidification; and
- vulnerability to extreme weather.

One can easily see how interconnected such risks are to social outcomes. On that front, the data has been harder (see Chapter 9 on the data challenges which remain), but our own research, for example highlights the following five categories for human rights considerations to take into account as involves:

- war and peace conditions and strategies;
- political and economic freedoms;
- community health and access to healthcare;
- racism and sexism; and
- business practices and working conditions.

Global governance is arguably even more complex, with a US model of sorts having emerged surrounding boards of directors and executive-suite conflict of interest, as well as compensation and shareholder rights issues among others.

Yet while US governance investors focus on issues such as companies not splitting their classes of stock or asking to split the Chairman-and-CEO role, in other settings such as family-run businesses, such mechanisms can help stave off those who don't want a company doing what's right for society.

In Germany, for example, companies own stakes in each other and sit on each other's boards, in what is one of the world's most successful economies, while such practices are often criticized in the US, so on a global basis, governance is also largely something of an art rather than a universal science.

We have long preferred, and still prefer ESGFQ[2] as a wider model than just ESG provides, which includes F as in the financial case, without which no sustainability strategy can be sustained, and Q as in quality of management, its culture and business plans, as distinct and separate from traditional corporate governance measures such as, say, on pay and board of directors composition.

Such an ESGFQ frame then encompasses all of the global financial system, bringing sustainability fully into consideration, without which we operate in a more limited economic dimension with so-called 'externalities' which can be ignored by those who simply want to circumvent the outcomes of business.

We can no longer afford to ignore these outcomes.

Such lists of ESG issues represent what an investor might consider on the performance of companies, but it is also a fairly robust list of issues affecting society in general, yet we keep coming back to climate change as the one starting point issue we seem to have in front of us, and if this is not dealt with it could well create a domino effect across many of these other issues as above.

Many of the aforementioned environmental and social issues are extremely important, but there is one overarching sustainability challenge that the world faces that is particularly daunting, and without changing one particular number, not much else may matter in the end.

That number is: **50**.

That's 50 as in the approximate gigatonnes (or Gt) of carbon dioxide emissions and other greenhouse gases being sent annually into the atmosphere (in carbon dioxide equivalent terms).

It is perhaps slightly odd that we don't understand this number with precision, but precision really doesn't matter. We also don't know what exact tipping points exist on the expected effects of climate change, but we know we need to get on with a much more rapid transition to a lower carbon economy.

To calculate this figure, emissions can be annually added up through the understood output of:

1 electricity generation;
2 transportation;
3 industrial processes;

4 agriculture, deforestation and land use (or so-called AFOLU); and
5 the operation of buildings.

Here's what US energy consumption recently looked like across the non-AFOLU sectors of the economy:

Energy produced that was consumed annually (as of 2015[3])

Petroleum	35%
Natural gas	29%
Coal	17%
Nuclear	8%
Renewable energy	11%

Across the following sectors of the economy

Transportation	27%
Industry	22%
Other residential and commercial buildings	12%
Electricity generation	39%

These percentages will differ by country and by region across the world; however, the systemic nature of this picture should quickly convey the clear and critical role of consumption in the ongoing generation of greenhouse gas emissions. For example, petroleum remains the source of over 90 percent of US transportation to the present day. Conversely, 71 percent of petroleum consumed in the US was used in transportation, roughly half through the driving of cars. Of coal use in the US, 91 percent was for the purpose of electricity generation, hence the potential importance of climate regulation, with the Clean Power Plan still working its way through the legal system.

Add in the other greenhouse gas emissions, especially methane – 25 times stronger than carbon dioxide – and net out all other effects such as forest carbon sinks, and we emit something like the previously mentioned 50 Gt in carbon dioxide equivalence if not more on an annual basis.

Scientists from the Intergovernmental Panel on Climate Change (IPCC) to independent expert bodies such as the International Energy Agency (IEA) to NGOs such as the Carbon Tracker Initiative all agree that we now operate under a de facto 'carbon budget'.

Best estimates put this carbon budget figure at 900–1,000 Gt, or if you do the sums, roughly 20 years or less of business as usual when factoring in where we are on an annual basis, and to change this requires a meaningful and much faster transition than we are experiencing.

The IPCC and IEA both suggested recently that we have used up over half the world's carbon budget and are rapidly using up the remainder. By the way, we would be remiss not to mention that the IPCC finds it 'extremely likely' or least 97 percent likely, that climate change is both real and largely an anthropogenic phenomenon.

It isn't that the science is settled; rather it's the reality we now must face as investors.

The challenge isn't to stop the production of fossil fuel; rather how to convert consumption so that we, over time, find annual use patterns that can keep us within necessary levels of global safety.

Unless consumption patterns change, the ongoing use of fossil fuel through the categories above will continue if not accelerate, especially as the developing world demands the lifestyles that those in developed nations have come to enjoy. What to do about this? We hope this book begins to enable paths forward for the necessary investment success we believe this requires.

At roughly 50 Gt of carbon dioxide and equivalents per year, with a carbon budget of 900–1,000 Gt as of 2011, we are likely closer to 650–700 Gt left to burn, at most, and as transitions take time, we really do need to hit the accelerator button on the low-carbon transition right now and in a major way.

This is a race against time, and investors hanging on to old ways may end up with little to show for it in the end, especially as energy prices come down and the gas pedal is increasingly pushed on the low-carbon transition that is needed.

Remaining of concern is the 'entrenched nature of the status quo' – existing cars that will continue to be driven, buildings that will continue to operate inefficiently, power plants that will continue to be built and operate on a suboptimal basis from an environmental perspective. This further locks in a climate-change affected future and increases the need for action now.

Many feel that we have at least 1.5 degrees Celsius of average temperature increase already 'baked in to the system'; even though the recent Paris Agreement will try to keep a 1.5 degree target in mind, it may be a utopian vision rather than something truly achievable. There are growing concerns that scientists have been too conservative on the effects of carbon emissions on global temperatures,[4] and many other societal outcomes are now fully expected, so the need to accelerate the transition gets even clearer.

These problems include, and are fully expected to happen and within many of your lifetimes:

- insufficient agricultural yields;
- spread of disease;
- millions of people experiencing fresh water stress;
- increased violent weather;
- sea level rise affecting large populations and infrastructure;
- mass extinctions and loss of biodiversity.

This last bullet point above is already happening as oceans absorb most of the increased heat, which affects the health of oceans, bleaching coral reefs and much more. Pollution running rampant is affecting air quality in many global cities, especially in India and China, and land- and water-based pollutants also are taking an increasing toll.

Many expect freshwater shortages to manifest first and foremost; and fertilizer and arable land depletion in the longer term, combined with an increase in population, loom on the horizon as further disasters we head towards in many ways full speed ahead.

As you start to examine sustainability, one realizes that there is an intertwined series of issues all playing out simultaneously, and the solutions therefore will require many different parallel strategies all happening at the same time to change the status quo of business, commerce and consumption.

Three other megatrends also continue to play out, and these also in some ways directly relate to sustainability and dramatically affect business value. They are:

- rapidly maturing globalization;
- the accelerating pace of technological change; and
- the need for economically resilient communities.

Globalization affects business success, including for individuals whose jobs are outsourced, but also has helped gradually maximize profits for shareholders.

The pace of technological change has caused a growing number of sectors to disappear or transform, such as print journalism and music publishing, and has also added pressure on middle-class families whose jobs are no longer as secure as they once seemed.

The rise of the global city-state adds a third pressure point to local communities being potentially left behind with the remnants of industries past.

These trends create social and political risks but also environmental opportunities, cities are more environmentally efficient, and with cities expected to house a majority of the world's population in the future, this creates a vital opportunity.

Investors can anticipate these trends to their benefit, not only on real estate valuations, but in other asset classes such as infrastructure and through companies positioning their products and services accordingly.

Technological change also brings badly needed environmental efficiency, and the opportunity to reduce waste through closed loops as well as energy consumption reducing trends such as cloud computing. The most innovative technology companies have been financially outperforming for some time now, and also are leaders in generating their own renewable energy. Some, such as Jeremy Rifkin, see technology companies becoming the electricity utilities of the future.[5]

Fifty-eight companies as of this writing have committed to become '100 percent renewable' on energy use.[6]

Among these, Ikea recently also committed to being a net exporter of energy by 2020.[7] Expect other large companies across sectors to follow, especially if low-carbon energy generation becomes its own diversification business opportunity, and it should, especially in an age of pinched margins. Those encouraging a race to the bottom on energy costs, such as Dan Esty of Yale when he headed the State of Connecticut's Department of Energy and Environmental Protection (DEEP),[8] have been part of this critical shift in dynamics, where the producers of future energy compete on quality and cost.

Automobile manufacturing and other technology companies are also strenuously competing to see who will lead on the electric/driverless cars of the future, along with other related enabling technologies. Companies such as Boeing have been strong financial performers through better fuel-efficient airplane design, as the developing world accelerates its desire for the middle-class lifestyles that the West has long enjoyed; even if the overall low-carbon transition on aviation will almost certainly take longer to play out, efficiency has and will be important.

Companies succeed by providing products that consumers want, and with sustainable growth and productivity baked in. This combined dynamic is now table stakes for market share and will be in furture, and there are methodologies for business and investment success which have emerged (see Chapter 16a on the value driver model, for example).

Globalization also ensures that the benefits of technology are shared and enjoyed elsewhere. Arguably the largest sustainability initiative in the history of Africa has been the introduction of the cellphone, with companies providing such solutions generating as much as nine times social benefit as financial profit, something of a 'holy grail' scenario of financial and societal benefit which is being rapidly advanced through what is largely called impact investing. Other forms of social entrepreneurship are also on the march. Companies in many sectors seek to build circular economies to eliminate waste streams while others take part in the sharing economy and through shared ownership.

Overall, we require these three things to happen simultaneously:

- an ongoing low-carbon energy transition at the pace required;
- an ongoing evolution of the environmental and social nature of existing businesses; and
- the rise of new/social businesses and the jobs they create.

These goals represent a single, intertwined dynamic that needs to be accelerated with intentionality for ongoing societal and financial success. This will require policymakers, investors, corporations and consumers to get on the same page.

Success will only be achieved through a positive systemic effort to make this happen by design, combined with methodologies to calibrate the pace of these transitions, ensuring that the balance is right.

You can see where we are headed in presuming that financial returns will increasingly be skewed towards innovative companies solving these problems while keeping a firm hand on the business case.

The strength of the US economy as a leading innovator shows that a global race has already in effect been underway. The economies of the future which can be both sustainable and financially successful will win out in the end.

Let the race to global competitiveness through sustainable investing begin.

Notes

1 www.genfound.org/media/pdf-genfound-wp2015-final.pdf. Accessed 8 September, 2016.
2 www.greenbiz.com/blog/2009/08/14/how-build-framework-sustainability-20. Accessed 8 September, 2016.
3 US Energy Information Administration, Monthly Energy Review (March 2015) www.eia.gov. Accessed 8 September, 2016.
4 https://www.scientificamerican.com/article/climate-science-predictions-prove-too-conservative/. Accessed 18 October, 2016.
5 www.foet.org/ongoing/documents/LeadingWayThirdIndustrialRevEUabridged5-14-08.pdf. Accessed 8 September, 2016.
6 http://there100.org/companies. Accessed 8 September, 2016.
7 www.theguardian.com/sustainable-business/2016/may/27/ikea-net-exporter-renewable-energy-2020-cop21. Accessed 8 September, 2016.
8 www.nhregister.com/general-news/20140115/connecticut-deep-commissioner-esty-to-return-to-yale-position. Accessed 8 September, 2016.

Appendix C

Additional value driver model case study[1]: Schneider Electric – business as a barometer for the planet and society

Strategy

In 1836, brothers Adolphe and Eugene Schneider purchased mining and manufacturing operations near Le Creusot, France. These would one day become the modern-day multinational company Schneider Electric (SE).[2] The company now provides energy management services and other infrastructure, building efficiency, solar energy solutions and automation processes, placing it at the heart of global potential for financial and environmental efficiency savings.

Results

SE already benefits from the dual trends of growing demand for these services, and their own specific offerings in these areas, with their most recent reports exhibiting significant growth from sustainability-advantaged revenue[3] (or S/G). The *sustainability quality* of revenue (i.e., the absolute percentage of total revenue defined as 'sustainability-advantaged') has grown from 29.9 percent in early 2011 to 63.3 percent by the third quarter of 2013. This, plus the fact that the company's share price increased by 50 percent during this period, signals that the strategy has been beneficial for SE's stakeholders, not least its shareholders. Computing an S/G rating for SE (which divides the growth rate of sustainability-advantaged revenue by the growth of the overall business) produces a score of 7.8. This means that growth from these sustainability-advantaged products has been faster than overall growth, and well above the two times growth rate that this analysis designated as a threshold for high performance.[4]

The company also focuses increasingly on sustainability-driven productivity (S/P) and deploys a 'Planet and Society Barometer' which acts as an overarching, public-facing monitor of progress on the most significant areas of risk management and sustainability. This is accessible at its website,[5] as well as featured prominently in ongoing financial reporting.[6]

How Schneider Electric did it

SE's efforts to create value via sustainability date back at least 12 years, when its sustainability department was first created to respond to what it saw as weak investor signals on the subject. It was also a way of demonstrating SE's commitment to sustainability, with a desire to create and measure itself against specific KPIs. SE was first selected for inclusion in the Dow Jones Sustainability Index in 2002, and it launched its NEW2004 ('New Energy World') initiative at the same time. Energy efficiency solutions went on to make up 30 percent of an €18.3 billion business by 2008.

Furthermore, SE began developing and maintaining its Planet and Society Barometer in 2005. It advanced SE's sustainable development goals of wasting less energy while practicing more environmentally friendly methods of industrial production and consumption.[7] Other aspects of the Barometer include helping the poorest nations gain access to energy while assisting their economic development, areas which could help garner future business for the company if successful. The Barometer has 14 aspects across planet, profit and people (as below), against which it scores itself on a scale of 1 to 10. SE improved from a score of 3 in early 2009 to 8 by 2011.[8] Most recently, SE is performing at 6.38 versus a goal of 8 by the end of 2014.[9] The company is ahead of recently stated targets in a number of key areas, listed below.

1 10 percent reduction of its 2011–2014 carbon dioxide emissions, which it aims to achieve through transportation mode selection, supply chain and logistics optimization and freight density, among other steps. The company has already exceeded this target, reducing emissions by 27.2 percent by the third quarter of 2013.
2 75 percent of product revenues gained from Green Premium-designated products. This goal was adjusted up from 67 percent. As of the third quarter of 2013, the company measured itself at 63.3 percent, up from 29.9 percent in the first quarter of 2011.
3 All industrial and logistics sites to become ISO 14001 certified within two years of acquisition or creation. This goal increased from the previous target of two-thirds of employees to be working in ISO 14001 certified facilities, a goal it surpassed in 2011.
4 Seven points above SE's annual growth gained by EcoXpert energy-efficiency products and services. This goal correlates directly with the aforementioned S/G calculation.
5 1 million households from the 'bottom of the pyramid'[10] gain access to energy via SE solutions.
6 90 percent of SE's Commodity Strategy suppliers adhere to ISO 26000 to identify issues and strategies and report on progress. Since 2004, SE has been supporting suppliers so they can adhere to the principles of the UN Global Compact. At the end of 2011, more than 50 percent of SE purchases were

made from companies who publicly committed to the Global Compact's ten principles.

7 Inclusion in specific socially responsible investment indexes, serving as independent confirmation of SE's sustainability strategy.
8 30 percent reduction by 2014 in SE's Medical Incident Rate, an indicator of safety, workplace hazards and reduction of injuries.
9 An increase in the number of employees endorsing SE as a 'great place to work'.
10 Score of 70 by 2014 relative to SE's Employee Engagement Index. It is currently on target for its anticipated goal, with a most recent score of 57 as of the third quarter of 2013.
11 30 percent of women in key positions by the end of 2014, up from 23 percent when first measured, via identification of high-potential employees in 2011.
12 One day of training per employee per year, a change from the previous target of 2,000 employees trained on energy management solutions.
13 30,000 people trained on energy management at the 'bottom of the pyramid'. Its current number (20,000 trained) far exceeds the original goal of 10,000.
14 300 training missions in communities over the first three years of Schneider Electric Teachers, a new program created in 2012.

With regard to S/P gains, the company is now focused on turning its own operational energy efficiency savings into tangible dollars saved for disclosure in its next annual report. In addition, the company is working on a sectoral breakdown to determine how much companies in different sectors have the potential to save in monetary terms. SE is a case where its own internal efforts on productivity can drive further revenue for the business. As a result, an S/P figure should be forthcoming which analysts and fund managers would be able to relate to savings benefiting the company's bottom line.

From a risk perspective, the company continued to actively measure and report on its established barometer via its website, while at the same time launching an internal water management plan. The company acknowledges that though this is not as material in terms of future risk to revenue as it might be for a beverage manufacturer or similar company, SE wishes to demonstrate that it is conscious of the most significant global issues regarding sustainability and is acting accordingly. Hence, it marked its progress through external ranking partners such as CDP, the Dow Jones Sustainability Index and the Global 100.

This case shows how the likes of Schneider Electric have been driving business success directly through sustainability initiatives. It demonstrates that concrete productivity savings can help drive further revenue. This could give analysts clues as to how companies such as SE who are moving toward measuring sustainability-driven productivity, may potentially add additional future value. Establishing key metrics and areas of focus from a risk perspective, as SE has done through its Planet and Society Barometer, can provide maximum transparency for the benefit of both internal and external stakeholders, while the company gains recognition for actively managing its risk areas.

SE offers investors an opportunity to observe its ongoing transformation into a company that integrates its thinking, strategy and reporting directly into business terms. In parallel to its progress in S/GPR terms, the company's share price has increased from just over €10 per share in early 2009 to over €61 per share in late 2013.

Notes

1 More of our value driver case studies can be found at UN Global Compact, www.unglobalcompact.org/library/811. Accessed 8 September, 2016.
2 www.schneider-electric.com/sites/corporate/en/group/profile/history/schneider-electric-history-animation.page. Accessed 8 September, 2016.
3 www.schneider-electric.com/sites/corporate/en/finance/presentations/financial-results.page. Accessed 8 September, 2016.
4 This and other thresholds presented here were deemed reasonable by the authors for the purposes of this analysis. They are illustrative and could vary in different company contexts.
5 www.schneider-electric.us/sites/us/en/company/sustainable-development-and-foundation/planet-and-society-barometer/planet-and-society-barometer.page. Accessed 8 September, 2016.
6 www.schneider-electric.com/documents/financial-results/en/local/2013-half-year-results/presentation-hy-2013-en.pdf. Accessed 8 September, 2016.
7 www2.schneider-electric.com/documents/sustainable-development-and-foundation/en/barometer-guide-en.pdf. Accessed 8 September, 2016.
8 www.schneider-electric.us/documents/sustainable-development-and-foundation/en/score_s409.pdf. Accessed 8 September, 2016.
9 http://www.schneider-electric.co.uk/sites/uk/en/company/sustainable-development-and-foundation/planet-and-society-barometer/our-sustainable-development-scorecard/sustainability-performance-evolution.page. Accessed 18 October, 2016.
10 'Bottom of the pyramid' activities comprise part of what Schneider Electric calls 'BipBop', or Business, Innovation and People at the Base of the Pyramid. www2.schneider-electric.com/sites/corporate/en/group/sustainable-development-and-foundation/access-to-energy/presentation.page. Accessed March 2016.

Index

Page numbers in *italics* refer to figures, page numbers in **bold** refer to tables and page numbers followed by b refer to boxes.

Printed in the United States
by Baker & Taylor Publisher Services